RETHINKING HOUSING BUBBLES

*The Role of Household and Bank Balance Sheets
in Modeling Economic Cycles*

Balance sheet crises, in which the prices of widely held and highly leveraged assets collapse, pose distinctive economic challenges. An understanding of their causes and consequences is only recently developing, and there is no agreement on effective policy responses. From backgrounds in experimental economics, Steven D. Gjerstad and Nobel Laureate Vernon L. Smith examine events that led to and resulted from the recent U.S. housing bubble and collapse, as a case study in the formation and propagation of balance sheet crises. They then examine downturns in the U.S. economy over the past century, including the Great Depression, and document substantive differences between the recurrent features of economic cycles and financial crises and the beliefs that public officials hold about them, especially within the Federal Reserve System. They conclude with an examination of similar events in other countries and assess alternative strategies to contain financial crises and to recover from them.

Steven D. Gjerstad is a Presidential Fellow at Chapman University in Orange, California. After receiving his Ph.D. in economics from the University of Minnesota, he worked for ten years on theoretical and computational models of market-price-adjustment processes and on experimental tests of those models. His work on price adjustment has appeared in *Economic Theory, Games and Economic Behavior,* and the *Journal of Economic Dynamics and Control.* More recently, his work examines adjustment processes in the aggregate economy, with an emphasis on financial crises and economic restructuring. That work has been published by the *Wall Street Journal,* the *Critical Review, The American Interest,* the National Bureau of Economic Research, and the *Cato Journal.*

Dr. Vernon L. Smith was awarded the Nobel Prize in Economic Sciences in 2002 for his groundbreaking work in experimental economics. Dr. Smith has joint appointments in the Argyros School of Business and Economics and the School of Law at Chapman University, and he is part of a team that created and runs the Economic Science Institute there. Dr. Smith has authored or co-authored more than three hundred articles and books on capital theory, finance, natural resource economics, and experimental economics. Dr. Smith has received an honorary Doctor of Management degree from Purdue University, was elected a member of the National Academy of Sciences in 1995, and received CalTech's Distinguished Alumni Award in 1996.

Rethinking Housing Bubbles

The Role of Household and Bank Balance Sheets in Modeling Economic Cycles

STEVEN D. GJERSTAD
Chapman University, California

VERNON L. SMITH
Chapman University, California

CAMBRIDGE
UNIVERSITY PRESS

CAMBRIDGE
UNIVERSITY PRESS

32 Avenue of the Americas, New York, NY 10013-2473, USA

Cambridge University Press is part of the University of Cambridge.

It furthers the University's mission by disseminating knowledge in the pursuit of education, learning, and research at the highest international levels of excellence.

www.cambridge.org
Information on this title: www.cambridge.org/9780521198097

First published 2014

Printed in the United States of America

A catalog record for this publication is available from the British Library.

Library of Congress Cataloging in Publication Data
Gjerstad, Steven D., 1959–
Rethinking housing bubbles : the role of household and bank balance sheets in modeling economic cycles / Steven D. Gjerstad, Chapman University, California, Vernon L. Smith, Chapman University, California.
pages cm
Includes bibliographical references and index.
ISBN 978-0-521-19809-7 (hardback)
1. Subprime mortgage loans – Corrupt practices – United States.   2. Housing – Prices – United States.   3. Banks and banking – Corrupt practices – United States.   4. Global Financial Crisis, 2008–2009.   I. Smith, Vernon L.   II. Title.
HG2040.5.U5G574   2014
338.5'42011–dc23   2013045961

ISBN 978-0-521-19809-7 Hardback

Contents

Acknowledgments

Chapter 4 was first published by the University of Chicago Press in 2014 as "Consumption and Investment Booms in the Twenties and Their Collapse in 1930" in *Housing and Mortgage Markets in Historical Perspective*, edited by Eugene N. White, Kenneth Snowden, and Price Fishback.

Selections from Chapters 5 and 10 first appeared in the May/June 2012 issue of *The American Interest* as "Underwater Recession," which was coauthored with Joy A. Buchanan. More extensive selections from the same two chapters were published as Chapter 5 in *The 4% Solution*, edited by Brendan Miniter.

Portions of Chapters 6 and 7 first appeared in 2009 in our paper "Monetary Policy, Credit Extension, and Housing Bubbles: 2008 and 1929" in the *Critical Review*.

Chapter 10 is a substantial revision of our keynote presentation at the Cato 30th Annual Monetary Conference, published as "Balance Sheet Crises: Causes, Consequences, and Responses" in the Fall 2013 issue of the *Cato Journal*.

Economic Crises, Economic Policy, and Economic Analysis

The committee determined that a trough in business activity occurred in the U.S. economy in June 2009. The trough marks the end of the recession that began in December 2007 and the beginning of an expansion. The recession lasted 18 months, which makes it the longest of any recession since World War II.
– Business Cycle Dating Committee, National Bureau of Economic Research, September 20, 2010

The crisis showed that the standard macroeconomic models used by central bankers and other policymakers ... contain ... no banks. They were omitted because macroeconomists thought of them as a simple "veil" between savers and borrowers.
– *The Economist,* January 19, 2013

1.1 Macroeconomic Policy: Failed Expectations

In a speech on January 10, 2008, when the National Bureau of Economic Research (NBER) had yet to declare that a recession had begun in the previous month, Chairman of the Federal Reserve Ben Bernanke stated: "We stand ready to take substantive additional action as needed to support growth and to provide adequate insurance against downside risks." Then, in response to a question following his speech, Bernanke replied that "The Federal Reserve is not currently forecasting a recession" but noted that it was, however, "forecasting slow growth."[1]

---

[1] Bernanke's speech is available from the Board of Governors of the Federal Reserve at www .federalreserve.gov/newsevents/speech/2008speech.htm. For an account of the questions and answers following the speech, see Associated Press (2008). Four weeks earlier, as the recession got underway in December 2007, the Federal Open Market Committee (FOMC) in its policy deliberations did not foresee anything more than a slowdown of growth or a moderate recession. The transcript of the FOMC meeting on December 11, 2007, includes statements by many of the FOMC members, and the consensus forecast was near-zero growth for 2008. Janet Yellin, President of the Federal Reserve Bank of San Francisco,

Then, on June 9, 2008 – six months into the Great Recession and with twelve months still to go – Bernanke reiterated in a prepared speech that "Although activity during the current quarter is likely to be weak, the risk that the economy has entered a substantial downturn appears to have diminished over the past month or so" (Bernanke, 2008).

At this juncture (June 9, 2008):

- New housing construction expenditures had declined without interruption for nine quarters; by the time Bernanke made his January 10 speech, it had registered a 44 percent decline, and by June 9, new housing construction was down 51 percent. At the time of the December 2007 Federal Open Market Committee (FOMC) meeting, new housing construction expenditures had fallen without interruption for six quarters and the total decline, at 36.1 percent, had reached a level exceeded only in the serious 1973–75 recession and the even larger combined decline in the double-dip recessions of 1980 and 1981–82.
- The net flow of mortgage funds had recently turned negative for the first time in any peacetime period since the Depression interval from 1932 to 1937.[2]
- During the entire post–World War II period, there had never been a decline in excess of 10 percent in expenditures on new housing construction that had not been followed soon afterward by a recession.

What became transparent in the economic policy narrative leading up to 2007 and its aftermath was the stunning inability of officials and economists – in the wake of declining residential construction expenditures – to anticipate the approaching economic catastrophe, to fully recognize its arrival when it had engulfed them, or to believe in and accept its severity.[3]

stated that her "modal forecast foresees the economy barely managing to avoid recession, with growth essentially zero this quarter and about 1 percent next quarter." Vice Chairman Geithner stated that "our modal forecast [has] several quarters of growth below potential with real GDP [growth] for '08 a bit above 2 percent." See Board of Governors (2007).

[2] There have been only three periods during the past 115 years when the net flow of mortgage funds has been negative: starting in the Great Depression in 1932 and continuing for several years into the recovery until 1937; from 1942 to 1944, when there were wartime restrictions on availability of construction materials; and from Q2 2008 through Q2 2013. Mortgage credit comprises about three quarters of all credit to households. Hence, the collapse of the housing and mortgage markets in 2007 and 2008 initiated the most serious episode of household deleveraging since the Depression.

[3] The two most serious declines in residential construction between the end of World War II and the Great Recession were associated with the two most severe economic downturns during that period (i.e., the 1973–5 recession and the 1980, 1981–2 double-dip recession).

Clearly, the role of households in economic cycles – operating through their acquisition of credit-financed new homes – had not been appreciated by the economics profession, the investment community, and policy makers. Our primary objectives in the chapters that follow are to examine the role of housing in past recessions, with a special focus on its role in severe cases that take the form of balance sheet recessions – that is, recessions that accompany severe deterioration in the balance sheets of households and financial firms – and to demonstrate that the role of housing in severe economic cycles has been largely neglected.

1.2 Unanticipated Events Drive Economic Policy

Five months before Bernanke's January 10, 2008, speech forecasting low growth (but not a recession), the FOMC suddenly reversed its policy. On August 7, 2007, the FOMC press release reiterated its ongoing primary concern about inflation; then, its August 10, 2007, press release switched to concern about "dislocations in money and credit markets." The latter was precipitated by a rapid surge in July 2007 in the cost of insuring AAA rated mortgage securities with credit default swaps.[4] The problems with insuring those risks raised the cost of issuing new securities and also informed market participants that insurers were concerned about the quality of existing securities. On August 9, 2007, BNP Paribas suspended withdrawals from three of its investment funds that were heavily invested in U.S. subprime mortgage securities after the prices of those securities fell more than 20 percent in less than two weeks.

This sharp policy reversal revealed the extent to which Bernanke and the Federal Reserve were engulfed by unanticipated events, but it also indicates their willingness to act once the unexpected collapse had necessitated a change in policy stance. Bernanke, specifically, and monetary policy experts, generally, were familiar with the argument in Bagehot (1873) that during a financial crisis, "advances should be made on all good banking securities." They were also familiar with the argument made ninety years later

---

Surely, the collapse of residential construction should have been a cause for greater concern in 2007 and 2008. Even the collapse of residential construction understates the severity of the situation because the previous downturns did not include a sharp decline of housing prices and the resulting sharp reduction in households' equity in their homes.

[4] The Markit ABX indices of credit default swaps on AAA rated mortgage-backed securities were trading near par on July 6, 2007, reflecting the market belief that these securities would incur no losses at all. By the end of July, these securities were trading at under $0.90, which reflects a market belief that losses on these securities could reach 10 percent.

by Friedman and Schwartz (1963) that the Federal Reserve had allowed a normal cyclical downturn to develop into the Great Depression through its failure to follow Bagehot's dictum to provide sufficient liquidity to the banking system.[5] Indeed, there would turn out to be powerful parallels between the events of late 1930 and late 2007, except for one commanding difference: The Federal Reserve adopted a "forceful policy response" to insure that conditions in the financial market did not deteriorate between 2007 and 2009 as they had between 1930 and 1932. But that policy response was constructed "on the fly" and did not incorporate much of the learning from other comparable crises, such as the relatively successful resolution of the Swedish and Finnish crises in 1992 or the far less successful response to the Japanese "lost decade." One of our key objectives in this book is to demonstrate that in balance sheet crises such as the Great Depression and the Great Recession, liquidity alone cannot solve the problem, and that the economics profession and monetary policy experts have not distinguished adequately between tight money markets that require an infusion of liquidity and balance sheet crises that involve widespread insolvency among households and financial institutions; neither have they determined the best policy responses to widespread insolvency.

1.2.1 Testing the Friedman-Schwartz Hypothesis

After serious problems developed early in August 2007 in the subprime mortgage sector and those problems began to affect financial institutions that were heavily invested in subprime mortgages, the Federal Reserve shifted decisively toward a policy of "liquidity enhancement."[6] However, that policy of traditional short-term injections of liquidity – vigorously pursued and greatly expanded in size and duration between August 2007 and

---

[5] We examine this argument in detail in Chapter 4 and reach a somewhat different conclusion. We argue in that chapter that economic conditions in 1930 were similar to those in 2007. Hence, the Federal Reserve was probably not in a position to completely avoid a major downturn. Yet, the unusual deterioration of conditions in the financial sector was likely a significant contributor to the severity of the Great Depression, exacerbating an already adverse and challenging economic environment.

[6] Although the total assets of the Federal Reserve grew slowly between August 2007 and August 2008, the composition of those assets shifted substantially away from U.S. Treasury securities and toward Repurchase Agreements and Term Auction Credit after August 2007. Changes to Federal Reserve holdings of these two types of assets can be tracked on a weekly basis in Federal Reserve Statistical Release H.4.1. We describe the Fed response to the financial market distress between August 2007 and September 2008 in "Federal Reserve Adaptation I" in Chapter 8, Section 8.1.1.

October 2008 – would be woefully inadequate. Federal Reserve policy would again and much more radically be shifted as a consequence of further financial market deterioration. Between September 10 and October 22, 2008, the assets and the liabilities of the Federal Reserve Bank system increased by well over 100 percent.[7] Bernanke had tested the Friedman-Schwartz hypothesis with dedication for more than a year after August 10, 2007. In September 2008, as the balance sheets of financial institutions came under increasing stress and scrutiny from funding sources, the liquidity enhancement measures pursued in the previous thirteen months proved entirely impotent, and the Federal Reserve perforce intervened on an unprecedented scale to maintain a functioning financial system. For the previous thirteen months, the Federal Reserve had been fighting a liquidity problem, not the insolvency problem that was infecting financial institutions. Moreover, these entities were no longer only depository institutions but also included investment banks heavily invested in mortgages, mortgage securities, and derivatives based on mortgage securities. These securities and derivatives both plummeted in value in July 2007. When the prices of these assets collapsed, the balance sheets of many financial firms were adversely impacted. In Chapter 3, we describe the expansion and collapse of the housing and mortgage markets. In Chapter 7, we examine the market for credit default swaps on mortgage securities. In Chapter 8, we examine the views of the Federal Reserve on those markets.

1.2.2 When the Test Failed, a "Forceful Policy Response" Followed

Four years after the crisis, in his March 27, 2012, retrospective lecture at George Washington University (GWU), Bernanke (2012b) said: "I think the view is increasingly gaining acceptance that without the forceful policy response that stabilized the financial system in 2008 and early 2009, we could've had a much worse outcome in the economy."

However, the "forceful policy response" he described at GWU reached far beyond his thinking in the earlier speeches of January 10 and June 9, 2008. It was an entirely new response driven by events that had overtaken previous policy but also, and significantly, the entire current pattern of thinking at the Federal Reserve and among economists. Moreover, in the new response, the U.S. Treasury had entered prominently into the policy arena, first with the $152 billion Economic Stimulus Act of 2008 early in

---

[7] We describe the Federal Reserve response to the crisis in more detail in "Federal Reserve Adaptation II" in Chapter 8 Section 8.1.2.

the year, followed by the $700 billion Emergency Economic Stabilization Act of 2008, and concluded with the $830 billon American Recovery and Reinvestment Act of 2009. These fiscal actions, totaling almost $1.7 trillion, came on the heels of the 2007–8 liquidity actions, followed by the 2008–9 solvency-promoting actions of the Federal Reserve.[8] A program that is costing so much and producing such high deficits requires close examination to determine whether it has benefited or harmed the economy. Beliefs and analyses on that issue differ widely. Following our assessment of the characteristics and causes of balance sheet crises, we turn in Chapter 10 to the question of the impact of alternative policies, including alternative fiscal policies in other countries that have experienced comparable downturns.

Neither the monetary nor the fiscal responses to the crisis satisfied anyone. The depth of the downturn, the slow recovery of output, and the persistent loss of jobs and income have been deeply disappointing. Policy makers faced economic challenges that did not respond to the old tools of low short-term interest rates or to fiscal expansion. The Depression could not provide a guideline because this time, the Federal Reserve had ostensibly acted as the circumstances dictated by providing all of the support for which the financial sector could hope, and the government had increased spending and reduced revenue, as Keynesians prescribe. Why have these classic prescriptions failed to produce the desired results? What is wrong with the premises underlying economic analysis and policy?

1.3 Balance Sheet Recessions: A Missing Perspective

In our view, the prominent role of balance sheets is the missing link in answering these questions and accounting for the abrupt turns and reversals as economic thinking and policy lagged behind the twisting curve of events. Both Keynesian and microeconomic equilibrium analyses model flows of goods, services, labor, and capital investment. When household and bank balance sheets are predominantly in positive equity, these flows behave with far more regularity than when they are weighed down by numerous balance

---

[8] Between 2002 and 2007, federal budget deficits averaged $304.8 billion. After the crisis, between 2009 and 2012, federal budget deficits were more than $1 trillion in each of the four years and averaged $1,273.4 billion per year. The figure for the earlier period was an average of 2.4 percent of GDP; for the later period, it averaged 8.4 percent of GDP. For budgets, see the Office of Management and Budget Historical Tables, available at www.whitehouse.gov/omb/budget/historicals. For GDP, see the National Income and Product Accounts from the Bureau of Economic Analysis in the Department of Commerce, available at www.bea.gov/iTable/index_nipa.cfm.

sheets in negative equity. It is this condition that looms large in economic calamities such as the Great Recession and the Depression. The Great Recession was preceded by a long period of expansion in the construction of new homes, driven by an expansion in the net flow of mortgage credit in excess of the growth in income that might otherwise have sustained an increased demand for new homes. Accompanying this mortgage credit expansion was a rise in inflation-adjusted home prices from 1997 into 2006. (See Figures 3.2 and 3.3 in Chapter 3 for charts of home sales, home prices, and the flow of mortgage credit.) When the collapse came, home values declined against fixed mortgage debt, and households and their creditor banks were plunged into rapidly escalating negative equity – a pit that massively disrupted the ordinary flows of economic activity across decision-making entities.[9] This large decline in household wealth contributed significantly to a disruption of the normal flows of goods and services as well as the payments for them, including the flows of payments for labor services. Reduction by households of their expenditures relative to income – especially for new housing units and consumer durable goods, the purchase of which can be readily postponed – contributed significantly to the disruption of normal flows.[10]

These developments are characteristic of balance sheet recessions. Businesses reduce their current outlays in step with declining consumer expenditures and they postpone new capital expenditures. Banks reduce lending and allow the incoming debt-service payments to reduce leverage. Precaution is everywhere present as households and the financial sector deleverage and non-financial businesses await renewed growth before they invest in inventories and new production capabilities.

In Chapter 5, we show that when the Federal Reserve reduces short-term interest rates by purchasing U.S. Treasury debt, that policy shift has its most significant effect on mortgage lending. However, in a downturn such as the recent Great Recession, no amount of bond purchases by the Federal Reserve could encourage banks to issue new mortgages. Simultaneously, households were saturated in debt and house prices were falling; hence, the demand for new home mortgages was extremely low. With aggregate output low, the demand for new investments by firms also was suppressed, so the impact of

---

[9] In Chapter 3, we examine the impact of the collapse of home prices in detail and how that collapse affected home equity. As Figure 3.7 shows, home equity fell more than 50 percent from early 2006 to early 2009.

[10] In Chapter 3, we also examine these usual flows and their disruption during the Great Recession. Figure 3.8 depicts this pattern of expenditures on new residential structures, household durable goods, and non-residential fixed investment.

monetary policy was severely blunted. Keynesians conclude that when monetary policy is ineffective, fiscal policy will stimulate the economy. However, we argue that the revenue side of fiscal policy is also blunted for a similar reason: Tax reductions to households do not stimulate household spending to the usual extent because households are in a defensive posture and they use the extra income to pay down debt or for precautionary savings. Other evidence suggests that fiscal stimulus cannot restore growth. Countries that responded to downturns like the one that the United States experienced in 2008 and 2009 with sustained deficit spending have been mired in slow growth for years, whereas countries that responded by curtailing deficit spending have returned quickly to a sustained period of rapid growth.

Because these large-scale domestic episodes are exceptional – twice now in eighty years in the United States – it is perhaps understandable that economic and policy thinking has not accounted for them. Consequently, our search for understanding includes an examination (see Chapter 10) of the responses that at different times have characterized many countries that share in common a collapsed investment boom that was fueled by credit. These countries vary in size, from Iceland to Japan, and constitute a rich set of "experiments" in economic surges and reversals, as well as the diverse policy responses that have been undertaken in response to them. Notable examples of such crises include Japan after the bubble collapsed in 1990–91, Finland and Sweden after their downturns in 1990–93, the East Asian crisis countries in 1997–98, the United States in the financial crisis, and the peripheral countries of the European Union in recent years. Comparison of crises and responses in these countries can help distinguish policies that promote recovery and growth from those that retard recovery and reduce growth.

1.3.1 Leverage Cuts Deep on the Downside

The impact of balance sheet stress on family net worth – as distinct from income flows in severe crises – is reflected in a report by Bricker et al. (2012), which the authors based on a comparison of the 2004, 2007, and 2010 editions of the Survey of Consumer Finances from the Federal Reserve. Table 1.1 summarizes the percentage changes in median and mean family income and net worth (i.e., the difference between families' gross assets and their liabilities) for one period late in the housing bubble (from 2004 to 2007) and for the period from its peak until near its low point (from 2007 to 2010). For brevity, we focus on the changes among the three most recent surveys because the 2007 survey fell near the peak of the economic

Table 1.1. *Changes in family income and net worth in survey periods comparing changes from 2004 to 2007 with changes from 2007 to 2010*

Percent changes in median and mean income and net worth measured relative to previous survey results

Survey years	2004 to 2007		2007 to 2010	
Measure	Median	Mean	Median	Mean
Income Change	Nil	+8.5	− 7.7	−11.1
Net Worth Change	+17.9	+13.1	− 38.8	−14.7

Source: Bricker et al. (2012). All changes are measured in inflation-adjusted dollars, and income is measured before taxes.

cycle. Therefore, these surveys provide snapshots of household income and wealth changes before and after the housing market collapse.

We observe that from 2004 to 2007, mean income rose 8.5 percent with no change in the median, indicating that the income of families above the middle improved relative to those below. Both groups suffered a decline from 2007 to 2010, with those above the middle falling more than those below (mean change –11.1 percent, median change –7.7 percent). As elaborated in the report by Bricker et al. (p. 4): "The changes for both periods stand in stark contrast to a pattern of substantial increases in both the median and the mean dating to the early 1990s."

From 2004 to 2007, however, median net worth grew notably more (+17.9 percent) than the mean (+13.1 percent), indicating that programs designed to enable those of lesser means to benefit from homeownership appeared to be working as intended. However, this relative improvement proved to be ephemeral. From 2007 to 2010, median net wealth fell (–38.8 percent) far more than the mean (–14.7 percent).

The Bricker et al. report noted (p. 17) that "Mean net worth fell to about the level in the 2001 survey, and median net worth was close to levels not seen since the 1992 survey." For the most recent 2007 to 2010 comparisons, the report further elaborated (pp. 1–2) on the striking changes in the median and mean measures of income and net worth shown in Table 1.1:

The decline in median income was widespread across demographic groups, with only a few groups experiencing stable or rising incomes. Most noticeably, median incomes moved higher for retirees and other nonworking families. The decline in median income was most pronounced among more highly educated families,

families headed by persons aged less than 55, and families living in the South and West regions.

The decline in mean income was even more widespread than the decline in median income, with virtually all demographic groups experiencing a decline between 2007 and 2010; the decline in the mean was most pronounced in the top 10 percent of the income distribution and for higher education or wealth groups.

Although declines in the values of financial assets or business were important factors for some families, the decreases in median net worth appear to have been driven most strongly by a broad house price collapse. This collapse is reflected in the patterns of change in net worth across demographic groups to varying degrees, depending on the rate of homeownership and the proportion of assets invested in housing. The decline in median net worth was especially large for families in groups where housing was a larger share of assets, such as families headed by someone 35 to 44 years old (median net worth fell 54.4 percent) and families in the West region (median net worth fell 55.3 percent).

These data reinforce the picture of households in Middle America as having achieved temporary gains in net wealth after the early 1990s, only to see those median gains erode back to the 1990s baseline.

1.3.2 The Role of Housing in Economic Fluctuation Is Not New

Fluctuations of residential construction have been a persistent element of economic cycles in the United States during at least the past ninety years. Moreover, residential construction has been a good leading indicator of economic downturns, and the extent of the downturn in residential construction is strongly correlated with the depth of the associated recession. The only two false positives coincided with the defense build-ups for the Korean War in 1950 and for the Vietnam War in 1967. Even in these two cases, a recession began as soon as the defense expenditures were curtailed.

The pattern of housing construction expenditures and economic cycles is conveyed most succinctly in Figure 1.1, which shows new housing expenditures as a percent of Gross Domestic Product (GDP) since 1920. Eleven of the last fourteen recessions were preceded by declines in new housing expenditures. The Great Recession and the Depression were the housing-collapse "bookends" that bracket twelve other less devastating recessions. Yet, even the less serious downturns exhibit patterns that are remarkably similar to those on each end. Moreover, rapidly increasing expenditures on new residential structures were a prominent aspect of every other recession recovery between 1934 and 2002; the single exception to that rule is

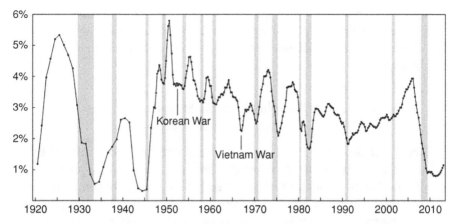

Figure 1.1. Expenditure on new single-family and multi-family housing units, as a percentage of GDP. Eleven of the past fourteen downturns (shown shaded) were led by housing; only one of fourteen recoveries (from the Great Recession) occurred without a strong recovery in housing.

the recovery from the Great Recession, which also has been the weakest recovery since the end of World War II.

Given this regularity, why has there not been broader recognition of the role of housing and its associated mortgage financing as a key element of economic cycles? This failure perhaps stems from the observation that new housing expenditures average only about 3 percent of GDP, as can be visually estimated in Figure 1.1. However, what is more compelling in Figure 1.1 is the remarkable volatility of housing, varying from less than 0.5 percent to nearly 6 percent of GDP. The Depression was preceded by a drop in new housing construction from 5.3 percent of GDP in 1925 to 1.7 percent in 1930, declining further to 0.5 percent in 1933. Furthermore, the Great Recession was preceded by a decline from 3.8 percent of GDP in 2005 to 1.6 percent in 2008 and down to 0.8 percent by 2010. This volatility, however, interacts with two factors that amplify its impact on both prosperity and recession. Housing is the most durable of all consumer goods. Its production is easily pushed forward when financing for it is plentiful or postponed when financing is scarce, when households are too indebted, or when housing is in oversupply.[11] When its production is pushed forward or postponed, this directly adds to or reduces aggregate output. As important, serious housing

---

[11]   We note that the National Income and Product Accounts (NIPA) lump housing (residential fixed investment) together with non-residential fixed investment by firms. However, we conceptualize housing expenditures as advance purchase of a stream of future consumption

cycles – such as the one in the United States between 1924 and 1934 or between 2001 and 2013 – have significant effects on household wealth. We explore both the income and the wealth effects in detail in Chapters 3 through 5.[12]

1.3.3 When Household Balance Sheets Are Damaged, so Are Bank Balance Sheets

The Great Recession is the economic consequence of an extensive balance sheet "crunch" in the household sector, wherein a large proportion of households – among which home equity is a significant component of total wealth – suffered a major reversal. At the end of 2012, 21.5 percent of all homeowners were in negative equity, with millions more experiencing a substantial reduction in the home equity "cushion" that buffers the uncertain gap between their income and their expenditures.[13] Many of these homeowners, even if still employed, are in debt-reduction mode and are wary of spending.[14] During the 14.5-year period from the beginning of 1997 through the second quarter of 2011, real home equity actually declined from more than $6 trillion to about $5.5 trillion. (Figure 3.7 in Chapter 3 is a graph of homeowners' equity from 1997 to 2013.)

Because the banking system is the primary holder of household mortgages and because those mortgages are collateralized by borrowers' homes, banks are exposed to losses when the many homeowners' values falls below the mortgage principal. Lenders also frequently experience a disrupted flow of mortgage payments when borrowers suffer from unemployment or reemployment at lower wages or salary. Consequently, banks' balance sheets deteriorated as their borrowers' losses grew.

---

against future household income. Therefore, throughout this book, we chart its course separately from non-residential fixed investment.

[12] Others have recognized the role of housing construction (e.g., Leamer 2007), the role of house prices (e.g., Reinhart and Rogoff 2008), and the role of leverage (e.g., Fostel and Geanakoplos 2008). However, we analyze the way that these factors combine to create unusually deep and protracted economic downturns.

[13] CoreLogic (2013) reported that 21.5 percent of homeowners were in negative equity as of the end of Q4 2012; Humphries (2012) reported estimates from another database in which 31.4 percent were in negative equity in 2011.

[14] No one has better stated this psychological state than Adam Smith (1759, p. 213): "We suffer more . . . when we fall from a better to a worse situation, than we ever enjoy when we rise from a worse to a better. Security, therefore, is the first and the principal object of prudence . . . It is rather cautious than enterprising, and more anxious to preserve the advantages which we already possess, than forward to prompt us to the acquisition of still greater advantages."

Once a bank's losses overwhelm its equity, bailouts are a common response, but bailouts in the form of massive government lending programs can lead to heavily indebted "zombie" banks. Zombie banks have so many bad assets and so much debt that they avoid new lending to preserve their access to liquid assets: They look like banks but they do not lend like banks. In market economic systems, bankruptcy is the natural consequence of excess risk-taking in asset bubbles. Bankruptcy is also the "surgical therapy" for excising negative equity in household and bank balance sheets and for allowing the system to resume its economic development. Thus, the Federal Deposit Insurance Corporation (FDIC) managed the failure of 465 banks from 2008 through the end of 2012 (51 banks failed in 2012, down from 92 in 2011). These were mostly small- to medium-sized regional banks, but the large national banks (e.g., Bank of America Corporation [BAC] and Citigroup [C]) suffered similar if not worse balance sheet stresses.

Despite being rescued from failure by joint action of the Federal Reserve and the U.S. Treasury beginning in October 2008, these banks' common stocks continued to sell at a substantial discount from book value: BAC common stock traded at 60 percent of book value and C at 72 percent of book value in April 2013, in sharp contrast with Wells Fargo & Company (WFC), which needed no rescue in 2008, and traded at 135 percent of book value – the norm for banks with healthy balance sheets.[15] Market expectations having been confirmed that these banks are "too big to fail" implies that their shares are likely to be overvalued, even at these discounts from book value. Hence, most of the largest banks are under continuing internal and external pressure to scrutinize more carefully all new mortgage loans. As a consequence, net mortgage lending declined in every quarter from Q2 2008 through Q2 2013 as old loans were being paid down in excess of the volume of new loans being made.

It is tempting to say that, this time, it was entirely different because of the "new finance" that gave birth to innovations in the form of mortgage-backed securities, runaway subprime loans, and uncollateralized derivatives (e.g., credit default swaps). In retrospect, many experts see these "excesses" as what caused the housing bubble. However, by 2001, the inflation-adjusted median price of a home exceeded its previous all-time national peak in 1989. Therefore, these significant and troubling new elements simply kited

---

[15] See Bair (2012), "Prologue" and *passim* for discussions of the contrasting issues with BAC, C, and WFC. Mitsubishi UFJ Financial, which infused capital into Morgan Stanley (Bair 2012, p. 3), sells for 76 percent of book. See Chapter 10 for a discussion of Japan's "experiment" with bank bailouts through accounting legerdemains after its real estate crash in the early 1990s.

pre-existing well-fueled price bubble expectations, assuring that the disaster to come would have mega proportions. Significantly, these supra-abnormal conditions failed to engender caution or prevent expert policy makers from being blindsided. We examine these policy failures, from both public officials and financial sector experts, in Chapter 8.

In the third of four lectures that he gave at GWU, Bernanke (2012b) dated the beginning of Federal Reserve action with the rescue of the large banks after their meltdown in September 2008, *not* to the failed prior liquidity actions that began more than a year earlier. Indeed, in his fourth lecture on the aftermath of the crisis, Bernanke (2012c) began with the statement: "A financial panic in fall 2008 threatened the stability of the global financial system." In his third lecture, Bernanke (2012b) had indicated that the Fed's response in 2008 had been conditioned by lessons from the Depression.

First, remember the Fed did not do enough to stabilize the banking system in the 1930s and so the lesson there is that in the financial panic, the central bank has to lend freely according to Bagehot's rules to halt runs and to try to stabilize the financial system. And the second lesson of the Great Depression, the Fed did not do enough to prevent deflation and contraction of the money supply, so the second lesson of the Great Depression is you need to have accommodative monetary policy to help the economy avoid a deep depression. So, and heeding those lessons, the Federal Reserve and the Federal Government did take vigorous actions to stop the financial panic, worked with other agencies, and worked internationally with foreign central banks and governments.

Several important issues are omitted from the Bernanke (2012b) retrospective. The primary lesson from the Depression had been the argument in Friedman and Schwartz (1963) that the Federal Reserve failed to supply adequate liquidity. Keenly aware of this, the Federal Reserve reversed itself and engaged decisively and vigorously in "liquidity enhancement" from August 2007 to October 2008. When these actions failed, the Federal Reserve moved far beyond providing liquidity and began to lift both public and private overvalued assets off of the balance sheets of insolvent financial institutions. Before October 2008, Bernanke clearly believed that not doing "enough to stabilize the banking system" meant not providing adequate liquidity. However, by late 2008 and early 2009, stabilizing the financial system had required lifting bad assets off of the balance sheets of major financial institutions. Clearly, the Federal Reserve went far beyond Bagehot's rules that "advances should be made on all good banking securities" by the central bank. Lending on that basis was pursued from August 2007 through September 2008 but proved inadequate. So the question arises: What is the appropriate response to widespread insolvency? Many alternatives have been tried. We examine several of these in Chapter 10 and find that the best responses have differed considerably from those followed by the Federal Reserve and the U.S. Treasury after the financial crisis in September 2008.

1.3.4 The Counterfactual Policy Paradox: Preventive Action or Blame for Error?

Even if the experts had seen it coming, any action that would have arrested the bubble would have been in danger of being perceived as the cause of the crash, not as an intentional pre-emptive move intended to avoid a bigger crash. This is the counterfactual paradox of economic policy, even if that policy is informed by good understanding and reasonable predictability. Thus, in his first lecture – which includes a discussion of the 1920s in the Fed's history – Bernanke (2012a) noted that the Federal Reserve "did not ease monetary policy...because it wanted to stop the stock market speculation." Surely this was an attempt to forestall perceived excesses that could be a source of trouble for the economy. Furthermore, as we discuss in Chapter 8, the private financial sector began responding a year and a half in advance of October 1929 to forestall recognized stock market excesses by raising margin requirements. What is more likely, from the perspective of our study, is that monetary tightening in 1928 and 1929 contributed to the further cooling of the housing-mortgage market boom that had set the stage for the approaching Depression. In a similar but opposite effect (as discussed in Chapter 5), the Federal Reserve under Alan Greenspan established an unusually low Federal Funds Rate, 2002–2004, designed to stimulate lagging business investment. However, the policy helped catapult housing expenditures into its final surge, 2002–2006.

1.3.5 When Monetary Policy Is Ineffective, Fiscal Policy Is also Ineffective

In the aftermath of a housing bubble, when households and banks are suffering from large reductions in equity, with many units in negative equity, economic activity will be less responsive to fiscal stimulus, as well as monetary stimulus, than when these sectors of the economy enjoy a buoyant foundation of strong balance sheet solvency. Yet, this phenomenon is not part of traditional macro or microeconomic thinking, and neither has it informed economic policy. Economic analysis focuses on the flows of economic activity, not the balance sheet conditions that underlie and facilitate or impede those flows. From this perspective, we envision the economic system as a network of flows connecting nodes, with decisions being made at each node. If these decisions are also constrained by negative equity balances and the prospect of further declines in home prices, then payment flows through the nodes are reduced by precautionary actions; debt reduction; and budget-stretching by households, banks, and firms. In the nodal-network metaphor, we think of the normal flows through the nodes as being diverted to refill the negative-equity "tanks" and correct the imbalance between an excess of liability over current asset value. Until that restoration process has rebuilt a sense of security dispersed across financial and economic units, the accustomed system flows will be retarded.

In this state of the economy, easy monetary policy is notoriously ineffective in stimulating either spending or lending – what Keynes called the liquidity trap – but economists have long believed that under these conditions, fiscal stimulus in the form of deficit spending can provide the needed mechanism for jump-starting economic recovery. The proposition that when monetary policy is ineffective, fiscal policy in the form of deficit financing must be used was prominently espoused by Harvard's Alvin Hansen in the 1940s and 1950s.[16] This belief system led to the Bush and Obama stimulus programs beginning in 2008. These programs are widely perceived as ineffective, and the hoped-for recovery response failed to live up to the expectations, even for those who promoted it. We think that the cause is the same as that which accounts for the ineffectiveness of monetary stimulus: the widespread preoccupation of households and banks with the daunting task of rebuilding balance sheets.

Beliefs about the effectiveness of fiscal policy originated primarily after 1939, when the expansion of government expenditures became prominently associated with the accompanying sustained recovery from the Depression.[17] Not a part of this pattern of thinking is that by the end

---

[16] One of the authors (Smith) sat in Alvin Hansen's Money and Banking course at Harvard, 1952–53. Sixty years ago, Hansen's arguments seemed plausible. Henry Wallich, an earlier (1940) student in Hanson's class, retained a life-long skepticism, noting in retrospect that "Hansen was sure that monetary policy had failed and that it had to be replaced with fiscal policy. He was sure also (Hansen was occasionally in error, but never in doubt) that the American economy had reached a phase of stagnation and that in the absence of growth generated by the private sector it was the government's job to maintain full employment, however unproductively, by sufficiently large deficits." See Wallich (1988, p. 112).

[17] Although he does not attribute an explicit causal connection, this popular interpretation is suggested by Bernanke in his first lecture, when he notes that: "The Depression continued until the United States entered World War II in 1941" (Bernanke, 2012a). Barro and Redlick (2011, p. 76) estimated the government spending multiplier over two years for a permanent change in defense spending (using a sample beginning in 1939) as about 0.80, significantly less than one (p-value, 0.004). Moreover, economic data from the period do not support the claim that wartime spending ended the Depression. From the cyclical

of 1939, the U.S. economy had been in balance sheet repair mode for a decade, and the net flow of mortgage credit, at long last, had been in positive territory for only one year. In these circumstances, it is a reasonable hypothesis – especially in light of what we learned from our experience after 2007 – that fiscal stimulus would have been far more effective in 1939 than in 1930, when balance sheet repairs had hardly begun. The intervening years brought a flood of restorative balance sheet actions: bank failures, household and business bankruptcies, and measures by the Home Owners Loan Corporation to reissue more than a million new mortgages with lower payments and, in some cases, with lower principal balances. At the time, all of these actions were seen by citizens and experts alike – just as they are now – as aspects of the economic distress, not as central to the process of healing balance sheets and resuming the flows of economic activity and growth.

1.3.6 Will New Models Save Us?

Against all of this background, *The Economist (2013)* offered a startling assessment that belated efforts (i.e., five years after the beginning of the Great Recession) were underway to introduce banks into macroeconomic models and that "big central banks are interested in these new ideas although staff economists are reluctant to abandon existing 'industry-standard' models." Existing models have the property of internal dynamic stability that helps to model responses to external shocks. However, the internal instability (or erratic cycling) suggested by the chart in Figure 1.1, and the associated linkage of the economy to housing and mortgage markets, far exceed the reach of these models, as even their most dedicated proponents acknowledge.[18] The challenge is to develop new models that account for cyclical movements at the level of major sectors, as shown in the figures in Chapters 3 through 5. To accomplish this, it seems necessary to develop models that incorporate

---

trough in 1933 to the next trough before the war in 1938, when government spending was low, real GNP grew at an annual rate of 6.7 percent. From the 1938 trough to the first trough after the war in 1947, when government spending was high, the annual growth rate remained at 6.7 percent per year. This record provides little support for the hypothesis that government spending increases economic growth. In Chapter 10, we provide evidence from international comparisons that strongly supports the opposite course – in an open economy with a floating currency, reduction of government spending and deficits facilitates rapid growth in the aftermath of a balance sheet crisis.

[18] Varadarajan Venkata Chari (2010) of the University of Minnesota and the Minneapolis Federal Reserve Bank, in testimony before the U.S. House of Representatives in July 2010, stated that "any interesting model must be a dynamic stochastic general equilibrium [DSGE] model" and went on to observe that "the [DSGE] models are not well suited to analyze extremely rare events." However, the rare events involve damaged balance sheets that are not part of the traditional general equilibrium models.

monetary policy and a financial sector that is engaged with households in important ways. A first step toward that goal is to establish the key features of these elements of economic activity. A second key objective of this book is to establish a base of facts about the interactions among real-sector activity, financial-sector activity, and monetary policy over the economic cycle so that future models of economic cycles and financial crises can be developed on a sounder empirical basis.

1.4 Experimental Markets and the Aggregate Economy

In this chapter, we have outlined key events in economic history from the 1920s to the Great Recession, and we offer the interpretation that severe economic slumps are a consequence of unusual balance sheet crises. In Chapter 2, we turn to an examination of learning from experimental market studies and, in particular, we identify differences in human behavior in two contrasting market types: (1) markets for consumer nondurable goods and services; and (2) markets for long-lived consumer durables, such as housing. We believe that these differences – which are not a part of standard economic thinking and modeling – are critical to understanding how certain markets, such as housing, that do not constitute a large share of total product nevertheless can be a source of severe instability and economic suffering. This is a frequent characteristic of market performance, easily as important as the more familiar characteristic that most markets are stable and efficient and steadily contribute to wealth creation.

References

Associated Press (2008). "Bernanke: Fed Ready to Cut Interest Rates Again." January 10. Available at www.nbcnews.com/id/22592939/#.UriqBvvwiSo.

Bagehot, Walter (1873). *Lombard Street.* London: Henry S. King & Co.

Bair, Sheila (2012). *Bull by the Horns.* New York: The Free Press.

Barro, Robert, and Charles Redlick (2011). "Macroeconomic Effects from Government Purchases and Taxes." *Quarterly Journal of Economics,* 126, 1, pp. 51–102.

Bernanke, Ben (2008). "Outstanding Issues in the Analysis of Inflation." Speech given at the Federal Reserve Bank of Boston's 53rd Annual Economic Conference, Chatham, MA. *Board of Governors of the Federal Reserve System,* June 9.

Bernanke, Ben (2012a). "Origins and Mission of the Federal Reserve." *Board of Governors of the Federal Reserve System* (March 20). Available at www.federalreserve.gov/mediacenter/files/chairman-bernanke-lecture1-20120320.pdf.

Bernanke, Ben (2012b). "The Federal Reserve's Response to the Financial Crisis." *Board of Governors of the Federal Reserve System* (March 27). Available at www.federalreserve.gov/mediacenter/files/chairman-bernanke-lecture3-20120327.pdf.

Bernanke, Ben (2012c). "The Aftermath of the Crisis." *Board of Governors of the Federal Reserve System* (March 29). Available at www.federalreserve.gov/mediacenter/files/chairman-bernanke-lecture4-20120329.pdf.

Board of Governors (2007). "Meeting of the Federal Open Market Committee on December 11, 2007." *Board of Governors of the Federal Reserve System.* Available at www.federalreserve.gov/monetarypolicy/files/FOMC20071211meeting.pdf.

Bricker, Jesse, Arthur B. Kennickell, Kevin B. Moore, and John Sabelhaus (2012). "Changes in U.S. Family Finances from 2007 to 2010: Evidence from the Survey of Consumer Finances." *Federal Reserve Bulletin,* Division of Research and Statistics, 98, 2, pp. 1–80. Available at www.federalreserve.gov/pubs/bulletin/2012/pdf/scf12.pdf.

Business Cycle Dating Committee (2010). *National Bureau of Economic Research,* September 20. Available at www.nber.org/cycles/sept2010.html.

Chari, Varadarajan Venkata (2010). "Testimony before the Committee on Science and Technology, Subcommittee on Investigations and Oversight." U.S. House of Representatives, July 20. Available at http://science.house.gov/hearing/subcommittee-investigations-and-oversight-hearing-science-economics.

CoreLogic (2013). "CoreLogic Reports 1.4 Million Borrowers Returned to Positive Equity in Q3, 2012." Irvine, CA, January 17. Available at www.corelogic.com/research/negative-equity/corelogic-q3-2012-negative-equity-report.pdf.

The Economist (2013). "Economics After the Crisis: New Model Army." January 19, p. 75.

Fostel, Ana, and John Geanakoplos (2008). "Leverage Cycles and the Anxious Economy." *American Economic Review,* 98, pp. 1211–44.

Friedman, Milton, and Anna J. Schwartz (1963). *A Monetary History of the United States.* Princeton, NJ: Princeton University Press.

Humphries, Stan (2012). "Despite Home Value Gains, Underwater Homeowners Owe $1.2 Trillion More than Homes' Worth." *Zillow Real Estate Research,* May 24.

Leamer, Edward E. (2007). "Housing *is* the Business Cycle." Federal Reserve Bank of Kansas City, Jackson Hole [Wyoming] Symposium, pp. 149–233. Available at www.kc.frb.org/publicat/sympos/2007/pdf/leamer_0415.pdf.

Reinhart, Carmen M., and Kenneth S. Rogoff (2008). "Is the 2007 U.S. Subprime Crisis So Different? An International Historical Comparison." *American Economic Review,* 98, pp. 339–44.

Smith, Adam (1759/1976). *The Theory of Moral Sentiments.* Oxford edition, edited by D. Raphael and A. Macfie. Indianapolis, IN: Liberty Fund, Inc., 1976.

Wallich, Henry C. (1988). "Some Uses of Economics." In *Recollections of Eminent Economists,* Volume 1, ed. J. A. Kregel. London: Macmillan.

2

Goods and Services Markets versus
Asset Markets

Cassano agreed to meet with all the big Wall Street firms and discuss the logic of their deals – to investigate how a bunch of shaky loans could be transformed into AAA-rated bonds. Together with [Eugene] Park and a few others, Cassano set out on a series of meetings with Morgan Stanley, Goldman Sachs, and the rest – all of whom argued how unlikely it was for housing prices to fall all at once. "They all said the same thing," says one of the traders present. "They'd go back to historical real-estate prices over 60 years and say they had never fallen all at once."
– Michael Lewis, *Vanity Fair,* July 2009

It's a pretty unlikely possibility. We've never had a decline in house prices on a nationwide basis. So, what I think is more likely is that house prices will slow, maybe stabilize, might slow consumption spending a bit. I don't think it's gonna drive the economy too far from its full employment path, though...
– Ben Bernanke, *CNBC Interview,* July 1, 2005

2.1 Two Types of Markets: The Good and the Sometimes Ugly

This chapter summarizes findings from two distinct types of experimental markets that are directly relevant to understanding the sources of both stability and instability in the macroeconomy: (1) the class of nondurable consumed goods and services that constitute about 75 percent of U.S. private expenditures (i.e., GDP minus government expenditures); and (2) asset markets, particularly those in which the items traded have long lives and whose market value, therefore, may be importantly influenced by the future price expectations of the participants (prominent examples include houses, securities, and commercial real estate). The parallels between the laboratory and the economy in each of these two cases suggest underlying modes and principles of human behavior that are similar – conditional on the differing characteristics of the items being traded in these two broad categories of economic activity.

In the laboratory and in the macroeconomy, output and prices in markets for nondurable goods and services are stable and their performance corresponds closely to the predictions of economic models. Yet, markets for many assets – both real and financial – have highly variable prices and production levels. Three key elements of the experimental asset market literature stand out, and all three were prominent features of the housing market in recent history. The most prominent characteristic of asset market experiments is that price bubbles are common in them. A second feature is that price bubbles in asset market experiments are exacerbated by liquidity – that is, the cash endowment levels and rate of inflow of new cash. Liquidity creates conditions in which buyers can access more funds and pay more for asset units. If buyers believe that the asset value will increase, then liquidity provides them with the resources that they need to purchase more asset units or pay higher prices. Similarly, housing bubbles have been closely associated with the availability of mortgage credit. A third feature of asset market experiments also appeared in the housing market bubble. Before an asset bubble collapses, trading volume typically declines substantially. This occurred in the housing market when new home sales fell sharply in the first quarter of 2006. Builders soon recognized the reduced sales volume and reduced their production of new homes early in 2006. After several quarters of reduced sales, time-to-sale began to escalate and, eventually, sellers accepted lower prices in order to complete a sale. The temporal pattern of changes to housing sales volume, production, and prices during the economic cycle is examined in Chapter 3.

The experimental literature associated with the two types of markets identified performance properties that differed from the ideas and expectations that prevailed among economics and finance researchers when the experiments were first reported. In the case of nondurable commodities and services, markets were stable under even more general conditions than economists had anticipated, but prices in asset markets were much less stable than they had expected. Although economists have now largely come to recognize these results, their implications for the aggregate economy have not been examined. Our primary objectives in this chapter are to describe the basic patterns of the two types of market experiments and to explore their implications for the aggregate economy, especially with regard to the impact of asset market bubbles on economic performance. Although asset market bubbles are often difficult for market participants and even keen observers to detect, it becomes painfully apparent when a bubble collapses. It can be compared to an avalanche or an earthquake: Pressure builds invisibly to our perception and it is difficult to predict the timing of its dramatic release, but we can search for characteristic features that precede and follow the event, and we can also take precautions that mitigate the damage when these events occur.

2.2 The Contrast between Markets for Nondurable Goods and for Long-Lived Durable Assets

In the 1950s and 1960s, the first laboratory market experiments explored the price discovery process for the delivery of nondurable goods and services that are produced, sold, and consumed and then disappear. In these "pay and consume" markets, the items are not retraded. Laboratory experiments that capture this feature, and in which value and cost information is private and dispersed among buyers or sellers, were found to be astonishingly efficient in discovering the welfare-maximizing equilibrium prices and exchange quantities. Contrary to common professional and theoretical expectations at the time, the number of agents did not have to be large; agents did not need complete information on supply and demand or to be capable of sophisticated or fully rational individual economic action.

This unexpected discovery boded well for the performance of market economies with strong institutional (property right) foundations, and there were abundant supporting parallel examples in studies of the history of Western economic development.[1]

It was against this experimental background and its gradual academic acceptance that the first asset market experiments were conducted in the 1980s. The initial experimental asset market designs were deliberately simple and transparent. Subject agents were endowed with cash and asset shares in a finite-horizon trading environment in which the expected dividend paid to the owner of an asset unit was common information. A prevailing belief among economists – fully shared by the experimenters at the time – was that these markets would quickly yield transactions at prices reflecting the "rational expectations" intrinsic dividend value of the shares. However, the belief was not supported by the first experiments. The original research plan had been to create a baseline so transparent that it would yield the expected "rational" result and then proceed to more opaque environments in an attempt to generate bubble behavior. However, the baseline experiments generated bubbles aplenty, so the question became one of examining their robustness and exploring various treatments that might eliminate them.

---

[1] For example, North (1990) and Rosenberg and Birdzell (1986) discussed this issue.

Contrasting these two strands of research, we see that in experiments, markets for perishable goods converge quickly to their equilibrium, whereas asset markets are prone to bubbles and collapses on the longer path to equilibrium. These two unexpected and puzzling discoveries were ultimately shown to be robust across a great variety of subject pools in hundreds of replications by many skeptical scholars.

The observed behavior of these asset markets is consistent with a mathematical model of bubbles based on two types of investment behavior: (1) fundamental-value traders who buy (sell) in proportion to the discount (premium) on intrinsic value; and (2) momentum- or trend-based traders who buy (sell) in proportion to the rate of increase (decrease) in the asset price. Some combinations of these trader types generate and sustain bubbles. In this model, placing greater weight on momentum trading causes bubbles to become more pronounced. The model also implies that if momentum traders have access to more liquidity – in the form of either higher endowments of cash or access to margin buying – the effect is to generate and sustain a larger bubble.

Although we claim that momentum trading and liquidity can fuel a bubble, the factors that cause people to generate ebullient price expectations both inside and outside of the laboratory – in a "crowd" – and the factors that trigger the sudden turnaround in those expectations in a crash remain mysteries. We can mathematically model price bubbles, and we have learned much about the conditions that exacerbate or dampen them in controlled laboratory environments. Yet, the sparks that ignite bubbles, the myopic self-reinforcing behavioral mechanisms that sustain them, and the factors that suddenly can extinguish them in a crash remain difficult to anticipate and to predict.

Financial economists often refer to price crashes as "fat left tails" of the probability distribution of price changes. However, this is misleading in that price changes are not independent events. In Chapter 3, we argue that the widespread belief that residential real estate was a secure investment combined with policies that attracted an unusual flow of foreign investment into the United States to create an unusual flow of mortgage credit into the housing market. Mortgage credit pushed prices up, creating the instability. The bubble and collapse were not "fat tail," "black swan," or "sunspot" events: The bubble was part of a positive feedback loop in which price increases attracted new buyers and lenders. This positive feedback loop pushed prices up to a level that could no longer be sustained. At that point, mortgage-fund growth and house price increases ceased. Soon afterward, many borrowers began to default. Mortgage financing then began to decline sharply and house prices fell as available mortgage funds diminished. By this point, the positive feedback loop that had prevailed during the bubble turned into a self-reinforcing negative feedback loop in the crash.

This chapter surveys the disparate results of these two streams of experimental learning that contrast commodity flow and asset markets. In the next three chapters, we use our findings from experimental markets to interpret output and price movements in important sectors of the macroeconomy over the course of the economic cycle. We also examine characteristics of the assets that lead to large differences in the macroeconomy between residential real estate and other asset classes.

2.3 Markets for Consumer Nondurables

In an early experimental study modeled after consumer nondurable goods and services markets – in which items are produced and sold, then disappear when consumed – Smith (1962) discovered that these markets are efficient under much more general conditions than economists had expected. These surprising experimental results understandably were met with resistance at the time.[2] Subsequently, hundreds of experimental studies exploring the phenomenon demonstrated the robustness and remarkable generality of this competitive equilibrium discovery process for nondurable goods and services.

2.3.1 The Experiment Procedures: Motivating Trade

In these experiments, buyers' "values" and sellers' "costs" are induced by the experimenter. The experimenter distributes a card to each seller with that seller's costs listed on it and then pays the seller an amount equal to the difference between the prices he receives and his costs for each unit sold. Similarly, the experimenter distributes a card to each buyer with her unit values listed on it, and the buyer earns an amount equal to the difference

---

[2] One aspect of the prevailing view of a competitive market was that many traders would be required to reach the competitive equilibrium price. Stigler (1957, p. 14) argued that "Perfect market competition will prevail when there are indefinitely many traders." Another prevailing viewpoint is that agents have common knowledge of market conditions – a view that goes back at least to Jevons (1888, para. 254), who argued that "A market, then, is theoretically perfect only when all traders have perfect knowledge of the conditions of supply and demand, and the consequent ratio of exchange; and in such a market, as we shall now see, there can only be one ratio of exchange of one uniform commodity at any moment."

between the induced value for each unit purchased and the price that she pays for each unit she acquires. Prices are determined through a voluntary process in which sellers call out public "ask" prices and buyers call out public "bid" prices. One common and useful market rule is that each new bid is required to improve on the terms of the current best (or "standing") bid; similarly, each new ask must improve on the best ask. As the bids are received, the experimenter writes them on a whiteboard in the hand-run version of the auction. At any time, each buyer has the option to accept the standing (i.e., the lowest) ask; similarly, any seller may accept the standing (i.e., the highest) bid. At that point, the accepted bid or offer is erased, the trade price is agreed on, and the traders' identities are written on the board. Thus, an exchange is bilateral between the buyer who accepts the standing ask and the seller who posted the standing ask, or between the seller who accepts the standing bid and the buyer who posted the bid. A similar trading procedure (or trading "institution"), known as an open-outcry continuous double auction, was used in the experimental test of competitive market performance reported in Smith (1962).[3] The bid, ask, and contract (i.e., acceptance) process plays out in real time in public in a rule-governed but completely voluntary process experienced in common by the participants. The open-outcry double auction is efficient and converges even faster than fully computerized double auctions, in which buyers and sellers interact with one another only through computer terminals. A computer interface for recording the oral bids, asks, and acceptances called out by the buyers and sellers provides a useful hybrid between an oral double auction and a fully computerized double auction. In this hybrid mechanism, as a bid or an ask is announced by a buyer or a seller, the experimenter enters it into a computer and it appears on a screen projected at the front of the room, as shown in Figure 2.1. At any time during the auction, there is a total accumulated quantity traded and a current standing best bid and ask, defining the bid–ask spread that appears at the top of the screen display (see Figure 2.1).

2.3.2 Prices Emerge from Decentralized Actions Governed by Rules

Figure 2.1 plots the bids, asks, and contract prices for a recent demonstration market much like those originally conducted more than fifty years ago.

---

[3] Experimental markets are far more complex today with participants interacting through computers. As they trade "electronically," all experiment data are processed and recorded in the computers. See, for example, Gjerstad (2007) and Plott and Smith (2008).

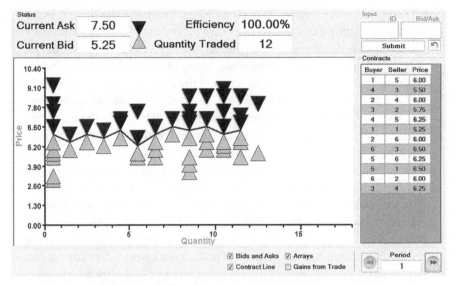

Figure 2.1. **Market screen display in an open-outcry market.** The downward arrows are a sequence of decreasing asking prices; the upward arrows are a sequence of increasing bid prices. Where they meet, a trade occurs. When the standing bid or ask is accepted, a contract between the buyer and seller results. A line connects successive contract prices. The table on the right identifies the buyer and seller who were paired in each contract and the price at which they traded. For example, the first trade at $6.00 paired Buyer B1 and Seller S5. During the trading activity, buyers' values and sellers' costs are not shown because they are private to each buyer and seller.

The demonstration market consists of twelve participants. All participants observe the display shown in Figure 2.1 that is projected onto a screen. The screen displays each bid, ask, and trade price as they occur. In this market, bids, asks, and acceptances of bids and asks that result in trades are made orally by buyers and sellers. Each unit purchased by a buyer yields a profit equal to the difference between her privately assigned value for the unit and the price paid to one of the sellers. Similarly, each unit sold yields the seller a profit equal to the difference between his privately assigned cost for the unit and the price received from a buyer. We think of each buyer as having a private maximum reservation price that she will pay for successive units that she might buy. Similarly, each seller has a private minimum reservation price that he will accept for units that he might sell. However, no one knows or can know in advance which trading prices will emerge. The purpose of the experiments was to understand how stable (or unstable) the prices and allocations are in goods and services markets and how they might come about in a world in which new goods and services are perpetually emerging and their market viability is subjected to market tests.

As each trade occurs, the buyer and seller fill in a private record sheet, allowing each individual to account for his or her profit on each trade and to determine total earnings. A seller profits by selling above his unit cost. Because the seller profits at any sale price that exceeds his unit cost, we also call this cost a "reservation price." Similarly, a buyer profits by paying less than her unit value, or reservation price. (In the economy, we observe this eagerness to "profit" dramatized when buyers crowd into retail stores for special sales.) A new trading period begins immediately after completion of the previous one, in sequence. The new period, or "trading day," may simply repeat the previous conditions with the same schedules of unit costs for sellers and unit values for buyers. Alternatively, these schedules may be altered in the new period, depending on the purpose of the experiment. In research experiments, total individual earnings are paid privately to each person, in cash, after completion of a session.

Markets with this structure have been observed to settle into a stationary pattern with the following four properties that have become a central part of our understanding of the nondurable goods market economy:

(1) Each individual is maximizing her earnings, given the behavior of others. At prevailing prices, each buyer purchases all units that she values at least as highly as the price she pays and no unit that she values as less than the prevailing prices. Sellers behave analogously.

(2) Prevailing market prices adjust so that the number of units sought (according to the first criterion) at the prevailing prices equals the number of units provided (also according to the first criterion) at those prices.

(3) The aggregate gain from exchange by the group members, as measured by their total earnings, is equal to the maximum possible amount.

(4) Participants in the experiment are unaware that their pursuit of criterion (1) leads to criteria (2) and (3).

2.3.3 Supply and Demand for Perishables: Invisible Guide to Best Social Outcomes

Figure 2.2 arrays all sellers' unit costs (ordered from lowest to highest) and all buyers' unit values (ordered from highest to lowest) onto the graph in Figure 2.1, which shows asks, bids, and transaction prices.[4] These arrays of costs

---

[4] We are indebted to our colleague Bart Wilson for making Figures 2.1 and 2.2 available to us.

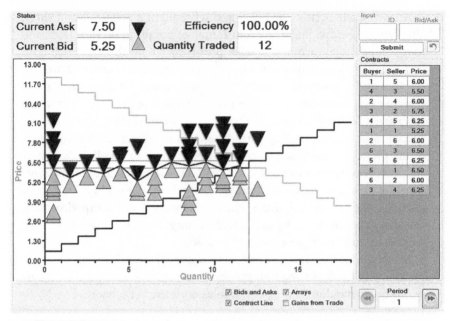

Figure 2.2. **Supply and demand in the market.** The experimenter assigns to each seller a private cost associated with each unit that the seller has available to sell (four units); to each buyer a private value is assigned associated with each unit the buyer desires to buy (four units). The upward-sloping supply schedule is formed by arraying these seller costs from lowest to highest. The downward-sloping demand schedule of prices is formed by arraying the buyer values from highest to lowest.

and values generate market supply and market demand functions.[5] Because each seller's unit costs, or reservation prices, are private information, the aggregate cost array that generates the market supply is distributed among all six suppliers; however, in aggregate, it is unknown to any single seller or to any buyer. This is an inherent property of markets in the world and a design condition in the experiments. Demand is similarly generated by the

---

[5] The graph of the array of costs is identical to the graph of the market supply, but the array of costs indicates for a given quantity "q" of output what the cost would be for the unit with the qth lowest cost, whereas the market supply indicates for a given price "p" how many units would be supplied at that price. For example, in the graph in Figure 2.2, the cost of the twelfth unit would be $6.10. If the price is $6.10, the number of units supplied to the market would be either eleven or twelve. Because the two concepts have the same graph, we can shift from discussions of the array of induced costs to the market supply function that results from the induced costs. Similarly, we can shift between discussions of the array of induced values and the market demand function that results from them.

ordered set of buyer values, or reservation prices, that the experimenter has dispersed among the six buyers so that the market demand is unknown to any individual buyer or seller.

We may think that a buyer (and, likewise, a seller) in the world surely must not be walking around with precise reserve prices in her head; indeed, we do not have to assume that a buyer is consciously aware of such a limit purchase price or a seller limit sale price. Those who attend an "English," or progressive buyer-bid, auction – commonly used for the sale of art objects, livestock, antiques, and numerous other commodities – invariably observe that there are many active bidders at the low initial bid prices but, as the bids rise, there are fewer active bidders, until finally one bidder wins. At every auction, it is thus revealed that people do indeed have reservation prices that may be vague, even subconscious, but that induce them to drop out of the bid competition as prices ascend.

In the experiment, each seller knows only his private cost information, which is a small subset of the cost information that is used to construct the overall market supply. Similarly, a buyer knows only her private value information, which is only a portion of all of the buyers' values that generate the market demand. With this fragmentary information, no one knows the market supply, the market demand, or the equilibrium price. The larger the number of market participants, the more fragmentary is each participant's knowledge of the whole. Similarly, in the economy, contemporary market theory is founded on the proposition that each individual is the most informed about his or her own private subjective circumstances and is not so well informed about the circumstances of others.

Hence, the designer of the experiment knows all sellers' unit costs and can use them to construct the market supply. The market supply is shown as the upward sloping step function in Figure 2.2. Similarly, the experimenter knows each buyer's unit values and can use them to construct the market demand. Market demand is shown as the downward sloping step function in Figure 2.2. Figure 2.2 superimposes these supply and demand conditions on Figure 2.1.

The equilibrium obtained from these supply and demand functions has several properties, as follows:

(1) For the price that prevails in the market, each seller trades all units with a cost below the market price, and each buyer purchases all units that she values above the market price.

(2) At the market price, the number of units that buyers want to purchase then equals the number of units the sellers want to provide.

(3) Conditions 1 and 2 characterize an equilibrium price and quantity of exchange; the conditions also guarantee that the surplus from exchange is maximized.

In the example shown in Figure 2.2, the gain from exchange is largest if and only if the twelve lowest cost units among all of the sellers are sold at mutually agreeable prices to the buyers with the twelve highest value units. That is, each unit with a unit cost below (and none equal to or above) $6.60 is sold, and each unit with a value above (and none equal to or below) $6.10 is bought. When these conditions are realized, in any market period, the market is 100 percent efficient – no improvement is possible. The top-right panel of Figure 2.2 shows that twelve units were traded and the efficiency was 100 percent.

In the example, equilibrium prices P* are between $6.10 and $6.60, and the quantity traded is twelve units. In replications of this experiment with a wide variety of different participant populations, it is common for eleven to thirteen units to trade, with efficiencies in excess of 95 percent of the possible cash profits from trade collected by the group.

In the table listing the trading prices as they emerge in sequence, note that four of the last five exchanges are at prices in the set P*. It is typical that most trades are close to the equilibrium price even in early "trading days" in some configurations of supply and demand, as explained in the following discussion.

2.3.4 Two Early Experiments: Falsifying an "Explanation"

The first reported experiment in Smith (1962) involved eleven buyers and eleven sellers, each with a capacity to trade only one unit. The arrays of unit values and unit costs from this experiment are shown on the left side of Figure 2.3. These unit costs and values remained unchanged, with the same values and costs held by the participants in Periods 2 through 5. The right side of the figure shows the trade prices in each of the five periods.

Before the experiment was conducted, economists strongly believed that many buyers and sellers were needed to reach a competitive equilibrium outcome; they also believed that each trader needed complete information about market supply and demand conditions. Consequently, the rapid convergence to a competitive equilibrium outcome in this experiment – even with information dispersed among buyers and sellers – came as a surprise to many economists and took decades to be widely accepted and understood.

In modern times, the perspective gained from the experiments had been independently proposed by Hayek (1945), whose critique of the state of

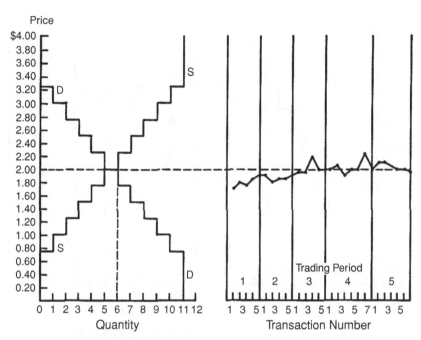

Figure 2.3. **First open-outcry auction experiment.** Eleven buyers and eleven sellers, each with a capacity to trade one unit, participated in a sequence of five consecutive repetitions of the auction. The supply and demand conditions in each trading period were identical. These conditions are shown on the left side of the figure. Trade prices in each of the five periods are shown on the right side of the figure.

mid-twentieth-century general equilibrium theory influenced the subsequent contributions of Hurwicz (2008) and his many collaborators on the theory of decentralized exchange processes.

At the time, Smith believed that the convergence toward equilibrium in Figure 2.3 may have been an artifact of the symmetrical supply and demand design model. This was tested in a subsequent experiment, shown in Figure 2.4, using an asymmetrical design in which, in equilibrium, sellers profit far more than buyers. The results suggested that although such a market might commence initially with prices well away from the equilibrium, in subsequent replications, the equilibrium is reached within a few periods.

Beginning in the mid-1970s, the first computerized laboratory experiments were pioneered and reported by A. W. Williams (1980). With the new technology, experimental market studies were greatly expanded in scope and complexity. Expansions in scope included many studies comparing different institutions (rules) under which people commonly exchange goods and services. Examples include comparisons between posted offer price

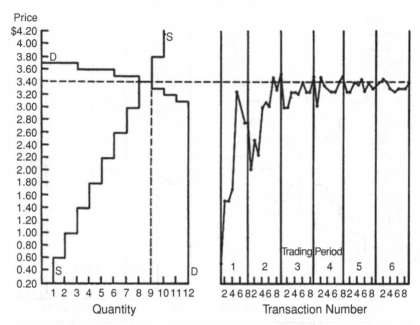

Figure 2.4. **An open-outcry market with asymmetric supply and demand.** Market with ten sellers and twelve buyers designed to test whether the equilibrium tendency in supply and demand markets (see Figure 2.3) is an artifact of symmetry. In the following experiment in equilibrium, the sellers' profit from exchange is much greater than the buyers' profit. Many trades in Period 1 are significantly below equilibrium but, with repetition, we observe convergence toward the equilibrium price ($3.40) as well as to the equilibrium exchange quantity (9).

markets – such as those that are common in retail trade – and double auction trading and comparisons between the double auction and an auction with sealed bids and offers. Although institutions matter, especially in the speed of convergence to efficient competitive outcomes, market experiments for nondurables tended to yield strong support for efficient performance and exchange at the equilibrium price.

New studies greatly expanded the complexity of the markets examined. These extensions allowed for interdependent demand in which the amount people are willing to pay for Good A depends on the price of Good B and vice versa. In these more complex markets, observed prices and exchange quantities converged to the competitive equilibrium predictions.[6]

---

[6] See Williams et al. (2000) and Gjerstad (2013). Moreover, for the single-commodity markets first studied experimentally in Smith (1962), Gjerstad and Dickhaut (1998) developed a model of heuristic learning by buyers and sellers about the prices that are likely to be

Taken together, all of these results demonstrate how well markets function when the items traded are not retraded later but instead are produced, purchased, and consumed and then disappear, and this sequential process is repeated again and again.[7] Everyone is a seller of something – services or skills that are inputs to production, if not products. Hence, the broader implication, articulated forcefully more than 230 years ago by Adam Smith (1776) in *The Wealth of Nations* (see Chapter 3 for reference), is that markets enable people to specialize: "The division of labour is determined by the extent of the market." Adam Smith's axiomatic principle that leads to the discovery of specialization and exchange is the human "propensity to truck, barter and exchange." This is what enabled wealth creation on an ever-widening social scale as markets were gradually extended to strangers and ultimately became global. The principle is alive and well in the numerous experiments, as demonstrated by the examples given herein.

2.4 Asset Markets

With the advent of computer-based experimental laboratories, researchers also turned to the examination of markets for assets – in particular, to much-simplified asset-trading environments but with properties like assets traded in stock markets. The first asset market experiments were conducted beginning in the early 1980s and were first published in Smith, Suchanek, and Williams (1988).

The mainstream financial literature had espoused the view that asset markets were efficient in the sense of "rational expectations"; that is, at any time, all of the historical and current information relevant to determining the value of the assets was incorporated into their current prices, except for pure random variation. As new information arrived, the asset price would respond and effectively incorporate the rational, forward-looking expectations of people's beliefs as to how that information affects value.

accepted by the other side of the market. They showed, in artificial-intelligence simulations, that when traders follow strategies based on these beliefs, market prices converge to the competitive equilibrium. Gjerstad (2007) also showed – by mixing algorithmic traders and human traders in the same market experiment – that these heuristic traders can perform as well as or even better than human buyers and sellers.

[7] The result in Gjerstad (2007) may appear to be the least compatible with the proposition that these markets function effectively because that paper demonstrated that simple, algorithmic agents with moderately sophisticated strategies outperform human subjects and reach efficient outcomes. Yet, this result also demonstrated that efficient outcomes do not require common knowledge of market conditions (as Jevons and subsequent theorists thought necessary).

2.4.1 Asset Markets: Unanticipated Bubbles on the Way
to Equilibrium

The initial experimental designs of the 1980s were meant to be simple and transparent and to serve as a microcosm of this world of rational expectations. Subject agents were endowed with cash and shares in a finite-horizon trading environment in which the dividend holding value of shares was common information. The research plan was to create a baseline set of experiments in which – as it was believed at the time – trading prices would reflect the common transparent information on fundamental value (FV) that was provided to subjects by the experimenter. Given this baseline, the research plan was to then introduce incomplete, less transparent information and treatments manipulating the information made available privately and publicly. The intention was to explore the conditions under which observed prices might deviate from FV and perhaps generate price bubbles.

The belief, however, that these original, simple asset market experiments would quickly yield transactions at prices reflecting the "rational expectations" intrinsic dividend value of the shares was not supported by the first experiment. The original research program, designed to observe a baseline no-bubble environment, was transformed by the initial results into investigations of robustness and the exploration of treatments that could enhance or retard bubbles. These first results were subsequently shown to be remarkably robust – as summarized herein – in a great variety of subject pools in hundreds of replications by many scholars.

Figure 2.5 shows a standard configuration for the earliest asset market experiments. The asset randomly paid one of four dividend amounts in each of fifteen periods. The amount was 0, 8, 28, or 60 cents, each with equal probability. The expected value of the dividend for one period was 24 cents; if the asset were held for all fifteen periods, its expected dividend payment was $3.60. The expected payoff fell 24 cents per period, so the value of the asset declined in each period, as shown by the step function in Figure 2.5. The figure also indicates the number of asset units and amount of cash that each of three distinct subject "types" had in the experiment. Subjects who began an experiment session with fewer asset units were given more cash; each subject received assets and cash worth $13.05, regardless of subject type.

Figure 2.6 illustrates a series of three experiments in which the same group of subjects was recruited to the laboratory to earn money and acquire experience across the three sessions on separate days. The results shown in the lower panel of the figure plot the mean double auction contract price for

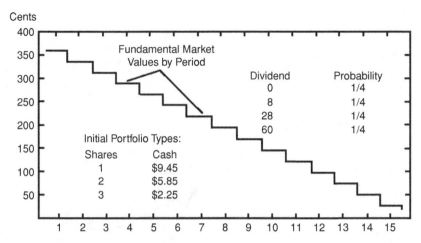

Figure 2.5. **Dividends and fundamental values in an asset experiment.** This figure displays the endowments of shares or cash for three portfolio types; the dividend probability distribution; and a chart showing the decline of 24 cents in the "fundamental market value" of an asset each period, as the initial right to fifteen draws is used up with each end-of-period dividend realization.

each of the fifteen periods of an experiment session across inexperienced, once-experienced, and – finally – twice-experienced subjects, and they are typical of the results from hundreds of experiments conducted by many investigators. A subject's earnings paid in cash at the close of the experiment is the sum of initial cash endowment, plus all dividends paid on shares held at the end of each period, plus all revenues from the sale of shares minus all expenditures from asset purchases.

2.4.2 Learning from the Bubble Generator

Numerous experimental treatments have been devised in an effort to eliminate bubbles, but the phenomenon has proven remarkably resilient. We describe a number of conditions that have been attempted to eliminate them and the effects of those treatments, as follows[8]:

(1) Common public information on fundamental value, including regular reminders of the asset's "fundamental" value at the end of each trading period, is not sufficient to induce common expectations and trading at a mean price that approximates fundamental value.

---

[8] Based on Smith, Suchanek, and Williams (1988) and Porter and Smith (1994).

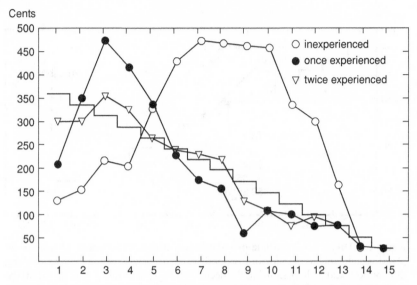

Figure 2.6. **Mean contract prices in three asset market experiment sessions.** This figure shows outcomes from three laboratory asset market experiment sessions using subjects who are inexperienced (i.e., their first time in an asset trading market), once-experienced (i.e., the same subjects return and repeat the same experiment), and twice-experienced (i.e., subjects return for a third session and repeat the experiment again). Each series represents one of the three sessions, and each dot represents the average contract price for a period in that session for that series.

Common information does not in itself resolve each individual's uncertainty about the behavior of others.

(2) For inexperienced subjects, a treatment in which the dividend is certain has no significant effect on the amplitude of bubbles or on share turnover (i.e., exchange volume per share outstanding), although the duration of the bubble is increased.

(3) Allowing short selling does not significantly diminish the amplitude and duration of a bubble but turnover is significantly increased.

(4) Allowing margin buying produces a significant increase in a bubble's amplitude for inexperienced but not experienced subjects.

(5) The use of subject pools of small-business owners, midlevel corporate executives, and over-the-counter market dealers has no significant effect on bubble characteristics for inexperienced subjects.

(6) Traders' price expectations cannot account for some of the most important features of the price paths in these experiments. Smith et al. (1988) examined traders' expectations by asking subjects at the end

of each period to forecast the mean price for the next period, with a monetary reward given at the end of the experiment to the best forecaster across all periods of the experiment. The consensus (mean) forecasts show that (a) bullish expectations arise early in the sessions; (b) after a period has ended, the mean forecast of the change in the next period is typically close to the change that just occurred in the previous period (i.e., forecasts are adaptive); and (c) mean forecasts invariably fail to predict price jumps and directional turning points. Although the mean forecasts miss the turning points, some individuals are better at forecasting than others, and there is a positive correlation (not necessarily causal) between forecasting accuracy and profits earned in an experiment.

(7) A more reliable predictor (than indicated by price forecasts) of the next period's mean price is obtained from the subjects' endogenous bid–ask activity: The difference between the number of bids and asks placed in a period is a good predictor of price changes in the next period. This difference is a simple unweighted count (i.e., all bids, asks, and contracts are for a single unit) of the total number of bids to buy, B_t, minus the total number of asks to sell, A_t. Thus, the parameters to be estimated are defined by the following linear equation:

$$P_{t+1} - P_t = a + b(B_t - A_t) + e_t$$

In this equation, the change in mean price from the current period to the next, $P_{t+1} - P_t$, is divided into the following three additive parts:

(a) A constant change, a, due to the passage of one time period, reducing by 1 the remaining number of dividend realizations.
(b) A change that is a proportion b of the excess bid activity $(B_t - A_t)$ in the current period, which is typically related positively to the group's average price change.
(c) A change due to otherwise unexplained random noise (e_t).

Most estimates of the coefficient a are negative and not significantly different than the one-period expected dividend value; that is, each period uses up one of the dividend draws and, on average, this is reflected in a decline in the one-period change in mean price. Also, most estimates of the coefficient b are positive and significantly greater than zero. Hence, mean price changes have the same sign as excess bids. If a peak in a bubble is imminent, this tends to be signaled by negative excess bids one period in advance.

These patterns in asset market experiments have parallels in housing market behavior: Sellers list their houses with high offers and
wait for a buyer to accept or make a counter bid. If buyers are actively
placing bids, then the house is not on the market for long, and new
listings can be placed at rising prices; this corresponds in the double
auction asset markets to the number of bids exceeding the number
of asks. If the housing market turns down, sellers continue to post
high asking prices, but buyers are less active. Consequently, the time
that houses are listed increases before they are sold, corresponding
to an excess of asks over bids in the experimental markets. In both
cases, price changes lag behind excess bid activity.

(8) Experience, particularly common group experience in two previous
experiments, is sufficient to yield prices that approximate declining fundamental value. Consequently, over time and through direct
experience, people come to have fundamental rational expectations.
They do not attain this state by mental construction – that is, by the
application of reasoning to common information that results in a
rational expectations outcome.

(9) "Inside traders" can earn excess profits and they can reduce the size
of a bubble if they know that bubbles are common. The excess-bids
equation provides a filter for predicting future price changes from
intraperiod data. Any prediction filter provides potential opportunities for profitable arbitrage. In theory, if a subset of knowledgeable
traders exploits those opportunities, such activity can be expected to
encounter diminishing returns that reduce arbitrage profits that, in
the limit, approach zero. This hypothesis was tested by Smith et al.
(1988), who recruited three graduate students to serve as "expert"
informed traders in an asset market experiment. In addition to seeing
past data on laboratory bubbles and being informed of the excess-
bids prediction results, these "experts" were given information on
the bid and ask counts at the end of each period. These informed
traders then participated in markets along with either six or nine
uninformed traders, recruited using the usual procedures. When
participating with nine uninformed traders who were inexperienced,
the informed traders were swamped by the bubble. They sold steadily
against the demand at prices above fundamental value up to the maximum permitted based on shares they owned and their capacity to
borrow shares to sell short. When prices collapsed, their purchases
to cover outstanding short sales prevented the market from declining to fundamentals. Thereafter, Smith et al. (1988) recruited six
experienced traders who typically produce lower volume bubbles,

and the three informed traders effectively arbitraged and dampened the lower volume bubble that they encountered.

(10) Two studies demonstrated that the introduction of futures markets can bring spot market prices in line with fundamental values. Porter and Smith (1995) reported an asset market with futures trading in Periods 1 through 7 for asset delivery in Period 8. In these markets, the spot price typically did not exceed the fundamental value until after Period 8. Bubbles did not occur until after the futures market concluded. Noussair and Tucker (2006) augmented the design in the Porter and Smith study by allowing futures markets for delivery in all subsequent periods. The presence of the futures markets stabilized prices in the spot market, but prices in the futures markets typically exceeded fundamental values by a wide margin throughout the experiment.

(11) Finally, we asked whether bubbles can be dampened or eliminated by imposing "circuit breakers" that suspend or otherwise modify trading under specified conditions – an old and recurring issue that was recently revived after the "flash crash" on May 6, 2010.[9] The stock market crash of October 19, 1987, generated renewed interest in stock market bubbles[10] and led to calls for some form of trading interruption in chaotic markets.[11] Calls for circuit breakers also motivated new experiments. The experiment in Figure 2.7 used the economic environment reported in Figure 2.5, but prices were constrained to a band of 48 cents above and 48 cents below the last price from the previous period.[12] The series used the same subjects in three different sessions, allowing a comparison of the effect of three different levels of experience to be examined, as in Figure 2.6. For brevity, we show only the second of these sessions in Figure 2.7. In the first session, when the subjects were inexperienced, the bubble in prices

---

[9] For a discussion of the "flash crash," see Patterson (2010).

[10] Soon after the 1987 stock market crash, the *Wall Street Journal* published a report on laboratory asset market experiments; see Bishop (1987).

[11] The 22.6 percent decline in the Dow Jones Industrial Average on "Black Monday" was the largest single-day percentage drop in history. The best known of the subsequent investigations was Brady et al. (1988), *The Report of the Presidential Task Force on Market Mechanisms*. Investigations ultimately led to the introduction of circuit breakers by the New York Stock Exchange (NYSE). Specific limits on market declines are laid out in a summary of rules on circuit breakers. As of August 2013, current NYSE circuit breaker rules are summarized and available at http://usequities.nyx.com/markets/nyse-equities/circuit-breakers.

[12] Figure 2.7 is an example from King, Smith, Williams, and Van Boening (1993). For a survey and report of further experiments on circuit breakers, see Ackert, Church, and Jayaraman (2001).

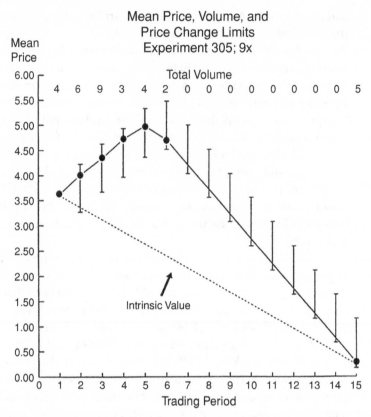

Figure 2.7. **Trade prices and quantities in an asset market session with price bands.**
Chart of mean price and volume in an asset market experiment in which price contracts
in each period are constrained by price change limits of 48 cents (i.e., twice the one-
period expected dividend value) above or below the previous period's closing price. The
bandwidth of each price constraint is indicated by the vertical bars containing the plotted
mean price for each of the fifteen periods of the experiment. This experiment was the
second in a series of three using the same subjects; each session used the parameters
shown in Figure 2.5. The previous session, in which the subjects were inexperienced,
recorded a larger price-volume bubble that reached a price peak in Period 12 and
collapsed to the lower price-control bound in each of the final three periods. In the
subsequent session with subjects twice-experienced, trades departed little from declining
dividend (intrinsic) value.

rose higher and trading volume was larger than in the second session,
and the bubble did not burst until Period 12. In the third session,
the subjects traded at very low volume on a price path that followed
closely the declining fundamental dividend value ("intrinsic value")
shown in Figure 2.7.

Circuit breaker rules, because they are implemented without full testing, are almost certain to harbor unintended consequences that are revealed too late to correct. For example, the experiment shown in Figure 2.7 resulted in no market activity for eight consecutive periods soon after the price decline began, even though the bubble size was moderate and the price decline at first was small.

2.5 Modeling Bubbles: The Interaction between Fundamental and Momentum Components of Trading Behavior

Asset market bubbles have been modeled by postulating that they form out of the interaction of two types of investment sentiment[13]: (1) *fundamental-value traders* buy in proportion to the percentage discount below and sell in proportion to the premium above the underlying asset value; and (2) *momentum traders* buy (or sell) in proportion to the current percentage increase (or decrease) in price. Simply stated, momentum sentiment is postulated to induce net purchases when prices are rising and net selling when prices are falling. Fundamental-value traders have objectives supported by *long-term rational expectations*, whereas momentum traders are driven by *myopically rational expectations* that cannot be indefinitely sustained. Because many of the latter may easily realize profits in excess of the former, they should not be described as irrational; however, they are indeed part of a collectively unsustainable dynamic; a similar unsustainable dynamic seems to characterize behavior in housing bubbles (described in detail in Chapters 3 through 5). Hence, the model distinguishes between long-term sustainable rationality and myopic unsustainable rationality.

The two types of behavior hypothesized in this model represent the primitive, unexplained characteristics of investors in an asset market environment. The parameters of the model, however, determine the dynamic path of prices, and the observed characteristics of that path may provide clues to the underlying forces driving a bubble. For example, if prices in an asset market are driven primarily by fundamentals, then prices should be expected to approach the intrinsic value of the asset at a diminishing rate (i.e., price change proportional to deviation from discount or premium). If the sequence of prices is accelerating or decelerating and diverging from intrinsic value, this implies that momentum effects must be predominating in determining the path. Of course, as with all such models of behavior, the

---

[13] For a derivation and exploration of the model, see Caginalp and Ermentrout (1991) and Caginalp and Balenovich (1994).

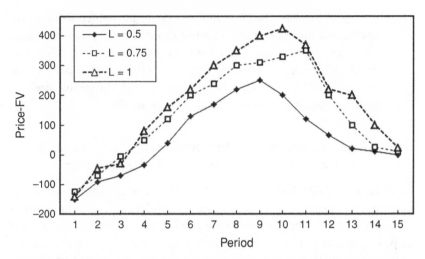

Figure 2.8. **Chart of mean contract-price deviations from fundamental value in three sets of four sessions (twelve sessions total).** In each set of four independent replications, the initial endowment of cash and shares is the same. The liquidity ratio in each set of sessions was fixed at one of the three levels: L = (Total cash)/(Total share value) = 0.5, 0.75, or 1.

model can provide only predictive sufficient conditions for a bubble. The observed path, in fact, might be due to entirely different aspects of behavior than those postulated by the model.

2.5.1 More Money, Bigger Bubbles

This model of bubbles also implies that prices can be sustained longer and more vigorously if momentum investors have more liquidity. This is testable and is consistent with the experimental findings reported previously in which larger bubbles result when inexperienced subjects are allowed to buy on margin. The intuition behind the model is that momentum trading requires liquidity if such purchases are to be sustained, especially as prices rise above fundamental value. A direct test of the model's qualitative predictions is to compare independent sessions that differ only in the subjects' endowment of cash relative to share value across comparison experiments. This liquidity ratio is as follows:

$$L = (\text{Total cash})/(\text{Total share value})$$

According to the momentum model, if L is larger, the bubble will be bigger. Figure 2.8 charts data from twelve sessions. Four sessions with independent groups of subjects were run under each of the three treatment levels of L: 0.5, 0.75, and 1.[14]

In contrast to the commodity-flow market, summarizing for asset markets in which the item can be resold, value can depend on buyer perceptions of the expectations of others about rising or falling future values, even if such expectations are not sustainable.[15] Smith et al. (1988) showed that human behavior in asset-trading markets leads to dramatically different convergence results than those in commodity-flow markets, even under conditions of high transparency. In their experiments, assets pay dividends over many periods. In early periods, prices rise and soon exceed the expected stream of dividend payments that the asset will yield. Halfway through an experiment session, asset prices are often 50 or even 100 percent higher than the expected dividend payments.

Although markets consisting of individuals who have previously been through two complete experiment sessions – so that they have had the same experience twice before – tend finally to converge, they generate substantial bubbles in the earlier sessions before trading near the fundamental rational equilibrium at the end of each session. Enigmas at first, the results were replicated with widely different groups of traders – college students, small-business owners, corporate-business executives, and over-the-counter stock traders – and by many skeptical new experimenters. However, the phenomenon is at the heart of human behavior. Twenty-five years of experimental research on asset market bubbles show that under a wide variety of treatments, asset prices typically deviate substantially from those predicted by the rational expectations market model.[16]

Sunder (1995, p. 474) perceptively noted in his review of experimental asset markets that "lack of repeat experience alone seems to be the simplest and most likely explanation of Smith, Suchanek, and Williams' results. Few asset markets with uncertainty get close to equilibrium in less than four or five replications or trials . . . Since a single experimental session may

---

[14] See Caginalp, Porter, and Smith (1998).

[15] More recently, Dickhaut et al. (2012) directly compared very simple markets with and without the capacity to retrade within each period. Without the capacity to retrade, as in the experiments shown in Figures 2.1 through 2.4, the item is like a nondurable consumer good – for example, hamburgers, airplane passenger trips, and hotel rooms – that are consumed within the period by buyers who are distinct from sellers. With retrade, depending on an individual's private utility value compared to the price, a person might be either a buyer or a seller. Also, it is now possible to profit from resale as well as from end-period consumption. The retrade markets converge to equilibrium much more slowly with higher volatility across period repetitions than the non-retrade markets.

[16] For an accessible recent review of asset trading experiments, see Postrel (2008).

have time enough for only one trial of a fifteen-period asset, several sessions are needed to impart the same level of experience..." This insight warns that the "unit of experience" in asset markets may properly be the entire episode of the bubble – an episode far longer than that which constitutes the relevant experiential feedback in a market for perishables. In the economy, of course, it can take a long time to obtain that "unit of experience."

2.5.2 It's Money All the Way to the End

Subsequent experiments reported in Smith et al. (2000), Noussair et al. (2001), and Kirchler et al. (2012) documented conditions on the economic environment that limit or contribute to the formation of asset market bubbles in laboratory experiments. These conditions highlight the critical importance of the inflow of new cash – which is represented in the experiments by the per-period cash dividend payments – and not only the endowment levels of cash relative to shares, as represented in the experiments shown in Figure 2.5. In Smith et al. (2000), bubbles disappear in a treatment in which fundamental value is constant across periods and implemented with a single, large, uncertain dividend paid in cash at the end of the session. In a second treatment, dividends are declared at the end of each trading period: half in the form of a current cash payment and half accumulated into an account paid at the end of the session. Thus, half of per-period dividend realizations are paid in cash and available to purchase shares, and half are delayed as a payment at the end. In this case, the bubbles are much smaller than when dividends are paid fully in cash at the end of each period. Noussair et al. (2001) investigated this phenomenon more fully, summarizing their results as implying that a constant fundamental value is not sufficient to eliminate bubbles when accompanied by frequent dividend payments. Kirchler et al. (2012) offered the important observation that because the Smith et al. (1988) environment is one of continual decline in fundamental value, with dividend realizations continuing at a constant average rate per period, the ratio of total cash in the system to the fundamental value grows very large. This explains why, as observed in Smith et al. (2000), bubbles are significantly moderated by delaying half of the payment of each period's dividend until the end of the session. The implication is that such payments are not available to fuel the postulated momentum elements in rising prices. Kirchler et al. (2012) reported new experiments that isolated the effect of declining FV in which they observe mispricing (i.e., deviations from FV) but no "overvaluation" (i.e., bubbles), and experiments in which bubbles occur when declining FV is combined with an increasing ratio of cash to asset value.[17]

2.6 Summary: Markets, Panics, and Manias – When Are Crowds Wise and When Are They Not?

In *The Wisdom of Crowds*, Surowiecki (2004) provided a lively account of several cases in which group (crowd) behavior remarkably and magically yields sustainably rational outcomes; he also recounted numerous cases in which such outcomes fail decisively to occur. He proposed the following four conditions that characterize the successful cases:

- diversity of individual information or opinion as it relates to outcomes
- independence of the individual's information from that of others
- decentralization of the dispersed individual information
- an aggregation principle or mechanism exists for producing outcomes from the dispersed information

---

[17] Kirchler et al. (2012, p. 876) also offered the interpretation that subjects are "confused" by the declining FV environment based on a questionnaire, as follows: "After each experimental session, we ask the following question: '*The fundamental value in period p is 50. What will the fundamental value most likely be in the next period?*' Subjects were asked to choose among values of 40, 45, 50, 55 or 60 . . . (in treatments with constant FV) . . . Nearly 70 percent estimate the FV correctly and the remaining 30 percent are symmetrically distributed around the correct estimation. In contrast, in markets with declining FVs . . . around 57 percent of subjects expect the FV to remain constant or increase and less than 30 percent of all subjects forecast the FV correctly. Subjects obviously are confused by the concept of a declining FV, even after having traded in the market for 10 periods. As most subjects in SSW-style markets believe that the FV will stay constant, prices do not fall, producing a 'bubble' as the FV declines." However, the hortative form "obviously" rather stretches the interpretation of the reported evidence beyond what can be inferred. What the post-experiment questionnaire shows is only that a strong positive relationship exists between the deviations of subjects' within-experiment transaction prices from FV and their subsequent responses to the previous question. We cannot say whether, or if, the subjects are "confused" except, of course, that their understanding does not conform to what the experimenter understands about FV. Subject answers to the question across the treatments consistently correspond to the prices they experienced earlier in trading; in this sense, the two measures represent belief consistency, especially after trading for ten periods. The data are consistent with the hypothesis, for example, that subjects believe an asset's correctly described value is the price it fetches in the market and that this is the appropriate response to the experimenter's FV question. No experiments were reported for experienced subjects, so we do not know how the question would have been answered if experience had brought convergence to FV, as in Smith et al. (1988). The puzzle of subjects' beliefs is particularly obscure in Kirchler et al. (2012) because, we recall, that in Smith et al. (1988) and (2000) and other studies, the experimenter calculated and informed the subjects as to FV, repeating this procedure in advance of each period of trading, but subjects' trading prices diverge from FV until they acquire experience.

Markets for perishables appear to approximately satisfy all of these conditions. Individuals have diverse and sufficiently independent tastes and incomes to yield diversity in the maximum prices that they are willing to pay or in the minimum prices at which they are willing to sell. Although many pricing institutions exist – one-sided or double-sided auctions, oral, written sealed or electronic bidding, posted offer or bid procedures – all provide means whereby information is aggregated into satisfactory outcomes based on voluntary action without centralized direction. When markets in nondurables are seized by fashion fads in food or clothing, they lead to a form of bubble in demand – as distinct from speculative retrading on price expectations – but the effects are limited to the particular industries affected until a new equilibrium is attained.

Experimental markets for assets, however, appear most prominently to violate independence and diversity – violations that underlie the concept of momentum- or trend-based investment behavior that introduces correlated behavior. If market participants in one group (Group A) expect prices to rise and act on their beliefs, then their behavior can cause prices to rise. Consequently, people in another group (Group B) will see rising prices, so their beliefs will have been affected by the beliefs of Group A. In this case, beliefs are self-reinforcing and independence is violated. This makes the prediction of a crash difficult because it subtly depends on dynamic features of interdependent expectations that appear to be not easily captured in the standard formulation of independent expectations. Similar considerations seem episodically to characterize the behavior of securities, land, and housing markets.

Sociologists have contributed significantly to the attempt to understand the collective behavior of individuals in small societies, groups, or "crowds," particularly in the context of panic behavior. The distinguished sociologist, Coleman (1990, pp. 198–9) observed: "The class of phenomena is broad. It includes runs on banks, panic in a crowded theater when a fire alarm is sounded, behavioral fads of the sort that sometimes sweep through a population of children (. . . the hula hoop . . . craze), acquisitive manias such as the stock speculation . . . in . . . John Law's Mississippi Scheme . . . hostile unorganized demonstrations, riots, crowd behavior . . . fashions in clothing . . . What makes these phenomena so fascinating and so puzzling is that they are so transient, evanescent, and apparently unpredictable."

Coleman (1990, p. 198) suggested three elements that these phenomena have in common: (1) the people involved carry out the same or similar actions at the same time (or over the same period); (2) the behavior is transient, changing, and not in equilibrium; and (3) individuals are not acting independently.

Momentum- or trend-based investment behavior in securities and housing markets are simply one way of modeling these elements. It is instructive to keep all of these considerations in mind as we examine the many behavioral, financial, and economic features of the Great Recession, the Depression, and the eleven other post–World War II recessions. These features are not part of the standard macroeconomic characterization of what is referred to as the "business cycle."

References

Ackert, Lucy F., Bryan Church, and Narayanan Jayaraman (2001). "An Experimental Study of Circuit Breakers." *Journal of Financial Markets*, 4, pp. 195–208.

Bernanke, Ben (2005). *CNBC Interview*, Available from Ludwig von Mises Institute at http://mises.org/daily/3588.

Bishop, Jerry E. (1987). "Stock Market Experiment Suggests Inevitability of Booms and Busts." *Wall Street Journal*, p. 41, November 17.

Brady, Nicholas F., James C. Cotting, Robert G. Kirby, John R. Opel, and Howard M. Stein (1988). *The Report of the Presidential Task Force on Market Mechanisms*. Washington, DC: Government Printing Office.

Caginalp, Gunduz, and D. Balenovich (1994). "Market Oscillations Induced by the Competition Between Value-Based and Trend-Based Investment Strategies." *Applied Mathematical Finance*, 1, pp. 17–19.

Caginalp, Gunduz, and G. Bard Ermentrout (1991). "Numerical Studies of Differential Equations Related to Theoretical Financial Markets." *Applied Mathematical Letters*, 4, pp. 35–8.

Caginalp, Gunduz, David Porter, and Vernon L. Smith (1998). "Initial Cash/Stock Ratio and Stock Prices: An Experimental Study." *Proceedings of the National Academy of Sciences*, 95, pp. 756–61.

Coleman, James S. (1990). *Foundations of Social Theory*. Cambridge, MA: Harvard University Press.

Dickhaut, John, Shengle Lin, David Porter, and Vernon L. Smith (2012). "Commodity Durability, Trader Specialization, and Market Performance." *Proceedings of the National Academy of Science*, 109, pp. 1425–30.

Gjerstad, Steven (2007). "The Competitive Market Paradox." *Journal of Economic Dynamics and Control*, 31, pp. 1753–80.

Gjerstad, Steven (2013). "Price Dynamics in an Exchange Economy." *Economic Theory*, 52, pp. 461–500.

Gjerstad, Steven, and John Dickhaut (1998). "Price Formation in Double Auctions." *Games and Economic Behavior*, 22, pp. 1–29.

Hayek, Friedrich A. (1945). "The Use of Knowledge in Society." *American Economic Review*, 35, pp. 519–30.

Hurwicz, Leonid (2008). "But Who Will Guard the Guardians?" *American Economic Review*, 98, pp. 577–85.

Jevons, William S. (1888). *The Theory of Political Economy*. London: Macmillan. Available at http://oll.libertyfund.org/title/625/10124/1504416.

King, Ronald R., Vernon L. Smith, Arlington W. Williams, and Mark Van Boening (1993). "The Robustness of Bubbles and Crashes in Experimental Stock Markets." In *Nonlinear Dynamics and Evolutionary Economics*, ed. R. H. Day and P. Chen. New York: Oxford University Press, pp. 183–200.

Kirchler, Michael, Jürgen Huber, and Thomas Stockl (2012). "Thar She Bursts: Reducing Confusion Reduces Bubbles." *The American Economic Review*, 102, pp. 865–83.

Lewis, Michael (2009). "The Man Who Crashed the World," *Vanity Fair*, July 8.

North, Douglas (1990). *Institutions, Institutional Change and Economic Performance*. New York: Cambridge University Press.

Noussair, Charles N., Stephane Robin, and Bernard Ruffieux (2001). "Price Bubbles in Laboratory Asset Markets with Constant Fundamental Values." *Experimental Economics*, 4, pp. 87–105.

Noussair, Charles and Steven Tucker (2006). "Futures Markets and Bubble Formation in Experimental Asset Markets." *Pacific Economic Review*, 11, pp. 167–84.

Patterson, Scott (2010). "How the 'Flash Crash' Echoed Black Monday." *Wall Street Journal*, p. C1, May 17.

Plott, Charles R., and Vernon L. Smith (2008). *Handbook of Experimental Economics Results*. Amsterdam: North Holland.

Porter, David, and Vernon L. Smith (1994). "Stock Market Bubbles in the Laboratory." *Applied Mathematical Finance*, 1, pp. 111–27.

Porter, David, and Vernon L. Smith (1995). "Futures Contracting and Dividend Certainty in Experimental Asset Markets." *Journal of Business*, 68, pp. 509–41.

Postrel, Virginia (2008). "Pop Psychology." *Atlantic Magazine*, December, pp. 1–2.

Rosenberg, Nathan, and L. E. Birdzell (1986). *How The West Grew Rich: The Economic Transformation of the Industrial World*. New York: Basic Books.

Smith, Vernon L. (1962). "An Experimental Study of Competitive Market Behavior." *Journal of Political Economy*, 70, pp. 111–37.

Smith, Vernon L., Gerry Suchanek, and Arlington W. Williams (1988). "Bubbles, Crashes, and Endogenous Expectations in Experimental Spot Asset Markets." *Econometrica*, 56, pp. 1119–51.

Smith, Vernon, Mark van Boening, and Charissa P. Wellford (2000). "Dividend Timing and Behavior in Laboratory Asset Markets." *Economic Theory*, 16, pp. 567–83.

Stigler, George J. (1957). "Perfect Competition, Historically Contemplated." *Journal of Political Economy*, 65, pp. 1–17.

Sunder, Shyam (1995). "Experimental Asset Markets: A Survey." In *Handbook of Experimental Economics*, Kagel, John and Alvin Roth (eds.). Princeton, NJ: Princeton University Press.

Surowiecki, James (2004). *The Wisdom of Crowds*. New York: Doubleday.

Williams, Arlington W. (1980). "Computerized Double-Auction Markets: Some Initial Experimental Results." *Journal of Business*, 53, pp. 235–58.

Williams, Arlington W., Vernon L. Smith, John O. Ledyard, and Steven Gjerstad (2000). "Concurrent Trading in Two Experimental Markets with Demand Interdependence." *Economic Theory*, 16, pp. 511–28.

3

Asset Performance

Housing and the Great Recession

[B]eing the managers rather of other people's money than of their own, it cannot well be expected, that they should watch over it with the same anxious vigilance with which . . . (they) frequently watch over their own.
    – Adam Smith (*Wealth of Nations*, Book V, Chap. 1, Part III)

In the 1950s, I went to work for a mortgage brokerage firm in LA. When my father learned about my new job, he expressed concern. "You're not going to bundle them, are you? That's what brought on the Depression."
    – Personal correspondence from William A. Fraser, Jr., April 7, 2009

Real estate bubbles occurred frequently during the past thirty years in both developing and advanced economies. Reinhart and Rogoff (2008) evaluated five major developed-country financial crises: Spain in 1977, Norway in 1987, Finland and Sweden in 1991, and Japan in 1992. They found that, averaged across the five crises, residential real estate prices peaked a year before the onset of the financial crisis; house prices had fallen by 22 percent four years after they had peaked. Rogoff and Reinhart (2009) extended their earlier analysis to twenty-two financial crises in both developed and developing countries and found that real estate prices fell in all of them, with a median decline of 35.5 percent. House prices declined more than 10 percent in twenty of the twenty-two crises. They also found that a typical financial crisis is associated with a substantial increase in unemployment and a decline in GDP that lasts for several years, followed by a large increase in government debt. Although their analyses indicated that house-price declines, unemployment, and equity market declines are all associated with financial crises, they did not indicate which factor or factors might have triggered the downturns and which are effects.

Data from the United States in the past several decades provide an opportunity to evaluate the sequence of events in the current economic cycle and compare it to past cycles. This comparison provides a clearer picture of the

50 *Rethinking Housing Bubbles*

chronology of a real estate bubble and collapse, the transmission of losses from the housing collapse to the financial sector, and the impact of the collapse on the broader economy. We consider interactions among a variety of factors – including house prices, mortgage lending, current account deficits, income growth, and mortgage delinquency – during a long, relatively stable period prior to the bubble, during its formation, and during the collapse of the bubble and the financial system. Our approach complements the cross-sectional approach of Reinhart and Rogoff (2008), and our conclusions broadly agree with theirs.

Comparison between the sequence of events in the real estate bubble and in asset market experiments illustrates the role of self-fulfilling expectations during the expansion and during the collapse of a bubble when growth expectations reverse.[1] By examining the sequence of events, we can form a clearer idea of how a financial crisis develops. In Chapter 4, we consider the Great Depression; in Chapter 5, we examine the ten post-war U.S. recessions that preceded the Great Recession. We find that – with the single exception of the 2001 recession – these events were preceded by substantial downturns in residential construction.

3.1 Expansion of the Real Estate Bubble and Onset of the Recession

Whereas the origins of the U.S. crisis lie in both institutional factors that encouraged risky mortgage lending and international capital flows that expanded the scale of risky lending – factors that developed before the period with the most rapid home price appreciation – the data show that the period of serious and sustained aggregate excess mortgage lending began in 2001 after home prices had reached their previous inflation-adjusted peak, which occurred in 1989. This phase of the economic cycle was primarily attributable to a large stimulus to mortgage finance that encouraged rapid accumulation of mortgage debt. Debt financing pushed up house prices;

---

[1] Some researchers fancifully suggest that expectations shift for no fundamental economic reason: A "sunspot" equilibrium is affected by an extrinsic random variable (i.e., a "sunspot") that has no impact on economic fundamentals but does affect agents' beliefs. We argue that during a bubble, it is myopically rational to believe that prices will rise further but that at some point, prices become implausibly disconnected from fundamentals. At that critical point, expectations of buyers shift: the momentum buying and momentum-motivated lending that generated asset price increases are reversed. Lewis (2010) described the shift in beliefs among a number of participants in the market for credit default swaps (CDS) on mortgage-backed securities (MBS). Participants such as Kyle Bass, Michael Burry, Steve Eisman, Greg Lippmann, and John Paulson were adamant in their belief that the market was poised for disaster. We examine the CDS market in more detail in Chapter 7.

then, higher house prices stimulated residential construction and home price appreciation justified further mortgage lending. This dynamic can readily persist as long as mortgage lenders believe that their investments are secure and a pool of new home buyers can be attracted by the prospect of capital gains. Other market participants gladly played along: mortgage originators, mortgage securitizers, rating agencies, and home builders could lock in their gains while the bubble inflated and hope to get out before the collapse. The bubble could persist even as credit was extended to many borrowers who were incapable of meeting their mortgage obligations in the long term because new mortgage credit was flowing into the market to buy them out or refinance their loans if they ran into trouble.

The precarious condition of the housing market, however, became apparent when by late 2006, many borrowers were unable to meet their obligations even in the very short term: Liu and Li (2006, Figure 4a) showed that for 2006-vintage, interest-only adjustable rate mortgages (ARM-IO), 3 percent of borrowers were sixty days delinquent within eight months of their closing date. In Q2 2006, after three quarters of sharp declines in sales of both new and existing homes, the flow of mortgage credit abruptly began to subside. Soon afterward, in December 2006 and January 2007, the cost of insuring the lower tranches (e.g., the BBB-rated tranches) of mortgage-backed securities (MBS) with credit default swaps (CDS) began to increase rapidly. When the cost of insuring the AAA rated tranches of new MBS increased dramatically in July 2007, the flow of funds into the mortgage market through privately issued mortgage securities soon collapsed: new private-label mortgage securities fell 52.0 percent in Q3 2007 and another 57.7 percent in Q4 2007.[2] This reinforced the decline in new mortgage credit, and the collapse of the housing market was underway.

The collapse of the bubble damaged household balance sheets, transmitted large losses to lenders, suppressed aggregate demand, and caused widespread unemployment. This chapter begins with a brief overview of the bubble formation, collapse, and its lingering repercussions. The remainder of the chapter examines the expansion and collapse in more detail.

3.1.1 Momentum Characteristics of the Developing Bubble

The "Great Recession" was preceded by an unusual stimulus to housing finance and housing construction. The largest housing price bubble in the United States in at least seventy-five years began in 1997 and expanded in

---

[2] Mortgage security issuance data are provided by *Inside Mortgage Finance* in its 2008 *Mortgage Market Statistical Annual*, Volume II, p. 13.

two phases. The first phase, 1997–2001, carried inflation-adjusted national housing prices to their previous peak, reached in 1989. The second phase, from 2001 into early 2006, was financed by a bulge in the net flow of mortgage credit to households, accompanied by an equally rapid increase in the inflow of foreign investment. Foreign investment surged from $157.2 billion in 1997 (1.60 percent of GDP) to $773.0 billion in 2006 (5.96 percent of GDP). During that period, the net flow of mortgage funds increased from $284.8 billion in 1997 to $1,040.4 billion in 2006.[3] The unusual level of mortgage credit pushed up prices; however, by the end of 2005, the pool of potential buyers was depleted after so much credit had been extended to weak borrowers.

Figure 3.1 shows the size and unusual characteristics of the recent bubble in comparison with two bubbles that peaked in 1979 and 1989. By 2001, the recent bubble already had exceeded the previous 1989 peak and was only beginning its ascent to levels that would dwarf the previous bubble. We also observe that the two previous bubbles followed price time paths that were concave; that is, prices rose to their peak at a decreasing rate per unit of time – prices decelerated as they rose to their top. However, the recent bubble exhibits a clear convex time path of accelerating price increases from 1997 to 2005. Year-over-year growth rates increased until the beginning of 2005 and remained near the peak growth rate until the quarter before the peak. This feature is consistent with the momentum trading model described in Chapter 2. In that model, the momentum component of demand increased in proportion to the rate of change in price: rapid price increases attract momentum buyers due to the prospect of capital appreciation, and their arrival in the market generates price appreciation.

The Case-Shiller U.S. Home Price Index (1987 to 2012) underestimates the scope of the problems: Its broad geographical coverage obscures the fact that so many of the losses occurred in markets such as Los Angeles, San Francisco, Phoenix, Las Vegas, Miami, and Tampa, where the bubbles and

---

[3] Current account data come from the Federal Reserve Flow of Funds historical data, Table F.107. Net flow of mortgage funds data come from Table F.218 in the same document. The net flow of mortgage funds to households is the increase in their total mortgage loans outstanding. It is approximately equal to new loan originations minus principal payments and prepayments (e.g., when a homeowner sells the home and a portion of the proceeds from the sale is used to retire the existing mortgage). These data are available at www.federalreserve.gov/releases/z1/Current/data.htm in the file atabs.zip. These values of the seasonally adjusted current account deficit and the net flow of mortgage funds are both inflation-adjusted to 2005 dollars using the series CPIAUCNS, which is available from Federal Reserve Economic Data (FRED) at http://research.stlouisfed.org/fred2/.

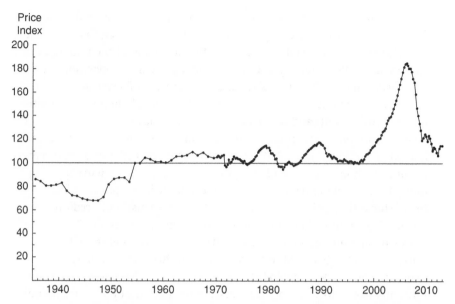

Figure 3.1. Inflation-adjusted house price index from 1935 to 2012 (Q1 1997 index = 100). Momentum elements in the 1997–2006 bubble are suggested by prices that rose at an increasing rate from 1997 through 2004.

collapses were the largest.[4] Section 3.3.5 examines these six markets in more detail. As an example of the extreme price movements in one market – that is, the lower-valued third of the Los Angeles market – the index increased 108 percent from the beginning of 2003 to the beginning of 2006. Then, from the middle of 2006 to the middle of 2009, the index fell by 56 percent.

3.1.2 The Course of the Recession

The crisis that ensued was characterized by a clearly ordered process of decline that provides a particularly useful guideline to rethinking the

[4] Data for 1935 through 1970 are FHA annual prices reported in an appendix to Davis and Heathcote (2007). Quarterly data from Q1 1970 through Q4 1986 are from the Freddie Mac Conforming Mortgage House Price Index (CMHPI), available at www.freddiemac .com/finance/cmhpi. Quarterly data from Q1 1987 through Q4 2012 are Standard & Poor's Case-Shiller National U.S. Home Price Index, available from Standard & Poor at www.standardandpoors.com/home/en/us. Each of these series is inflation-adjusted by the Consumer Price Index (CPI) series CPIAUCNS. (See Footnote 3 for the CPI data source.) The inflation-adjusted series are then spliced together so that they have the same value or average in the first year of each overlap (i.e., 1970 and 1987). The index value is set to 100 in Q1 1997, the first quarter following the long decline in real house prices from Q3 1989 to Q4 1996.

Depression (see Chapter 4) and to reexamining the Finnish depression (1990–3), the economic collapse in Thailand, and other serious economic downturns (see Chapter 10). Events in the unraveling of the bubble were sharply delineated, starting with a precipitous decline in new home unit sales beginning in Q4 2005. The sales decline was followed by (1) sharp declines in expenditures on construction of new single-family and multi-family housing units and in the net flow of mortgage funds starting in Q2 2006; (2) a rapid house price decline beginning early in 2007; (3) a credit market seizure in August 2007 that accelerated the collapse of mortgage lending and house prices (and brought Federal Reserve action to supply liquidity to the banking system); (4) a rapid collapse in the prices of financial firms' stocks that gathered momentum after the August 2007 credit market seizure; (5) continued deterioration of the financial system in 2008; (6) an aggressive and unprecedented Federal Reserve intervention (see Chapter 8) starting in September 2008 and continuing into 2014; and (7) sharp declines in output and employment in Q4 2008 and Q1 2009. These events differ significantly from those in a typical recession because most recessions do not involve the serious stresses in the financial system in Steps (3) through (5) or the central bank response of Step (6). To better understand the Great Recession, we examined all of the economic downturns in the United States since the Depression, with the objective of determining why the Great Recession was so much more severe. To our surprise, our examination of the post-war recessions from 1948–9 through 1990–1 (reported in Chapter 5) revealed that all involved some measure of the problems in Steps (1), (2), and (7). We found strong evidence that economic cycles emanate from the household sector and then move into the business sector as aggregate demand falls.

In the aftermath of these events, many households suffered extreme balance sheet damage that has suppressed borrowing for new housing assets and durable goods consumption. Households' decreased expenditures on new housing units and durable goods, in turn, led to a sharp decline in non-residential fixed investment. Large decreases in housing construction, durable goods expenditures, and non-residential fixed investment all contributed to decreased employment and output, which led to a rapid decline in tax revenues and an increase in government expenditures.[5]

---

[5] In 2009, federal government receipts fell $419.0 billion from their level in 2008 and outlays increased $535.1 billion. Individual and corporate income taxes together account for 94.6 percent of the decline in receipts: individual income taxes fell $230.4 billion (55.0 percent of the decline in receipts) and corporate taxes fell $166.1 billion (39.6 percent of the decline).

3.1.3 Lingering Repercussions of the Bubble and Recession

As of Q3 2013, almost six years after the start of the recession, all three major components of durable goods output – housing construction, consumer durables, and non-residential fixed investment – remained below their peak levels (in inflation-adjusted figures). Seven years after the peak level of residential construction, it remained at a historically low level.[6] Our objectives in this chapter are to (1) demonstrate that important features of the residential real estate bubble are similar to those found in the laboratory asset market bubbles described in Chapter 2, and (2) outline how the housing bubble affected household balance sheets, the financial sector, and – ultimately – the broader economy. We describe the general course of the downturn and then argue that the effects of the recession have persisted because the problems generated by the massive real estate bubble – namely, damaged household balance sheets and a saturated housing market – will require years to resolve. In subsequent chapters, we use the insights from this recession to reevaluate the Depression (see Chapter 4) and postwar U.S. recessions (see Chapter 5). We show that a decline in residential construction is a good predictor of the onset and depth of a recession and that the recovery of residential construction is a good predictor of the strength of the general recovery. In Chapter 10, we examine downturns from other countries that were similar to the Great Recession in order to consider which policies have been associated with strong recoveries.

Increases in Medicare, health costs, and social security – which were largely independent of the bubble and crisis – amounted to $159.0 billion (29.7 percent of the increase in outlays). Income security outlays (primarily unemployment benefits) increased $101.9 billion (19.0 percent of the increase in outlays). The largest increases in outlays were due to homeowner and business credit, which increased by $257.8 billion. These two items together account for 48.2 percent of the increased government outlays: mortgage credit accounts for 18.6 percent of the increased outlays and commercial credit accounts for 29.5 percent of the increase. Of the $954.1 billion increase in the federal deficit in 2010, $756.2 billion can be attributed to problems that ensued from the real estate bubble, the financial crisis, and the unusually severe recession that followed. Government receipt and outlay data are from the Historical Tables of the 2011 Budget of the United States Government, available at www.gpoaccess .gov/usbudget/fy11/hist.html.

[6] In the first sixty years of quarterly national accounts, from 1947 to 2006, construction of new single-family and multi-family residences averaged 3.03 percent of GDP. During that period, the figure fell below 2.0 percent of GDP in seven quarters: all four quarters of 1982 and the first three quarters of 1991. It has now been below 1.5 percent of GDP for twenty-one quarters beginning in Q3 2008 through the last data available in Q3 2013. The level in Q3 2013 was 1.20 percent of GDP. This is what we mean by a historically low level of residential construction.

3.2 Parallels in Behavior: Laboratory and Housing Market
Asset Bubbles

Critical features of both the expansion of a bubble and its collapse were similar in the real estate market during the past decade and the asset market experiments described in Chapter 2. Asset bubbles are exacerbated by market liquidity: When buyers have more money, the bubble is more pronounced. In the housing bubble, liquidity was provided by mortgage finance, with most of the excess flow of mortgage funds coming – directly or indirectly – from foreign investment.

As a bubble expands, trade quantities increase as prices rise. Eventually, buyers become scarce as prices deviate too much from fundamentals and, at the prevailing high prices, the trade quantity collapses. When sellers realize that few buyers are willing to trade at the prevailing prices, they reduce their offer prices or accept lower bids to hasten sales, and the price collapse begins. These patterns from experimental asset market bubbles also appeared as the housing bubble expanded and collapsed.

3.2.1 Liquidity Influences the Magnitude of the Bubble
and Its Subsequent Collapse

During the formation and expansion of the housing bubble, the flow of funds into mortgage finance increased dramatically, especially through foreign investment. During the expansion, the large increase in mortgage lending pushed up prices.[7] Unit sales of both new and existing homes peaked in Q3 2005 (as shown in Figure 3.2); mortgage finance flows peaked two quarters later in Q1 2006 (as shown in Figure 3.3) – the same quarter that house prices peaked.

As house prices fell against fixed mortgage debt, homeowners' housing equity collapsed and, for many homeowners, housing equity turned negative. This is the source of the damage to household balance sheets that plagued the economy for five years. Damage to household balance sheets was transmitted to bank balance sheets through delinquency and foreclosure. Delinquency reduced mortgage payments to banks and, in foreclosure, the assets that collateralized loans (i.e., the mortgaged houses) were often worth less than the loan amounts.

---

[7] Figure 3.7 shows that household mortgage debt and residential real estate value moved up together until early 2006.

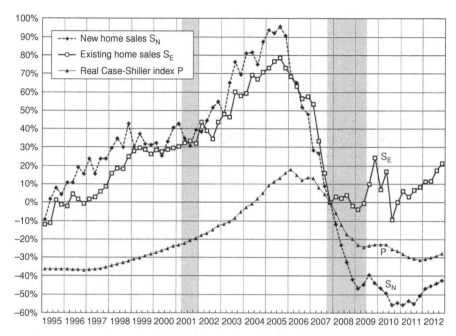

Figure 3.2. Changes to new home sales, existing home sales, and home prices, 1995–2012 (relative to Q4 2007 levels).

The rapid expansion of mortgage financing during the formation of the bubble also fueled the increased construction of new housing units. This is shown in Figure 3.2 by the run-up in sales of new home units from 1995 to 2005. These sales abruptly reversed in 2006 and, by the second half of 2010, they had fallen by 77 percent – to their lowest level since at least 1963. Moreover, the construction of new housing units would remain depressed and would not rise above their recession low until Q2 2012.

3.2.2 Trade Quantities Fall While Prices Continue to Rise or Flatten Out

When an experimental asset bubble peaks, prices usually remain at or near their peak value, whereas the trade quantity declines; even after prices reach a peak, sellers expect to receive a high price but willing buyers eventually become scarce. After a period of declining trade quantity, prices commonly begin to collapse and volume typically continues to fall as prices collapse. In the experiments, we observed all bids and asks and found that the turning point in a bubble is foreshadowed by a reduction of the number of bids

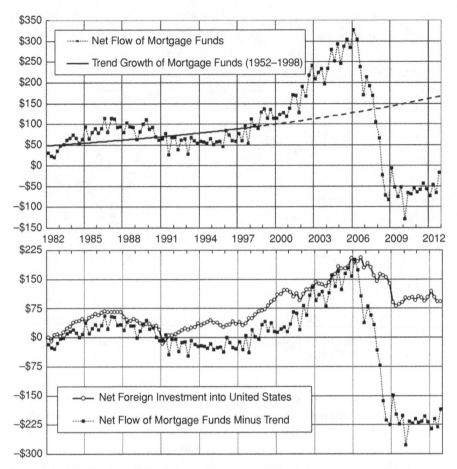

Figure 3.3. Mortgage funds and foreign investment flows into the United States (in billions of 2005 dollars per quarter).

relative to asks. At the peak, both ask prices and the number of asks remain high, but fewer of them are accepted. These experimental price and trade-quantity patterns were present in the expansion and the collapse of the housing bubble.

This stickiness of asking prices is paralleled in the housing market by the slow decline in housing prices between Q3 2005 and Q4 2006, even as sales fell and the median number of months between construction and sale of new homes rose. During this period, the Case-Shiller Home Price Index fell only six tenths of 1 percent; however, sales of new homes fell 24.3 percent and sales of existing homes fell 11.7 percent. When seasonally adjusted sales of new homes peaked in July 2005, builders had 4.2 months of supply. By the end of Q1 2007, when prices first began to decline sharply, their months of supply had almost doubled to 7.9 months, even as construction had fallen sharply. By January 2009, builders' months of supply reached 12.1 months.[8]

Declines in both new and existing home unit sales are apparent in Figure 3.2. The figure shows the percentage difference between sales (or prices) in each quarter and sales (or prices) when the recession began in Q4 2007. Sales of new residential units were the most volatile of the three series. Unit sales peaked in Q3 2005 at a level 95.7 percent higher than their level in Q4 2007, whereas existing home sales peaked in the same quarter at a level 78.6 percent higher than their level in Q4 2007. We notice, however, that home sales declined for two quarters (i.e., Q4 2005 and Q1 2006) as their prices continued to rise.[9]

3.2.3 Prices Turn and Collapse While Trade Quantity Continues to Decline

In a pattern also found in asset market experiments, prices turned down after the trade quantity fell. Following the Q1 2006 peak, home prices declined slowly from Q1 2006 to Q4 2006 (i.e., a cumulative decline of only 2.5 percent), whereas home sales continued to fall rapidly.[10] In the sharp collapse from Q4 2006 to Q1 2009, both sales and prices fell rapidly for nine quarters. By the end of 2010, sales of new homes had declined more than 55 percent below their level when the recession began in Q4 2007. From the new home sales peak in Q3 2005 through Q1 2011, new home sales declined in nineteen of twenty-one quarters to a level only 22.8 percent of their peak level. Even at the end of 2013, three years after the bottom, new

---

[8] See www.census.gov/const/fsalmon.pdf for data on builders' months of supply of new houses.

[9] At least two factors might lead to a large quantity decline prior to a price decline. Sellers may be unaware of the lengthening time to sale because they may not have aggregate sales data and because market conditions are local. Moreover, Stein (1995, p. 382) described an aspect of the housing market that, in some cases, may accentuate the tendency for sellers to adhere to their asking prices. When house prices fall, a family with reduced equity will be unable to trade up and may even be unable to sell and make a comparable purchase in a new location. Such a family is motivated to hold to its asking price.

[10] The real home price index shown in Figure 3.2 is the Case-Shiller U.S. National Home Price Index inflation-adjusted by the CPI series CPIAUCNS. Sales of new single-family housing units come from the U.S. Census Bureau, "Houses Sold by Region," available at www.census.gov/const/soldreg.pdf. Data on sales of existing homes are from the National Association of Realtors, "Single-Family Existing-Home Sales and Prices," available at www .realtor.org/research/research/ehsdata.

home sales had recovered only a small fraction of the declines. In 2013, they were slightly more than half of the average level between 1987 and 2007.

3.3 Mortgage Finance Supported the Bubble Until It Was Withdrawn

During the housing bubble expansion, the flow of mortgage funds increased rapidly. As the amount of credit grew unusually large, mortgage finance was extended to increasingly less credit-worthy borrowers for purchases at prices that grew more rapidly than household income, which ultimately would be required to support the mortgage payments. The increased extension of mortgage credit was accompanied by lower down payments: In 2005, 45 percent of first-time home buyers made no down payment at all.[11] Deterioration of lending standards was particularly apparent in the rapid growth of Alt-A lending between 2000 and 2005.[12] Standards for Alt-A loans were deteriorating along a number of dimensions during this period as loan originations soared, especially for interest-only and negative-amortization loans. According to Liu and Li (2006), total Alt-A originations increased by a factor of twenty-four, from $14.2 billion in 2000 to $341.5 billion in 2005. During this same period, interest-only and negative-amortization loans increased from 2.2 to 72.7 percent of the Alt-A pool; in the Alt-A pool, interest-only and negative amortization loan originations increased by a factor of 797, from $311 million (in 2000) to $248.2 billion (in 2005).[13]

3.3.1 Self-Sustaining Expectations in the Housing, Mortgage, and Derivatives Markets

Declining lending standards led to an increase in mortgage delinquency, especially toward the end of 2006. Delinquency predictably frightened investors, which contributed to the rapid decline in the flow of mortgage funds that began in Q2 2006. As Figure 3.3 shows, the flow of mortgage funds peaked in Q1 2006 and then began a rapid decline that soon led to a

---

[11] This figure comes from the National Association of Realtors (2006 Exhibit 5–3).

[12] The Alt-A category is considered riskier than prime loans because the borrowers typically had one or more risk factors, such as less than full documentation of income or assets, high loan-to-value ratio, or a blemished credit history.

[13] Bair (2011) reported that as Assistant Secretary for Financial Institutions at Treasury: "This is what we were seeing in 2001 and 2002 – negative amortization features, steep prepayment penalties, so that you'd force them [borrowers] into refinancing and then you'd charge them a really steep prepayment penalty to refinance out of these loans that had these steep presets."

collapse of house prices. The sharp reduction in the flow of mortgage funds came two quarters in advance of the first sign of trouble in the market for the CDS that insured MBS. With the collapse in the price of CDS, the cost of insuring MBS soared. This increased the cost of issuing new MBS because the rating agencies (i.e., Standard & Poor's, Moody's, and Fitch) required that an MBS pool include CDS insurance to qualify for higher ratings. When the price of insurance on the AAA rated tranches of MBS increased rapidly in July 2007, problems developed for the investment banks that created and marketed the securities. To obtain high ratings, the banks needed to include CDS insurance in the bundle of assets in the pool. However, the cost of that insurance increased astronomically, beginning with the low-rated tranches between December 2006 and February 2007. For example, on November 30, 2006, the cost of buying insurance on $10 million of BBB- rated MBS issued in the second half of 2006 would have been $180,000 plus a $242,000 annual premium. By February 28, 2007, the cost for the same insurance had risen to $3,337,000, plus the $242,000 annual premium. In July 2007, a similar cost surge for insurance on the AAA rated tranches preceded the credit market seizure of August 9, 2007. On July 9, 2007, insurance on $10 million of AAA rated securities issued in the second half of 2006 could be purchased for $50,000 plus an $11,000 annual premium. On August 3, 2007, that same insurance would cost $936,000, plus the $11,000 annual premium.[14]

The rapid increase to the cost of insuring MBS led to a rapid decline in their issuance. In Q2 2007, new private-label MBS issues amounted to $258.5 billion. In Q3 2007, the figure fell 52.0 percent to $124.1 billion. The collapse continued in Q4 2007, when new issues fell another 57.7 percent to $52.5 billion. As securitization was collapsing, origination of alternative mortgage products was collapsing almost as quickly, from $247 billion in Q2 2007 to $77.5 billion in Q4 2007.[15] These collapses figured significantly in the collapse of the net flow of mortgage funds, which fell $47.1 billion from Q2 2007 to Q4 2007, and new MBS issues fell $206.0 billion. The decline in the flow of mortgage funds, in turn, reinforced the collapse of house prices.

This is a clear example of the type of self-sustaining expectations fundamental to the behavior found in the asset market experiments discussed in

---

[14] We first reported our analysis of the cost of insuring MBS with CDS in the *Wall Street Journal* in Gjerstad and Smith (2009a). We expanded on that analysis in Gjerstad and Smith (2009b).

[15] Figures on MBS issuance are taken from the *2008 Mortgage Market Statistical Annual*, Vol. II, p. 13. Figures on origination of alternative mortgage products are taken from Vol. I, p. 6, in the same source.

Chapter 2. As prices were rising, those price increases justified the invest-ments by both homeowners and mortgage financers. Moreover, capital gains from house price appreciation could be used to "paper over" developing problems with unsound underwriting practices because teetering borrow-ers could refinance into a larger mortgage, extracting equity to alleviate their immediate financial distress. Mortgage default rates and house price appreciation data strongly suggest that this was occurring. In Arizona, the serious delinquency rate in Q3 2006 was 0.63 percent, which was the sec-ond lowest figure in the fifty states, Puerto Rico, and Washington, DC. The rate in California was 0.74 percent, which was the fourth lowest fig-ure. Three years later, in Q3 2009, the situation had changed dramatically. Arizona and California had serious delinquency rates of 12.21 and 11.70 percent, respectively, which were the third and fourth *highest* figures in the country.[16]

When prices fell even modestly, speculative (i.e., momentum) buyers withdrew from the market and mortgage financers restricted their loans to only the most financially stable buyers. The resulting decline in lending then led to a more precipitous decline in home prices and exposed the fundamental weakness of borrowers in the cities that had experienced the largest price gains. In these markets, as delinquency rates soared, prices collapsed.

3.3.2 Money Mattered: The Flow of Mortgage Funds Grew Dramatically During the Bubble

The massive flow of mortgage credit into the housing market is charted in the upper panel of Figure 3.3. The exponential trend of mortgage fund growth from 1952 to 1998 is shown as the solid line in the top panel. The lower panel of Figure 3.3 charts the difference between the flow of mortgage credit and its exponential trend. A positive value for this difference indicates an above-normal flow of funds into the residential mortgage market; the flow of funds into the market grew to an elevated level between 2003 and 2006. The figure also demonstrates that the excess flow of mortgage funds corresponds closely to foreign capital inflows, shown in the lower panel, especially between late 2001 and late 2006.[17]

---

[16] Figures on serious delinquency are from the Mortgage Bankers' Association *National Delinquency Survey* in the Third Quarter 2006 and the Third Quarter 2009 issues.

[17] Sources for the home mortgage and current account data in Figure 3.3 are provided in Footnote 3 in this chapter. Both series are inflation-adjusted to 2005 prices.

The surge in housing prices to their peak in Q1 2006 – shown in Figures 3.1 and 3.2 – is clearly supported by a corresponding surge in the flow of mortgage credit into housing above its long-term trend, as shown in Figure 3.3. The net flow of mortgage credit was above its long-term trend for thirty-six consecutive quarters, from Q4 1998 through Q3 2007. The net flow of mortgage funds was positive from Q1 1952 through Q1 2008; it was negative for twenty-one consecutive quarters from Q2 2008 through Q2 2013 before turning positive again in Q3 2013. As Figure 3.1 shows, real house prices had cyclical peaks in 1979 and 1989. Figure 3.3 shows the close correspondence of these peaks with net flow of mortgage credit. Both of the previous price peaks followed long periods in which the net flow of mortgage credit was above trend. However, the deviation was not as long or as large in the two previous periods of house price appreciation as it was during the thirty-six quarters from Q4 1998 to Q3 2007.

House prices increased most rapidly between Q1 2003 and Q3 2005, when the Case-Shiller U.S. National Home Price Index increased 30.4 percent (i.e., an average annual increase of 11.2 percent per year for 2.5 years). As house prices escalated, the flow of mortgage funds increased commensurately from $208.9 billion in Q1 2003 to $304.3 billion in Q3 2005. The positive feedback loop between home prices and the net flow of mortgage funds is an inherently unstable dynamic system.[18]

The growth of both home prices and the net flow of mortgage funds should correspond more closely to income growth if their growth rates are to be sustainable. When home prices and mortgage funds cause the growth of one another in a positive feedback loop – fed by credit creation and an inflow of foreign investment – then both can grow much faster than income; eventually, however, they must return to growth rates in line with income. Figure 3.4 shows the sharp increase in the ratio of median house price to median family income between 2001 and 2005.

---

[18] Economists prefer stories about self-correcting or stabilizing feedback loops. In a typical narrative about self-correcting dynamics, home builders would respond to higher house prices by increasing production. Increased supply would then lead to house price declines, restoring equilibrium. We know that this self-correcting feedback effect occurred because home construction surged during the bubble. However, for several years, the destabilizing feedback between house price appreciation and the increased mortgage lending was stronger than the self-correcting loop. Home price appreciation drew in new buyers and lenders, and the increased flow of mortgage funds contributed to home price increases. This positive feedback system is inherently unstable; when home price appreciation turned negative, so did the flow of mortgage funds. Wheat (2009) described system dynamics models that incorporate both stabilizing and destabilizing feedback loops by evaluating three models of the housing bubble.

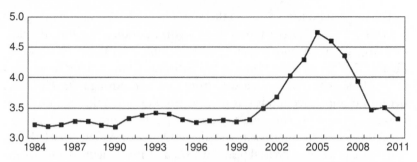

Figure 3.4. Ratio of median sale price of existing homes to median family income.

The rapid influx of new mortgage credit increased total outstanding mortgage debt of U.S. households from $5.84 trillion at the end of Q4 2001 to $9.00 trillion at the end of Q1 2006, a 54.1 percent increase. This rapid growth of mortgage credit corresponded to an increase in the value of residential real estate, from $14.96 trillion at the end of Q4 2001 to $22.24 trillion at the end of Q1 2006 – an increase of 48.7 percent.[19]

On the surface, this looks like a bargain: Housing value increased by $7.28 trillion whereas mortgage debt increased by only $3.16 trillion. During this period, about 4.5 million new homes were sold, with a value of about $1.3 trillion; therefore, the value of the existing housing stock increased about $6 trillion. Assuming that the $1.3 trillion in new housing value was financed with 60 percent equity, the mortgage debt of the 73.2 million existing homeowners increased about $2.65 trillion. Therefore, their equity increased about $3.35 trillion in slightly more than four years – an average increase of almost $46,000 per household. However, when the bubble burst, most of the house price increase disappeared but the debt burden remained.

The large flow of mortgage financing to lower-income borrowers also pushed up house prices more in the lowest priced tier, as Figures 3.5 and 3.6 demonstrate. In the self-reinforcing loop from prices to credit in the bubble, rapid price increases in the low-price tier encouraged lending to borrowers in that market segment – many of whom had low income, few assets, and a weak credit history. In the next section, we examine the source of this mortgage credit. In the subsequent section, we show that this large flow of mortgage credit in support of increased homeownership disproportionately

---

[19] Mortgage debt and residential real estate values are from the Federal Reserve Flow of Funds historical data, Table L.218 in ltabs.zip and Table B.100 in btabs.zip. These files are available at www.federalreserve.gov/releases/z1/Current/data.htm. Figures are inflation-adjusted to 2005 dollars with the series CPIAUCNS.

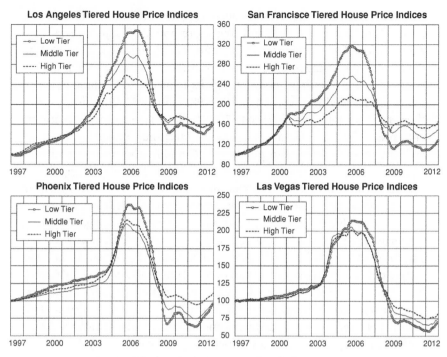

Figure 3.5. Prices changes in three price tiers for four Western cities.

encouraged mortgage borrowing and refinancing among those buyers in the weakest financial condition.

3.3.3 Money from Abroad: Foreign Investment Inflated the Bubble

Trade imbalances and international capital flows contributed importantly to this debt-fueled asset price surge in the United States. The inflow of foreign

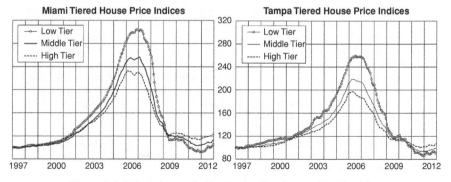

Figure 3.6. Prices changes in three price tiers for two Florida cities.

investment is charted in the lower panel of Figure 3.3. The pronounced surge in such inflows between 1997 and 2006 corresponded first to the run-up in equity prices during the technology sector boom and then, after 2001, to the run-up in housing prices evident in Figure 3.2. Between 2001 and 2006, accumulated U.S. current account deficits totaled $3.52 trillion, whereas net mortgage lending exceeded its 1952–98 trend by $2.43 trillion. During those six years, foreigners invested $786.8 billion in government-sponsored enterprise (GSE) (i.e., Fannie Mae, Freddie Mac, and Ginnie Mae) MBS; we estimate that foreigners also purchased $676 billion in private residential MBS.[20] Slightly more than 60 percent of the excess flow of mortgage funds can be attributed directly to foreign investment.[21] Foreign investment in mortgages was significant, but foreign investment in other financial instruments indirectly freed domestic funds for investment in mortgage lending.

During the past decade, a large fraction of the world's current account surpluses have been invested in the United States. For example, in 2004, sixty-eight countries ran current account surpluses that totaled $930.4 billion. The United States absorbed $630.5 billion of that total, or 67.8 percent of all current account surpluses in the world.[22] Why should two thirds of the world's net international investments find their way to the world's wealthiest nation, and why should their investments support consumption? We examine this issue in more detail in Chapter 10. However, the short answer is that in 1997, there was a sudden stop of the capital flows that had been going into the fast-growing economies of East Asia. Those economies quickly began

---

[20] Foreign investment in GSE securities is from Table F.107 in the Federal Reserve Flow of Funds document. For our estimate of foreign investors' purchases of private-label MBS, we start from their purchases of corporate bonds, which totaled $1,729.6 billion in those six years (Flow of Funds, Table F.107). During this period, corporate bond issues amounted to $4,536.2 billion (Flow of Funds, Tables F.2 and F.3), of which $1,773.8 billion were private mortgage securities (Flow of Funds, Table F.126); therefore, 39.1 percent of corporate bonds issued were MBS. Assuming that foreigners made the same percentage of their corporate bond investments in MBS as domestic investors, their MBS purchases would have amounted to $676.3 billion.

[21] The inflow of foreign investment equals the trade deficit minus net earnings on foreign investment. Elliot and Min (2004) provided a concise summary of the current account, the financial account, and their relationship to the international investment position. Higgins et al. (2005) showed that despite the fact that foreign investment in the United States exceeds U.S. investment in foreign assets, the United States has net earnings on its international investment position. Whitaker (2006) described the similar position in the United Kingdom by noting that "the United Kingdom can, surprisingly, generate net investment income from net debt."

[22] These figures are calculated from data in the World Economic Outlook Database from the International Monetary Fund. Data are available at www.imf.org/external/pubs/ft/weo/2010/02/weodata/weoselgr.aspx.

to repay prior debts and many other countries began to accumulate foreign currency reserves as a precaution against the type of sudden stop that Thailand, South Korea, Malaysia, and Indonesia had suffered from during and after the East Asian crisis. Much of this capital ended up flooding into the United States after 1997.

3.3.4 Housing Affordability Fell as Credit Pushed Up Prices

When developing countries switched course and became net suppliers of capital, most of that capital was invested in the United States. Much of this investment made its way into the U.S. mortgage market, especially after the investment boom in the technology sector subsided in 2000 and 2001. As the huge volume of foreign investment flowing into the U.S. mortgage market pushed up house prices, house prices became disconnected from fundamentals – such as the income that would be required to make mortgage payments during a period of several decades.

Until the late 1990s, the rough guideline for housing affordability in the United States had limited housing expenditures (i.e., principal, interest, taxes, and insurance) to about 30 percent of income. For example, before the mid-1990s, federal housing agencies would not purchase conventional mortgages unless those expenses were no larger than 28 percent of the borrower's income (29 percent if the mortgage was insured by the Federal Housing Administration).[23] These mortgage underwriting restrictions limited access to mortgage financing. Rajan (2010) argued that the widening income distribution in the United States created political pressure to make the "American dream" accessible to the growing number of households whose real incomes had remained stagnant or fallen in the past thirty years. Rajan argued that credit was the palliative offered to those whose incomes had stagnated. We present evidence later in this section that credit grew faster in lower-income segments of the population and that house prices grew fastest in the lowest priced tier of the market.

The massive infusion of credit led to a rapid increase in home prices that was unconnected to income growth. As shown in Figure 3.1, inflation-adjusted house prices increased by 85.0 percent from Q1 1997 to their peak in Q1 2006 – a 7.1 percent annual increase in excess of inflation. During that same period, median real household income grew 3.7 percent, from $45,022 in 1997 to $46,695 in 2006 – an increase of only 0.3 percent per

---

[23] See Schwartz and Wilson (2008, p. 2).

year.[24] Hence, house prices grew 7.1 percent faster than the prices of all other goods and 6.8 percent faster than income during the nine-year period.[25]

The ratio of median house price to median household income, shown in Figure 3.4, indicates a substantial decline in housing affordability during the bubble. The ratio averaged 3.29 between 1984 and 2000; during those seventeen years, the ratio never deviated by more than 4 percent from that average. However, between 2001 and 2005, the ratio shot up to a level 44.1 percent above its long-term average.[26]

Teaser rates, ARM loans, and negative-amortization loans all drew borrowers into unsustainable financial positions. Their predicament is apparent if we consider what would be required if they had a conventional loan. A fully amortizing thirty-year fixed-rate mortgage with a 6 percent interest rate requires annual payments of $7,200 per $100,000 borrowed. The median household income in 2005 was $46,326 and the median house price was $240,900. If that house were financed 100 percent with a mortgage (as it was for 45 percent of first-time home buyers in 2005), the annual mortgage payments would be $17,345. With a household income of $46,326, the mortgage payments would need to be made from an after-tax income of about $40,000. With property taxes and insurance added to mortgage payments, housing costs would exceed 50 percent of median income for a household owning a median-priced house.

Only two thirds of American households own their home, so this benchmark might overstate the problem faced by the median household because

---

[24] Median household income is reported annually by the U.S. Census Bureau, in income Table H-08, available at www.census.gov/hhes/www/income/data/historical/household/index.html. These figures are inflation-adjusted to 2005 prices using series CPIAUCNS.

[25] Throughout this book, we use the inflation-adjusted price of homes to identify housing bubbles over time. This implies that the fundamental value of homes is related to the price of other consumer goods, with price bubbles measured relative to this fundamental value. There are other useful measures of house price deviations from fundamental value – for example, the ratio of price to income as shown in Figure 3.4, or the ratio of home price to rental values. Figure 3.4 shows an increase in the price-to-income ratio starting in 1986 that subsequently peaked in 1989. The start of this house price bubble has been attributed to the Tax Reform Act of 1986 based on the reported upward shift in the (linear) relationship between median house price and median family income. The assertion is based on the fact that the 1986 Act created tax incentives for larger mortgages by eliminating the tax deductibility of non-housing related interest on consumer debt. (See "The U.S. Housing Bubble Is Back," *Seeking Alpha*, March 19, 2013, available at http://seekingalpha.com/article/1285281-the-u-s-housing-bubble-is-back.)

[26] Median household income data and median house price data are available from the U.S. Census Bureau. The median sale price for sales of existing homes is from various issues of the *Real Estate Outlook* by the National Association of Realtors. For the median household income data source, see Footnote 24.

those with income at the 67th percentile would own the median-valued home if income and home value were perfectly correlated. However, Lloyd (2007) and Lewis (2010) provided anecdotes that suggest that lower-income borrowers may have been purchasing more expensive homes. Lenders, and especially mortgage originators, frequently pushed loans on people with dubious employment and credit histories and few or no assets. Lloyd recounted the story of a couple in Watsonville, California, who earned about $300 each per week picking strawberries and who purchased a $720,000 house in Hollister. Lewis (2010, p. 98) told of a nanny who owned five townhouses in Queens and could not afford to make mortgage payments on any of them.

3.3.5 Low-Priced Homes Had a Bigger Bubble

Statistical analysis by Mian and Sufi (2009) suggested that these anecdotes were not unusual. They examined relationships among credit quality, mortgage lending growth, and household income growth at the ZIP code level between 2002 and 2005. They found that income growth was slower in ZIP codes with lower credit quality; however, mortgage credit grew more quickly in those ZIP codes. Their evidence suggests that aggregate figures on home price appreciation might not fully reveal the extent of the problems that developed during the past decade: So much of the new lending went to households with low incomes and weak credit histories that were not in a position to weather a downturn in the housing market. The tiered Case-Shiller Home Price Index movements during the course of the bubble and collapse are consistent with the pattern of credit growth that Mian and Sufi found.

Across every city covered by the tiered price indices, during the bubble home prices grew and fell fastest in the low-price tier. Mian and Sufi (2009) showed that credit grew faster in the low-income tier, and the Case-Shiller tiered indices showed that prices grew fastest in that tier during the bubble and fell fastest in the low-priced tier during the collapse. More risk was concentrated in the low-price tier, wherein homeowners were least able to withstand a decline in asset values. There also was a significant geographical concentration of risk. Figures 3.5 and 3.6 show the tiered Case-Shiller U.S. Home Price Indices for four Western cities and two Florida cities, respectively.[27]

---

[27] Tiered Case-Shiller U.S. Home Price Indices divide homes into three tiers. In December 2010, the Los Angeles low-price tier consisted of homes that sold for less than $309,109; the high-price tier consisted of homes that sold for more than $506,475.

By March 2011, nominal prices in the lowest tier had fallen from their peak by 52.0 percent in Los Angeles, 59.4 percent in San Francisco, 70.7 percent in Phoenix, 67.3 percent in Las Vegas, 55.1 percent in Minneapolis, 52.3 percent in Chicago, 56.2 percent in Atlanta, 65.1 percent in Miami, and 60.2 percent in Tampa. The middle-price tier had fallen 60.2 percent in Las Vegas, 58.9 percent in Phoenix, 54.5 percent in Miami, and 50.4 percent in Tampa. In Las Vegas, the high-price tier had fallen 54.6 percent. None of the other ten cities with tiered price indices had a decline of more than 50 percent in any tier. Although even the aggregate figures showed a serious decline in housing affordability during the course of the bubble, price increases were concentrated unevenly both geographically and by income. In several cities, house prices grew much faster than in the country as a whole, and prices grew faster yet in the low-price tier in those cities.

3.3.6 Mortgage Leverage Was Extreme During the Bubble

The National Association of Realtors (2006, Exhibit 5–3) reported that in 2005, 45 percent of first-time home buyers made no down payment. On stocks, margin loan requirements are commonly 50 percent, and a loan can be called within 24 hours (see Chapter 8), whereas an "underwater" mortgage goes unrecognized on a financial firm's balance sheet as long as the loan servicer receives mortgage payments. This hidden mortgage-lender risk accumulates if the collateral values continue to erode against fixed debt. If a homeowner stops making payments, the foreclosure process can be prolonged, and the value of the collateral may continue to decline during the process. In its October 2013 Mortgage Monitor report, Lender Processing Services (LPS) estimated that the average borrower in foreclosure had not made a payment for 900 days. It also estimated that among buyers whose payments are 90 days or more past due (but who are not yet in foreclosure), the average number of days since the last payment reached 512 in October 2013.[28] Illiquidity in the housing market, combined with declines in asset values and high leverage, generated significant losses that threatened financial-system solvency.[29]

---

[28] LPS Applied Analytics produces its *Mortgage Monitor* report monthly, which is available at www.lpsvcs.com. Data on average days since last payment appear of p. 26 of the October 2013 report.

[29] In Chapter 8, we examine the development of margin rules for lending on equities and on real estate especially before and after the Depression. Many financial sector problems in the United States during the past thirty years developed when these rules were abandoned.

3.3.7 Mortgage Delinquency Reversed the Flow of Mortgage Funds

The rapid increase in serious delinquency in late 2006 and 2007 finally broke the myopically rational positive feedback loop in which mortgage credit drove house prices higher, and higher prices justified additional mortgage credit. Then, mortgage financing abruptly reversed: between Q1 2006 and Q1 2007, the net flow of mortgage funds fell by 36.2 percent. Five quarters later, the net flow of mortgage funds turned negative for the first time since 1944. MBS peaked earlier than the flow of mortgage funds, but their sharp decline came later than the decline in the net flow of mortgage funds. New private-label MBS issues peaked at $327.5 billion in Q3 2005, but new issues had fallen only to $258.5 billion in Q2 2007. In Q3 2007, just as the problems in the CDS market hit the AAA rated tranche of the securities, new MBS issues collapsed dramatically. (Chapter 8 describes how this event precipitated the abrupt change in Federal Reserve policy when the Fed embarked on an extended period of enhanced liquidity injections into the financial system.) New issues fell 52.0 percent in Q3 2007 to $124.1 billion. The collapse continued in Q4 2007, when new issues fell another 57.7 percent to $52.5 billion. By Q2 2013, nominal residential mortgage debt had fallen for twenty-one consecutive quarters; the decline finally ceased in Q3 2013. Real residential mortgage debt outstanding had fallen by $2.05 trillion below its peak level in Q4 2007.[30] The process of paying down this debt has been slow; only a small fraction of the debt accumulated since 2001 had been shed by Q2 2013.

3.3.8 Leverage Cuts Brutally on the Downside

As the flow of mortgage funds into the market leveled off in early 2006, house prices also leveled off, and many homeowners who relied on price increases to refinance their mortgage became financially distressed. Mortgage delinquencies began to rise rapidly toward the end of 2006 as house prices flattened out. Increases in serious delinquency were especially acute in states where house price appreciation had been the greatest. Among subprime ARM loans, serious mortgage delinquency increased fastest in three states that previously had seen the fastest home price appreciation. Between

---

[30] The inflation-adjusted outstanding mortgage debt level peaked in Q4 2007 at $9,881 billion. In Q3 2013, it had fallen $2.05 trillion to $7,826 billion. These figures are inflation-adjusted to 2005 prices by series CPIAUCNS.

Q3 2006 and Q2 2007, serious mortgage delinquency increased by a factor of 3.02 in Arizona, 2.75 in California, and 2.68 in Nevada.[31]

Figures 3.1 and 3.2 show that prices collapsed soon after the flow of mortgage funds began to subside in Q2 2006. Without credit flowing into the housing market, there was nothing to support house prices, and the decline gathered downside momentum – similar to what is described in the asset market experiments reported in Chapter 2.

In 2006, delinquency alerted investors to the problems in the mortgage market and led to a decline in the flow of mortgage funds that was soon followed by the collapse of house prices. However, as house prices collapsed, delinquency rose dramatically. During the bubble, rising prices concealed much of the risk in the mortgage market. As Buffett (2001) famously noted in his letter to Berkshire Hathaway investors, "[Y]ou only find out who is swimming naked when the tide goes out."

The Mortgage Bankers' Association estimated that serious delinquency fell after the 2001 recession to a minimum of 1.82 percent in Q3 2005. By Q3 2006, the figure had risen modestly to 2.00 percent and rose thereafter in every quarter until Q4 2009, when it reached 9.67 percent.[32] Deterioration in the performance of some mortgage products was far worse. The percentage of seriously delinquent subprime ARM loans went from a minimum of 5.13 percent in Q2 2005 to 7.72 percent in Q3 2006. Even the minimum delinquency rate of 5.13 percent is extraordinarily high, but lenders in 2005 – in case of borrower default – would either refinance the borrower into a larger loan or take possession of collateral that had appreciated in value. However, by Q4 2009, the subprime ARM serious delinquency rate had risen for eighteen consecutive quarters to 42.70 percent. By that time, in case of borrower default, lenders would take possession of collateral that had greatly eroded in value, and the market was far less liquid than it had been before the price collapse.

Because so many mortgages had been written with slender down payments, the other side of the house price collapse was its impact on banks, which suffered an impaired flow of mortgage payments from distressed homeowners, asset value losses on foreclosed homes, and further exposure to risk in the portfolio of housing loans and mortgage bonds still active on their books.

---

[31] These figures are calculated from the Q3 2006 and Q2 2007 *National Delinquency Survey* from the Mortgage Bankers' Association.

[32] Seriously delinquent loans are those that are ninety days past due as well as loans in the foreclosure process.

3.4 Housing Equity, Negative Equity, and the Transmission of Borrowers' Losses

During the bubble, large loans were issued to many existing homeowners who had experienced house price appreciation. Home equity loans thus allowed many existing homeowners to incur mortgage obligations that kept pace with the rising value of their home. When home prices fell, the net wealth of most homeowners fell at an even faster rate than prices. If a homeowner has 20 percent equity and prices fall by 10 percent, the homeowner's equity falls by 50 percent. If prices fall by 50 percent, as they have in many cities in the Case-Shiller U.S. Home Price Index, the homeowner's equity position turns to negative 60 percent. Although this example may seem extreme, in January 2011, Case-Shiller U.S. Home Price Indices had fallen below peak values by 57.7 percent in Las Vegas, 55.4 percent in Phoenix, 49.7 percent in Miami, and 46.0 percent in Tampa. As shown in Figures 3.5 and 3.6, the percentage declines in house prices were much greater in the low-price tier. Homeowners who were unable to make mortgage payments or who lost homes through foreclosure generated large losses for lenders and investors in mortgage securities.

3.4.1 Households' Equity in the Housing Stock

By the close of Q4 2011, Americans owned housing assets worth $13.94 trillion, $3.21 trillion greater than at the end of 1997. However, on the liability side of the ledger, Americans had mortgage debt of $8.40 trillion, up from $4.54 trillion at the end of 1997.[33] At the end of 2011, household inflation-adjusted housing equity was lower than at any time since the beginning of 1985. Between 1997 and 2011, the number of owner-occupied homes increased 11.7 percent, from 67.4 million to 75.3 million units.[34] Most of the mortgage lending was used to bid up the prices of existing homes. Debt per household has increased dramatically, even after we take into account the increased number of households; debt-service costs have risen with debt. With the drop in housing value against fixed mortgage debt, equity collapsed disproportionately between 2006 and 2011. By Q2 2012,

---

[33] These figures are all inflation-adjusted to 2005 dollars by the CPIAUCNS series. The mortgage debt and housing value data sources are provided in Footnote 19.
[34] At year end in 1997, there were 67.42 million owner-occupied homes in the United States. At year end in 2011, that number had increased to 75.32 million. See U.S. Census Bureau, *Housing Vacancies and Homeownership*, Historical Table 8, available at www.census.gov/housing/hvs/data/histtabs.html.

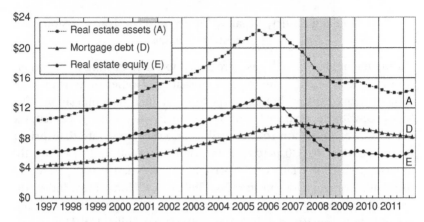

Figure 3.7. Mortgage debt pushed up housing values and housing equity rose with them from 1997 to 2006, but when values plummeted, debt remained high.

homeowner equity had finally recovered to its level in 1997 – although the total value of all homes had risen from $10.7 trillion to more than $14 trillion.

The effect of the debt build-up and of the price bubble and collapse is indicated in the chart in Figure 3.7, which shows the dollar value of households' residential assets, their mortgage debt, and their housing equity (i.e., residential assets minus mortgage debt). Although real estate assets are only 30 percent of households' total assets, unlike financial assets, they are widely distributed across households – and for many households, they are highly leveraged. Housing assets, mortgage debt, and housing equity grew in roughly similar proportions throughout the formation of the bubble from 1997 until Q1 2006. When house prices collapsed in 2007 and 2008, a large portion of the previous run-up in asset value was lost, but the debt remained. Equity declined from $13.25 trillion in Q1 2006 to $9.63 trillion at the start of the recession and declined further to only $5.54 trillion in Q1 2009, from which it finally recovered to its 1997 level in Q2 2012.[35] The modest recovery in 2009 and early 2010 was driven by special home-buyer subsidy programs that arrested the decline in home asset values – but only temporarily because such programs tend to shift future demand into the present.

The aggregate nature of the chart in Figure 3.7 underestimates the loan-to-value ratio among mortgaged properties because one third of homeowners

---

[35] These housing equity figures are all inflation-adjusted to 2005 dollars by series CPIAUCNS.

have no mortgage. The First American Negative Equity Report for Q3 2010 estimated that mortgaged homes were worth $12.71 trillion and mortgage debt on those homes totals $8.85 trillion. Homeowners' equity is the difference between the estimates, or approximately $3.86 trillion. Even this aggregate equity figure does not indicate the extent of mortgage distress being experienced by some households because of the wide distribution in the loan-to-value ratio from one mortgaged property to another.

3.4.2 Negative Equity Became Widespread After Prices Fell

In its first negative equity report in Q3 2008, First American Corporation estimated that there were more than 7.6 million negative equity mortgages. That number increased rapidly to more than 11 million, where it remained through 2011. Even at the end of 2012, CoreLogic estimated that 10.4 million mortgaged homes were in a negative equity position,[36] which is 21.5 percent of the 48.5 million mortgaged properties in its database.[37] Nevada had the highest negative equity percentage – 52.5 percent of homeowners – and total residential mortgage debt in Nevada exceeded the value of all mortgaged residential properties. California had the largest number of negative equity homeowners at 1.70 million, followed by Florida at 1.67 million and Illinois at 632,000.

Homeowners with negative equity of 25 percent or more default much more frequently than homeowners with positive equity or even small negative equity positions, and they generate larger losses for lenders. In Q4 2012, about 4.4 million homeowners (about 9.1 percent of homeowners) had a loan-to-value ratio of 1.25 more. These losses are readily transmitted to the financial sector when homeowners are delinquent in their mortgage payments or when properties revert back to the lenders in foreclosure at a value below the outstanding mortgage. CoreLogic estimated that even in Q4 2012, four years after the financial crisis in September 2008, there was an aggregate of $628 billion in negative equity among homeowners. LPS estimated that as of December 2012, 5.29 million mortgages were

---

[36] CoreLogic produces a quarterly estimate of negative equity by state. It also estimates the percentage of households in negative equity positions from 0 to 5 percent, 5 to 10 percent, 10 to 15 percent, 15 to 20 percent, 20 to 25 percent, and finally, above 25 percent. The report is available at www.corelogic.com/research/negative-equity/corelogic-q4-2012-negative-equity-report.pdf.

[37] According to LPS, there were 50.65 million first-lien mortgages in the United States as of May 2012; therefore, the First American database includes about 95.8 percent of mortgaged residential properties.

noncurrent. Of those non-current mortgages, 1.72 million were in foreclosure and another 1.55 million were more than ninety days past due but not yet in foreclosure. The combination of the number of delinquent loans and the extent of negative equity on those loans suggested that even at the end of 2012, more than four years after the financial crisis, the banks had not yet experienced the full extent of their losses.[38] Reilly (2011) noted that in the spring of 2010, proposed rules from the Financial Accounting Standards Board (FASB) would have forced banks to value the loans on their books at market price; however, banks were able to defeat the proposal and value their loans at "original cost less a reserve to reflect the possibility of loss."

In March 2010, First American Corporation estimated, for ten cities, the length of time until the average borrower with negative equity would reach positive equity. It expects that the average borrower with negative equity in Q4 2009 will reach positive equity by 2015 or later in each of the ten cities that it examined. Its estimates were based on the assumption that home prices increase at 3 percent per year. The Case-Shiller U.S. National Home Price Index has appreciated at an average rate of 4.3 percent per year since Q4 2010. Even with home price appreciation that has exceeded the estimate, the number of negative equity homeowners has fallen only 42 percent from 11.1 million in Q4 2010 to 6.4 million in Q3 2013.

3.4.3 Borrowers' Losses Were Transmitted to the Financial Sector

Two risk factors in mortgage lending contributed to the large losses suffered by banks. Mortgage loans have become increasingly leveraged during the past twenty years. Even the extreme case of 100 percent leverage has become the norm for first-time buyers. This exposes lenders to extreme risk because the borrower has nothing at stake in case of default and has no equity to buffer losses in case of a decline in the asset value.

Illiquidity poses another risk for both homeowners and lenders. Sales of both new and existing units were falling sharply during the price collapse, and inventories of unsold homes were growing rapidly while house prices fell. Homeowners who needed to sell because their equity was eroding or

---

[38] Many mortgages have been securitized, and expected losses on those securities are reflected in the decline in their value. However, even these losses are not completely reflected on the banks' balance sheets due to changes in mark-to-market accounting rules. Newman (2009) noted that "in the wake of the banking crisis, many changes have taken place – or are taking place – in mark-to-market accounting. The FASB in the United States has relaxed mark-to-market rules after political pressure from banking and financial services lobbies."

because their mortgage payments strained their budget faced a challenging dilemma. They could lower the price to try to hasten a sale or hold to their asking price as home prices continued to fall. If they were already in a negative equity position, either alternative could lead to a larger loss to lenders.

Stock market prices of financial firms and mortgage lenders eventually reflected the accumulation of bad loans on their books. The Keefe, Bruyette, and Woods BKX Index of financial firms peaked in January 2007. By January 2008, the index had fallen 23.2 percent. The rapid declines in the share prices of financial firms came in 2008 and early 2009. By February 2009, the index value was only 19.5 percent of its peak value twenty-five months earlier. Although the index recovered substantially after its trough, as of November 2013, it stood at 49.9 percent of its peak value.

NIPA data indicate that financial-sector profits in 2010 were 79.6 percent of profits in 2006.[39] Yet, even with these high profits, the value of the Keefe, Bruyette, and Woods BKX Index in January 2011 was only 35.1 percent of the Index level in January 2007. This pattern persisted into 2013. In the two years from Q4 2011 to Q3 2013, financial-sector profits have exceeded the peak pre-crisis level from Q2 2006 in every quarter, yet the value of the BKX index is only 49.9 percent of its peak pre-crisis level. There are several possible explanations for the significant difference in asset prices given the small difference in financial sector profits. The market may have recognized that financial sector equity prices were too high in January 2007. It is also possible that equity markets were not convinced that financial institutions had set aside adequate reserves to account for the losses that they already experienced on their assets and will experience in the future.

3.5 Housing and Key Components of GDP in the Great Recession: The Two Types of Markets Again

In this chapter, we have examined the development of the housing bubble, drawing attention to the large influx of foreign investment. We have compared the broad patterns of price and trade-quantity movements during the bubble to their patterns in asset market experiments. We have also described how borrowers' losses were transmitted to lenders, leading to the most serious financial crisis since the Great Depression. Next, we turn our

---

[39] These figures on financial sector profits come from NIPA, Table 6.16D, which is available from the Bureau of Economic Analysis at www.bea.gov/national/nipaweb/SelectTable.asp.

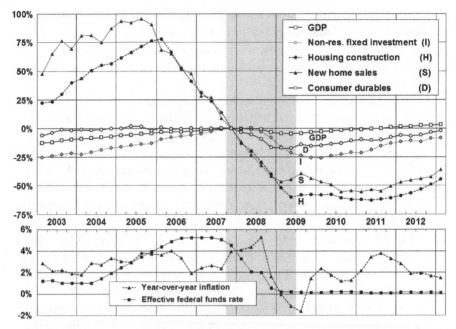

Figure 3.8. Percentage changes to GDP and its major components. Housing (H) represents the percentage difference between real expenditures on new housing units in the indicated quarter and its level at the start of the recession in the Q4 2007. For example, housing was 76.3 percent higher in Q4 2005 than it was in Q4 2007; it was 49.0 percent lower in Q4 2012 than it was in Q4 2007. Other series are interpreted similarly. For example, non-residential investment (I) was 25.5 percent lower in Q1 2003 and 25.7 percent lower in Q4 2009 than it was in Q4 2007. Series are inflation-adjusted with GDP deflators. See Footnote 40 for a discussion of GDP deflators.

attention to the changes in GDP and its major components prior to, during, and following the Great Recession.

Figure 3.8 provides a comparative empirical perspective on the housing sector and its relation to other components of GDP in the Great Recession. The expenditure chart in Chapter 4 on the Great Depression, as well as all of the expenditure charts in Chapter 5 on post-war recessions, follow the same measurement principles used in Figure 3.8. The charts follow a common design intended to convey the relative magnitude of changes to GDP and its major components before, during, and after the peak of an economic cycle. The purpose is to facilitate understanding of comparative movements of these components and to establish pattern regularities across different cycles. Thus, Figure 3.8 charts percentage changes in GDP, non-residential fixed investment (I), value of new residential construction (H), and consumer durables (D).[40] The change for each category is computed relative to its level at the beginning of the recession in Q4 2007. The graph also includes a series with changes in sales of new residential units (S), also relative to their level in Q4 2007.

The contrast between the two fundamental types of markets – perishable goods and services versus the class of durable goods – is quite striking: consumption of nondurable goods and services had a maximum decline of 1.7 percent during the recession, whereas housing (H), which declined the most, fell 60.0 percent from the start of the recession to its end and fell 78.8 percent from its peak to its trough. The slower decline in non-residential fixed investment (I), after the recession started, likely reflects that industry did not recognize the strain that households were under and the extent that their distress would affect aggregate demand: Firms were blindsided along with the experts. The fall of I intensified even as consumer durable goods (D) stabilized for three quarters before the recession officially ended. As discussed in Chapter 5, D and I are more likely to be coincident than leading indicators of economic decline.

The impact of financial developments on the housing sector as described in this chapter is particularly apparent in Figure 3.8. Housing construction expenditures began to fall in Q2 2006; unit sales of new homes – also shown in Figure 3.8 – turned down six months earlier in Q4 2005. For an extended period, the slowdown in the housing industry did not spill over into the broader economy because banks continued to lend even though at a reduced rate – net mortgage lending would not turn negative until 2008.

It took seven more quarters after residential construction began to decline (in Q2 2006) before durables fell, ten quarters before the financial system collapsed at the end of Q3 2008, and another quarter before investment declined substantially in Q4 2008. Non-residential fixed investment – primarily firms' investments in plants and equipment – did not fall substantially until long after the housing market decline was underway. The major investment decline began to set in three quarters after the recession began.

---

[40] These four series all come from the NIPA data provided by the U.S. Department of Commerce. For brevity, we refer to personal consumption of services and nondurable goods (NIPA Table 1.1.5, lines 5 and 6) as "consumption" (C); households' durable goods expenditures (NIPA Table 1.1.5, line 4) as "durables" (D); expenditures on new single-family and multi-family housing units (NIPA Table 5.3.5, line 19) as "housing" (H): and non-residential fixed investment (NIPA Table 1.1.5, line 9) as "investment" (I). All series are converted from nominal to real figures by dividing by GDP deflators, which we calculate by dividing NIPA Table 1.1.5, line 1, by Table 1.1.6, line 1. The data are available at www .bea.gov/national/nipaweb/SelectTable.asp. Consumption (C) not shown in Figure 3.8.

Chapters 4 and 5 demonstrate that the delayed decline in I is a feature common to all economic cycles in the United States since the Great Depression. The shaded area in Figure 3.8 shows the recession. Consumer durable goods expenditures recovered slowly after they bottomed out, along with GDP, in Q2 2009. Housing had a tepid, temporary recovery due to temporary tax incentives in 2009 but then resumed its decline in late 2010 and the first half of 2011. Investment bottomed out two quarters after consumer durables. Investment recovery also has been weak, and all three of these components of GDP (i.e., H, D, and I) remained below their peak levels nearly six years after the beginning of the recession. It seems likely that all three of these types of durable expenditures will continue to grow slowly at best, possibly for several more years. Household balance sheets are stressed from debt accumulation and asset value declines, the housing market is saturated from the building boom of the past decade as well as the rash of foreclosures and short sales, and business capacity is not strained enough to generate a significant increase in non-residential fixed investment.

Almost certainly, the eight-year period embracing 2006 through 2013 and perhaps beyond will be seen historically as the great episode of household and bank deleveraging from the excesses of 1997 to 2006. The decline in mortgage lending, combined with declines in other lending, played a crucial role in the onset of what is arguably our largest deleveraging cycle and our first deflationary episode since the Great Depression.[41]

3.6 Summary: The Great Recession Has Unusual Persistence

Reviewing the housing bubble, its collapse, the recession that followed, and the lingering effects of the collapse, we see a number of broad patterns. Many of these patterns occurred during other financial crises and during the stagnation that frequently follows a financial crisis. The large run-up in mortgage credit pushed house prices higher, especially in the Southwest and in Florida but also to a substantial extent in other cities, and even in the small urban areas of the central valley in California. The geographical concentration of price increases, the large price increases in the lowest

---

[41] The CPI in February 2011 was only 0.6 percent above its level in July 2008. Because the CPI utilizes homeowners' equivalent rent rather than home prices, the rapid decline in housing purchase costs is not fully reflected in the CPI. If housing costs were fully reflected in the CPI, it would probably have fallen by about 8 percent between July 2008 and February 2011, which constitutes significant deflation. Smith and Gjerstad (2010) examined the velocity of money between 1919 and 2009, with particular attention to the collapse of velocity in 1930 and in 2008.

price tier, and the high leverage in mortgage lending had the effect of concentrating a significant risk in a fairly small fraction of the housing market. Low down payments and lax underwriting standards contributed importantly to rapid house price increases: Under normal circumstances, the time required by newly formed households to acquire a down payment and build a credit and employment history effectively regulates the flow of potential home buyers into the market. When this natural regulatory mechanism was short-circuited and new home buyers entered the market faster than new homes could be built, house prices surged. The other effect of reduced down payment requirements and relaxed underwriting standards has received more attention: When risky loans soured and house prices turned down, many borrowers had an inadequate equity buffer, and losses were transmitted to lenders and investors in mortgage securities. When the equity cushions of homeowners disappear, banks are exposed to losses and their balance sheets also become stressed.

The illiquidity of houses as collateral added to lenders' problems when house prices collapsed. As lenders worked through the arduous and slow foreclosure process, missed payments and eroding collateral added to lenders' losses throughout the foreclosure process. In addition to their losses on mortgages held on their books, financial institutions suffered major losses from the collapse of the market for mortgage securities in the fall of 2008. This combination of factors precipitated the most serious financial crisis in the United States in the past seventy-five years.

The house price collapse produced balance sheet losses not only among financial firms but among households as well. The economy suffered from a long, sharp collapse of expenditures on new residential units but, in addition, households' concerns about their declining housing assets and damaged balance sheets precipitated declines in consumer expenditures on durable goods. Finally, firms recognized the developing downturn and cut their investment in inventories and in non-residential fixed investments starting in Q1 2008. Employment peaked just as the downturn reached consumer durables and firms' inventory investments and then accelerated with the rapid collapse in non-residential fixed investment that began in Q3 2008.

The extreme saturation of the housing market that resulted first from the rapid expansion of residential construction during the boom and then from the rash of foreclosures and short sales during the collapse contributed to the extreme and persistent suppression of residential construction. During the post-war period prior to the Great Recession, the fraction of GDP dedicated to construction of single-family and multi-family residential structures had its low point in Q2 1982, at 1.66 percent of GDP. At the bottom of the Great Recession, the figure sank to 0.89 percent of GDP but by Q2 2011, it had fallen well below even that post-war low to 0.80 percent of GDP. Residential construction, which is typically an important contributor to post-war recoveries, remained sharply suppressed into 2013, and the number of homes in the foreclosure process and the number of mortgages that are seriously delinquent but not yet in foreclosure both suggest that the residential construction recovery will be slow. This situation sharply contrasts with a typical post-war recovery. Chapter 5 on the post-war recessions discusses the fact that residential construction – normally sensitive to interest rates – typically recovers more than any other sector in the first year after the end of a recession. The current recovery has had to proceed without one of the main contributors to previous post-war recoveries.

In addition to suppression of residential construction, the balance sheets of millions of households remained stressed for years after the housing bubble burst. As late as Q1 2013, about 9.6 million homeowners from the First American Corporation database were in a negative equity position. As of March 2013, LPS estimated that 3.2 million homeowners were either in the foreclosure process or at least ninety days past due on their mortgage but not in the foreclosure process. This left at least 6.4 million homeowners in a negative equity position who were current or nearly current on their mortgages. These homeowners were able to make their mortgage payments, but it is likely that their impaired asset position suppresses their demand for consumer durables and even for some nondurables and services. This situation likely will be rectified only after several years of balance sheet repairs. The effect of household balance sheet problems on mortgage and consumer credit has been substantial. The value of mortgage loans outstanding fell in every quarter from Q2 2008 until Q2 2013, after sixty-three years of uninterrupted expansion. Nominal consumer credit outstanding fell 7.0 percent during the two years beginning in July 2008. In the post-war era, nominal consumer credit outstanding has fallen only twice before: by 1.0 percent in the first half of 1975 and by 1.9 percent between November 1990 and November 1991. Clearly, this reflects a combination of unwillingness among households to take on new debt and a tightening of lending standards by banks.

Reduced household demand for durable goods and for new residential units has impacted the need for new investment in business capacity. Non-residential fixed investment has partially recovered since its trough in Q4 2009 but, as of Q3 2013, it remained at 4.2 percent below its peak level from Q4 2007. This suppressed level of investment also affected borrowing by businesses. Commercial and industrial loans at commercial banks peaked in October 2008 and then fell 24.9 percent before bottoming out in October 2010.

All of these factors have contributed to an unusually persistent recession; a robust recovery with a return to real GDP growth in the historical range of 3 to 3.5 percent will require absorption of the excess housing stock and strengthening of both household and bank balance sheets. Unfortunately, there is no "silver bullet" that will fix these problems. Both require time, and household balance sheet repair also will require discipline. Personal savings as a percentage of disposable income rose after the recession began, from an average of 2.2 percent between 2005 and 2007 up to 4.6 percent between 2008 and March 2013.[42] At the same time, households reduced their mortgage debt considerably. However, the process is far from complete, and the sizable government debts only shift the burden of indebtedness from households individually to households and firms collectively. Therefore, more fiscal discipline will be required to simultaneously strengthen household, financial institution, and government balance sheets.

References

Bair, Sheila (2011). *The Financial Crisis, Frontline Interview*, by Martin Smith. Accessed November 15. Available at www.pbs.org/wgbh/pages/frontline/oral-history/financial-crisis/sheila-bair.

Buffett, Warren (2001). "Chairman's Letter to the Shareholders," Berkshire Hathaway. www.berkshirehathaway.com/letters/2001pdf.pdf.

Davis, Morris A., and Jonathan Heathcote (2007). "The Price and Quantity of Residential Land in the United States." *Journal of Monetary Economics*, 54, pp. 2595–620.

Elliot, John and Erica Wong Min (2004). "The External Balance Sheet of the United Kingdom: Recent Developments." *Bank of England Quarterly Bulletin*, Winter, pp. 485–94.

Gjerstad, Steven and Vernon L. Smith (2009a). "From Bubble to Depression?" *Wall Street Journal*, April 6.

Gjerstad, Steven and Vernon L. Smith (2009b). "Monetary Policy, Credit Extension, and Housing Bubbles: 2008 and 1929." *Critical Review*, 21, pp. 269–300.

Higgins, Matthew, Thomas Klitgaard, and Cédric Tille (2005). "The Income Implications of Rising U.S. International Liabilities." Federal Reserve Bank of New York, *Current Issues in Economics and Finance*, 11, pp. 1–11.

Lewis, Michael (2008). "The End." *Portfolio*, December.

Lewis, Michael (2010). *The Big Short: Inside the Doomsday Machine*. New York: W.W. Norton and Company.

---

[42] Both of these period averages are much lower than historical savings rates. For example, between 1950 and 1992, the savings rate averaged 8.5 percent.

Liu, David, and Shumin Li (2006). "Alt-A Credit – The Other Shoe Drops?" *RiskView*, December, First American Real Estate Solutions.

Lloyd, Carol (2007). "Minorities Are the Emerging Face of the Subprime Crisis." *San Francisco Chronicle*, April 13.

Mian, Atif, and Amir Sufi (2009). "The Consequences of Mortgage Credit Expansion: Evidence from the U.S. Mortgage Default Crisis." *Quarterly Journal of Economics*, 124, pp. 1449–96.

Mortgage Bankers Association (2006–2010). "National Delinquency Survey." Various issues.

National Association of Realtors (2006). *Profile of Home Buyers and Sellers*.

Newman, Jeremy (2009). "In Defense of Mark-to-Market." *Forbes.com*, August 18.

Rajan, Raghuram (2010). *Fault Lines: How Hidden Fractures Still Threaten the World Economy*. Princeton, NJ: Princeton University Press.

Reilly, David (2011). "Banks Have Their Way with FASB." *Wall Street Journal*, January 26.

Reinhart, Carmen M., and Kenneth S. Rogoff (2008). "Is the 2007 U.S. Subprime Crisis So Different? An International Historical Comparison." *American Economic Review*, 98, pp. 339–44.

Rogoff, Kenneth S., and Carmen M. Reinhart (2009). "The Aftermath of Financial Crises." *American Economic Review*, 99, pp. 466–72.

Schwartz, Mary, and Ellen Wilson (2008). "Who Can Afford to Live in a Home? A Look at Data from the 2006 American Community Survey." U.S. Census Bureau, Housing and Household Economic Statistics Division. Available at www.census.gov/hhes/www/housing/special-topics/files/who-can-afford.pdf.

Smith, Adam (1776/1981). *An Inquiry into the Nature and Causes of the Wealth of Nations*, ed. R. H. Campbell and A. S. Skinner. Indianapolis, IN: Liberty Fund.

Smith, Vernon L., and Steven D. Gjerstad (2010). "Housing, Depressions, and Credit Collapses." *Financial Times*, January 24.

Stein, Jeremy C. (1995). "Prices and Trading Volume in the Housing Market: A Model with Down-Payment Effects." *Quarterly Journal of Economics*, 110, pp. 379–406.

Wheat, I. David (2009). "Empowering Students to Compare Ways Economists Think: The Case of the Housing Bubble." *International Journal of Pluralism and Economics Education*, 1, pp. 65–86.

Whitaker, Simon (2006). "The UK International Investment Position." Bank of England, *Quarterly Bulletin*, third quarter (Q3), pp. 290–6.

4

The Great Depression

As explanations of the so-called business cycle, or cycles, when these are really serious, I doubt the adequacy of over-production, . . . over-confidence, over-investment,
over-saving, over-spending, and the discrepancy between saving and investment. I
venture the opinion . . . that in the great booms and depressions each of the above-
named factors played a subordinate role as compared with two dominant factors,
namely over-indebtedness to start with and deflation following soon after.

Over-investment and over-speculation are often important, but they would have
far less serious results were they not conducted with borrowed money.

The same is true as to over-confidence. I fancy that over-confidence seldom does
any great harm except when . . . it beguiles its victims into debt.
– Irving Fisher (1933, pp. 340–1)

4.1 Interpretations of the Great Depression

Similarities between the financial crisis in September 2008 and the collapse of the financial system during the Great Depression are widely noted.
Yet, the comparability of the origins and transmission of the crises have
been neglected. The recent downturn, which originated with a pronounced
housing boom and collapse, led to severe household balance sheet problems
that were transmitted to lenders and mortgage security investors. Damage
to household balance sheets weakened household demand – especially for
housing and durable goods – which adversely affected employment, production, and nonresidential fixed investment. This pattern, however, is not
recognized in the dominant view as a possible cause of the Great Depression. Contrary to prevailing views of its origins, we argue in this chapter
that changes in the levels of mortgage finance and residential construction
and the broader economy preceding and during the initial phases of the
Great Depression shared many features with the recent Great Recession.
Based on data collected by Wickens (1937), we estimate that by the end of

the Great Depression, losses on mortgage loans exceeded estimates of losses in the Great Recession, either as a percentage of loans outstanding or as a percentage of aggregate output.

4.1.1 Friedman and Schwartz versus Real Business Cycle Interpretations

The interpretation of the Depression that Friedman and Schwartz articulated in *A Monetary History of the United States* is probably the most influential. Friedman and Schwartz (1963, p. 300) argued that during the Depression, the "monetary collapse was not the inescapable consequence of other forces, but rather a largely independent factor which exerted a powerful influence on the course of events." They further argued (p. 301) that "different and feasible actions by the monetary authorities could have prevented the decline in the stock of money – indeed, could have produced almost any desired increase in the money stock." However, they also admitted that while "monetary expansion . . . would have reduced the contraction's severity . . . the contraction might still have been relatively severe." Much effort has been expended to understand the monetary contraction that took center stage in 1931. In this chapter, we focus on the background for the stresses that emerged in the financial system. Before the serious deterioration of the banking system developed at the end of 1930, the United States had already experienced a deep downturn in output. In the aftermath of a debt-fueled residential real estate bubble, expansionary monetary policy could not entirely eliminate the effects of the resulting household balance sheet problems, financial sector losses, and collapse in mortgage lending. Misallocation of resources and investment losses could not be reversed by central bank provision of liquidity in an environment wherein a significant portion of households and their lenders face insolvency.

In contrast to the monetary policy explanation of Friedman and Schwartz, the real business cycle literature initiated by Kydland and Prescott (1982) contends that economic downturns have their origin in serially correlated negative productivity shocks that reduce aggregate output. Although this view has been influential, in its current form, it is implausible. It would be difficult to argue that the decline in U.S. automobile and light truck production from 10.47 million units in 2007 to only 5.56 million units in 2009 resulted from a shock to productivity. If a productivity shock drove the decline of this magnitude, then the relative scarcity of automobiles should have resulted in an increase in automobile prices. In fact, the Consumer Price Index (CPI) component for new automobiles and light trucks fell

0.5 percent from 2007 to 2009.[1] Construction of new single-family and multifamily residences fell 78.7 percent between Q1 2006 and Q1 2011, during a period when the Case-Shiller U.S. National Home Price Index fell 35.5 percent. If the contraction of output in these two sectors resulted from a shock to productivity that disrupted supply, it should have led to rising prices. The pattern of decline seems more consistent with a demand shock initiated by a shock to household credit, and the credit shock had an underlying economic explanation.

4.1.2 Economic and Banking Conditions in 1930

The rapid accumulation of mortgage debt, the housing bubble and collapse, and their impact on the financial and real sectors up to the time of the financial crisis in September 2008 share many similarities to events from the end of the 1920–21 recession to the collapse of the banking system that began in late 1930. The fact that the recent financial crisis and recession did not lead to an economic calamity equal to the Great Depression is strong evidence that an aggressive monetary policy response can mitigate the consequences of a financial crisis. Yet, the depth and duration of the recent recession and the slow recovery suggest that expansionary monetary policy cannot entirely compensate for the contraction caused by a residential real estate bubble and collapse. It also suggests that there may have been more to the Depression than "a largely independent" monetary collapse, as Friedman and Schwartz (1963) argued.

A serious downturn had already occurred before the first banking crisis. By the end of 1930, Gross National Product (GNP) had fallen 9.5 percent from its peak in 1929. As Wicker (1996) noted, the number of bank suspensions and the level of deposits in suspended banks were only slightly higher between January and October 1930 than they had been throughout the 1920s. The wave of bank suspensions in November 1930 was concentrated primarily in the St. Louis Federal Reserve District; in December, 60 percent of the deposits of suspended banks were in three banks: two in New York and one in Philadelphia.

Receivers' reports from the liquidation of failed national banks compiled by the Comptroller of the Currency (1929, 1941) provided strong evidence that the large majority of suspended banks both before and during the

---

[1] Automobile production figures are available at http://oica.net/category/production-statistics. The CPI new-automobile and light-truck component series is CUSR0000SS4501A from the Bureau of Labor Statistics.

Depression were insolvent. After November 1930, the frequency of insolvent banks entering receivership escalated. The contention by Friedman
and Schwartz that the banking system was facing only liquidity problems
and not solvency problems is difficult to reconcile with the record of liquidated national banks.[2] The extent of insolvency versus illiquidity during the
Depression is placed in context by first examining it during the boom years.
The 103 national bank receiverships that were completed in the 12 months
ending October 31, 1929, paid only 49.2 cents on each dollar of unsecured
liabilities, even after stock assessments were collected that amounted to 9.8
percent of unsecured liabilities. Only 21 of these 103 liquidations resulted
in repayment of more than 75 percent of unsecured liabilities.[3] Given that
asset values had not yet suffered when the liquidations were completed,
the results should have been better if there were only a liquidity problem.
Insolvency persisted at a similar level in 1930 and became far more preva-
lent in 1931. For all national banks that entered receivership in the year
ending October 31, 1929, 66.1 percent of $41.8 million in unsecured liabil-
ities was paid during liquidation. In 1930, 61.1 percent of $47.0 million in
unsecured liabilities was paid. In 1931, the percentage of unsecured claims
paid increased to 72.2 percent, but the level of unsecured claims surged to
$294.2 million.[4] The percentage of failed banks that were deeply insolvent
did not change appreciably from 1925 to 1933, but the number of banks
that entered liquidation – and the deposits and other liabilities involved –
escalated sharply in the reporting period beginning on November 1, 1930.
Although we do not have data on the condition of state banks, they were
more encumbered with illiquid assets, especially real estate; therefore, it is
unlikely that their record with respect to solvency was better than that of the
failed national banks. The hypothesis that the banking system collapsed due
to a contagion of fear and widespread runs on solvent banks seems suspect,

---

[2] In an article titled "Bernanke Is Fighting the Last War," Carney (2008) interviewed Anna
     Schwartz. As the title suggests, her position was that circumstances in 2007–2008 were
     quite different from those in 1930 and afterward. "'If the borrowers hadn't withdrawn
     cash, they [the banks] would have been in good shape. But the Fed just sat by and did
     nothing, so bank after bank failed. And that only motivated depositors to withdraw funds
     from banks that were not in distress… [T]hat's not what's going on in the market now,'
     Ms. Schwartz says."
[3] These data on the results of liquidations that were completed in 1929 are drawn from Table
     43 in Comptroller of the Currency (1929).
[4] These data on the results of liquidations by the year the bank entered receivership are
     compiled in Table 83 in Comptroller of the Currency (1941) for all liquidations closed by
     October 31, 1941. We added to these figures by collecting the results of other liquidations
     that were completed and reported in later years.

so an examination of the sources of banks' losses is warranted. Losses on residential real estate lending comprise one important category of losses.

4.1.3 Mortgage Leverage and a Housing Collapse Amplify Distress in a Downturn

The same pattern of contraction evident in the 2008 crisis – beginning with declining expenditures on residential construction followed first by declining house prices and then by declining nonresidential fixed investment – was clearly present before the effects of monetary contraction appeared late in 1930 and accelerated in 1931. In fact, the 40.4 percent decline in residential construction from 1925 to 1929 was the largest decline from housing peak to economic cycle peak in any economic downturn between the 1920–21 recession and the 2001 recession.[5]

As discussed in Chapter 5, typical recessions begin with a downturn in expenditures on residential construction, which directly affects employment and consumption. However, if home prices do not decline substantially, the problems are not further compounded by households' losses on their real estate assets, with corresponding negative impacts on bank equity.[6] In the 2007–2009 recession and the Great Depression, significant house price declines against fixed mortgage debt reduced household wealth and damaged the balance sheets of financial sector firms. This, in turn, amplified the usual downturns in consumer durables expenditures and nonresidential fixed investments.

One consequence of the focus in the past half-century on monetary policy mistakes is a clearer understanding of the importance of an aggressive central bank response to a developing crisis. Another consequence of the focus on monetary factors, however, was a lack of attention to and concern about the housing bubble and the precarious build-up of household debt that accompanied it. If the Federal Reserve had given more attention to the risk accumulating in the housing and mortgage markets, it might have obviated the need for the aggressive policy measures that were subsequently pursued.

In this chapter, we demonstrate that the real estate boom in the 1920s began to unwind three years before the general contraction began:

---

[5] The only larger decline in residential construction between housing peak and economic-cycle peak during the past ninety-four years in the United States was the 43.9 percent collapse between Q1 2006 and Q4 2007.

[6] For a discussion of the somewhat typical 1973–5 recessions and the 1980 and 1981–82 recessions, see Chapter 5.

Households' consumption of durable goods; firms' investments in inventories, equipment, and structures; the stock market; and output all continued to climb for three years after the contraction in residential real estate began. The broader economic collapse coincided with the collapse of credit to households, which had supported residential real estate purchases and consumer durable goods consumption.[7] All of these events preceded the first banking crisis in late 1930, as well as the missed opportunities by the Federal Reserve to counteract the declining money supply.

4.1.4 Household Balance Sheet Stress and the Consumption Decline in 1930

Prior to subsequent problems with monetary policy, a serious contraction was already underway in 1930 before the escalation of bank failures in late 1930 and in 1931. Temin (1976) noted that the consumption decline in 1930 was much sharper relative to the declines in household income and wealth than it was during the other two interwar recessions in 1920–21 and 1937–38.[8] Friedman and Schwartz (1963) argued that a series of monetary policy failures – starting with the failure to provide liquidity during the first banking crisis in November and December of 1930 – turned a normal cyclical downturn into an inexorable economic collapse. Temin's observation that the decline in consumption in 1930 was unusually large is consistent with the hypothesis that household balance sheets were stressed before the monetary collapse in 1931. Particularly unusual, in comparison with other downturns in the last century, was the decrease in nondurable consumption (Figure 4.1). This decline, suggesting unusual household belt-tightening, preceded the monetary collapse described by Friedman and Schwartz, which leaves open the possibility that both consumption decline and an inadequate monetary response are consistent with the broad course of events. White (1984) argued that the first banking crisis was indistinguishable from the

---

[7] Figure 4.2 shows that mortgage lending collapsed well before the money supply declined and before the first large failures of financial firms occurred in November and December 1930 – the serious decline in the money supply began in early 1931.

[8] We note, however, that declines in total wealth alone do not measure the precise impact on households of a decline in home values against fixed mortgage debt. During the Great Recession, mean household wealth fell 14.7 percent between 2007 and 2010, but median household wealth fell 38.8 percent. (These figures are calculated from the 2007 and 2010 editions of the Survey of Consumer Finances from the Federal Reserve.) For many households, home equity is a major store of wealth, and a collapse of housing prices can affect the wealth of a large fraction of households to an even greater extent than it decreases national wealth.

banking troubles that had plagued rural areas throughout the 1920s. White (p. 119) noted that "Friedman and Schwartz argue that the surge of failures was prompted by a loss of confidence in the banking system, while Temin believes that the failures and depression grew out of a downturn in the real sector." He concluded (p. 137) that "depictions of events by Temin and by Friedman and Schwartz are not really in conflict. The weakening of assets and the lack of easy credit put the squeeze on all banks, and many weak ones were doomed."

Although we cannot unambiguously identify the cause of the collapse in consumption, the build-up of household debt almost surely had a significant role. The period prior to the Depression contrasts sharply with the period leading up to the 1920–21 recession. Before the 1920–21 recession, the price level – including housing prices – rose sharply. The CPI and nominal GNP doubled from December 1915 to June 1920. Consequently, even as households took out new mortgage loans, real household mortgage debt fell more than 20 percent between 1915 and 1920. During the deep 1920–21 recession and again in the shallow 1923–34 recession, whereas fixed investments and inventories fell, real household expenditures on nondurable goods and services, durable goods, and new residential structures all increased. As we demonstrate in the next section, all major components of household expenditures declined sharply in the early years of the Great Depression. Although there were sharp monetary contractions in both the 1920–21 recession and the Great Depression, the persistence of the monetary contraction in the Depression was most likely catalyzed by the stressed balance sheet conditions among households.

4.2 Changes in Output by Sector

During the 1920s, residential and commercial construction, manufacturing, and consumer durable goods production all expanded rapidly, but mortgage and consumer credit were the factors that expanded most sharply. The expansion had two distinct phases: a strong expansion from 1921 to 1925 supported by a rapid expansion of residential construction and consumer durable goods expenditures, followed by a moderate expansion from 1925 to 1929 that continued despite declines in residential construction that began in 1927. These two phases indicate the important role that residential construction played over the entire decade from 1921 to 1930, so it is worthwhile to decompose the growth and decline in the economy during that period into its major components. We examine changes in GNP and four of its major components: consumption of nondurable goods and

Table 4.1. *Annual growth rates of GNP and
components, 1921–1933*

	1921–1925	1925–1929	1929–1933
GNP	6.1%	3.7%	– 7.8%
C	3.4%	4.7%	– 4.6%
D	12.9%	2.7%	– 15.6%
D + H	17.7%	– 1.7%	– 19.8%
H + I	17.6%	0.6%	– 27.6%
H	29.4%	– 10.9%	– 40.1%

services (C), investment in new residential structures (H), expenditures on durable goods (D), and fixed investment less investment in new residential structures (I).[9]

Table 4.1 shows annual growth rates of GNP and several of its primary components between 1921 and 1933. Looking at the growth rates of these components from 1925 to 1929, nothing appears surprising as we move down the table from GNP to the sum of residential fixed investment and nonresidential fixed investment (H + I). Toward the end of the expansion, H + I flattened out for a long period, from 1925 to 1929. However, non-residential fixed investment (I) grew by 5.3 percent per year during those four years; it was residential construction that was collapsing. Given its size relative to the economy, this should not have been a serious problem. However, residential construction had an outsized role in the household balance sheet because it became increasingly leveraged during the decade, and the price collapse during the Depression seriously reduced household wealth and solvency.

Changes in output by sector in the Great Depression are uncharacteristic of recessions primarily in magnitude but also by the fact that there was a major decrease in consumer spending on nondurable goods and

[9] For brevity, we refer to personal consumption of services and nondurable goods as "consumption" (C); household durable goods expenditures as "durables" (D); expenditures on new single-family and multifamily housing units as "housing" (H); and nonresidential fixed investment as "investment" (I). Expenditure on new single-family and multifamily housing units is from Grebler, Blank, and Winnick (1956, Table B-3); consumption and durable goods expenditures are from a revision of Kuznets (1961) in Swanson and Williamson (1972, Table A1); investment is from Swanson and Williamson (1972, Table A2, Column 3) minus expenditure on new housing units from Grebler, Blank, and Winnick (1956, Table B-3); and GNP is from Swanson and Williamson (1972, Table 1). All series are converted from nominal to real figures by dividing by GNP deflators from Balke and Gordon (1989, Table 10); these deflators are HSUS Series Ca215.

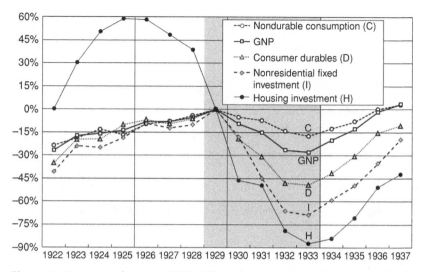

Figure 4.1. Percentage changes to GNP and its major components relative to 1929 levels.

services. With the single exception of the 2001 recession, consumer durables, residential construction, and investment all declined in every postwar recession; however, the percentage of declines have never matched those during the Depression.[10] During the Great Depression, durable goods expenditures declined 49.2 percent, investment declined 68.6 percent, and housing declined 92.5 percent. In the average of eleven postwar recessions from 1948 to 2007, the corresponding declines were 11.4 percent (durables), 11.8 percent (investment), and 32.5 percent (housing).[11]

In the Depression, real GNP declined 27.7 percent and every major component of output declined: Even nondurable consumption fell by 17.3 percent – a figure dramatically larger than the decline in consumption of nondurable goods and services in any downturn since the Depression.[12] Figure 4.1 shows the movement of GNP and several of its major

[10] In the 2001 recession, nonresidential fixed investment was the only sector that declined. This has happened only once before in the past ninety-four years, in the 1923–24 recession, when a downturn in consumption was averted by large infusions of mortgage credit, just as in 2001. See Figure 4.2 for a depiction of the highly unusual growth of net mortgage credit in 1923 and 1924.

[11] These figures on the average size of sectorial changes in postwar recessions are drawn from Table 5.2 in Chapter 5.

[12] Real expenditures on nondurable goods and services have fallen in only three postwar recessions (i.e., 1980, 1981–82, and 2007–2009). The only year-over-year decline in household consumption of nondurable goods and services between 1934 and 2012 was the 1.4 percent decline in 2009.

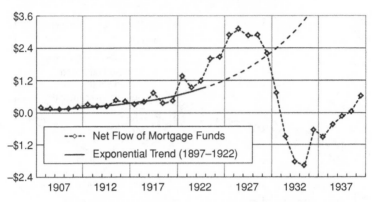

Figure 4.2. Net flow of mortgage funds, 1905–1939 (in billions of dollars).

components between 1922 and 1937. Each data point in a series measures the difference between the value of the series in that year and its value at the peak of the economic cycle in 1929. For example, residential construction was 30.3 percent higher in 1923 than it was in 1929; it was 46.4 percent lower in 1930 than it was in 1929. In Figure 4.1, housing peaked in 1925 at a level 58.7 percent higher than the 1929 level. Other major components of GNP – and GNP itself – all continued to rise until 1929. Every major component of GNP fell in 1930, but none fell as much as housing. By 1933, housing was only 12.5 percent of its 1929 level and a paltry 7.5 percent of its peak level in 1925.

4.3 Residential Mortgage Debt Boom and Increasing Leverage

Grebler, Blank, and Winnick (1956, Table L-6) reported residential mortgage debt outstanding from 1896 to 1952. Mortgage debt increased fairly steadily from 1896 to 1922. The rapid decline in foreign lending after World War I, combined with the pent-up demand for housing, led to a surge in residential mortgage finance starting in 1919. From 1919 to 1929, nominal residential mortgage debt rose from $7,998 million to $29,440 million, an increase of 268 percent. Mortgage debt outstanding grew rapidly from 1923 to 1928 and then slowed in 1929 and 1930. From 1931 to 1937, total mortgage lending outstanding fell in every year. Figure 4.2 shows the net growth of mortgage funds outstanding from 1905 to 1939.

The nominal declines in mortgage debt outstanding between 1931 and 1937 were remarkable in view of the historical record of mortgage lending in the United States. Residential mortgage debt increased every year from 1897 to 1952 except in the period from 1931 to 1937 and during the war years of 1942 to 1944. Combining the Grebler, Blank, and Winnick (1956) annual data from 1896 to 1952 with the Federal Reserve Flow of Funds quarterly data from 1952 on, mortgage loans outstanding increased in every reporting period from 1945 until Q1 2008. It subsequently declined for twenty-one consecutive quarters, from Q2 2008 through Q2 2013 before finally increasing in Q3 2013. Clearly, new residential mortgage credit is a bellwether for the condition of household and financial-sector balance sheets. The two worst economic and financial crises of the past century in the United States were associated with the only two peacetime collapses of residential lending; in both cases, the lending collapse preceded the collapse of the financial system and the general economic downturn.

Residential mortgage credit growth during this period was much higher than during any other period in the past 110 years. Nominal mortgage debt increased at an average annual rate of 13.9 percent between the end of 1919 and the end of 1929. During the same period, the CPI fell 11.4 percent; therefore, the net effect was a rapid growth of real household mortgage debt. This rapid build-up of mortgage debt enabled increased residential construction.

Mortgage bonds financed large construction projects to a greater extent than at any previous time, with results that ultimately proved costly to investors. Losses on Chicago residential apartment building bonds began before 1929. More than 10 percent of apartment building bonds were in default by the end of 1929 and 35 percent were in default at the end of 1930. Almost every indicator in the residential real estate market turned down before the stock market bubble began in 1928. Sales, prices, net flow of mortgage funds, and residential construction all peaked in 1925 or 1926, but the net flow of mortgage funds continued at an elevated level in 1927 and 1928 as house prices, housing sales, and new residential construction were all falling. From this, we can conclude that household leverage – that is, the fraction of home sales paid for with mortgages – was rising in 1927 and 1928. However, there is important direct evidence, which we examine next.

In 1934, the U.S. Department of Commerce conducted a Financial Survey of Urban Housing in fifty-two cities. The survey included a broad range of questions about household and housing finance. Wickens (1937) tabulated the results of these surveys in up to eighty tables per city for twenty-two of the fifty-two cities in the original survey. Table 29 of the survey, which was tabulated for each of the twenty-two cities, provided the total number of respondents who acquired their home in each year from 1901 to 1933, with the amount of the original purchase price that was financed by a mortgage, grouped into percentage ranges. The three highest ranges were 70 to 84 percent, 85 to 99 percent, and 100 percent. There is widespread belief that mortgages were limited to 50 percent of the purchase price in the 1920s (see Field 2014 for an example); however, the results of the survey indicate high levels of mortgage leverage.

Aggregated across the 27,795 respondents who originally purchased their home between 1920 and 1929, 23.4 percent of all home buyers (whether they had a mortgage or purchased entirely with equity) had mortgages at the time of purchase that were 85 percent of the purchase price or higher. The time trend also was consistent with increasing leverage: The percentage of new purchases made with 85 percent or more borrowed money increased every year from 1920, when it was 16.3 percent, until 1926, when it reached 26.4 percent.

If we set the threshold lower, 42.7 percent of homeowner occupants in the survey had borrowed 70 percent or more of their purchase price. The survey also reported the number of homeowners who did not take out a mortgage when they purchased their home. If we consider only those homeowners who took out a mortgage at the time of purchase, 55.8 percent of those borrowed 70 percent or more of their purchase price. Most measures of the nominal decline in housing prices are close to 30 percent for the period from 1930 to 1933; therefore, by this measure, about half of mortgaged properties could have been at risk of being "underwater" (i.e., with a mortgage greater than the value of the home).

Research on the housing market in Franklin County, Ohio, complements the evidence we report herein from aggregate data and from the Financial Survey of Urban Housing. The Bureau of Business Research (1943) conducted a study at The Ohio State University to examine deed and mortgage recordings from 1917 through 1937. The study reported tax assessment values of properties with new mortgages by year and type of structure. We use these data to determine the loan-to-value ratio for the years from 1921 to 1930, which are reported in Table 4.2.[13]

---

[13] The data on number of residential mortgages are from Table 21 in the Bureau of Business Research (1943) survey. Data on the ratio of mortgage to assessed value and average assessed value are calculated from data in Table 24 for appraised value of mortgaged residential structures and from Table 27 on the amount of residential mortgages. We restrict our attention to 1921 through 1930 because the same data source also includes assessed values on properties acquired under Sheriff's Deeds and on the sales prices for those properties, and those prices and assessed values are close. For 1921 through 1930, the average ratio of

Table 4.2. *Mortgage leverage in Franklin County, Ohio, 1921–1930*

Year	Number of mortgages	Mortgage to assessed value	Average assessed value	Index of assessed values
1921	8,599	61.6%	$3,998	0.76
1922	12,097	62.1%	$4,352	0.83
1923	14,303	62.1%	$4,906	0.94
1924	13,526	57.6%	$5,227	1.00
1925	16,896	64.2%	$4,885	0.93
1926	18,195	67.8%	$4,798	0.92
1927	15,735	68.8%	$4,890	0.94
1928	14,120	69.1%	$4,968	0.95
1929	9,997	65.4%	$4,936	0.94
1930	8,400	66.6%	$4,806	0.92

As with the data from the Financial Survey of Urban Housing, the deed and mortgage survey data show a gradual increase in loan-to-value ratios, and the average mortgage debt is well above the 50 percent commonly believed to be the norm in the 1920s. Table 4.2 shows that, averaged across all mortgages recorded in 1928 in Franklin County, Ohio, debt amounted to 69.1 percent of assessed value.[14] Data on properties with junior liens in the Bureau of Business Research (1943) survey indicate that the loan-to-value ratio was far worse for homes with junior liens. Table 69 of the survey indicates the number of properties with junior liens, the assessed value of the properties, the principal amount of the junior lien, and the amount of the senior lien. For properties that had two or more liens, the principal of the junior liens gradually escalated from 21.4 percent of assessed property values in 1917 to a peak of 46.1 percent in 1925. Between 1917 and 1924, the average amount of the sum of the two liens was 85.4 percent of the assessed

sales price to assessed value was 1.018. These ratios are calculated from data in Tables 87 and 96.

[14] Some mortgages issued in 1928 would have been refinanced from earlier purchases, and the assessed value may have been from a previous year. Even so, according to the price series in Grebler, Blank, and Winnick (1956, Appendix C), the average price of homes was almost unchanged between 1920 and 1928. Table 2 also shows that average assessed values for mortgages recorded in Franklin County (Ohio) were consistent between 1923 and 1929, with one brief "blip" in 1924. Consequently, the fact that not all assessed values were current probably would not have significantly affected this measure of the loan-to-value ratio. Furthermore, the level of the loan-to-value ratio from mortgage recordings in Franklin County is also consistent with those reported in the Financial Survey of Urban Housing for twenty-two cities.

property values. Between 1925 and 1930, the sum averaged 109.1 percent of the assessed property values.

The roles of debt-fueled construction and durable goods booms were mentioned in the early literature but received limited attention in subsequent accounts of the Depression. Persons (1930) attributed the boom to excessive lending on real estate and consumer durables, and Fisher (1933) outlined a theory of the impact of deflation on debt; however, during sixty postwar years of relatively stable domestic financial markets, their concerns faded. Now that the pattern has been repeated several times in the past twenty years in developed countries – such as Japan, Finland, and Sweden and, more recently, the United States, United Kingdom, Spain, and several other European countries – it is easier to appreciate a more universal role for the impact on the economic cycle of residential construction and durable goods booms that are based on unsustainable mortgage and consumer credit expansion. This new as well as the neglected older evidence allows economic developments from 1920 into the 1930s to be reexamined with a fresh and more accurate perspective.

4.4 Housing-Sales and House-Price Declines, 1926–1933

The pattern of housing market decline during the late 1920s was similar to the pattern from 2006 to 2009. A broad measure of sales volume compiled by the FHA peaked in 1925 and then fell in each year from 1926 until 1933. In a pattern that has been replicated in the recent downturn, home prices began to fall after the sales volume decline.

4.4.1 Housing Sales Decline

Fisher (1951, pp. 157–62) described a project devised by the Division of Research and Statistics at the FHA to make a complete survey of deed recordings in the District of Columbia and eight U.S. counties.[15] Figure 4.3 shows a six-month moving average of the monthly aggregated deed recordings for these nine jurisdictions from 1922 through 1940.[16]

---

[15] The survey methodology is described in Works Progress Administration (1938). A deed recording is the formal record of ownership transference, whether by sale, inheritance, foreclosure, or a voluntary conveyance of property to a lender.

[16] The series begin in 1895 in six of the nine jurisdictions and commence by 1898 in the other three. The series extend through 1935 in all nine jurisdictions and through 1946 in four of them. The areas covered are the District of Columbia and eight U.S. counties. The counties and their principal cities are San Francisco (San Francisco, California); Ada

Figure 4.3. Six-month moving average of deed recordings in eight counties and Washington, DC (in thousands).

Other than regular seasonal variation, the series declined sharply from its peak in July 1925 until it bottomed out in February 1934. Annual deed recordings fell 64.8 percent from the annual peak in 1925 to the annual trough in 1933. Although annual peaks varied from one location to another, in six of the nine locations, they took place in 1924 (Allegheny, Pennsylvania), 1925 (San Francisco, California; Cuyahoga, Ohio; and Salt Lake, Utah), and 1926 (Essex, NJ; and Washington, DC).

Several years before the FHA data were collected and evaluated, Vanderblue (1927b) examined the number of real estate transfers and conveyances in Miami, Orlando, and Jacksonville, Florida.[17] Real estate transfers in all three cities exhibited a similar pattern of gradual but strong growth from 1919 that continued until it reached a feverish pitch in the last three months of 1924 and the first nine months of 1925. The peak in Miami was reached in September 1925; real estate transfers had collapsed 75 percent by the time the September 1926 hurricane devastated Miami. The patterns of

(Boise, Idaho); Washoe (Reno, Nevada); Essex (Newark, New Jersey); Burleigh (Bismarck, North Dakota); Cuyahoga (Cleveland, Ohio); Allegheny (Pittsburgh, Pennsylvania); and Salt Lake (Salt Lake City, Utah). The graph in Figure 3 extends beyond 1935. Fisher estimated deed recordings for several counties: Ada and Burleigh (1936–40), Allegheny (1937–40), Washoe (1939–40), and Salt Lake (1940). See Fisher (1951, Tables A1 and A2).

[17] Vanderblue (1927a) described general economic conditions in Florida from the 1890s through 1926.

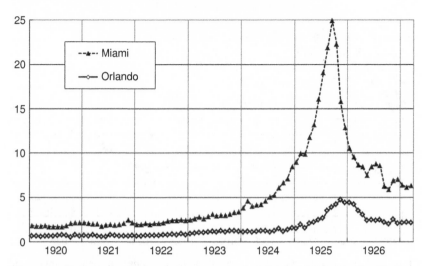

Figure 4.4. Real estate transfers and conveyances in Miami and Orlando, Florida (seasonally adjusted, in thousands per month).

real estate transfers in Orlando and Jacksonville were similar: Jacksonville peaked in October 1925 and Orlando in November 1925.

The Florida real estate boom was an amplified version of the more general boom throughout the country, much as the recent booms in Las Vegas, Phoenix, and Miami were amplified versions of similar booms around the country. Figure 4.4 shows that real estate transactions in Miami had increased by a factor of five in only fourteen months – from five thousand transfers in July 1924 to twenty-five thousand in September 1925. Although the increase was remarkably rapid in Miami, its peak differed by only one month from the peak for the average of the nine widely dispersed jurisdictions shown in Figure 4.3.

4.4.2 House Price Movements, 1926–1933

House price data are fragmentary and are obtained by a variety of methods from diverse geographical areas. Yet, most show a similar temporal pattern and similar magnitudes. House prices peaked in 1926, fell moderately for at least two years, and then began a sharp decline before reaching a trough in 1933. Sales volume closely tracked price declines, as indicated by extensive data from the FHA.

Fisher (1951, p. 55, Table 7) reviewed evidence from a sample of 3 percent of urban mortgage loans in New York, New Jersey, and Connecticut, which

Figure 4.5. One-year moving average of asking prices in Washington, DC.

was compiled by the Home Owners' Loan Corporation. This survey compared appraisal values for homeowners who were refinancing their home in 1933 and 1934 to the purchase prices in 1925–1927. The median price decline between 1925 and 1933–34 was 31.0 percent. For homes purchased in 1926 and 1927, the median decline to 1933–34 was 26.9 percent.

The National Housing Agency used newspaper ads to compile asking prices for homes in Washington, DC, for the period from 1918 to 1948. Figure 4.5 shows a one-year moving average of those prices from 1920 through 1940.[18] The 1929 average asking price was 7.2 percent below the 1925 average asking price; by 1933, the average asking price was 26.3 percent below the 1925 average asking price. Figure 4.3 shows that across nine jurisdictions, deed transfers fell substantially for three years before the significant decline in house prices and for four years before the stock market crash in 1929.

Grebler, Blank, and Winnick (1956, pp. 345–9) summarized the results of a survey conducted in twenty-two cities by the U.S. Department of Commerce in 1934 and published in Wickens (1937). The survey was based on interviews of property owners who were asked (1) the current value of their property, (2) the year it was purchased, and (3) the original purchase price. The median price of single-family owner-occupied homes was determined

---

[18] The Washington, DC, monthly ask price series is provided in Fisher (1951, p. 53, Table 6). Annual averages for the series are provided in HSUS Series Dc828.

from these survey data and then this median price was used to develop an index of house prices for each year from 1890 to 1934. This series peaked in 1925. By 1929, it had fallen only 8.2 percent; by 1933, it had fallen 30.5 percent.[19]

All three of these series show similar declines from annual peaks in 1925 to lows in 1933. The Washington, DC, asking-price series is the only monthly series, and it shows a peak in June 1926 – almost a year after the sales series began to fall (although the sales series included eight counties in addition to Washington, DC). The two series that included 1929 prices also displayed similar declines from the peak to 1929. Overall, given the widely different geographical coverage of these indices and the variety of methodologies, the resulting measures of house price peaks, troughs, and percentage declines are surprisingly similar, and they portray a situation in which large household home equity losses must have been widespread and severe. The price declines also demonstrate the potential for serious losses on residential mortgages, especially when combined with evidence on the extent of mortgage leverage from Section 4.3.

Wickens (1941) used census data for 1930 and data from the Financial Survey of Urban Housing for 1934 to estimate prices (see Table A 10) for fifty U.S. cities. He estimated that the average value of a house fell 32.9 percent, from $6,619 in 1930 to $4,439 in 1934. He also used 1930 census data to estimate the value of the housing stock for the entire country. The estimate of the total value of the housing stock in 1930 (from Table A 2) was $122.58 billion, with owner-occupied homes valued at $64.68 billion and rented housing units valued at $57.90 billion. Wickens's Table A 8 shows the value of owner-occupied housing in 1934 at $42.42 billion and the value of rental housing as $36.75 billion. Between 1930 and 1934, rental-unit value dropped 36.5 percent and owner-occupied-unit value dropped 34.4 percent. The total value of residential units fell 35.4 percent between 1930 and 1934, according to Wickens's estimates.

Table 4.3 reproduces cost-of-living and rent indices from 1914 to 1941 from Colean (1944, Table 41, p. 421). Rental-price movements tracked house-price movements over the course of the boom and decline, but the magnitude of the decline in rents was larger than the decline in any of the four price indices reported in this section.

Rent dropped 13.5 percent in nominal terms between 1924 and 1929; it dropped another 30.7 percent in nominal terms between 1929 and 1933.

---

[19] The survey is described in Grebler, Blank, and Winnick (1956, Appendix C, pp. 345–8). It is also available as HSUS Series Dc826.

Table 4.3. *Cost-of-living and rent indices, 1921–1940*

Year	Cost-of-living index	Rent	Year	Cost-of-living index	Rent
1921	102.3	97.7	1931	87.2	82.4
1922	97.4	95.9	1932	77.9	72.4
1923	100.0	100.0	1933	74.9	63.8
1924	101.3	106.3	1934	79.4	64.8
1925	103.7	104.1	1935	82.2	70.3
1926	104.3	101.3	1936	84.1	77.9
1927	102.0	97.8	1937	87.8	86.5
1928	100.6	93.7	1938	85.7	87.0
1929	100.1	92.0	1939	84.5	86.3
1930	96.7	89.5	1940	87.0	86.9

The cumulative nominal rent decline was 40.0 percent between 1924 and 1933. In real terms, rent dropped 12.4 percent between 1924 and 1929 and 7.3 percent between 1929 and 1933. The cumulative real rent decline was 18.8 percent between 1924 and 1933.

Hoyt (1933, p. 377) found a broadly similar pattern of rent price movements in Chicago between 1915 and 1933. His index increased from 100.0 in 1915 to 205.6 in 1925, with almost all of the increase occurring between 1919 and 1924. From 1925 to 1929, the index fell 12.3 percent; between 1930 and 1933, it fell 39.7 percent to a level almost identical to the 1919 level.

It is worth noting that the nominal rent decline during the Depression period would have hurt a landlord who purchased a property with a mortgage before the property value and the rental income fell. At the same time, real rents fell much less during the Depression than real income so that renters also were hurt between 1929 and 1933.

4.5 Mortgage Bond Defaults, Mortgage Delinquency and Foreclosure, and Unemployment

Mortgage bonds grew rapidly as a source of financing for apartment buildings and other commercial structures in the 1920s. After their spectacular rise, they had an even more precipitous collapse. The previous section shows that rent and residential real estate prices were falling before the general decline in 1930. It is also apparent from the reviewed data that rental prices fell earlier and farther than purchase prices. Colean's rent index fell

11.6 percent and Hoyt's Chicago rent index fell 12.3 percent between 1925 and 1929. If these rental price strains were felt by the property owners who borrowed on mortgage bonds, then the early collapse of the bonds is understandable. The rapid accumulation of debt also had adverse consequences for households when the mortgage market collapsed from 1929 to 1931 and house prices collapsed along with it. In this section, we examine the performance of mortgage bonds and the foreclosure record as indicators of the distress in the residential real estate market.

4.5.1 Mortgage Bond Defaults

The record of real estate bond issues provides a useful indication of real estate market trends. Bond issues increased rapidly, especially after 1921. The rapid growth of bond issues, their poor performance, and the pattern of early deterioration of residential mortgage bonds followed by later deterioration of commercial mortgages are all familiar characteristics from the recent real estate downturn. Several studies of these developments were carried out during the Depression.[20]

Data from the Commercial and Financial Chronicle analyzed by Johnson (1936a) showed that by 1925, new real estate bond issues reached $695.8 million and accounted for 22.9 percent of corporate bond issues. As with the many other series on real estate activity that we have reviewed, the growth rate declined sharply after 1925. In 1928, real estate bonds were 1.7 percent below their peak in 1925, but then real estate bond issues began a precipitous fall. In 1929, real estate bond issues fell 51.2 percent to $333.9 million. Declines of 48.8 and 32.8 percent in 1930 and 1931, respectively, were followed by a virtual cessation of new issues in 1932, when newly issued bonds fell 96.8 percent. Johnson found that total real estate bond issues between 1919 and 1933 amounted to $4,114.9 million.[21] For the period from 1919 to 1931, Johnson found data on the performance of 1,090 bond issues that exceeded $1 million, with a total issuance of $2,684 million. He evaluated bond performance by year of issue and classified them in one of three categories: called, matured, and outstanding. Bonds outstanding

---

[20] For an interesting history of real estate bonds, see Boysen (1931), who discussed the development of real estate bonds issued on Chicago apartment buildings starting in 1901.

[21] Goldsmith (1955) estimated that the total of outstanding real estate bond issues reached $6,500 million in 1931. The significant difference between their figures is most likely attributable to the fact that Goldsmith provided an estimate, whereas Johnson counted them from contemporary records. Goldsmith's estimate was provided in Grebler, Blank, and Winnick (1956, Table L-2).

Table 4.4. *Defaults on Chicago real estate bonds, 1925–1934*

Year	Number of defaults	Amount (Thousands)	Cumulative defaults (Thousands)	Percent defaulted
1925–28	7	$8,275	$8,275	1.66%
1929	22	$29,320	$37,595	7.55%
1930	50	$64,095	$101,690	20.42%
1931	104	$162,116	$263,806	52.97%
1932	67	$146,725	$410,531	82.54%
1933	20	$38,003	$448,534	90.17%
1934	5	$22,706	$471,241	94.74%

in 1936 were further separated into those that were current and meeting all obligations and those that were not meeting obligations or defaulted.

According to Johnson (1936b), New York accounted for 36.3 percent of the bonds issued; 25.9 percent were issued on Chicago real estate. Koester (1939a, 1939b) evaluated the performance of 285 Chicago real estate bonds issued between 1919 and 1930. The market grew rapidly from the first issue for $1 million in 1919, doubling approximately every year until 1925, when the growth slowed and eventually peaked at $109,305,000 in 1928. Koester examined 338 mortgage bonds compiled by Moody's that amounted to $546,983,500. Detailed information was available on 302 of these bonds, with a total issue amount of $536,478,500.[22] Of the 302 issues, 285 issues totaling $497,391,000 had a corporate structure with bonds and equity. Koester restricted her analysis to this pool with a homogeneous legal organization. Some moderate losses on these bonds appeared between 1925 and 1928. By the end of 1930, more than one fifth of the bonds were in default, in advance of the banking and monetary crises of 1931 (Table 4.4).

Apartment and apartment hotels defaulted earlier than hotel and office buildings. Office bonds had the best record, but even their record was deplorable: 87.7 percent of the office building bonds were in default by the end of 1934. The cascade of defaults on these bonds, from apartments to commercial real estate, is consistent with other aspects of the transmission of the downturn from households to businesses. Koester (1939b) examined prices for the Chicago real estate bonds and found that the basic price patterns conformed to the pattern of defaults through much of the downturn.

---

[22] All of the excluded issues were less than $475,000. Public price and performance data on these bonds were incomplete, probably because the bonds were closely held.

Prices of bonds on apartment hotels fell earliest and farthest; apartment and hotel bonds fell almost as much. Commercial property and office building bonds fell the least but, even so, the declines were dramatic. When apartment hotel bonds reached their minimum price in July 1933, they traded at 8.2 cents on the dollar. Apartment bonds reached their minimum of 11.36 cents on the dollar in January 1934. Office bonds fared the best of the five categories, but even they traded at only 13.0 cents on the dollar at their minimum in January 1934. Recovery of bond prices was limited even by the end of the price series that Koester evaluated in January 1939. Between July 1933 and January 1939, the highest average price for any of the categories was 31.93 cents on the dollar, for commercial buildings in January 1937. The high level of defaults and the low prices indicate extensive losses on the Chicago real estate bonds.

Johnson (1936b) analyzed the performance of bonds issued between 1919 and 1931 in nine cities, including Chicago. His sample of Chicago bonds differed only slightly from the sample analyzed by Koester. He found that in 1936, the recoverable value of Chicago real estate bonds was 39.0 cents on the dollar.

4.5.2 Mortgage Delinquency and Foreclosures

As in the recent debacle, mortgage delinquency was a significant factor in the Depression. Wickens (1941, Table D 44, p. 284) reported that in a survey of more than thirty thousand homeowners in fifty-two cities, 41.9 percent of respondents were behind in their mortgage payments on January 1, 1934. The distress was not confined to low-valued homes. The rate of delinquency among homeowners with homes valued at more than $15,000 was, at 41.8 percent, almost identical to the average for the full sample. The frequency of delinquency among owners of rental properties was, at 45.7 percent, even higher. The situation in some cities was dire. For example, in Cleveland, 61.9 percent of homeowners and 66.0 percent of rental housing owners were delinquent. Those delinquent payments must surely have generated problems with banks' incomes and their liquidity position.

Wickens (1941, Table D 9, p. 215) also reported the percentage of mortgaged properties for owner-occupied homes (56.2 percent) and rental property owners (39.8 percent), as well as the average dollar amount of past-due payments to lenders for delinquent homeowners ($467) and for delinquent rental property owners ($582) (Table D 45, p. 287). Together with the number of owned and rented homes, this is enough information to estimate the total delinquent payments.[23] The results are that homeowners had about $1.16 billion and rental property owners had an additional $1.31 billion in delinquent payments. These delinquent payments amounted to 10.7 percent of the $23.08 billion in nonfarm residential mortgage debt (excluding mortgage bond debt) outstanding at the end of 1933. A comparison with the current situation provides perspective on this number. Combined with the amount of residential mortgage debt from the Federal Reserve Flow of Funds, LPS provides enough information to develop a reasonable estimate of delinquent mortgage payments. Delinquent residential mortgage payments appear to have peaked at $85.24 billion in Q3 2012. This figure amounts to only 0.9 percent of the $9,442.12 billion in mortgage debt outstanding at that time.[24] This comparison should demonstrate that mortgage delinquency could have been an important factor in the financial distress during the Great Depression because it was probably an order of magnitude greater (i.e., as a percentage of outstanding mortgage debt) than it was in the recent crisis.

Unfortunately, there is no national foreclosure data until 1926. Foreclosures increased steadily from this first year through 1933 and thereafter began to decrease.[25] Foreclosures began to rise sharply before the period of rapidly falling house prices and rapidly increasing unemployment began in 1930.

For comparison, the number of foreclosures during the recent crisis peaked at 1.1 million in 2010, which would correspond to about

[23] Table 965, p. 886, in the 1943 edition of the *Statistical Abstract of the United States* includes the number of owner-occupied homes (10,549,972) and the number of rental homes (12,367,100) in 1930.

[24] From the amount of residential mortgage debt provided in the Federal Reserve Flow of Funds and the number of mortgaged properties in the LPS *Mortgage Monitor*, it is possible to determine the average mortgage for each quarterly reporting period. In Q3 2012, the average home mortgage principal balance was $188,598. If we assume that the typical delinquent mortgage was a fully amortized thirty-year loan with a 6 percent interest rate, then one missed monthly payment amounted to almost exactly $600 per $100,000 principal balance. LPS reports the number of residential mortgages thirty days past due and the number sixty days past due in its *Mortgage Monitor*. For mortgages ninety or more days past due, it reports both the number and the average number of days past due. It also reports the number of mortgaged residential properties in the foreclosure process and the average number of days that they are delinquent. From this information, it is possible to estimate the number of delinquent monthly payments. For example, multiplying the number of mortgages that are thirty days past due by the average principal balance per mortgage and the average monthly payment on that balance yields the estimate of delinquent payments for that category of delinquency.

[25] Foreclosure statistics are taken from HSUS Series Dc1255 and Dc1257.

Table 4.5. *Foreclosures and foreclosure rates, 1926–1941*

Year	Total foreclosures	Foreclosures per thousand mortgaged structures	Year	Total foreclosures	Foreclosures per thousand mortgaged structures
1926	68,100	3.6	1934	230,350	12.2
1927	91,000	4.8	1935	228,713	12.1
1928	116,000	6.1	1936	185,439	9.8
1929	134,900	7.1	1937	151,366	8.0
1930	150,000	7.9	1938	118,357	6.3
1931	193,800	10.2	1939	100,410	5.3
1932	248,700	13.1	1940	75,556	4.0
1933	252,400	13.3	1941	58,559	3.4

20.6 foreclosures per thousand mortgaged residential properties. In 2012, the rate was approximately 14.4 per thousand mortgaged residential properties. In a July 2013 National Foreclosure Report from CoreLogic, it was estimated that 4.5 million foreclosures have been completed since September 2008, which is about 8.3 percent of the mortgaged properties at the time of the financial crisis. The rates shown in Table 4.5 for the Great Depression would imply that there was about the same percentage of home foreclosures between 1929 and 1936 as there was between 2008 and 2012. Standard & Poor estimates that the recoverable value on the average foreclosure is about 55 percent of the loan principal. By the end of 1933, accumulated foreclosures from 1929 had reached about 5.1 percent of the properties with mortgages in 1929. If lenders' losses were comparable to the recent estimates from Standard & Poor, losses would have been about $615 million, or 2.7 percent, of the residential mortgage principal outstanding at the end of 1933. Combined with losses from delinquency, the losses in the Depression would have been about 13.4 percent of mortgage loans; in the Great Recession, the figure would be about 4.5 percent of mortgage loans. Although these figures are approximations, they certainly suggest that losses on mortgage lending must have been severe and an important source of financial distress during the Depression. Moreover, foreclosure statistics underestimate both homeowner and lender distress because many homeowners surrendered their home before the foreclosure process was undertaken or completed. Fisher (1951, p. 48), citing Hoad (1942), noted that "during the eight-year period, 1931–38, 10.1 percent of all single-family homes in the [Toledo] area were foreclosed, and 9.6 percent were surrendered in lieu of foreclosure."

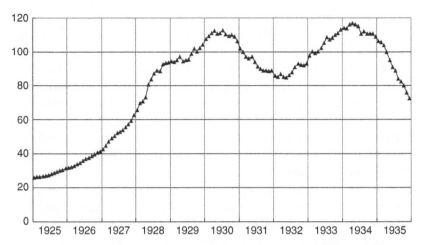

Figure 4.6. One-year moving average of monthly foreclosures in Washington, DC.

More disaggregated data reported by the Bureau of Business Research (1943) for Franklin County, Ohio, can be used to determine which vintages of loans had the most serious foreclosure rates. Table 60 in that report shows that the percentage of mortgages resolved by foreclosure or court judgment by the end of 1937 increased monotonically from 0.5 percent in 1919 to 9.9 percent in 1928. If we assume that the hazard rate of foreclosure or court judgment was stationary for each vintage from 1917 to 1937, then the percentage of loans that would ultimately be judged to be in default each year increased from 0.03 percent for those issued in 1919 to 1.09 percent for those issued in 1928. The rate then began to fall slowly to 0.66 percent by 1932. By 1934, it reached 0.04 percent per year.

Additional evidence on the years prior to 1926 was provided by Badgley (1936), who published a monthly series on deed recordings and foreclosures from 1893 to 1936 for Washington, DC. Figure 4.6 shows a one-year moving average of Badgley's foreclosures series. We note that foreclosures were increasing fastest during a period that was otherwise considered part of the economic boom, in 1927 and 1928.

In 1929, the unemployment rate was lower than in any other year in the 1920s. Yet, Table 4.5 shows that the rate of foreclosures nearly doubled between 1926 and 1929. This result would be puzzling but the experience of the recent housing bubble suggests a possible reason for rising foreclosures in a time of rising income and expanding employment. We compiled considerable evidence that leverage was increasing as the real estate market was slowing down. Figure 4.2 shows that as late as 1928, the net increase in outstanding mortgages remained close to its peak level from 1926. Figure 4.3 shows that deed recordings in eight counties and Washington, DC, peaked in 1925 and had been falling rapidly for three years. The total number of deed recordings in 1928 was 31.4 percent below the level in 1925. Moreover, as Figure 4.1 shows, new residential construction – which would absorb a large amount of new mortgage funds – was also falling by 1928. New residential construction had fallen 14.3 percent from 1925 to 1928. Yet, through this developing downturn in residential construction and sales, the net flow of mortgage funds actually increased slightly between 1925 and 1928. From this, it follows that the leverage was increasing as the Depression approached. It is possible or even likely that during the mid to late 1920s, underwriting standards were eroding. As house prices began to decline in 1927 and 1928, an increasing number of homeowners were unable to meet their obligations, even before the general downturn began.

4.6 Urban Bank Stress from Real Estate

Among the banks that experienced serious problems, we have evidence that they were heavily exposed to residential real estate. According to Lucia (1985) and O'Brien (1992, p. 378), the Bank of United States had 45 percent of its assets in real estate in 1930, compared to an average of 12 percent for other New York City banks. The final banking crisis from January to March 1933 originated in Detroit with the Guardian Union Group and Detroit Bankers Group. Union Guardian Trust had $30 million in real estate assets at the end of 1930, and it had 72 percent of its assets in real estate at the end of 1932, six weeks before it failed. According to Wigmore (1985, p. 437), "Within the Guardian Group as a whole approximately one third of its total assets were in loans or investments related to real estate at the end of 1932." These figures are extremely high relative to other commercial banks. According to Grebler, Blank, and Winnick (1956, Table N-10, p. 485), the average percentage of assets in residential mortgage loans for commercial banks in 1933 was 5.5 percent, and the average level of commercial bank lending on all real estate was only 8.7 percent.

The other main bank in the Guardian Union Group was the Guardian National Bank of Commerce. That bank's deposits of $198 million in December 1930 had fallen to $113.9 million when it was closed. Wigmore (1985, p. 438) also noted that "The banks in the Detroit Bankers' Co. had over 40 percent of their assets in real estate loans or investments at the end of 1932, although their emphasis on individual home mortgages had produced a more sound portfolio." The largest bank in the Detroit Bankers

Group was the First National Bank of Detroit, which had deposits of $398.8 million when it closed.[26] In Senate hearings in late January 1934, Ferdinand Pecora quoted from the bank examiner's report of September 25, 1931, on the condition of the First National Bank of Detroit[27]:

This report reflects a very unsatisfactory condition, showing classified loans and doubtful paper aggregating approximately the surplus and profit of the bank, without taking into consideration a large amount of slow assets. This condition has been brought about by two major causes, namely, the general business depression, and the shrinkage in the inflated value of real estate, and poor management.

In the first instance, Detroit has suffered along with other large cities from the depression, and more particularly because of the slowing down of the motor industry. The city has a large floating population, relying to a great extent on this one industry for its income. When this source of income is materially reduced, all other branches of business are to some extent affected.

This condition has been reflected to a very marked degree in the value of real estate. Real estate values of two years ago have been cut in half, with little activity on this basis. Large buildings have not shown any market whatever. Foreclosures and receiverships are numerous.

From this quote, it appears that the First National Bank of Detroit also was heavily invested in real estate. Therefore, the two largest banking conglomerates in Detroit – where the final banking panic of January to March of 1933 incubated – were both fragile institutions with large real estate portfolios.

Dolbeare and Barnd (1931) compared the condition of ten banks that failed in the summer of 1929 with a group of eight banks that survived into 1931. The successful banks were chosen first from among the strongest Florida state banks. Eight of the failed banks were chosen because they were similar in size and located in the same cities as successful banks in the study, and two of the failed banks were chosen because they were similar in size to other successful banks in the study. Characteristics of the failed and successful banks were compared at call dates in June and December of each year from June 1922 to December 1928. Two comparisons stood out: (1) the real estate loans of failed banks, on average, grew 288.1 percent between June 1924 and December 1925; and (2) the real estate loans of the successful banks grew by 40.0 percent, on average, between June 1924 and December 1925. The volume of real estate loans as a percentage of assets averaged 12.3 percent in the failed banks and 15.2 percent in the successful

---

[26] For the final report on the condition of the First National Bank of Detroit, see Table 36 in the *Eightieth Annual Report of the Comptroller of the Currency* (1942).

[27] See United States Congress (1934), p. 5242.

banks during the boom period. Although the failed banks had fewer real estate loans as a percentage of assets, the real estate loans of failed banks grew much faster during the bubble period than those of successful banks. Failed banks also grew much faster during the boom. On average, deposits in failed banks grew by 220.7 percent, whereas deposits in successful banks grew by only 90.6 percent. Total loans of failed banks also grew faster during the boom period – 166.0 versus 56.6 percent – but most other characteristics of the two groups were similar. Loans as a percentage of total assets averaged 57.4 percent in the failed banks versus 56.0 percent in the successful banks during the boom period. During the boom period, cash as a percentage of total assets averaged 29.4 percent in the failed banks versus 32.4 percent in the successful banks. Deposits as a percentage of total liabilities averaged 89.0 percent in the failed banks versus 90.1 percent in the successful banks during the boom period. These results leave open the possibility that it was growth of all lending that was a key factor in the bank failure, but they also contribute to the body of evidence showing the greater relative vulnerability of bank balance sheets to lending on real estate in the 1920s.

Field (2014) argued that banks' loans to brokers were probably a more serious source of losses than real estate loans. He noted the large volume of these loans and the fact that they constituted a significant share of total lending by member banks. Despite the large amount of loans for securities purchases, evidence from loans to brokers suggests that deleveraging in this sector was conducted quickly and with minimal losses. Loans to brokers on the NYSE peaked in October 1929 at $8.55 billion. By the beginning of December 1929, the figure had fallen by 53 percent to only $4.02 billion.[28] Through the course of this rapid deleveraging, only one brokerage failed (i.e., Mandeville, Brooks & Chaffee). Its liabilities were estimated at $4 million to $5 million.[29] It was seven months later before the next brokerage, Woody & Co., failed, with liabilities estimated at $3 million.[30] This indicates the ease with which loans on securities could be closed out and the relative safety of these loans, because the bonds and equities that secured the loans could be liquidated if margin calls went unmet.

In sharp contrast to loans on securities, mortgage loans cannot be called, even as collateral collapses (see Gjerstad and Smith 2009 and Chapter 8). Section 4.4.2 discussed how rapidly house prices fell during the Depression, and Section 4.5.2 described the escalation of foreclosures. We estimate

---

[28] See New York Stock Exchange (1930).
[29] See *New York Times* (1929).
[30] See *New York Times* (1930).

that delinquent mortgage payments in January 1934 amounted to 10.7 percent of outstanding mortgage principal and that losses on foreclosures may have amounted to another $615 million, or about 2.7 percent of outstanding principal, at the end of 1933. Residential mortgage debt outstanding (excluding mortgage bond debt) peaked in 1931 at $27.65 billion. At the beginning of 1934, when losses on mortgage lending had reached approximately 13.4 percent of outstanding loans, mortgage loans outstanding had been reduced by only $4.57 billion to $23.08 billion, a decline of 16.5 percent. The process of deleveraging in the real estate market was arduous, costly, and slow. Mortgage lending continued to fall for four more years, until it reached a low of $21.92 billion in 1936 and 1937. This is remarkable in view of the fact that mortgage debt outstanding in the United States has fallen during only three periods during the past 115 years: 1932–6, 1942–4, and from Q2 2008 through Q2 2013.

4.7 Summary: Channels of Contraction

There are five primary channels through which the construction and consumer-credit booms accentuated the economic cycle. The first and most direct channel was reduced residential construction. The second channel was the damage to household balance sheets from the fall in home prices and the negative impact from damage to household balance sheets on household demand for consumer durables and nondurables. The third channel was the reduction in firms' inventories, production, and fixed investment that resulted from the household consumption decline. The fourth channel was the feedback effect from declining production and investment to declining household income, which then circled back to affect each of the first three factors. The fifth factor was the damage to bank balance sheets, which accentuated the troubles of both firms and households when loans could not be extended or rolled over due to the need for banks to deleverage.

4.7.1 Reduced Residential Construction

In the peak year of 1925, residential construction amounted to 5.3 percent of GNP. Between 1921 and 2010, residential construction as a percentage of GDP (or GNP between 1921 and 1929) has exceeded 5 percent in four years: 1924, 1925, 1926, and later in 1950, when the stock of housing was depleted from the low level of residential construction during World War II. Even during the recent boom, residential construction reached a maximum level of only 3.8 percent of GDP in 2005. The excess supply of structures constructed during the boom had to be absorbed before the construction industry could revive; therefore, the decline in residential construction was the first and most direct channel by which the residential real estate downturn affected economic activity.

4.7.2 Damage to Household Balance Sheets

Housing market data show that real estate prices peaked in 1925 and 1926 and then began a slow decline that gathered momentum from 1929 to 1932. Many households borrowed when house prices were at or near their peak. Figure 4.2 shows that from 1925 to 1928, the net flow of mortgage funds held steady at their flat four-year peak of about $3 billion per year. As prices slid, household wealth fell, whereas total debt burdens not only remained high but also continued to increase, even as new residential construction declined rapidly. For households in which much of total wealth was consumed by their down payment, the house price decline wiped out their accumulated wealth, or worse. Short loan terms were a structural feature of the mortgage market, not only in commercial bank lending generally but also in bank residential lending. These short contract terms probably created an additional source of contraction in mortgage lending and an additional source of downward pressure on housing prices when loans that came due were not rolled over.[31] In addition to their short term, many mortgages at that time were either non-amortizing (i.e., interest only, as in the current crisis) or partially amortizing (i.e., balloon payments, if not rolled over). All of these loans would have involved balloon payments at the end of their term. For the period 1925–9, about 14.3 percent of mortgages issued by life insurance companies were fully amortizing; in the same period, about 10.3 percent of mortgages issued by commercial banks were fully amortizing.[32] Savings and loan associations commonly issued fully amortizing loans: 94.9 percent

---

[31] Grebler, Blank, and Winnick (1956, Table 67) listed average lengths of mortgage contracts for life insurance companies, for commercial banks, and for savings and loan associations from 1920 through 1947. For the period from 1920 to 1934, the average contract length for commercial banks was only 3.0 years. The averages for life insurance companies and for savings and loan associations were longer, at 6.8 and 11.2 years, respectively. However, these figures are the average contract length when the loan was issued; therefore, the average length remaining on the loan when the banking troubles began would have been significantly shorter, and many borrowers would have been affected when banks tried to retain liquid assets by declining to roll over loans.

[32] Data on amortization were reported in Grebler, Blank, and Winnick (1956, Table 66, p. 231).

of their loans between 1920 and 1929 were fully amortized. By 1935–9, the share of fully amortized mortgages at commercial banks had risen to 69.0 percent.

The combination of short loan terms and the use of non-amortizing loans must have exacerbated the distress of both homeowners and lenders as the Depression developed. A significant fraction of borrowers would have faced the necessity to refinance sometime between 1930 and 1935, when credit market conditions were stringent. When a borrower tried to refinance after prices had fallen, lenders either had to extend a new loan with a higher loan-to-value ratio, reduce the amount of the loan, or decline to renew it. As foreclosures were rising and prices were falling after 1926, this was an unattractive proposition for lenders, even before credit market conditions began to deteriorate significantly late in 1930. The need to refinance during a period of falling home prices must have led to distress sales when home-owners were unable to find new lenders on expiration of their existing loans. Because many loans were not amortizing, lenders risked losses on a loan when the value of a home fell below the homeowner's equity. Lost equity and the prospect of a distress sale would naturally create uncertainty among households and lead to increased precautionary savings and reduced consumption. Estimates of personal savings in Swanson and Williamson (1972, Table 3) reinforced this impression: The average level of personal savings between 1929 and 1931 was 97.5 percent higher than the average level for 1926 through 1928.

An increase in precautionary savings due to household balance sheet problems leads to declining household consumption, especially of durable goods. This, in turn, leads to reduced production levels and reduced employment. As reduced employment adds to household distress, it reinforces both the decline in durable goods consumption and the frequency of mortgage default and distress sales of housing. Reduced consumption from lost home-owner equity, its effect on production and employment, and the contribution of reduced employment to homeowners' mortgage distress comprises the second channel through which a downturn in the housing market affects economic activity.

4.7.3 Reduction of Firms' Inventories, Production, and Fixed Investments

As demand for consumers' durables collapsed, firms reduced inventories; however, when demand failed to recover quickly, demand for producers' durables also began to fall. Investment decline impacts producers of raw materials and production equipment more than any other sector.[33] The decline in the demand for residential housing and for consumer durables leads to a desire by firms' to reduce inventories, production, and employment. Reduced production then leads to a decline in demand for producer durables (i.e., plants, equipment, and structures). The large collapse in consumer durable goods demand that resulted from household balance sheet problems generated the third transmission channel into the real economy when producers' durable goods investment collapsed.

4.7.4 Feedback Effect on Households' Incomes

All of these effects have a pronounced impact on production, which feeds back to cause additional problems in the labor market. Labor market problems, in turn, circle back to cause further problems in the housing market and reduce durable goods expenditures by consumers. Compensation to employees and proprietors' real incomes fell 11.3 percent from 1929 to 1930, whereas real GNP fell only 9.5 percent. At the same time, the uncertainly associated with employees' compensation grew rapidly as unemployment rose from 2.89 percent in 1929 to 8.94 percent in 1930. In 1931, the plight of employees and proprietors grew considerably worse: Their real income fell 16.6 percent, far in excess of the 6.3 percent decline in real GNP. In 1932, the gap between the decline in employee compensation and proprietors' incomes grew even larger: Their real income fell 24.9 percent, whereas real GNP fell 13.3 percent. As their incomes fell in 1931 and 1932, employees faced increasing uncertainty as the unemployment rate increased to 22.89 percent. The brunt of the Depression fell on households, and their rapidly declining incomes led inevitably to a rapid collapse of demand for the products of industry.

4.7.5 Damage to Banks' Balance Sheets

The fifth transmission channel runs directly from households and investors to bank balance sheets. We estimate in Section 4.5.2 that by January 1934, delinquent residential mortgage payments reached 10.7 percent of residential mortgage debt outstanding. Once housing equity losses among some households reach the critical threshold, wherein their equity is exhausted

---

[33] Raw material and capital equipment output declined precipitously. Steel production (HSUS Series Dd399) fell 75.5 percent between 1929 and 1932, and locomotive production (HSUS Series Dd429) fell 96.4 percent from 1,770 in 1926 to 63 in 1933.

and borrowers with inadequate collateral default on their payments, banks accumulate further losses. Distress among mortgage holders was not limited to owner occupants; it also included rental property owners and mortgage bond holders. In the 1920s, a significant fraction of residential property was rented. Rental prices fell slightly more than property values, and the average loan term on rental properties was shorter than on loans to owner-occupants. Real estate bonds issued in the 1920s on large apartment buildings, hotels, office buildings, and commercial properties accounted for an increasing share of real estate financing, and their performance was extremely poor. Transmission of losses into banks came from all sectors of the real estate market.

All classes of lenders deleveraged sharply during the course of the Depression. There are four reasons that banks reduce their private lending during a severe downturn. When bank capital declines as a result of losses, deleveraging is the simplest and most direct way to decrease the asset-to-equity ratio. When lending declines, a bank's assets are reduced but its equity is not directly affected. This improves the equity-to-asset ratio, even in the absence of direct capital investment. A second reason for a lending reduction is that when a loan is called or not rolled over, the funds obtained can be invested in liquid assets, such as Treasury securities or excess reserves with the Federal Reserve Bank, which provide protection against illiquidity in the face of depositors' demands. A third reason for deleveraging is that borrowers are scrutinized more carefully in a downturn because loan collateral might decline in value, and investments will produce an inadequate return during a downturn more frequently than during a boom. A fourth – and significant – reason that bank lending will decrease is outside of the control of the banks: Many sound borrowers do not have solid investment opportunities; therefore, borrower demand for loans declines. All four of these forms of bank deleveraging have been particularly characteristic of domestic developments during the Great Recession and the slow recovery from it. Bernanke (1983) focused on a related transmission channel from failed or suspended banks to borrowers. He argued that businesses that had established relationships with a failed bank faced reduced access to capital markets. Although this is true, even solvent and surviving banks reduced their lending during the Depression. Chapter 10 discusses how policies that protect the book value of bank assets from mark-to-market accounting can be inimical to the restoration of bank lending and to economic recovery.

In his discussion, Temin (1976) argued that the consumption decline in 1930 was large relative to declines in wealth and income, especially when compared to consumption declines in the other two interwar recessions in

1920–1 and 1937–8. The unemployment rate shot up from 2.9 percent in 1929 to 8.9 percent in 1930. The foreclosure rate increased from 3.6 per thousand mortgaged nonfarm homes in 1926 to 7.1 per thousand in 1929 and 7.9 per thousand in 1930. Surely, the fear of losing first a job and then a home could readily lead to a sharp decline in expenditures on housing and durable goods. As household expenditures fell, production, investment, and employment fell also, and the cycle of collapse was underway.

The accumulating household balance sheet stress after 1926 did not have a visible impact on corporate profits or the value of corporate equities even as late as October 1929. The national income accounts from 1919 to 1941 in Swanson and Williamson (1972) indicated that the sum of dividends and undistributed corporate profits were higher in 1929 than in any other year between 1919 and 1940. However, the capacity of households to buy the goods and services that industry produced was dependent on debt accumulation, and the capacity of households to absorb more debt was limited. Therefore, the profits that industry had been earning would soon collapse and the value of the capital that industries had accumulated would be reduced by the collapse of household demand.

During the Depression, the decline in expenditures on new residential units plus the decline in consumption accounted for 72.9 percent of the total decline in GDP.[34] This figure is striking, but it must understate the contribution of households to the contraction. Consumer durables sales fell 49.3 percent in real terms between 1929 and 1933. With such a dramatic decline in consumer durables sales, investment in plants and equipment collapsed almost completely. Nonresidential fixed investment declined 68.6 percent, which was a precipitous collapse, especially in comparison with the average decline of 11.8 percent during postwar recessions and the maximum decline of 22.5 percent during the 2007–2009 recession.

4.8 Conclusions

The evidence presented in this chapter about the Depression, combined with the evidence from Chapter 3 on the Great Recession, indicates that our two most severe financial crises and our two most persistent economic downturns of the past century both followed large declines in the value of residential real estate prices. It is possible that another factor caused the downturns in residential real estate prices, the financial crisis, and the

---

[34] This figure is calculated from NIPA Table 1.1.6, comparing 1929 and 1933 figures for GDP and for residential investment and personal consumption expenditures.

prolonged recession. However, we also describe a direct mechanism by which residential real estate losses are transmitted to the financial sector, and we indicate why the losses to households suppress consumption – especially of durable goods – and how suppressed consumption reduces capacity investment by firms.

In the Great Depression, as in the Great Recession, the deterioration of the residential real estate market preceded the peak of the economic cycle and the broader downturn by two to three years; in both cases, the damage to household balance sheets originated in residential real estate losses. Much of the damage suffered by financial sector firms resulted from transmission of households' real estate losses to financial sector firms.

This begs the question: "Why are losses on residential real estate so pernicious?" There are at least four primary reasons. Residential real estate is illiquid, especially in a downturn when sales begin to decline. It is often highly leveraged and, in the Depression, we saw that mortgage credit was growing while sales and construction of new homes were falling. Therefore, leverage was increasing toward the end of the boom as prices began to fall. A third reason is that residential real estate assets are a large portion of national wealth and a large fraction of the wealth of many households. Therefore, a downturn in residential real estate values has a substantial impact on household balance sheets and on consumption levels, especially of durable goods and new housing assets. Finally, housing assets are immobile; therefore, there is no geographical redistribution of overbuilding in one area to other areas. For many real assets, redistribution is almost immediate, as with ships, airplanes, or locomotives. Even overbuilding of production capability, such as factories, would lead to a revaluation of the assets, but the factories often would remain utilized for export. Residential real estate is unusual in having few alternative uses when it is overbuilt. For all of these reasons, policies related to development and financing of residential real estate should be carefully considered.

References

Badgley, L. Durward (1936). Real Estate Transfer Index, Washington, DC, 1893–1936.

Balke, Nathan S., and Robert J. Gordon (1989). "The Estimation of Prewar Gross National Product: Methodology and New Evidence." *Journal of Political Economy*, 97, pp. 38–92.

Bernanke, Ben S. (1983). "Nonmonetary Effects of the Financial Crisis in Propagation of the Great Depression." *American Economic Review*, 73, pp. 257–76.

Board of Governors of the Federal Reserve System (1943). *Banking and Monetary Statistics, 1914–1943*. Washington, DC: Board of Governors of the Federal Reserve System.

Boysen, Louis K. (1931). "A History of Real Estate Bonds." *Chicago Real Estate Magazine,* 6 (23 May), pp. 12–13.

Bureau of Business Research (1943). *Real Estate Transactions in Franklin County, Ohio: 1917–1937, Special Bulletin X-56.* Columbus: Ohio State University, College of Commerce and Administration.

Carney, Brian (2008). "Bernanke Is Fighting the Last War." *Wall Street Journal,* October 18.

Colean, Miles L. (1944). *American Housing: Problems and Prospects.* New York: The Twentieth Century Fund.

Comptroller of the Currency (1929, 1941, 1942). "Annual Report of the Comptroller of the Currency." Washington, DC: U.S. Government Printing Office.

Dolbeare, Harwood, and Merle O. Barnd (1931). "Forewarnings of Bank Failure: A Comparative Study of the Statements of Certain Failed and Successful Florida State Banks, 1922–1928." Gainesville: University of Florida, *Business Administration Series,* Vol. 1, No. 1.

Field, Alexander J. (2014). "The Interwar Housing Cycle in the Light of 2001–2012: A Comparative Historical Perspective." In *Mortgage Markets in Historical Perspective.* Chicago: National Bureau of Economic Research, University of Chicago Press.

Fisher, Ernest M. (1951). "Urban Real Estate Markets: Characteristics and Financing." Washington, DC: National Bureau of Economic Research.

Fisher, Irving (1933). "The Debt-Deflation Theory of Great Depressions." *Econometrica,* 1, pp. 337–57.

Friedman, Milton, and Anna J. Schwartz (1963). *A Monetary History of the United States.* Princeton, NJ: Princeton University Press.

Gjerstad, Steven, and Vernon L. Smith (2009). "From Bubble to Depression?" *Wall Street Journal,* April 6, p. A15.

Goldsmith, Raymond W. (1955). *A Study of Saving in the United States, Volume 1.* Princeton, NJ: Princeton University Press.

Grebler, Leo, David M. Blank, and Louis Winnick (1956). *Capital Formation in Residential Real Estate.* Princeton, NJ: Princeton University Press.

Hoad, William M. (1942). "Real Estate Prices: A Study of Residential Real Estate Transfers in Lucas County, Ohio." Ph.D. thesis. Ann Arbor: University of Michigan.

Hoyt, Homer (1933). *One Hundred Years of Land Values in Chicago: The Relationship of the Growth of Chicago to the Rise of Its Land Values, 1830–1933.* Chicago: University of Chicago Press.

Johnson, Ernest A. (1936a). "The Record of Long-Term Real Estate Securities." *Journal of Land and Public Utility Economics,* 12, pp. 44–8.

Johnson, Ernest A. (1936b). "The Record of Long-Term Real Estate Securities: By Cities of Issue." *Journal of Land and Public Utility Economics,* 12, pp. 195–7.

Koester, Genevieve (1939a). "Chicago Real Estate Bonds, 1919–1938: I. Corporate History." *Journal of Land and Public Utility Economics,* 15, pp. 49–58.

Koester, Genevieve (1939b). "Chicago Real Estate Bonds, 1919–1938: II. Market Behavior." *Journal of Land and Public Utility Economics,* 15, pp. 201–11.

Kuznets, Simon (1961). *Capital in the American Economy: Its Formation and Financing.* Princeton, NJ: Princeton University Press.

Kydland, Finn and Edward C. Prescott (1982). "Time to Build and Aggregate Fluctuations." *Econometrica,* 50, pp. 1345–70.

Lucia, Joseph (1985). "The Failure of the Bank of United States: A Reappraisal." *Explorations in Economic History*, 22, pp. 402–16.

New York Stock Exchange (1930). *New York Stock Exchange Yearbook, 1929–1930*. New York: New York Stock Exchange Committee on Publicity.

New York Times (1929). "Brokerage Concern Put in Receivership." November 19, p. 2.

New York Times (1930). "Brokerage Insolvent, Face Jury Inquiry." June 20, p. 17.

O'Brien, Anthony Patrick (1992). "The Failure of the Bank of United States: A Defense of Joseph Lucia: Note." *Journal of Money, Credit and Banking*, 24, pp. 374–84.

Persons, Charles E. (1930). "Credit Expansion, 1920 to 1929, and Its Lessons." *Quarterly Journal of Economics*, 45, pp. 94–130.

Swanson, Joseph A., and Samuel H. Williamson (1972). "Estimates of National Product and Income for the United States Economy, 1919–1941." *Explorations in Economic History*, 10, 53–73.

Temin, Peter (1976). *Did Monetary Forces Cause the Great Depression?* New York: W.W. Norton and Co.

United States Congress (1934). Stock Exchange Practices: Hearings before the Committee on Banking and Currency, Part 11, Detroit Bankers Company. Washington, DC: U.S. Government Printing Office.

Vanderblue, Homer B. (1927a). "The Florida Land Boom." *Journal of Land and Public Utility Economics*, 3, pp. 113–31.

Vanderblue, Homer B. (1927b). "The Florida Land Boom." *Journal of Land and Public Utility Economics*, 3, pp. 252–69.

White, Eugene Nelson (1984). "A Reinterpretation of the Banking Crisis of 1930." *Journal of Economic History*, 44, pp. 119–38.

Wickens, David L. (1937). Financial Survey of Urban Housing: Statistics on Financial Aspects of Urban Housing. Washington, DC: U.S. Government Printing Office.

Wickens, David L. (1941). Residential Real Estate: Its Economic Position as Shown by Values, Rents, Family Incomes, Financing, and Construction, Together with Estimates for All Real Estate. Washington, DC: National Bureau of Economic Research.

Wicker, Elmus (1996). *The Banking Panics of the Great Depression*. Cambridge: Cambridge University Press.

Wigmore, Barrie A. (1985). The Crash and Its Aftermath: A History of Securities Markets in the United States, 1929–1933. Westport, CT: Greenwood Publishing Group, Inc.

Works Progress Administration (1938). "Real Estate Activity Surveys: Intensive Analysis of Deeds and Mortgages Recorded in a Recent Period." Washington, DC: WPA Technical Series. Research, Statistical, and Survey Project Circular No. 7, Volume I. September 28.

5

The Postwar Recessions

"[T]he investment component of output is about six times as volatile as the consumption component."
— Edward C. Prescott (1986a)

"[T]echnology shocks account for more than half the fluctuations in the postwar period, with a best point estimate near 75 percent."
— Edward C. Prescott (1986b)

"[R]esidential investment causes, but is not caused by GDP [movements], while non-residential investment does not cause, but is caused by GDP [movements]."
— Richard K. Green (1997)

In this chapter, we examine the ten postwar recessions from 1948–9 to 2001 that preceded the Great Recession. The role of housing investment expenditures in both the Great Recession and the Depression is also manifest in the post–World War II period but with less catastrophic consequences. Recurrent patterns of interaction between housing investment and monetary policy are prominent elements of postwar U.S. economic cycles. Examination of these interactions clarifies one of the primary channels through which monetary policy affects output, especially in the period immediately preceding a recession, during the recession, and in the immediate aftermath of a recession.

In a typical postwar economic cycle, inflation and interest rates remain relatively low as new housing construction expands. Then, inflation begins to set in as housing expenditures slow down. In response to developing inflation, monetary policy is tightened and housing begins a sharper decline. The resulting downturn in the household-expenditure cycle – and in economic activity more generally – reduces inflationary pressure but also leads to a turn in the investment cycle as firms encounter reduced demand for housing and consumer durable goods. As aggregate demand slows, firms reduce their investments in structures, equipment, and inventories. The combination of the leading household-expenditure cycle and the coincident or lagging investment cycle forms an economic cycle. Seven of the ten postwar downturns closely fit this pattern. The 1948–9 and 1953–4 recessions fit this pattern in most respects, but wage and price controls after World War II and large defense expenditures prior to the 1953–4 recession somewhat disrupted the usual patterns. The 2001 recession also deviated from this pattern; however, there is substantial evidence that the pattern was disrupted by the huge influx of foreign investment into the housing market, as discussed in Chapter 3.

5.1 The Major Downturns

In the postwar era, in addition to the Great Recession, three downturns stand out for their duration and depth: the 1973–5 recession and the "double-dip" recessions of 1980 and 1981–2.

5.1.1 The 1973–1975 Recession

The upper panel of Figure 5.1 charts percentage changes in GDP relative to its level in Q4 1973 at the peak of the economic cycle. The panel also shows the percentage changes in the value of residential construction (which we frequently refer to as housing), in the value of nonresidential fixed investment, and in the number of new homes sold. As with the GDP series in the figure, each series represents percentage changes relative to their values at the beginning of the recession in Q4 1973. The lower panel of the figure charts the year-over-year inflation rate and the effective federal funds rate. Measured by the average depth multiplied by its duration, the recession from Q4 1973 to Q1 1975 was the third largest of the postwar era, exceeded only by the Great Recession and the 1981–2 recession. Although the recession has often been attributed to the Arab oil embargo that began in October 1973, housing had declined for two quarters before that event, and the $103.8 billion housing decline from housing peak to housing trough was more than double the additional cost of imported oil. The housing decline also was more than 2.5 times as large as the $40.7 billion investment decline. The decline in housing combined with consumer durables, at $177.2 billion, was 4.35 times larger than the investment decline. Also, as discussed in Chapters 2 and 3, it is critically important to distinguish perishables (i.e., consumer nondurables) from durable retraded assets when evaluating market performance and the roots of dynamic instability for the economy. In this regard, oil is merely one more consumer perishable.

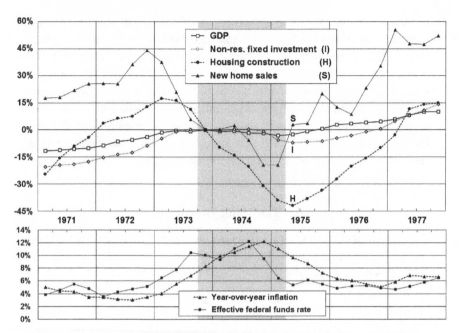

Figure 5.1. The upper panel charts the percentage changes to GDP, to residential construction (H), to nonresidential fixed investment (I), and to new home sales during and after the recession of 1973–5. The housing decline was the second largest of the postwar era, as was the decline in durables, whereas the investment decline was delayed and moderate. In a common pattern, shown in the lower panel, inflation rose sharply after housing peaked and inflation peaked during the recession.

The 50.6 percent decline in housing was the second largest of the postwar era, exceeded only by the decline of the Great Recession. Consumer durables spending joined housing in peaking three quarters before the recession began. The 17.5 percent decline in durable goods consumption was the largest of any postwar recession before the Great Recession. The 7.4 percent investment decline, however, was surprisingly small given the depth of the recession. Moreover, investment peaked three quarters after the recession began and six quarters after the sum of residential construction and consumer durable goods peaked. Because the decline in households' expenditures on housing and durable goods is so much larger than and precedes the decline in firms' fixed investments, this recession is not consistent with the idea that firms are the primary drivers of the economic cycle. As we demonstrate in this chapter, most other postwar U.S. recessions share this characteristic; therefore, we suggest that the economic cycle is a composite of a leading household-consumption cycle and a coincident or lagging investment cycle.

Monetary policy impacted both the onset of and the recovery from the recession. Monetary policy was loose throughout 1972. Then, between February 1973 and February 1974, inflation increased from less than 4 to 10 percent. In response to surging inflation, monetary policy was tightened in Q1 1973, housing began to fall in Q2 1973, and the cyclical peak came in Q4 1973, two quarters later. Inflation peaked a year into the recession, almost two years after housing began to decline; the peak inflation rate occurred just before housing reached its trough. The housing decline continued until two quarters after monetary policy was eased in Q4 1974. Once the federal funds rate was reduced to a level comparable to the 1972 level, a rapid recovery in housing and in the economy began.

5.1.2 The 1980 and 1981–1982 Recessions: The Fed-Housing Economic Cycle Revealed

Between August 1979 and August 1982, monetary policy was tightened and relaxed twice in quick succession. This unusual pattern of monetary policy shifts created, in effect, a monetary policy field experiment that provides an excellent test of our hypotheses about the interactions between monetary policy and the real economy.

Housing peaked six quarters before the peak of the economic cycle in Q1 1980. The housing decline was moderate until one quarter before the peak but then dropped sharply for three consecutive quarters while monetary policy was tight. However, when short-term interest rates were reduced greatly in May 1980, new home sales surged in the next quarter. Housing construction briefly recovered soon after new home sales recovered. However, when short-term interest rates increased sharply again between October and December 1980, new home sales fell once again.

Housing fell 40.6 percent during the first decline from Q3 1978 to Q3 1980; during the second decline, from Q1 1981 to Q2 1982, housing fell 36.0 percent. Throughout an almost four-year period, from Q3 1978 to Q2 1982, housing fell 55.2 percent.[1] During those fifteen quarters, real GDP grew by a total of 2.6 percent – a growth rate of about 0.7 percent per year – considerably below the 3.8 percent average growth rate from Q1 1947 to Q3 1978.

---

[1] Although the housing decline in the 1981–2 recession was smaller than the decline in the 1973–5 recession, if we consider the 1980 and 1981–2 "double-dip" recessions as one recession interrupted by a sharp monetary stimulus between May and September 1980, then the decline during the course of the double-dip recessions was larger. The 55.2 percent housing decline between Q3 1978 and Q2 1982 associated with the double-dip recessions of 1980 and 1981–2 exceeded the 50.6 percent decline between Q1 1973 and Q2 1975.

Investment rose 9.9 percent during this period when housing collapsed by 55.2 percent. During the course of the two combined recessions, housing – which peaked six quarters before the cyclical peak in Q1 1980 – fell $120.9 billion before it reached bottom in Q2 1982. Investment peaked in Q4 1981 – thirteen quarters after the housing peak and two quarters before the trough – and fell $131.5 billion in the next six quarters. Between Q4 1978 and Q2 1982, the sum of housing and durables fell $201.7 billion. Households' interest-rate sensitive components of consumption had a stronger impact on the development of this serious downturn than nonresidential fixed investment: Housing and durables peaked twelve quarters before investment, and the dollar amount of the decline exceeded the investment decline by 53.4 percent. Moreover, as in the 1973–5 recession, household expenditures led the cycle and firms' fixed investments lagged.

Monetary policy left a clear imprint on real-sector development during the six-year period represented in Figure 5.2, and the most pronounced impact was on housing. When President Carter appointed Paul Volcker as Chairman of the Federal Reserve on August 6, 1979, the Fed targeted money supply growth rates, using the federal funds rate as the instrument to affect the money supply. In an effort to reduce inflation, Volcker increased the federal funds rate from 9.6 percent when he took office to 19 percent eight months later. Monetary tightening was followed by a sharp decline in new home sales with a one-quarter lag, and housing construction began a sharp decline one quarter after new home sales fell sharply. In the first three quarters after short-term interest rates were increased, new home sales fell 35.9 percent and housing construction fell 34.8 percent.

By April 1980, the money supply was contracting rapidly, but the Fed had sought to reduce only its growth rate. In an adaptive response, the federal funds rate was reduced from 19.4 percent in early April 1980 to 9.5 percent seven weeks later in late May; the Federal Reserve then kept the rate below 10 percent until the end of August. The effect on housing was a sharp reversal. New home sales increased 35.9 percent in the first quarter after the short-term interest rate was reduced. The monetary policy shift slowed the housing decline in the third quarter and was followed by an increase in the fourth quarter. However, just as the recovery began, the short-term interest rate was again increased from less than 11 percent at the end of September 1980 to more than 20 percent by early January 1981. Housing started down again in Q2 1981, this time falling 36.0 percent in five quarters to a new postwar low of less than 1.7 percent of GDP in Q2 1982.

In the first two quarters of 1980, when Volcker's tightened monetary policy first began to have a strong effect on housing, the inflation rate averaged

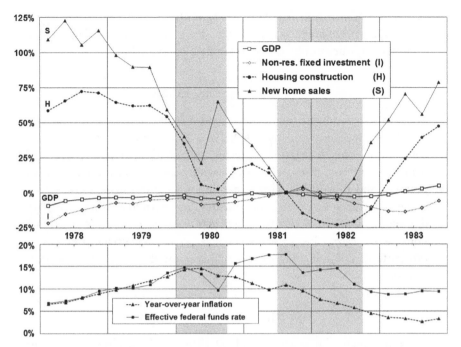

Figure 5.2. Percentage changes to GDP, to housing construction, to investment, and to new home sales before, during, and after the "double-dip" recessions of 1980 and 1981–2. These combined recessions included major declines in housing and consumer durables and a three-year-long period – from Q3 1979 until Q3 1982 – when real GDP fell. During that three-year period, housing fell 51.1 percent, yet investment fell only 2.8 percent during the same period. New home sales responded quickly and sharply to both increases and decreases in short-term interest rates; with each shift, housing construction responded with a lag.

14.4 percent. By Q4 1982, when the recovery began, inflation averaged 4.7 percent. Monetary policy had been tight in ten of eleven quarters from Q4 1979 to Q2 1982, bringing inflation under control. When monetary policy was finally eased sharply in Q3 1982, new home sales responded immediately, increasing 78.7 percent between Q2 1982 and Q2 1983. Housing again responded strongly with a short lag: Housing construction increased 92.0 percent between Q3 1982 and Q2 1984.

This episode demonstrates a key argument of Friedman and Schwartz (1963): Monetary policy has a clear impact on the real economy – an argument that has been widely accepted for thirty years. However, this natural experiment, in which monetary reins were tightened and then eased twice in quick succession, demonstrates another and more specific proposition, as follows: *Monetary policy operates primarily through interest-rate sensitive components of household consumption, especially housing.* This point is reinforced by our examination of other postwar recessions.

5.2 The Minor Recessions

The two major downturns in the second half of the twentieth century – the 1973–5 recession and the 1980, 1981–2 double-dip recession – both conform to our description of economic cycles. Housing peaks well before downturns; inflation develops with a lag as housing levels off or declines; and monetary policy tightening – a natural response to developing inflation – accelerates the housing downturn and initiates a sharp decline in inflation. As inflation subsides, monetary policy is eased and housing increases sharply. Most postwar economic cycles conform to this pattern. The following subsections describe the seven other postwar recessions.

5.2.1 The 1948–1949 Recession

Housing growth between 1945 and Q2 1948 was the strongest of the past century. Between 1932 and 1945, housing averaged only 1.3 percent of GDP. The stock of housing was depleted during the Depression and World War II. Pent-up demand and households' accumulated wartime savings led to a long surge of housing construction between 1947 and 1956. During those ten years, housing averaged 4.1 percent of GDP. The housing expansion between late 1945 and Q2 1948 was more rapid than any other major component of GDP. By Q2 1948, housing expenditures reached 4.4 percent of GDP.

During the rapid recovery that followed World War II, the CPI increased by 28.9 percent between June 1946 and June 1948. Federal Reserve open market operations were limited as a policy instrument from the Depression until the Treasury–Federal Reserve accord in March 1951. During this period, the Fed was required – through the bond-price support program – to passively monetize short-term Treasury debt.[2] With limited means to control the money supply, inflation escalated after the war, and the Federal Reserve was forced to resort to changes in banks' reserve ratio (i.e., the

---

[2] Hetzel and Leach (2001) provided an excellent account of the economic issues and political context that led to the Treasury–Federal Reserve accord on March 4, 1951.

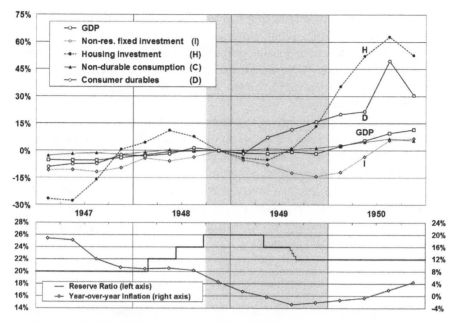

Figure 5.3. Percentage changes to GDP, to housing construction, to investment, and to consumer durable goods expenditures before, during, and after the 1948–9 recession. Bank reserve ratios were increased in each of the first three quarters of 1948. Housing peaked in Q2 1948 and continued to fall until the reserve ratio was lowered in May 1949.

ratio of the sum of reserves on deposit with the Fed plus vault cash to their customers' deposits) to control lending.[3]

The major surge in housing came in 1946, when it increased by a factor of four over the 1945 level. Inflation rose rapidly at the same time but had already peaked in Q1 1947 at 18.9 percent, although much of the rise resulted from the lifting of wartime wage and price controls.[4] Nevertheless, the Fed decided to raise the reserve ratio in three equal steps – on February 27, June 11, and September 24, 1948 – from 20 to 26 percent. Banks reacted

---

[3] For a history of reserve ratios, including changes to required reserves, see Feinman (1993).

[4] Friedman and Schwartz (1963, pp. 557–8) noted several effects of wartime price controls, including shortages of products with small price increases and substitution to available products with greater increases and "changes in quality or in the services rendered along with the sale of a commodity" with the result that "the elimination of price controls in 1946 did not involve any corresponding jump in 'prices'; rather, it reflected largely the unveiling of price increases that had occurred earlier." This is the only postwar economic cycle in which inflation fell before housing peaked. A combination of the measurement problems described by Friedman and Schwartz and actual price increases on the lifting of price controls most likely impacted the unusual course of prices in this economic cycle.

with a contraction of lending that further curtailed inflation but also led to a recession. The money supply peaked in the same month that the reserve ratio was first increased; housing peaked in Q2 1948, several months later. The cyclical peak in GDP lagged the first reserve ratio increase and the decline in the money supply by ten months, and it lagged the housing decline by two quarters.

With inflation rapidly falling and a recession underway, the Fed lowered the reserve ratio two percentage points on May 5, 1949, and then lowered it one half of a percentage point four times between August 11 and September 1, 1949. Housing and durables began to recover soon after the first reserve ratio reduction; the general recovery began in Q1 1950 as housing surged. As in the recovery from every postwar recession – including even the abortive recovery in the second half of 1980 – housing and durables responded first, and most, to monetary easing.

5.2.2 The 1953–1954 Recession

The 1953–4 recession was the fourth largest of the postwar era (also measured by its average depth multiplied by duration). A substantial and sharp decline in housing reached bottom in Q1 1952, five quarters before the cyclical peak, and then remained near the new lower level for the next eight quarters. That decline might be considered a false-negative indication of a recession, and the recession that did follow five quarters later might be considered one that was not led by a housing decline. However, the $37.0 billion decline in housing between its peak in Q3 1950 and its trough in Q1 1952 was swamped by the $173.7 billion increase in national defense expenditures during the same period. Had defense expenditures remained fixed at the level in Q2 1950 (i.e., the last quarter before hostilities began), we can reasonably expect that GDP would have peaked in Q4 1950 and declined from Q1 1951 through Q2 1952, just after housing reached the trough.

After the outbreak of the Korean War, households anticipated another long war and the possibility of wartime restrictions on durable goods. Purchases of durables surged 24.0 percent between Q2 and Q3 1950. Inflation once again shot up, this time from a year-over-year rate of −1.4 percent in Q1 1950 to 8.9 percent in Q1 1951. The year-over-year inflation demonstrated here understates the surge in inflation in late 1950 and early 1951: The annualized three-month CPI increase reached 17.2 percent on February 1, 1951.

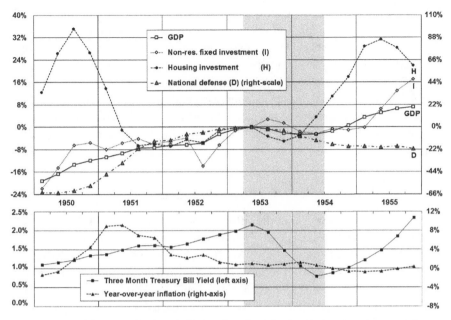

Figure 5.4. Percentage changes to GDP, to housing construction, to investment, and to consumer durable goods expenditures before, during, and after the 1953–4 recession.

The Federal Reserve responded by increasing the reserve ratio, as it had in 1948, but this time from 22 to 24 percent, in two equal steps on January 11 and January 25, 1951. Wage and price controls, instituted by the Truman Administration on January 26, 1951, may have contributed to the slowdown of inflation but did not stop it. Although housing had already been falling, the housing decline accelerated after the increase in the reserve ratio. Inflation peaked three quarters after housing peaked, despite the major increase in defense expenditures that sustained GDP growth for two more years. In most postwar economic cycles, inflation develops as housing levels off and then subsides as housing contracts. The same pattern occurred in this period, but it is surprising that in this episode, inflation subsided during the housing contraction even as the government generated a large fiscal stimulus – defense expenditure increased 4.7 times as much as housing declined – in an effort to contain communist expansion on the Korean peninsula. Even in this unusual episode, in which aggregate output continued to rise due to fiscal stimulus, the inflation cycle was more closely related to the housing cycle than to movements in aggregate output.

Defense expenditures continued to increase for five quarters after housing reached the trough – in effect, forestalling the recession until the July 1953 Korean armistice. Defense expenditures fell substantially in the seven quarters following the armistice, from 14.9 percent of GDP in Q2 1953 to 11.7 percent of GDP in Q1 1955. During the course of the recession, GDP fell less than the total decline in defense expenditures. Many components of private expenditures fell only slightly during the recession, but – in a typical pattern – the recession ended only when housing began to increase rapidly in the middle of 1954.

5.2.3 The 1957–1958 Recession

The 1957–8 recession was the fifth largest postwar recession. It was the deepest of the postwar era (slightly deeper than the Great Recession) but, unlike the Great Recession, it was short and the recovery from it was sharp. When the Federal Reserve reduced the effective federal funds rate from an average of more than 3.25 percent in Q4 1957 to less than 1 percent in Q2 1958, housing responded quickly. In the five quarters after the trough of the recession, GDP increased 10.2 percent – an 8.1 percent annual growth rate.

When investment peaked in Q3 1957, at the peak of the economic cycle, the sum of durables and housing had already declined in seven of the previous eight quarters, and the $48.5 billion decline at that point exceeded the $43.9 billion investment decline during the course of the recession that followed. From peak to trough, the $73.8 billion decline in housing plus durables was 68.1 percent larger than the investment decline. The timing of the declines reinforces the idea that the household-expenditure cycle forces the investment cycle.

Housing fell in eight of the nine quarters prior to the beginning of the recession. Expenditure on consumer durables fluctuated before the recession, but they had fallen 7.8 percent in the two years prior to the cyclical peak. By contrast, nonresidential fixed investment increased in eight of the nine quarters prior to the recession. During and after the recession, investment fell 16.2 percent, which was the largest percentage decline in any postwar recession prior to the 2001 recession. Yet, this large investment decline was not as significant in percentage terms as the decline in housing, which fell 30.4 percent.

As in the period preceding the 1973–5 recession and the 1980 and 1981–2 recessions, inflation was low, whereas housing surged from Q1 1954 until Q2 1955; inflation only began to rise as housing fell before the recession began. As inflation rose in 1956, monetary policy was tightened moderately

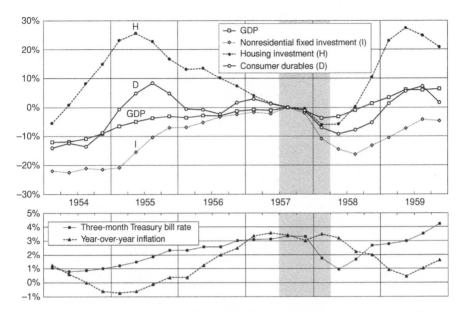

Figure 5.5. Percentage changes to GDP, to housing construction, to investment, and to consumer durable goods expenditures before, during, and after the sharp recession in 1957–8.

and housing continued to decline. Inflation peaked eight quarters after housing began to decline, a delay of one quarter more than in the 1980 and the 1973–5 recessions. As in those recessions – and, as discussed herein, in the 1969–70 and 1990–91 recessions – most of the inflation reduction came after the recession ended.

5.2.4 The 1960–1961 Recession

In the 1960–61 recession – as in all postwar recessions other than 2001 – the housing decline preceded the investment decline. Also as in all recessions except 1948–9 and 2001, the fall in housing plus durables was considerably larger than the investment decline. Housing had already declined $16.6 billion when investment peaked in Q2 1960, one quarter after the cyclical peak. From the housing peak to the trough, the $23.3 billion decline was 30.2 percent larger than the $17.9 billion investment decline. From the peak to the trough, the sum of housing and durables fell $47.3 billion, which was more than 2.6 times as large as the investment decline.

The 1960–61 recession was mild, in both depth and duration, and may have been avoided had the monetary tightening of 1959 been discontinued several months earlier. Recovery from the 1957–8 recession was – like the two

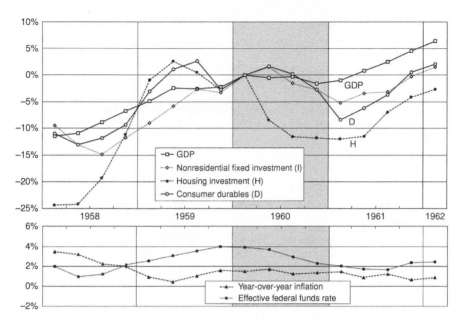

Figure 5.6. Percentage changes to GDP, to housing construction, to investment, and to consumer durable goods expenditures before, during, and after the 1960–61 recession.

previous recessions – very sharp. The strong recovery led to some concern that inflation might begin again, as it had in 1956 and early 1957 at the end of the 1954–7 expansion. Consequently, the Federal Reserve increased the federal funds rate from less than 0.7 percent in July 1958 to an average of slightly more than 3 percent in Q2 1959, when housing peaked.

Although housing peaked in Q2 1959, the Fed continued raising the federal funds rate until October 1959, when it reached 4 percent and where it remained until May 1960. By that time, a recession had taken hold, with a major plunge in housing from Q1 to Q2 1960. The Fed responded with a looser monetary policy starting in Q3 1960. By Q2 1961, the federal funds rate was less than 2 percent. The sharp recovery in housing began the next quarter and continued for eleven quarters; however, inflation remained low until the late stage of the expansion, when it began to rise in 1968 and early 1969.

5.2.5 The 1969–1970 Recession

In the 1969–70 recession, housing and durables began to decline before the recession, and both dropped more sharply than investment after the

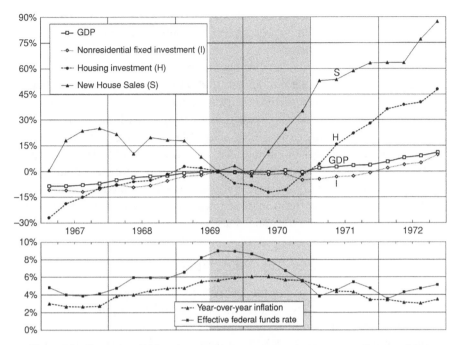

Figure 5.7. Changes to GDP, to housing construction, to investment, and to new home sales before, during, and after the 1969–70 recession. Although this cycle was moderate, all of the typical patterns are shown. New home sales plateaued first, inflation developed soon afterward, and monetary policy was tightened. Then the housing downturn intensified. Once the recession was underway, fixed investment fell. When short-term interest rates were reduced, new home sales increased immediately and residential construction increased soon afterward, leading the recovery.

recession began. From peak to trough, housing fell 20.2 percent, durables fell 11.3 percent, and investment fell 5.1 percent. Housing plus durables fell $59.0 billion, 2.5 times more than the $23.3 billion investment decline.

This mild recession demonstrates a particularly close connection among inflation, monetary policy, and the effect of the latter in reducing expenditures on housing (and, to smaller extent, consumer durables). Thus, as inflation approached 4 percent in Q1 1968 (for the first time since Q4 1951), the Federal Reserve responded by tightening monetary policy in the first half of 1968. Housing responded predictably to the change: New home sales peaked in Q4 1967 and fell in the first two quarters of 1968. Because the short-term interest rate was held steady at a new higher level, new home sales also stabilized at a new lower level. As inflation continued to rise gradually in 1969, short-term interest rates were increased during the first half of

1969, and new home sales began a sharper decline. The decline in new home sales was soon followed by a decline in residential construction: Housing peaked two quarters before the peak of the economic cycle. Inflation was rising steadily but moderately throughout the period of monetary tightening. As the effective federal funds rate and three-month Treasury bill rates increased in the middle of 1969 to their highest levels since the Treasury–Federal Reserve accord, inflation continued to rise, reaching 5 percent for the first time since the end of 1951, in Q2 1969. Housing reacted to tightening monetary policy, declining 20.2 percent between Q1 1969 and Q2 1970. Three quarters after the housing decline began, monetary policy was gradually eased. A sharp increase in new home sales immediately followed the reduction to short-term interest rates and the recovery of residential construction followed with a one quarter lag.

5.2.6 The 1990–1991 Recession

Housing peaked long before the 1990–91 recession began, fluctuated but fell only moderately between the end of 1986 and the beginning of 1989, and then declined more sharply during the five quarters before the peak of the economic cycle in Q2 1990. Investment peaked three quarters before the peak of the economic cycle. From the peaks to the troughs, housing fell 34.8 percent, investment fell 13.4 percent, and durable goods fell 12.8 percent.

In Q2 1986, fourteen quarters into the expansion, the federal funds rate was less than 7 percent for the first time since 1978, and inflation was less than 2 percent for the first time since 1965. Even with the relatively loose monetary policy, housing flattened out at the end of 1986 and remained flat through 1987. By late 1988 and early 1989, inflation was rising again and housing was fluctuating, but overall housing was down only slightly from the peak in Q4 1986. When the Fed tightened monetary policy in the first half of 1989, housing began a sharper decline. The Fed responded with a slight easing in the second half of 1989, which it maintained through 1990 while the recession was developing. Similar to several other recessions – 1960, 1970, 1974, 1980, and 2008 – inflation peaked during the recession.[5] The Fed began a sharper easing of monetary policy in Q1 1991, just as

---

[5] In the few cases when inflation did not peak during a recession, it peaked just before the recession began. Inflation peaked at 3.73 percent in March 1957, five months before the 1957–8 recession began, but it was still at 3.62 percent ten months later during the recession. Inflation peaked just before the 2001 recession at 3.5 percent, but in the first quarter of the recession, it was still at 3.4 percent. In the 1981–2 recession, the peak came during the preceding half of the double-dip recession.

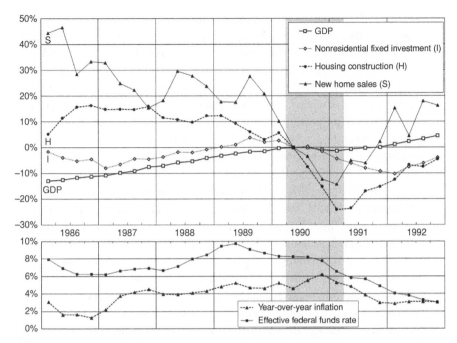

Figure 5.8. Percentage changes to GDP, to housing construction, to investment, and to new home sales before, during, and after the 1990–91 recession.

inflation began to subside. In the quarter after short-term interest rates were reduced sharply in Q1 1991, new home sales rapidly increased. The collapse of residential construction ended in the same quarter that new home sales increased, and a steady, moderate increase in residential construction followed one quarter later.

5.2.7 The 2001 Recession: Finally, a Business Investment Recession

The 2001 recession stands out as the clear anomaly of the postwar era, although it was more concordant with the common belief that business investment drives the economic cycle. However, as described in Chapter 3, the large influx of mortgage credit began just as the recession was developing, and that credit probably sustained household expenditures late into the housing expansion. In 1999, new home sales reached a peak and began a gradual decline; in 2000 residential construction also peaked and began a gradual decline after years of expansion. However, both mortgage credit and house prices were growing rapidly throughout the recession so that purchases of durable goods and expenditures on new homes fell very little leading into and during the recession. Investment reached a plateau between Q2 and Q4 2000 and started to decline in Q1 2001. (The crash of the technology sector stock bubble started in Q1 2000 and extended through Q4 2002.) The Federal Reserve's concern about investment spending was revealed in a press release (Board of Governors, 2001) on March 20, 2001, which stated that "persistent pressures on profit margins are restraining investment spending." The Fed responded as the slowdown developed by lowering the effective federal funds rate from 6.5 percent at the end of Q4 2000 to 5 percent by the end of Q1 2001. The federal funds rate was reduced another percentage point in each of the three quarters of the recession between Q2 2001 and Q4 2001, reaching 1.77 percent by the end of 2001. Even with this rapid reduction in the federal funds rate, investment continued to decline. During the first three quarters of 2002, the federal funds rate remained around 1.75 percent, but investment continued to fall. The housing recovery failed to deliver the usual stimulation to the recession recovery. In the four quarters following the end of the recession, housing construction increased only 7.8 percent – far below its 28.3 percent average increase in the four quarters after the previous nine postwar recessions.

In its November 2002 meeting, the FOMC lowered the federal funds target rate to 1.25 percent because "the generally disappointing data since the previous meeting . . . pointed to a longer-lasting spell of subpar economic performance than they had anticipated earlier" (Board of Governors, 2002). The report concluded that "a relatively aggressive easing action could help to ensure that the current soft spot in the economy would prove to be temporary and enhance the odds of a robust rebound in economic activity next year."

Housing had been growing modestly as investment declined, although not enough to offset reduced investment. On June 25, 2003, the FOMC lowered the federal funds target rate to 1 percent, noting in a press release (Board of Governors, 2003) that the economy "has yet to exhibit sustainable growth" and "with inflationary expectations subdued, the Committee judged that a slightly more expansive monetary policy would add further support for an economy which it expects to improve over time." In Q2 2003, investment turned the corner, after ten quarters of monetary easing, and began to increase, but the federal funds rate remained at 1 percent for the next year. Investment growth was slow, even with the expansionary monetary policy, but housing surged 21.9 percent in the four quarters when the federal funds rate was 1 percent, from Q2 2003 to Q2 2004. In most other postwar recessions, housing recovered sharply when the recession ended; however,

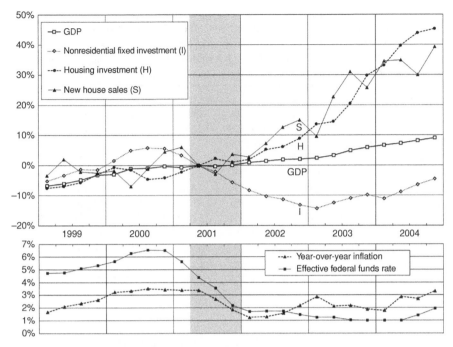

Figure 5.9. Percentage changes to GDP, to housing construction, to investment, and to new home sales before, during, and after the 2001 recession.

this recession still supports the general rule: The investment recovery was delayed until the housing recovery.

Even when this substantial increase in residential construction came (between Q2 2003 and Q2 2004), it was delayed for a year and a half after the recovery began. This suggests that the housing bubble was not primarily the result of monetary stimulus: The Federal Reserve simply lowered short-term interest rates to a level that generated a recovery of residential investment that approached the housing recovery in other postwar recessions. Cross-country evidence in Bernanke (2010) supported this view. He found that countries with low monetary policy rates (relative to the Taylor rule) had house price increases barely higher than countries with higher policy rates. He also replicated analysis in Fatás et al. (2009), which showed that countries with large trade deficits typically had high house price appreciation. A country finances a trade deficit primarily by issuing or selling financial instruments; during the U.S. housing bubble, mortgage securities formed a significant portion of the instruments issued to finance our trade deficits. A significant portion of the funds that supported the U.S. housing

Table 5.1. *Two measures of the severity of postwar recessions (depth and average depth multiplied by length) with changes to key components of GDP during and after the downturn*

Recession	Depth	Average depth times length	Housing change	Durables change	Investment change	Housing recovery	Investment recovery
2007–9	–3.66%	–3.87%	–77.1%	–18.0%	–22.5%	6.1%	–3.5%
1981–2	–2.87%	–3.31%	–36.0%	–8.8%	–15.8%	75.5%	–3.5%
1973–5	–3.19%	–2.89%	–50.6%	–17.5%	–7.4%	19.4%	1.1%
1953–4	–2.65%	–2.35%	–31.1%	–7.5%	–5.0%	26.8%	9.1%
1957–8	–3.73%	–2.20%	–30.4%	–16.2%	–16.2%	31.3%	0.5%
1948–9	–1.75%	–1.34%	–14.6%	–3.4%	–14.3%	34.4%	25.0%
1980	–2.23%	–1.18%	–40.6%	–16.8%	–5.0%	–2.4%	8.6%
1960–1	–1.58%	–0.84%	–21.1%	–10.7%	–6.6%	13.4%	2.6%
1990–91	–1.36%	–0.80%	–34.8%	–12.8%	–13.4%	15.4%	–6.2%
1969–70	–0.63%	–0.43%	–20.2%	–10.9%	–5.1%	41.1%	4.4%
2001	–0.27%	–0.07%	–1.1%	–2.9%	–19.0%	7.8%	–8.0%
AVERAGE	–2.17%	–1.73%	–32.5%	–11.4%	–11.8%	24.4%	2.7%

bubble came from foreign investors, and many of the mortgages that formed these securities were issued to borrowers in weak financial condition, who eventually were unable to meet the terms of the loans. Thus, the large flow of foreign investment into the mortgage market together with incentive problems in the mortgage industry combined as significant factors in the formation of the housing bubble. The incentive flaws in the fee structure for mortgage originators are discussed in Chapter 7 and corrective measures are proposed in Chapter 9.

From the end of June 2004 until the end of June 2006, the Fed raised the federal funds rate half of one percentage point per quarter. Even so, housing increased for six more quarters, as investment funds sought out the high returns of mortgage securities rather than the anemic returns of short-term Treasury bills. The combination of massive foreign investment, expansionary monetary policy, and loose mortgage underwriting standards that invigorated housing kept the 2001 recession the mildest of the postwar era. However, it also set the stage for the Great Recession.

5.3 Summary of GDP Component Changes

The graphs in this chapter illustrate that in recessions, housing typically declines first. Table 5.1 shows that housing declines have been substantially greater in percentage terms than investment declines. Another way to consider whether housing or investment is more clearly associated with recessions is by reviewing the correlation between the severity of the recession and the extent of housing declines and then comparing those results to the correlation between the severity of the recession and the extent of investment declines.[6] The correlation between recession severity and housing contraction is 0.796; between recession severity and investment contraction, it is 0.313. The results do not change significantly if we use recession depth rather than recession severity in the correlations. The correlation between recession depth and housing contraction is 0.751; between recession depth and investment contraction, it is 0.202. Serious recessions are more clearly associated with major declines in housing than with major declines in investment.

The last two columns of Table 5.1 present the growth of housing and investment in the four quarters following each postwar recession. Housing recovered more rapidly than investment in all recessions except the abortive recovery between Q3 1980 and Q3 1981. The average growth of housing in the first four quarters of recovery was 24.4 percent, whereas the growth of investment was only 2.7 percent.

Magnitudes of declines reveal only part of the story. We show that housing declines preceded investment declines in the Depression and in every postwar recession except 2001. Green (1997, p. 266) examined the hypothesis that housing causes recessions and recoveries more formally, using Granger causality tests. He found that "residential investment appears to Granger cause GDP... while nonresidential investment appears not to Granger cause GDP. Thus, residential investment seems to lead the nation into and out of recession, while nonresidential investment does not. The question remains as to why this should be true." Leamer (2007, p. 193) suggested a reason: "If we choose to stimulate [housing construction] today, tomorrow our ability to stimulate will be less." This is a reasonable hypothesis, and evidence suggests that the quantitative impact of housing stimulation is significant. In Q1 2006, residential construction reached $4,446 per household; by Q2 2009, it had fallen 78.0 percent to $979 per household. In earlier economic cycles, large changes also occurred. In Q1 1973, residential construction reached $3,031 per household, then fell 52.9 percent to $1,429 in

[6] We rank severity by the number of quarters that the economy is below peak output multiplied by the average percentage that GDP is below peak during the period when output is below the peak. The depth of a recession overstates the impact of a short, sharp recession like 1957–8 and understates the effect of a longer, shallower recession like 1981–2. The order of postwar recessions differs only slightly in the two measures.

Table 5.2. *Total GDP declines (in billions of 2005 dollars) in eleven postwar recessions*

Recession	GDP	Housing	Durables	Housing + durables	Investment
1948–9	–$29.5	–$11.8	–$5.8	–$14.4	–$27.2
1953–4	–$59.8	–$37.0	–$70.2	–$105.9	–$5.1
1957–8	–$97.7	–$35.1	–$41.3	–$73.8	–$43.9
1960–1	–$45.1	–$23.3	–$27.0	–$47.3	–$17.9
1969–70	–$26.8	–$26.8	–$43.0	–$59.0	–$23.3
1973–5	–$157.8	–$103.8	–$84.1	–$177.2	–$40.7
1980	–$131.9	–$88.8	–$90.8	–$168.7	–$29.6
1981–2	–$163.8	–$55.0	–$42.8	–$86.3	–$131.5
1990–91	–$109.4	–$77.4	–$92.4	–$148.0	–$119.5
2001	–$31.2	–$12.0	–$30.4	–$23.4	–$275.4
2007–9	–$489.7	–$392.3	–$202.0	–$579.6	–$358.2
TOTALS	–$1,342.7	–$863.3	–$721.8	–$1,482.6	–$1,072.3

Note: The table shows declines in housing, durables, and investment. The decline in housing plus consumer durables is slightly lower than the decline in housing plus the decline in durables in each recession because the peaks and troughs in these two series differ slightly.

Q2 1975. A new cycle began almost immediately, with an increase to $2,839 per household in Q4 1978 and a long 68.7 percent decline to $1,173 in Q2 1982. As discussed herein, monetary policy stimulates housing construction and adds temporarily to output, in amounts that add meaningfully to household income, even before considering multiplier effects.

Housing averages a much smaller percentage of GDP than investment. Between Q1 1947 and Q1 2013, it averaged only 3.0 percent of GDP, whereas investment averaged 10.6 percent of GDP. Yet – as shown in Table 5.2 – in seven of the eleven postwar recessions, the dollar decline in housing exceeded the investment decline. The dollar decline in housing plus consumer durables exceeded the investment decline in one other recession. In the combined double-dip recessions in 1980 and 1981–2, the sum of housing and consumer durables declined $201.7 billion – substantially more than the $131.5 billion decline in investment. This leaves two postwar recessions, 1948–9 and 2001, in which investment declines dominated the downturn.

Between 1997 and 2007, large trade deficits were financed by selling financial instruments to foreign suppliers, and a major portion of their investment found its way into the U.S. housing market, which allowed the country to sustain a housing construction boom for a longer period than usual.[7] However, housing reacts to and corrects for excessive and prolonged

[7] The $773.0 billion current account deficit in 2006 amounted to $6,758 per U.S. household, based on the Census Bureau estimate of 114,384,000 households. This is a serious financial stimulus program, even if brought to us by the "invisible hand" of trade.

stimulation. Given the major role of housing fluctuations in economic activity, a better approach to economic stabilization would include an effort to stabilize housing rather than attempts to work through periods of weak economic growth with esoteric methods – such as channeling foreign capital inflows to weak borrowers – to stimulate housing and the economy.

5.4 Conclusions

The Depression, the typical postwar recession, and the recent Great Recession all followed similar sequences: Housing increased rapidly during the expansion but fell before the general contraction began. In many recessions, durable goods expenditures began to fall at the same time as or soon after housing fell. Firms' fixed investments have fallen in thirteen of the past fourteen downturns; however, a downturn in investment served as a leading indicator in only two of the past fourteen downturns. In the 1990–91 downturn, housing began a sharp decline a year before the peak of the economic cycle, whereas investment had its first substantial decline in the quarter before the economic cycle peak. Another exception, in 2001, was associated with a massive capital inflow into the mortgage market and extremely weak mortgage-underwriting standards that sustained the housing boom through the recession. Rather than being a leading indicator, investment often has been a lagging indicator of both imminent recessions and recoveries. In five of eleven postwar recessions, investment rose for at least one quarter after the recession began. In 1953, 1960, and 1981, investment peaked one quarter after the recession began. In 1974, investment peaked three quarters after the recession began. Even in 2008, investment peaked one quarter after the recession began; by that time, housing had already fallen 55.6 percent after nine consecutive quarterly declines.

Housing led eleven of the last fourteen recessions, whereas investment led the declines only in 1990 and 2001. Magnitudes of movements in housing reinforce its important role in what is universally referred to as the "business cycle." During postwar recessions, the average percentage decline in housing – at 32.5 percent – was 2.75 times as large as the 11.8 percent average decline in investment. When we aggregate households' interest-rate sensitive expenditure on housing and durables, the declines (in dollar amounts) are 38.3 percent larger than investment declines. The timing strongly indicates that the investment cycle is a delayed response to downturns in interest-rate sensitive elements of household expenditures.

Relative to GDP, the importance of fluctuations in housing, investment, and housing plus consumer durables is depicted in Figure 5.10, which

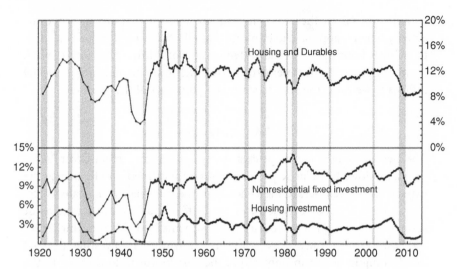

Figure 5.10. Expenditures on housing, on investment, and on housing plus durables as percentages of GDP in the past ninety years.

shows the size of these sectors as a percentage of GDP in the past ninety years.

Monetary policy has left a clear imprint on developments in the real economy. In the immediate aftermath of most recessions, housing expands more rapidly than any other component of GDP, and inflation falls. Through the first part of the expansion, housing increases and inflation remains low. In the latter part of the expansion, housing ceases to respond to loose monetary policy but inflation begins to develop. In response to developing inflation, the Fed tightens monetary policy to rein in inflation, housing begins a sharper decline, and the economy enters a recession. In most cases, consumers' durable goods expenditures begin to fall soon after the decline in housing; however, the decline in investment comes several quarters later, coincident with the start of the recession. Tightened monetary policy, as well as the general contraction that follows, eases inflationary pressures; as inflation subsides, the Fed returns to a looser monetary policy. At that point, housing begins a rapid resurgence and the economy emerges from recession. As a recovery gains momentum, businesses respond to growing demand by increasing their capacity via increased investments in structures and equipment. This general pattern has played out in most postwar recessions, with only minor variations in the sequence of events. A genuine understanding of economic fluctuations must recognize these basic facts of household-expenditure and investment cycles.

References

Bernanke, Ben (2010). "Monetary Policy and the Housing Bubble." Paper presented at the 2010 American Economic Association meeting.

Board of Governors of the Federal Reserve (2001). Press Release. March 20. Available at www.federalreserve.gov/boarddocs/press/general/2001/20010320.

Board of Governors of the Federal Reserve (2002). "Minutes of the Federal Open Market Committee." November 6. Available at www.federalreserve.gov/fomc/minutes/20021106.htm.

Board of Governors of the Federal Reserve (2003). Press Release. June 25. Available at www.federalreserve.gov/boarddocs/press/monetary/2003/20030625/default.htm.

Fatás, Antonio, Prakash Kannan, Pau Rabanal, and Alasdair Scott (2009). "Lessons for Monetary Policy from Asset Price Fluctuations." In *World Economic Outlook* (Fall, Ch. 3). Washington, DC: International Monetary Fund.

Feinman, Joshua N. (1993). "Reserve Requirements: History, Current Practice, and Potential Reform." *Federal Reserve Bulletin*, 79, pp. 569–89.

Friedman, Milton, and Anna J. Schwartz (1963). *A Monetary History of the United States.* Princeton, NJ: Princeton University Press.

Green, Richard K. (1997). "Follow the Leader: How Changes in Residential and Non-Residential Investment Predict Changes in GDP." *Real Estate Economics*, 25, pp. 253–70.

Hetzel, Robert L. and Ralph F. Leach (2001). "The Treasury–Fed Accord: A New Narrative Account." *Economic Quarterly*, Federal Reserve Bank of Richmond, pp. 33–55.

Leamer, Edward E. (2007). "Housing *Is* the Business Cycle." Federal Reserve Bank of Kansas City, Jackson Hole [Wyoming] Symposium.

Prescott, Edward C. (1986a). "Theory Ahead of Business Cycle Measurement." Federal Reserve Bank of Minneapolis *Quarterly Review*, 10, pp. 9–22.

Prescott, Edward C. (1986b). "Response to a Skeptic." Federal Reserve Bank of Minneapolis *Quarterly Review*, 10, pp. 28–33.

6

What May Have Triggered or Sustained the
Housing Bubble (1997–2006)?

As home prices rose and hunger for high-yield investments grew, Sadek [founder of Quick Loan Funding] found his niche pushing mortgages to borrowers with poor credit. Such subprime home loans grew to $600 billion, or 21 percent, of all U.S. mortgages last year from $160 billion, or 7 percent, in 2001, according to *Inside Mortgage Finance*, an industry newsletter. Banks drove that growth because they could bundle subprime loans into securities . . . "I never made a loan that Wall Street wouldn't buy," Sadek says. He worked hard to build the business, he says, and the company did nothing illegal . . . with the support of Citigroup, which funded the loans, he pioneered lending to homebuyers with credit scores of less than 450.

Citigroup spokesman Stephen Cohen said the bank doesn't comment on its relationships with clients.

"We made most of our money from selling loans to banks," Sadek says . . . like many subprime companies, [he] specialized in . . . thirty-year mortgages that start with lower "teaser" interest rates and ratchet higher after two years.

A key selling point was the 50 percent rise in home prices nationally from 2001 to 2006.

Bob Ivry, *Bloomberg News*, December 18, 2007

Since late 1997, more than $2 billion worth of community reinvestment loans have been packaged and marketed into securities . . . Every dollar taken off the originator's books through securitization is a dollar available for new loans . . . securitization reflects a growing confidence among secondary market investors – many of whom, after all, are under no CRA obligation of their own – in the quality of these loans. I think that it proves we're on the right track.

John D. Hawke, Jr.; Comptroller of the Currency; May 5, 1999

We observed in Chapter 2 that, by far, the most important source – the fundamental "cause" – of stock and housing price bubbles and their collapse is the "bubble mentality" that episodically characterizes people's behavior in markets for retradable assets in which people repeatedly get caught in loops of self-reinforcing, myopically rational but unsustainable expectations of rising asset prices. Although the timing of the beginning and collapse of equity and housing-mortgage bubbles is essentially unpredictable, past experience implies that they are reliably bound to occur and reoccur. This interpretation is made possible from experimental asset market learning, in which fundamental value can be defined independently of observed prices and deviations attributed to behavior, and that behavior can be studied and modeled.

We divide the ten-year period from 1997 through 2006 into two five-year phases. The first phase is the interval that marked when the price bubble began, 1997, to the end of 2001, when the inflation-adjusted Case-Shiller U.S. National Home Price Index rose above its previous peak in 1989. (See Figure 3.1; we also note in Figure 3.4 that the ratio of median household price to median household income had risen to a new high in 2001 before surging higher in 2002.) By the end of 2001, the housing bubble was as large as any in the previous fifty years; a phenomenon of this magnitude demands explanation and understanding. The second phase is the interval that sustained and carried the index to new heights from 2002 to 2006, when the index abruptly halted its advance and thereafter went into rapid decline. The subsequent five-year course of the housing-mortgage market accounts for the extreme severity of the Great Recession among all postwar recessions.

In this chapter, we identify and examine several promising trigger developments in both the public and private sectors that either coincide with these two five-year intervals or precede them as an "incubation period." Because none of these events and developments can be identified clearly as external and autonomous – independent of prevailing economic and political sentiments – each is best viewed as characterizing the components of the eventual financial crisis.

Hindsight is hazardous when trying to identify factors that may have incubated and finally sparked the housing bubble – we have no controlled experiments. Moreover, knowing that the takeoff in housing prices occurred after 1997, we are looking for explanatory events around that point in time – and "looking" implies the high likelihood of "finding" in the absence of controls in the identification process. However, the exercise is potentially informing for both historical comparisons of the type addressed in Chapters 4 and 5 and, more powerfully, the design of new experiments. Interpreted in terms of the modeling of bubbles (see Chapter 2), these factors would be possible independent variables in both the fundamental- and momentum-based components that determine the dynamic path of prices.

6.1 What May Have Triggered the Housing Bubble (1997–2001)?

For the upswing of house prices from 1997 through 2001, we suggest the following four possible stage-setting events:

- The bipartisan Taxpayer Relief Act of 1997, which exempted home resales from capital gains taxes up to a maximum of $500,000.
- Government housing programs: Fannie Mae, Freddie Mac, and Ginnie Mae. Beginning in 1996, U.S. housing agencies were assigned target goals to direct their funding to low-income borrowers (subsequently, targets were increased to 50 percent in 2000 and 52 percent in 2005).
- Laws intended to help the poor own homes by requiring mortgage-lenders to be performance-rated on their efforts to lend to borrowers with incomes below 80 percent of the median family income. Accusations regarding these issues have centered on the Community Reinvestment Act (CRA).
- The U.S. trade deficit, resulting in a large inflow of foreign investment capital beginning in the early1990s. Chapter 3 (see Subsections 3.3.2 and 3.3.3) examined the inflow of foreign investment, comparing it with the net flow of mortgage funds; therefore, this topic is not discussed further in this chapter. Chapter 10 revisits the topic of foreign investment flows in the context of the crisis experiences of several other countries.

6.1.1 The Taxpayer Relief Act of 1997

Federal tax policy has long biased consumer-credit expenditures in favor of mortgage debt by allowing interest to be deducted from earnings to arrive at taxable income. Interest on credit card and other consumer debt is not deductible in calculating tax liability. Mortgage interest deductibility was not new and is not likely to have jump-started the developing mortgage crisis. In combination, however, with laxity in private and public mortgage standards, it provided a "loophole" for borrowers to obtain excess tax deductible cash-to-mortgage funds and home equity loans to pay down credit card and other consumer debt. The major new development – part of the political consensus to facilitate homeownership – was the Taxpayer Relief Act (1997), which for the first time allowed housing assets (up to $500,000 on each sale after a two-year holding period) to be excluded from the capital-gains tax.[1]

---

[1] See Smith (2007); see also Bajaj and Leonhardt (2008). Although the Act was overwhelmingly supported by both parties in both the Senate and the House, it contained other features, such as a general reduction in the capital gains tax that likely would have been more appealing to Republicans than Democrats.

Housing and corporate securities each constitute large components of all U.S. wealth; any asymmetric reduction in taxes on homes implies that a larger fraction of capital will flow into home investment away from other forms of capital investment in pursuit of higher after-tax returns. The new tax incentive would be expected to increase the fundamental or permanent component of the demand for homes and the long-run equilibrium stock of homes. However, in moving to that equilibrium, any increase in the expected rate of home price appreciation also would raise the short-run momentum demand for homes.[2]

6.1.2 Evaluating the Role of Public Housing Policy: Government-Sponsored Enterprises and the Community Reinvestment Act

This section begins with a brief review of the tier structure of house prices because this phenomenon, in city after city, may relate directly to the intentions that motivated various public housing programs, as well as the structure of private mortgage funding.

Which households were most and which least affected by the house price bubble and its collapse? As illustrated in Figure 3.5, the charts showing the tier structure of house prices in four of the cities in the Case-Schiller Home Price Tiered Index exhibit the following characteristic feature: The cheaper the home, the greater is the percentage increase in prices during the upswing and the greater is the percentage reversal in the course of the decline. This tier structure reflects the differential structure of demand in which the lowest one-third price tier included homes concentrated in the low- to middle-income (LMI) category class – officially defined as families with incomes less than 80 percent of the median income. LMI families were targeted by both public and private programs designed to assist them in obtaining access to mortgage terms that would facilitate homeownership. The following sections discuss these programs against the background of the remarkable cross-city consistency of this price tier structure.

6.1.2.1 Fannie Mae and Freddie Mac

The Federal National Mortgage Association (FNMA) (or Fannie Mae, started in 1938) and the Federal Home Loan Mortgage Corporation (FHLMC) (or Freddie Mac, originated in 1968) were subsequently

---

[2] Econometric estimates focus on the incentive effects of the Tax Relief Act on home sales – that is, the tax elasticity of sales – not on the effect of the tax relief on expectations and momentum elements that are central to the incubation of bubbles. For an econometric estimate of the effect of the Act on home sales, see Shan (2008).

reconstituted as mixed public–private entities, financed privately via listed equity and bond financing in 1970.[3] As GSE, they were long considered to be implicitly guaranteed by the government to give them access to low borrowing cost; they were further favored by exemption from state and local taxation. The perception that the government would not let the GSE fail – subsequently confirmed when the Housing and Economic Recovery Act of 2008 authorized government support for GSE bond and equity issues[4] – allowed them to borrow at preferential rates. "Consequently, the GSE's ability to borrow at a preferential rate provides them with strong incentives both to expand the range of assets that they acquire and to increase the size of their portfolios to the greatest extent possible" (Bernanke, 2007). The belief that the GSE bonds and mortgages were implicitly guaranteed proved to be correct: The Federal Reserve began supporting the market for GSE obligations, and they entered government conservatorship in September 2008. That this guarantee could have exacerbated the bubbles is evident, but this had long been a widely accepted truism and was not likely to be a special factor igniting the bubble.

In 1996, the GSE were assigned target goals by the U.S. Department of Housing and Urban Development (HUD) to direct 42 percent of its mortgage financing to LMI borrowers; subsequently, these targets were increased to 50 percent in 2000 and 52 percent in 2005.[5]

---

[3] "In 1968, the Housing and Urban Development Act . . . reorganized Fannie Mae as a for-profit, shareholder-owned company with government sponsorship and established Ginnie Mae as an independent government corporation in HUD. Ginnie Mae's primary function was to guarantee the timely payment of principal and interest from pools of FHA-, USDA/RD-, and PIH-insured and VA-guaranteed mortgages. Ginnie Mae has the full faith and credit backing of the federal government. Although now a for-profit, shareholder-owned company, Fannie Mae continued its activities, which were mainly purchasing FHA and VA mortgages. According to some financial analysts, Congress largely reorganized Fannie Mae as a private company for budgetary purposes (that is, to remove its financial obligations from the federal budget)" (U.S. Government Accountability Office Report, 2009). The programs referred to in the quote are Federal Housing Administration (FHA), U.S. Department of Agriculture Rural Development (USDA/RD), and Public and Indian Housing (PIH) programs. Ginnie Mae is discussed in Section 6.1.2.2.

[4] The takeovers of Fannie Mae and Freddie Mac were authorized by the Housing and Economic Recovery Act of 2008 (P.L. 110-289) on July 30, 2008. On September 7, 2008, Fannie Mae and Freddie Mac were placed into the conservatorship of the Federal Housing Finance Agency, and the U.S. Treasury was authorized to purchase an unlimited amount of bond and equity in the agencies in order to stabilize their prices. For additional details on the support arrangements, see Jickling (2008). FNMA shares reached a low of 18.5 cents in July 2010, down from the high of $126 in December 1995.

[5] See Table 1 in Profiles of GSE Mortgage Purchases in 1999–2000, HUD, Office of Policy Development and Research, April 2002. For a subsequent update, see Profiles of GSE Mortgage Purchases in 2005–2007, HUD, Office of Policy Development and Research, April 2008.

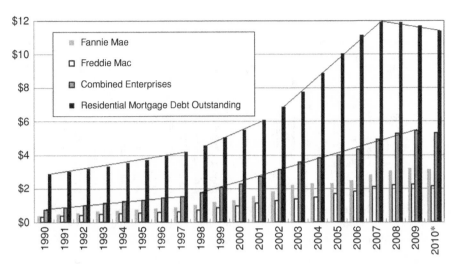

Figure 6.1. Residential mortgage debt: Total, Fannie and Freddie, and combined GSE. *Source:* Federal Housing Finance Agency, Research and Analysis, market data, "Enterprise Share of Residential Mortgage Debt Outstanding." Revised 11/2/11.

Other than the fact that these actions were a complex blend stemming from as well as contributing to the "bubble mentality" that emerged in the housing-finance markets, what was the course of total mortgage debt growth – and GSE participation in that growth – in the years preceding and following our benchmark year of 1997? Figure 6.1 shows total outstanding residential mortgage debt, Fannie Mae and Freddie Mac, and for the Combined Enterprises from 1990–2010.

GSE and private mortgage lending both grow (1990–1997). In Figure 6.1, the bar chart for the period 1990 to 1997 defines the natural background for the bubble from 1997 to 2006. We recall that housing prices had peaked in 1989, declined until 1997, and then rose to a new peak in 2006. The figure illustrates the trend line for both total loans outstanding (i.e., privately issued mortgages plus GSE issues) and GSE issues for 1990 to 1997. As shown, the trend for each is tightly linear and increasing, with total loans expanding slightly faster than for the combined enterprises. Afterward, there is a sharp "kink" in these trends. Hence, not only is 1997 a pivotal year based on the turnaround in house prices, we also see that the pivot was further corroborated in abrupt changes in the rate of increase in both the private and public issuance of mortgage debt.

GSE and private lending growths kink upward (1997–2001) but private lending grows even more (2002–2006). Next, we examine the course of total and GSE

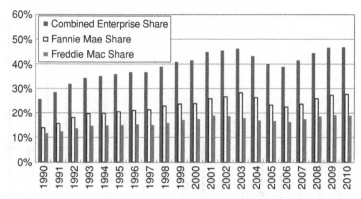

Figure 6.2. Residential mortgage debt: Percent shares held by Fannie, Freddie, and combined GSE. *Source:* Federal Housing Finance Agency, Research and Analaysis, market data, "Enterprise Share of Residential Mortgage Debt Outstanding." Revised 11/2/11.

debt growth from 1997 to 2006. We review this growth during the two five-year time intervals identified previously: first, 1997–2001, demarcated by the start of the recent bubble and the year (i.e., 2001) in which house prices rose to their preceding peak year (i.e., 1989); and second, the period from 2002 to 2006, when house prices surged to set a new all-time historical high. Figure 6.1 shows that total loans outstanding experienced an even larger growth rate kink in the second five-year interval (with a growth rate of 12.8 percent per year) than in the first (with a growth rate of 9.1 percent per year), whereas the combined enterprises grew at a rate of 13.6 percent per year in the first interval but at only 8.4 percent per year during the bubble phase of the housing market. Just as 1997 was the pivotal year for the beginning of the bubble, the pivot point at which the bubble shifted into high gear appeared midway between 2001 and 2002.

GSE shares of total peaked in 2003 and recovered in 2007. Figure 6.2 also provides a chart of the corresponding percentage share distributions among the mortgage market funding sources, based on the same data used in Figure 6.1. The combined enterprise share peaks in 2003, three years before the bubble ended in 2006. The torrid housing market years were 2004 to 2006, and they were financed by corresponding growth in the total loan share by the private financial sector. Furthermore, the decline in enterprise share in 2004–2005 is associated with the GSE accounting irregularities that surfaced prominently in the period 2004–2005 (U.S. Government Accountability Office, 2009).

Bhutta (2009) sought to identify the specific effect of government legislation on the GSE's allocation of credit to "underserved" lower-income and minority neighborhoods by focusing on one of the early GSE Underserved Areas Goal (UAG) in the 1992 Federal Housing Enterprises Financial Safety and Soundness Act. By controlling for correlation biases in previous studies (which had found no effects), and consistent with the previous trend comparisons, Bhutta found a modest, statistically significant 4 percent increase in loan purchases by GSE occasioned by the UAG with no evidence of offsetting effects from private or Federal Housing Administration (FHA) loans being crowded out by GSE actions. This paper, lauded for its analytical care, illustrated the great technical difficulty in isolating the specific effect of GSE policies in an environment of bubble expectations that were widely shared by private and public enterprises and by policy experts (Gerardi et al., 2010).

Growth in adjustable rate mortgages was mostly private. A pernicious factor in the housing bubble was the trend away from the traditional fully amortized fixed rate mortgage (FRM) and toward adjustable-rate mortgages (ARMs) available in several versions in which the interest rate was periodically reset (e.g., every six months) based on a market index (e.g., London InterBank Offered Rate plus a premium). The payments could involve a principal component that paid down the loan, but they were often interest-only loans, with a balloon payment due after a specific period (e.g., ten years). Conversely, toward the late stage of the bubble, the negative-amortization loan emerged, in which the principal balance due grows from its initial level. The chart in Figure 6.3 shows mortgage originations by funding source and sold into the secondary market: private-label securities (PLS) and government enterprise (Ent); type of loan payment: ARM or FRM; and year from 2001 through 2008. We note that the first category (PLS: ARM) grows more rapidly than the third category (PLS: FRM) in the period from 2001 to 2005. We also note that the enterprise FRM greatly dominates over the enterprise ARMs sold. These results are consistent with the hypothesis that to compete with the GSE, the private-label lenders expanded in the riskier segments of the mortgage markets.

6.1.2.2 Ginnie Mae

Ginnie Mae – a third federal entity designed to promote homeownership – is a wholly owned government corporation within HUD that was established in 1968. Ginnie Mae (2009, p. 1) does not engage in direct mortgage lending to home buyers: By providing investors with the full faith and credit guaranty

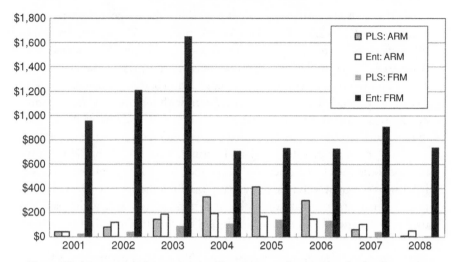

Figure 6.3. Mortgages originated and sold to the secondary market, by funding source (private-label securities, PLS, and GSE, ENT); payment form (adjustable-rate mortgages, ARMs, and fixed-rate mortgages, FRMs); and year of origination, 2001 to 2008 ($ billions). *Source:* Federal Housing Administration, "Data on the Risk and Performance of Single-Family Mortgages from 2001 through 2008 and Financed in the Secondary Market," September 13, 2010 (Figure 1, p. 6).

of the U.S. Government on the timely payment of principal and interest, Ginnie Mae enables qualified mortgage lenders to sell their mortgage loans at favorable prices in the secondary market and attract new sources of capital. Lenders then can use the proceeds to make new mortgage loans available.

In 1970, Ginnie Mae developed and guaranteed the first modern mortgage backed securities (MBS). It accounted for as high as 26 percent of the MBS market in 1994 – a share that declined as low as 4 percent in 2005 and 2006 but expanded rapidly to 22 percent in 2008 in the wake of the collapse of the private MBS market and more aggressive action by Ginnie Mae (Ginnie Mae, 2009, p. 9, Figure 4). By September 2009, Ginnie Mae's share of the entire MBS market (i.e., agency and nonagency) was 23 percent; in October 2009, MBS issuance by Ginnie Mae exceeded that of both Fannie Mae and Freddie Mac (Ginnie Mae, 2009, p. 9). These post-crash changes also reflect the actions by the U.S. Treasury and the Federal Reserve to support the MBS holdings of the GSE (Federal Housing Finance Agency, 2010).

As discussed previously, the data are consistent with the proposition that the GSE were not primary direct movers in the housing finance boom. However, was the private financing of the bubble indirectly supported by Ginnie Mae through its guarantees of MBS?

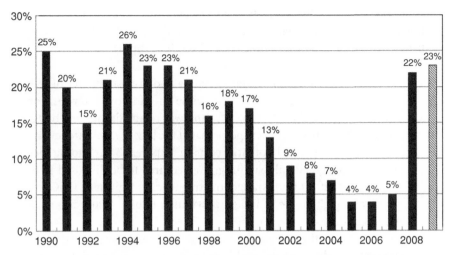

Figure 6.4. Ginnie Mae share of MBS issuance, 1990–2009. *Source:* Ginnie Mae Report to Congress, HUD, November 6, 2009, p. 13; from *Inside Mortgage Finance.* Data for 2009 are from the first nine months of the year.

Figure 6.4 plots Ginnie Mae's share of the total MBS market for each year from 1991 to 2009. Although the agency increased its issuance of MBS in 2000–2007, its relative role declined as the private MBS market surged, particularly in the torrid end years of 2004–2006. This private-label mortgage market development was fueled by the astonishing growth in derivatives written as protection in the event of default on MBS portfolios, fostered by the widespread perception that mortgages were safely "insured" against default. Chapter 7 examines how and why these instruments failed. These data are consistent with the proposition that warrants emphasis: The implicitly guaranteed mortgages issued by Fannie Mae and Freddie Mac and by Ginnie Mae's explicit guarantee of qualifying private-label MBS packages could not compete with the perceived-equivalent form of private MBS hedged by derivatives. However, in 2008 and 2009, Ginnie Mae's role was dramatically expanded under new federal bailout programs and action by the U.S. Treasury and the Federal Reserve (Federal Housing Finance Agency, 2012).

6.1.2.3 Evaluation of the GSE by the Government Accountability Office

A useful report evaluating the GSE was issued in 2009 for the consideration of Congress in its deliberations on what might be done to restructure (including privatizing or terminating) the mixed private and public housing support enterprises. Primarily, this report was critical of the GSE role in the housing crisis as those entities evolved over the decades. The principle problems identified are as follows (U.S. GAO, 2009, pp. 18–28):

- The Federal Housing Enterprises Safety and Soundness Act of 1992 resulted from Congress's desire to revise and improve the regulatory structure of the GSE, but a key feature was retained: their off-budget status. This status effectively perpetuated the lack of transparency concerning GSE risks and potential costs to taxpayers by excluding them from the many federal loan programs required to be disclosed in the federal budget. This off-budget treatment was a legitimate GAO criticism although, as we indicated previously, Bhutta (2009) found the effects of the Act to be minor.
- It is likely that the GSE, as per their charters, contributed to mortgage market liquidity and reduced interregional interest rate differentials. However, this conclusion is confounded by the fact that such outcomes also were implied by the competition that results from the removal of restrictions on the ability of depository institutions to pay market rates and to engage in interstate expansion.
- The scale of GAO operations in conventional mortgage markets enabled it to standardize and efficiently facilitate mortgage-underwriting procedures. However, it is not evident that the GSE have been able to stabilize mortgage markets in periods of stress, which are also part of their chartered directives. Thus, in the current crisis, GSE support for the mortgage market was possible only as a consequence of the major (i.e., $1.45 trillion) assistance received from the Federal Reserve and the U.S. Treasury. The GSE and Ginnie Mae together accounted for nearly 60 percent of all new MBS issued in the critical year of 2006, with the remainder from private-label issues. This share rose to 97 percent in 2008 as the private label MBS issuance fell from about $700 billion in 2007 to about $40 billion in 2008, whereas GSE issuance remained more than $1 trillion.
- Also questionable is the effectiveness of the GSE in expanding home-ownership for targeted low income and minority groups – a central part of their charge. Thus: "Although the enterprises generally satisfied the numeric purchase goals through 2007, HUD and independent researchers have had difficulty identifying tangible benefits for targeted groups associated with the enterprises' purchase program. In setting higher housing goals beginning in 2005, HUD stated that the intent was to encourage the enterprises to facilitate greater financing and

homeownership opportunities for the groups targeted by the goals. *HUD concluded that, although the enterprises had complied with previous goals, they continued to serve less of the affordable housing market than was served by conventional conforming primary market lenders during those years.* Furthermore, recent research indicates that, although the enterprises have enhanced their product offerings to meet the housing goals, the effects of the housing goals on affordability and opportunities for target groups have been limited" (U.S. GAO 2009, p. 23; italics added).

• Many commentators and researchers, including the GAO, long maintained that the GSE had incentives to pursue profitability at the expense of risk under the shelter of an implied guarantee of their financial obligations. These incentive distortions were revealed first in the GSE accounting irregularities of 2004–2005 and then in the aggressive purchase (and retention) of mortgage assets with poor quality underwriting standards (e.g., Alt-A mortgages), in which the levels of debt were high relative to home values or borrower income. From 2003 through 2006, there was a rapid increase in GSE purchases of private-label MBS as a percent of their retained mortgage portfolio. The accounting manipulations were designed to show growth in profitability to enhance their appeal to investors and general reporting standards governing derivatives. (See U.S. GAO, 2009, pp. 26–7.)

6.1.2.4 Public Housing Policy: The CRA

In 1995, the CRA – originated in 1977 to combat mortgage discrimination (called racial "redlining") – was amended to require all mortgage-lending banks to be rated in accordance with their demonstrated efforts to lend to people of modest means. This CRA update was a product of a bipartisan – if volatile – political consensus in the Clinton Administration to expand homeownership rates among minorities and the poor. Both of the Bush Administrations were part of this bipartisan consensus, extending over two decades (Rosenthal, 1989; Business Editors, 2002).

The CRA: From defending minority property rights to the management of increased lending. Essentially, under the CRA, the regulatory agencies had been channeled into management by command and control, as distinct from the property rights enforcement task of implementing penalties designed to discourage discrimination in mortgage lending markets – itself a difficult directive to apply in an even-handed manner in the original (1977) legislation. The intense political controversy was fueled by issues concerning the heavy handed invasiveness of the agencies in this management process.

To convey a sense of the scope of the CRA legislation, we examine some of the rules, and their motivation, as summarized in two U.S. Treasury reports, and originally promulgated in the *Federal Register* by the regulatory agencies charged with implementing congressional intent (Litan et al., 2000).[6]

In 1999, Congress passed the Financial Services Modernization Act of 1999 (or the Gramm-Leach-Bliley Act), which contained a provision requiring the U.S. Treasury within two years to prepare reports on how the Act impacted the provision of services as intended under the previous CRA (i.e., 1977, amended in 1995).[7] The initial report was released in April 2000

---

[6] The second and final report was issued nine months after the first by the U.S. Treasury (Litan et al., 2001). For the CRA Regulations and HMDA Final Rules, see the *Federal Register* (May 4, 1995). The regulatory agencies consisted of the Board of Governors of the Federal Reserve System, the FDIC, the Office of the Comptroller of the Currency, and the Office of Thrift Supervision.

[7] This provision was a residue of an intense partisan debate over the Act. For example: "Gramm had maintained that he did not want anything in the bill that would expand the application of the Community Reinvestment Act because it was, he said, unnecessarily burdensome to banks. He had sought a provision that would exempt thousands of smaller banks from the law. He also wanted a provision that would expose what he has described as the 'extortion' committed by community groups against banks by requiring the groups to disclose any special financial deals the groups extract from the banks. But the White House found that provision unacceptable and had its own ideas about community lending. It wanted the legislation to prevent any bank with an unsatisfactory record of making loans to the disadvantaged from expanding into new areas, like insurance or securities. The White House had insisted that the President would veto any legislation that would scale back minority-lending requirements. Four days of intense negotiations between Summers, Gene Sperling, the President's top economic policy adviser, and Gramm, while moving the two sides closer, failed to resolve the differences... Ultimately, the following provisions were drawn up and both the White House and Gramm said they could accept them:

"Banks will not be able to move into new lines of business unless they have satisfactory lending records. Community groups will have to make disclosures to regulators about certain kinds of financial deals with banks that they have pressed to make loans under the Community Reinvestment Act. Wholesale financial institutions, a new kind of business that takes large, uninsured bank deposits, cannot be affiliated with commercial banks. Small banks with satisfactory or excellent track records of lending to the underserved would be reviewed less frequently under the Community Reinvestment Act. As a practical matter, smaller banks are reviewed about every three years. The deal struck today allows all rural banks and banks with less than $250 million in assets to undergo examination once every five years if their last exam resulted in an 'outstanding' grade and every four years if they last scored 'satisfactory'" (Labaton, 1999).

The Financial Services Modernization Act (S.900) commanded huge bipartisan support. The final bill resolving the differences between the Senate and House versions passed the (followed by the final report in January 2001) and it provides a unique perspective on how Treasury perceived developments under the CRA, unvarnished by the hindsight afforded in the collapse of the mortgage market seven years later.

The 1995 amended version of the CRA sought to better achieve the full potential of the purpose of the original legislation, which was to meet the credit needs of local communities, especially LMI residents. This was to be accomplished by placing more emphasis on performance and its measurement, as distinct from the vagaries of process. New rules thereby were to be promulgated that would apply to the standards that the regulatory agencies used in evaluating compliance with CRA requirements. The new rules were an attempt to make that management task more effective and the political controversy was about how invasive the agencies would be.

In issuing the new rules, the regulatory agencies articulated clarifications of the history of the CRA, including community perceptions – that is, complaints – of the laxity of the enforcement agencies in penalizing poor performance, which culminated in the 1995 amendments. The CRA provided an impetus for various deposit institutions to expand their services, open new branches, and increase lending to all members of the local community. However, many consumer and community groups criticized the regulatory agencies for not more aggressively penalizing depository institutions whenever their outcome performance was poor in lending responses to LMI borrowers.

An explicit part of the statement of new rules was that mortgage institutions would face sanctions if, in the judgment of the regulators, the needs of LMI borrowers were not being met. The sanctions would be applied through the power of regulators to deny or condition applications for expanding operations. Thus, an institution's rating in meeting the credit needs of the entire community under the new standards would be taken into account whenever that institution applied for new branches, mergers, office relocations, consolidations, and other changes in business activity. Based on the institution's performance rating, any such application could be denied or conditioned to merit approval.

That the announcement by the agencies in the *Federal Register* was essentially reaffirming but streamlining and simplifying regulatory procedures already in place was indicated in a *New York Times* article a month earlier that reported Republican opposition:

Senate by a vote of 90–8 and the House by 362–57. For details, see S.900 legislative history, available at http://thomas.loc.gov/cgi-bin/bdquery/z?d106:S900.

House and Senate Republicans, including the banking chairmen, united today behind bills that would scale back substantially banking laws that provide for consumer protection and more lending in poor neighborhoods.

The bills, introduced today, would make more than 60 changes in Federal laws. Some of the changes are broad, like an exemption for small and medium-sized banks from the Community Reinvestment Act, which requires that financial institutions lend in poor neighborhoods as well as in rich ones....

Robert L. Gnaizda, the general counsel of the Greenlining Institute, a San Francisco–based group of civil rights and minority business organizations, said the proposed legislation would gut the Community Reinvestment Act because it would also bar challenges under the law to any big bank that earned a "satisfactory" rating or better on its most recent evaluation by regulators. Virtually all large financial institutions receive such a rating. *The act currently allows community groups to block regulatory approval of bank mergers and other deals if the banks involved cannot provide fresh proof of their compliance with the act* (Bradsher, 1995; italics added).

The referenced bills were introduced in a failed attempt to head off the regulatory agency changes announced later in the *Federal Register*. Indeed, as discussed previously, the issues debated in the CRA legislation of 1995 were still prominent four years later (see footnote 7).

Consumer loans, not only mortgage lending, were on the CRA stimulus table. Although the role of the CRA in the mortgage market crisis is our primary focus, it is important to note that the language referring to the "credit needs of its entire community" had broader implications. Thus, the breadth of regulatory intentions is indicated by explicitly allowing an institution to elect to be evaluated on the basis of its consumer loan activity. Consumer loans were defined (to avoid double counting) to exclude home mortgages and small business or farm loans and to include motor vehicle loans, credit card loans, home equity loans, and other secured and unsecured consumer loans. Thus, institutions could elect to be evaluated on a loan-product-by-product basis.

As we interpret these rules, financial institutions were under broad instructions to show performance in increasing mortgage and other types of credit to LMI segments of their local communities. More was potentially at stake than loans to facilitate homeownership among those of lesser means. To an extent that is difficult to quantify, the great expansion of mortgage credit in 1997–2006 was accompanied by credit card and other forms of debt that were facilitated by these directives.

Surges in Fannie Mae cash-out financing. For perspective on home equity as a source of financing other activities, we use data available from reports

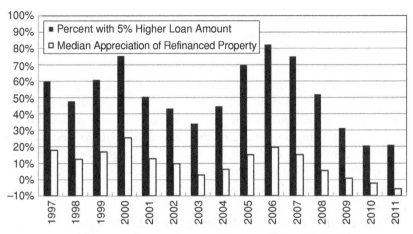

Figure 6.5. Freddie Mac cash-out refinancing: Percent of loans refinanced at 5 percent or more of the previous principal balance, and median percent appreciation on the loan property, 1997–2011. *Source:* Freddie Mac (2011), "Cash-Out Financing," Office of the Chief Economist, Fourth Quarter. Note: "Higher loan amount" refers to loan amounts that were at least 5 percent greater than the amortized unpaid principal balance of the original loan. The remaining percent of loans involved all loans not in this category.

by Freddie Mac on the enterprise's "cash-out" refinancing of loans. Figure 6.5 charts the percentage of loans refinanced at a level of 5 percent or more above the previous principal balance, as well as the median appreciation of the property on which the loan is refinanced, for 1997 through 2011. Mortgage refinancing surged in the late stages of the dotcom stock market bubble (1998 through 2000) and then fell sharply with the dotcom crash (2001 through 2003). An even larger percentage increase followed in the refinancing of loans at 5 percent or higher levels and corresponding median property appreciation during the final assault on the housing price peak (2004 through 2006) before the crash of 2007 through 2011 finally arrived.

In reporting the data in Figure 6.5, we caution that it provides no detail about how the home equity cash-out money was used. There is an implication that the cash-out sums in 1998–2000 were related to the final stages of the dotcom bubble, but we do not know what this cash was used for – buying securities, paying down credit card debt, education, business start-ups, buying automobiles, or shopping. Although anecdotal evidence abounds, the same ignorance of detail applies to the even larger surge in cash-out financing in the final ascent of the housing boom.

Justification and rationalization: Externalities and market failures. A prominent feature of the April 2000 CRA report was the perspective that the CRA was viewed as an attempt to correct for "externalities" or "market failures," with the explicit intention to provide opportunities for private profit that otherwise would not be available. The report is replete with confidence in the ability of public planners to implement programs that would be good for LMI districts and do well for investors.

Thus, it was suggested that depository institutions, in effect, may be leaving money on the table by investing in distant ventures to the detriment of their local communities. By giving institutions better incentives to seek local lending opportunities, the CRA could revitalize deteriorating inner-city communities. This could correct, it was argued, market failures through legal intervention in the form of mandates and incentives leading to profitability that otherwise would not be available (Litan et al., 2000, p. 45).

Moreover, the report views developments under the CRA as consistent with the intention to correct for externalities. By entering into loan-pooling arrangements and partnering with neighborhood groups, lending institutions can obtain access to information and its interpretation that allows LMI lending costs to be shared (Litan et al., 2000, pp. 48–9). The CRA was compared with environmental regulations as an "action-forcing device" that benefits both actors and society as a whole; everybody can gain (Litan et al., 2000, p. 51).

The report also refers to regulatory concerns about subprime lending and certain bank failures, perhaps due in part to this lending and to securitization programs, implying that regulators indeed had the intention to guard against excessive credit risk (also "externalities") by requiring banks active in this lending to increase their capital reserves (Litan et al., 2000, p.107):

In March 1999, the federal banking agencies issued joint guidance on the risks of subprime lending. The regulators generally require depositories with significant proportions of subprime mortgages to set aside relatively more capital for possible credit losses on these loans.

These events and expressed concerns all occurred well before "bubble fever" had set in, which speaks well for the sensitivity of plan implementers to the possibility that their actions might add to financial risk unless appropriate actions were taken.

A regulator's perspective. One of the chief regulators in this era, the Comptroller of the Currency, summarized CRA intentions and extolled with some exuberance the virtues of securitization as a means of enabling mortgage originators to make new loans as fast as old loans were repackaged and sold to investors (Hawke, 1999; italics added):

Empirical evidence suggests that information barriers have impeded the efficient operation of financial markets. CRA created incentives for banks to reduce the barriers that obstructed the flow of market information. For example, when lenders shied away from some low- and moderate-income borrowers, it was in part because they didn't know enough about them – and because they thought that the cost of obtaining additional information was not worth it. . . .

CRA was designed to . . . overcome the market imperfection of inadequate information, and to help lenders and creditworthy borrowers connect. . . .

We can measure this progress in at least two ways. First, there is the growing volume of CRA-qualifying loans and investments. Since 1993, financial institutions have made CRA commitments and pledges totaling more than one trillion dollars.

The second . . . is the success of CRA asset-backed securities in the capital markets. Since late 1997, more than $2 billion worth of community reinvestment loans have been packaged and marketed into securities . . . *Every dollar taken off the originator's books through securitization is a dollar available for new loans. And, more to the point, securitization reflects a growing confidence among secondary market investors – many of whom, after all, are under no CRA obligation of their own – in the quality of these loans.* I think that it proves we're on the right track.

6.1.2.5 Evaluating the CRA

The January 2001 CRA report (Litan et al., 2001, p. ES-3) provided data that credits the performance of CRA lenders in accounting for the substantial increase in home purchases by those in the LMI classification from 1993 through 1999:

CRA lenders and their affiliates increased home purchase loans to LMI individuals and communities by 94 percent between 1993 and 1999 and refinancing loans by 51 percent between the two refinance boom years of 1993 and 1998. A portion of these significant increases is attributable to the performance of non-bank affiliates acquired by banks and thrifts during this period: 16 percentage points of the 94 percent growth in home purchase loans, and 12 percentage points of the 51 percent growth in refinances. In addition, a growing share of lending by CRA lenders was accomplished through the affiliates they had created or acquired before 1994. This shift underscores how the decisions by banks and thrifts of which affiliates to include for the purposes of assessing their organization's CRA performance can affect the overall data on CRA-eligible lending.

A second principle conclusion from the same report (Litan et al., 2001, p. ES-4) is that the CRA can be credited with significant expansion into the subprime lending market:

CRA lenders and their affiliates, adjusting for differences in product specialization, increased their purchase lending to LMI individuals and communities faster than independent non-bank lenders. Even after netting out non-bank affiliates acquired after 1993, CRA lenders and their affiliates increased their prime home purchase lending by 9.0 percent and their subprime and manufactured housing lending by 79.6 percent while independent non-bank lenders increased theirs by only 6.7 percent and 36.6, respectively. Had CRA lenders and their affiliates grown their prime and other lending at the slower rates of independent non-banks, they would have advanced about one-fifth fewer home purchase loans to low and moderate income individuals and communities.

These considerations support the possibility that the CRA helped to fuel the housing bubble by pressuring private institutions into high-risk lending, but it is an exaggeration that it caused the bubble in the environment that was manifest from 1997 to 2006. Moreover, it is unclear that the private sector needed any pressuring, given its poorly aligned incentives to perform due diligence with originations being paid for with upfront fees. Online blogs are full of arguments that both blame the bubble on the CRA and absolve it from blame. However, a credible voice of experience (i.e., a Governor of the Federal Reserve System from 1991 to 1997) stated that the CRA played a role in the crisis, that its flaws were partly due to changed circumstances, and, implicitly, noted how difficult it is to design "good" policies that will not turn out to have undesirable consequences (Lindsey, 2009):

All bubbles are built on the fundamentals of human nature. Therefore, I am not saying the CRA caused the subprime crisis. But, it would be equally wrong to deny [sic, recte assert] that the CRA played no part of that process. Nor does it follow that the flaws in CRA design mean that the policy is a bad one. The world does not provide us with pristine policy options, only tradeoffs. Just as it was probably logical from a macroeconomic viewpoint to allow for the general expansion of credit in the 1990s and 2000s, so too was it logical to have a CRA program.

Another credible voice is that of a current member of the Federal Reserve Board of Governors, who commented on a Board of Governors report that included an examination of the CRA as a potential cause of the housing-mortgage crisis. The report concerned loans originating in 2005 and 2006, and a December 3, 2008, speech by Governor Kroszner (2008) noted the following:

The research focused on two basic questions. First, we asked what share of originations for subprime loans is related to the CRA. The potential role of the CRA in the subprime crisis could either be large or small, depending on the answer to this question. We found that the loans that are the focus of the CRA represent a very small portion of the subprime lending market, casting considerable doubt on the potential contribution that the law could have made to the subprime mortgage crisis.

Second, we asked how CRA-related subprime loans performed relative to other loans. Once again, the potential role of the CRA could be large or small, depending on the answer to this question. We found that delinquency rates were high in all neighborhood income groups, and that CRA-related subprime loans performed in a comparable manner to other subprime loans. As such, differences in performance between CRA-related subprime lending and other subprime lending cannot lie at the root of recent market turmoil.

That profitable lending by private investors was possible in LMI neighborhoods is illustrated by the ShoreBank model in Chicago, the ultimate failure of which is reported in detail by Bair (2012, pp. 284–90). ShoreBank was a $2.2 billion state bank with roots in the Chicago community since 1939 but whose mission changed in 1973 – before the CRA – when it was purchased by a community development organization committed to providing financing for low-income housing and business in poor local neighborhoods. It was highly successful until the early 2000s when, as Bair interpreted the situation, ShoreBank began to focus less on bank basics and more on "trendy" areas, such as microloans in developing countries, where it had no expertise. ShoreBank suffered particularly from the collapse in low-tier home prices in Chicago[8] because the bulk of its loans had been made in those neighborhoods that were most heavily impacted. What makes this case interesting is that ShoreBank's business model had been able to demonstrate profitability in those neighborhoods for many years but then got caught up in the torrid price-acceleration years of 2002 through 2006. By 2009, its financial condition had deteriorated sufficiently for the FDIC and Illinois state bank regulators to order the bank to raise capital; however, valiant attempts to do so ultimately failed. The bank failed and was sold under the FDIC's standard whole bank with a loss-share agreement (under which the buyer assumes the whole bank and the FDIC shares a portion of the losses on some bank assets); it survived after balance sheet restructuring as the Urban Partnership Bank under new owners.

Using a different approach from other studies, Agarwal et al. (2013) asked whether the CRA led to risky lending. They suggested that around examination periods, a bank has a particularly strong incentive to show that it is compliant with CRA guidelines. In loan-level comparisons with a control group, they found that for a given census track and month in the six-quarter interval containing a bank examination, there is a 5 percent

[8] Available at http://blog.redfin.com/local/chicago/2010/05/case-shiller_chicago_home_prices_return_to_rapid_declines.html.

average increase in lending. Moreover, these "treatment group" loans are 15 percent more likely to be delinquent one year after their origination.

As we interpret this evidence and testimony, the CRA is neither absolved of playing a role in the crisis nor faulted as a root cause. The CRA plainly had the charge of scoring and providing sanctions to private lenders for their efforts in expanding loans to those of modest means. Indirectly, that affected all potential mortgage loans to the groups targeted and was part of an emergent consensus that served to promote an increase in the demand for homeownership based on mortgage credit expansion. Moreover, there is mixed evidence to support the hypothesis that these pressures were an important contributor to the unraveling of the housing bubble. The behavioral essence of bubbles is that fixing "blame" or "cause" is not a useful exercise. If bubbles are driven primarily by widespread, shared myopic expectations reinforced by and causing rising prices, then parsing who or what accounts for the rising prices poses an exceptionally challenging identification problem.

6.2 What May Have Sustained and Continued the Housing Bubble (2002–2006)?

We identify the following three primary sources that sustained the bubble:

- The continuing large inflow of foreign capital.
- The unprecedented (for fifty-two years up to that time) ease in monetary policy, 2001–2003. Chapter 5 discusses the role of monetary policy in the context of the recession of 2001. This section further examines this episode of monetary ease: Exceptionally low interest rates were associated with an increase in home purchase loans and a surge in loans to refinance existing mortgages.
- Uncollateralized Credit Default Obligations (i.e., derivatives) widely thought of as providing "insurance" against mortgage default (see Chapter 7).

6.2.1 Unprecedented Monetary Ease (2001–2003) versus Foreign Investment

If the Taxpayer Relief Act of 1997 provided expectations in support of the run-up in housing prices, a significant and sustained change in monetary policy beginning in 2001 is potentially implicated in strengthening and imparting longer life to the mortgage market growth that fueled the housing price bubble.

Here is what we said in our first examination into the crisis that became known as the Great Recession:

In January 2001, after four years of real house-price increases averaging 7.2 percent per year in the Case-Shiller ten-city composite index (about 6 percent above the inflation-adjusted trend for the previous eighty years), the Federal Reserve started to ratchet down the federal funds rate. By December 2001, the federal funds rate had been reduced to its lowest level since 1962. The average federal funds rates in 2003 and 2004 were lower than in any of the years since the Fed began reporting this rate in 1955; the average federal funds rate had been lower than the average rate of 2002 in only one year since 1955: the recession year of 1958. In other words, the years 2001–2004 saw *the longest sustained expansionary monetary policy of the past fifty-four years.* (Gjerstad and Smith, 2009, pp. 276–7; italics in the original)

At the time, we saw this monetary ease as the main source of fuel for the housing bubble after 2001, and, consistent with this interpretation, noted in particular that "... during the expansion phases of the two earlier bubbles (1976–79 and 1986–89), the Fed was increasing the federal-funds rate, and those two bubbles were much milder..." (Gjerstad and Smith, 2009, p. 277). However, further examination, particularly of the inflow of foreign investment, eroded this initial interpretation. The key chart is displayed in Figure 3.3 (see Chapter 3) in which the lower panel plots foreign investment juxtaposed with the net (of trend) flow of mortgage funds. This chart shows how these two sources of funds can account for the house price cyclical peaks in 1979, 1989, and 2006 (between the housing price peaks of 1989 and 2006 was the dotcom stock market bubble that collapsed in 2000–2003).

Also, it was long after the recession ended between Q3 2003 and Q2 2004 – during the year when the federal funds rate was held to only 1 percent – that housing expenditures finally surged 21.9 percent. Even this delayed housing recovery was distinctly below the 28.3 percent average increase in residential construction during the first four quarters after the nine postwar recessions occurring between 1948–49 and 1990–91. By pointing to the lack of response to monetary easing that followed the 2001 recession, and the repeated extension of that easing, we are trying to explain it rather than justify it. In conjunction with other factors, such as the large current account deficit, the lax underwriting standards, and the originate-and-distribute model for mortgages, the cure was worse than the disease.

The very low interest rates in the 2001 recession had other consequences that set the stage for the Great Recession: They had a pronounced effect

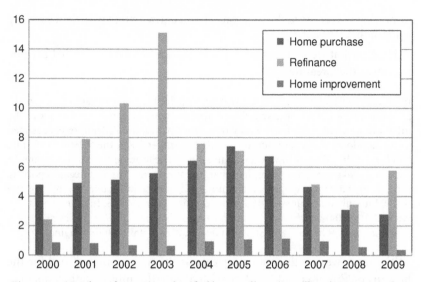

Figure 6.6. Number of mortgages classified by use of loan (in millions): Home purchase, refinance, and improvement (2000–2009). *Source:* Based on an overview of the 2009 HMDA data (2B) reported in R. B. Avery et al., 2011. "The HMDA Data: The Mortgage Market in a Time of Low Interest Rates and Economic Distress," *Federal Reserve Bulletin*, February 15.

on home refinancing. Low interest rates tend to impact home refinancing more immediately than home purchases, which take longer to "gestate." The contrast between purchase and refinancing effects is shown in Figure 6.6 using data filed under the Home Mortgage Disclosure Act (HMDA) for 2000 through 2009 (Avery et al., 2011).[9] From 2001 to 2003, the growth in home purchase mortgages moderated, whereas mortgage refinancing activity surged. During those three years, as shown in Figure 6.5 (looking only at Freddie Mac mortgages), on average, about 40 percent were refinanced at a 5 percent or higher loan amount; home refinancers were "doubling down" in response to watching their homes appreciate in price.

6.2.2 Derivatives

Financial innovation in the new century included derivatives that were designed to limit the risk of investment in MBS. In the rush to embrace

---

[9] See also Financial Crisis Inquiry Commission (2010), "The Mortgage Crisis," Preliminary Staff Report, April 7, p. 8.

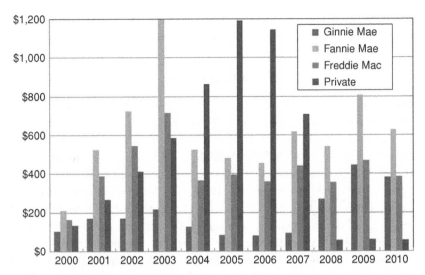

Figure 6.7. MBS issuance by Ginnie Mae, GSE, and Private Label, 2007–2010 ($ billions). *Source:* Government National Mortgage Association (2011). Annual Report, November 7–11, p. 11.

these new "insurance" instruments and exempt them from Securities and Exchange Commission (SEC) registration and margin rules, they escaped outdated collateralization rules. Chapter 7 examines the consequences of these new developments during the course of the bubble and its collapse.

6.3 Sweeping Up the Broken Glass

Although our concern in this chapter is to emphasize and discuss possible initiating events and programs that produced the bubble, the crash and its aftermath are also evident in the charts provided: the decline in lending after 2007 (see Figures 6.1 and 3.3); the increased share of loans taken by the GSE (see Figure 6.2); and the surge in Ginnie Mae's share of MBS (see Figure 6.4). We close the narrative of that government "adventure" with a look at its end-game: Figure 6.7 charts the MBS issued by Fannie Mae, Freddie Mac, Ginnie Mae, and private-label securities in the crash years of 2007 through 2010. The largest issuance is private in 2007 at slightly more than $700 billion, which collapses to slightly more than $50 billion in 2008, 2009, and 2010. Taking up most of the slack is Fannie Mae, followed by Freddie Mac and Ginnie Mae, as the government became the funding agent of last resort for almost all new mortgages – a condition likely to be continued as long as households and banks are stuck in balance sheet disequilibrium.

6.4 Conclusions

In this chapter, we divide the course of the housing bubble into two five-year intervals for examination: from 1997 to 2001, during which the national median price of a home accelerated to its previous inflation-adjusted all-time high; and the period from 2002 to 2006, when the median price surged and then flattened before its collapse into the Great Recession. Recognizing that bubbles are not fundamentally "caused" or driven only by external events and circumstances, we seek first to identify several promising "trigger" developments in both the public and private sectors that either coincided with or preceded the bubble as an "incubation interval."

These events and developments include the bipartisan Taxpayer Relief Act of 1997, which exempted home resales from capital gains taxes. Both the timing of this event and the substantial incentive it provided for the diversion of capital investment into homes combine to make it a prime trigger suspect.

Although there can be no question that the housing bubble excesses were importantly influenced by continuing public subsidy programs – that is, the GSE and Ginnie Mae – these programs had long been providing perverse incentives to stimulate housing. The evidence we provide is consistent with the proposition that to compete with the GSE, the private-label lenders expanded in the riskier segments of the mortgage markets. These risks were camouflaged by the perception that they were hedged by derivative insurance and by the failure of lenders to understand the implications of poor upfront incentives for due-diligence in loan originations. These issues are examined in more detail in Chapter 7.

The CRA's pressure to expand loans in LMI neighborhoods became a new source of potential risk enhancement in the 1990s. As we interpret the evidence and testimony, it was bad policy to use threats of coercion to prod lenders in the absence of better controls for the increased risk. The CRA cannot be absolved of a contributing role in the crisis and neither can it be faulted as a root cause.

In the end, the government's implicit and explicit guarantee programs bore the brunt of the collapse in the value of mortgage debt because of the collapse in underlying housing asset values. Moreover, private mortgages held by the financial sector led to massive intervention by the Federal

Reserve and the U.S. Treasury, which sheltered incumbent investors from facing the failed consequences of their unsound investments (discussed in Chapter 8).

References

Agarwal, Sumit, Efraim Benmelech, Nittai Bergman, and Amit Seru (2013). "Did the Community Reinvestment Act (CRA) Lead to Risky Lending?" National Bureau of Economic Research Working Paper No. 18609.

Avery, Robert B., Neil Bhutta, Kenneth P. Brevoort, and Glenn B. Canner (2011). "The HMDA Data: The Mortgage Market in a Time of Low Interest Rates and Economic Distress." *Federal Reserve Bulletin,* February 15.

Bajaj, Vikas, and David Leonhardt (2008). "Tax Break May Have Helped Cause Housing Bubble." *New York Times,* December 19.

Bernanke, Ben S. (2007). "GSE Portfolios, Systemic Risk, and Affordable Housing." March 6. Available at www.federalreserve.gov/newsevents/speech/bernanke20070306a.htm.

Bhutta, Neil (2009). "GSE Activity and Mortgage Supply in Lower-Income and Minority Neighborhoods: The Effect of the Affordable Housing Goals." Finance and Economics Discussion Series, Divisions of Research & Statistics and Monetary Affairs. Washington, DC: Federal Reserve Board.

Bradsher, Keith (1995). "Republicans Seek a Cutback in Lending Rules for Banks." *New York Times,* March 31.

Business Editors (2002). "Fannie Mae Chairman and CEO Raines Says Bush Administration Housing Budget, Initiatives Will . . . Fuel Housing." Atlanta: Business Wire, February 8.

Federal Housing Finance Agency (2010). Mortgage Market Note 10–2: "The Housing Goals of Fannie Mae and Freddie Mac." February 1. Available at www.fhfa.gov/webfiles/15408/Housing%20Goals%201996-2009%2002-01.pdf.

Federal Housing Finance Agency (2012). "Current Data on Treasury and Federal Reserve Purchase Programs for GSE and Mortgage-Related Securities." January 2. Available at www.fhfa.gov/Default.aspx?Page=77&ListNumber=0&ListYear=2012#Year_2012.

Federal Register, May 4, 1995. "Rules and Regulations." 60, Number 86, pp. 22155–223. Available at www.fdic.gov/regulations/community/community/crapreamb.txt.

Financial Crisis Inquiry Commission (2010). "The Mortgage Crisis." Preliminary Staff Report, April 7.

Gerardi, Kris, Christopher Foote, and Paul Willen (2010). "What Role (if any) Did the Federal Government and the GSEs Have in the Housing Boom?" Real Estate Research, Federal Reserve Bank of Atlanta, April 21.

Ginnie Mae (2009). "Annual Report." U.S. Department of Housing and Urban Development, November 6. Available at www.ginniemae.gov/inside_gnma/company_overview/budget_performance/Annual_Reports/annual_report09.pdf.

Ginnie Mae (2009b). "Report to Congress."

Gjerstad, Steven, and Vernon L. Smith (2009). "Monetary Policy, Credit Extension, and Housing Bubbles: 2008 and 1929", *Critical Review,* 21, pp. 269–300.

Hawke, John D. (1999). "Remarks before the Neighborhood Housing Services of New York." New York, May 5. Available at www.occ.gov/static/news-issuances/news-releases/1999/nr-occ-1999-41.pdf.

Ivry, Bob (2007). "'Deal with Devil' Funded Carrera Crash before Bust (Update3)." *Bloomberg News*, December 18.

Jickling, Mark (2008). "Fannie Mae and Freddie Mac in Conservatorship." Congressional Research Service Report, September 8.

Kroszner, Randall S. (2008). "The CRA and the Recent Mortgage Crisis." Speech given at Federal Reserve Board. Available at www.federalreserve.gov/newsevents/speech/kroszner20081203a.htm#fn4#fn4.

Labaton, Stephen (1999). "Agreement Reached on Overhaul of U.S. Financial System." *New York Times*, October 23. Available at http://partners.nytimes.com/library/financial/102399banks-congress.html.

Lindsey, Lawrence B. (2009). "The CRA as a Means to Provide Public Goods." Federal Reserve Bank of San Francisco. Available at www.frbsf.org/community-development/publications/community-development-investment-review/2009/february/cra-community-reinvestment-act-public-goods.

Litan, Robert E., Nicolas P. Retsinas, Eric S. Belsky, and Susan White Haag (2000). "The Community Reinvestment Act after Financial Modernization: A Baseline Report." U.S. Department of the Treasury, April. Available at www.treas.gov/press/releases/docs/crareport.pdf.

Litan, Robert E., Nicolas P. Retsinas, Eric S. Belsky, Gary Fauth, Maureen Kennedy, and Paul Leonard. (2001). "The Community Reinvestment Act after Financial Modernization: A Final Report." U.S. Department of the Treasury, January. Available at http://bflo-housing.wikispaces.com/file/view/CRA+after+Financial+Modernization.pdf.

Rosenthal, Andrew (1989). "Bush Offers Housing Plan to Aid Poor, Homeless and New Buyers." *New York Times*, November 11.

Shan, Hui (2008). "The Effect of Capital Gains Taxation on Home Sales: Evidence from the Taxpayer Relief Act of 1997." Finance and Economic Discussion Series 2008–53, Board of Governors of the Federal Reserve System.

Smith, Vernon L. (2007). "We Have Met the Enemy, and He Is Us." AEI-Brookings Joint Center Policy Matters, Paper 07–32, December 20.

U.S. Government Accountability Office (GAO) (2009). "Analysis of Options for Revising the Housing Enterprises' Long-Term Structures." Report to Congressional Committees, GAO-09–782, September. Available at www.gao.gov/assets/300/295025.pdf.

7

The Bubble Bursts

Subprime Mortgages, Derivatives, and Banking Collapse

The parties to these kinds of contract are largely sophisticated financial institutions that would appear to be eminently capable of protecting themselves from fraud and counterparty insolvencies.
– Lawrence Summers, Congressional testimony, July 30, 1998

With respect to their safety, derivatives, for the most part, are traded among very sophisticated financial institutions and individuals who have considerable incentive to understand them and to use them properly. The Federal Reserve's responsibility is to make sure that the institutions it regulates have good systems and good procedures for ensuring that their derivatives portfolios are well managed and do not create excessive risk in their institutions.
– Ben Bernanke, Senate confirmation hearings, November 15, 2005

We were on the March 22 call with Fitch regarding the subprime securitization market's difficulties. My associate asked several questions. "What are the key drivers of your rating model?" They responded, FICO scores and home price appreciation (HPA) of low single digit (LSD) or mid single digit (MSD), as HPA has been for the past fifty years. My associate then asked, "What if HPA was flat for an extended period of time?" They responded that their model would start to break down. He then asked, "What if HPA were to decline 1 percent to 2 percent for an extended period of time?" He then asked, "With 2 percent depreciation, how far up the rating's scale would it harm?" They responded that it might go as high as the AA or AAA tranches.
– Robert Rodriguez, June 28, 2007

Every time there's been a fire, these guys [derivatives traders] have been around it.
– Nicholas Brady (Lowenstein, 2000, p. 105)

The collapse of the housing finance market is in many ways the most fascinating – and certainly the most painful – part of the story of the bubble's unraveling. In previous chapters, we present a brief primer on the private mortgage market as it developed following the popular initiatives of the Clinton and Bush administrations to expand homeownership and eliminate the capital gains tax (capped at $500,000 for each sale) on homes, the policy actions of government sponsored enterprises (GSE), the continuing large inflows of foreign capital, and the unprecedented (at the time) monetary ease of 2002–2004. The focus now turns to the private housing-mortgage market institutions that served to amplify the housing price run-up, particularly in the period after 2001.

7.1 Financial "Innovations" in the Mortgage Market: Mortgage-Backed Securities and Credit Default Swaps

The private sector originators of the loans that were bundled into securities included Countrywide, Indymac, and Washington Mutual, all of which ended in bankruptcy or were distress buyouts.[1] Commercial banks (including their nondepository investment bank partners) such as Citibank and Bank of America received substantial balance sheet support from the U.S. Treasury and the Federal Reserve System after September 2008, but even with this support, they continued into 2012 and 2013 to exhibit weak balance sheets as signaled by their low share-price-to-book-value ratios. The private-sector loans did not have the explicit guarantees of the government; however, because these institutions were perceived as "too big to fail," a large fraction of the loans were acquired at face value by the Federal Reserve through actions that were never thoroughly analyzed.[2] Hence, the true risks

---

[1] Countrywide, a mortgage origination company was bought on July 1, 2008, for $2.5 billion by Bank of America (BAC) after the mortgage market collapsed. Its only asset was its "expertise" in loan originations, which had become worthless. By the fourth anniversary of the purchase, it had led BAC to incur costs of " . . . more than $40 billion in real-estate losses, legal expenses and settlements with state and federal agencies, according to people close to the bank" (Fitzpatrick, 2012). For the Washington Mutual failure, see Bair (2012, pp. 75–8); for the Indymac failure, see Bair (2012, pp. 79–82). The latter cost the FDIC, through deposit guarantees, "more than $7 billion, by far the most expensive bank failure for us of the crisis" (p. 80). A significant "haircut" had to be given their uninsured deposits of some $1 billion. As chairperson of the FDIC, Bair (2012, p. 75) reported that on March 26, 2008, she met with other banking agencies to review thirteen banks with the largest threat of failure: Washington Mutual topped this list with assets of $300 billion. Ultimately, its assets and deposits were sold as an "open bank unassisted transaction" (i.e., multiple bidders competing to acquire these assets) to JPMorgan for $1.8 billion. All losses were borne by shareholders and bondholders at no cost to the government.

[2] As reported by Sheila Bair, who was in attendance at the meeting of the leading Washington, DC, government policy makers and the nine leading private banking and financial institutions that were to be rescued: "All the banks survived; indeed, the following year, their executives were paying themselves fat bonuses again. In retrospect, the mammoth assistance to those big institutions seemed like overkill. I never saw a good analysis to back it up. But that was a big part of the problem: lack of information" (Bair, 2012, p. 6).

were revealed to be more significant than perceived by any of the participants. Although we see clearly in retrospect that risks had steadily accumulated in financial institutions, the recognition first in private financial markets and then in the financial and government policy communities, was sudden and struck panic into market participants if not also the monetary authorities. As indicated in Chapter 6, we believe that the financial excesses were partly motivated by the need to compete effectively with the GSEs. Although the "innovations" in financial instruments were at the center of the financial meltdown and the housing market bubble, they have merits along with serious flaws. If those flaws are to be corrected, it is important to understand the difference between fundamental incentive failures and secondary responses that were derived from the failures.

Part of that institutional development came in the form of the issuance of mortgage-backed securities (MBS) by commercial banks and investment banks, such as Bear Stearns (which was rescued by the government in the belief that the action would avoid a financial meltdown) and Lehman Brothers (which was allowed to fail).

Although MBS had been used in the private sector,[3] we note that Ginnie Mae has the dubious distinction of claiming credit for being the first to use these instruments in their current form – an ominous expression of pride in the light of subsequent events:

Forty years ago, President Lyndon B. Johnson signed the Housing Bill of 1968 establishing Ginnie Mae. The explicit full faith and credit guarantee of the U.S. Government for timely payment of principal and interest on Ginnie Mae mortgage-backed securities (MBS) attracts global investors, allowing Ginnie Mae to provide liquidity and remain a viable outlet for mortgage lenders in the secondary market. Even in the current credit crisis, Ginnie Mae remains a source of stability in the market. Since the time that Ginnie Mae created the very first MBS in 1970 and revolutionized the housing finance industry, it has... guaranteed approximately $2.9 trillion in MBS.[4]

The other part of the innovation was the development of the credit default swap (CDS) market. These instruments were perceived as the hedging

---

[3] Mortgage bonds have been used to pool capital for real estate ventures since at least 1901. Boysen (1931) provided an interesting history of real estate bonds, which he thought might indicate their contribution to real estate troubles in the Depression. He concluded that "In summing up the experiences of the last two years, we are obliged to come to the conclusion that the majority of real estate bond issues, as previously made, cannot stand adversity." This may understate the problem because the bonds were an instrument in the original construction of real estate assets in excess of the growth in income.

[4] See "Ginnie Mae Report to Congress; Fiscal Year 2008." U.S. Department of Housing and Urban Development, November 7, 2008, p. 1.

linchpin – that is, default "insurance" – supporting the private MBS market that internationalized the credit financing of local residential housing. It was the collapse in the Markit ABX index for AAA rated securities in July 2007 that led quickly to the collapse of the market for the loans written by many subprime lenders, as well as a collapse in the market for the structured MBS into which these loans were gathered by investment banks. CDS instruments enjoyed "exempt status," constituting a vast, publicly unregistered and uncollateralized market as derivative securities that became prominent in the mortgage market expansion after 2001.

As an information vehicle, the CDS market can be interpreted as an "early-warning" signal for distress in the MBS market when the ABX index for BBB – rated securities declined sharply beginning in February 2007, six months before the first credit-market seizure in August 2007 and eighteen months before the financial meltdown.[5] (The ABX index for AAA rated securities declined in July 2007, just three weeks before the credit-market seizure.) The signal was ignored until it spread to the AAA-rated index. We hasten to add, however, that there were much earlier warning signals that were summarily ignored by financial markets and all of the policy experts. By mid-year 2007, (1) new housing construction expenditures had declined for five quarters (see Chapter 3, Figure 3.8); (2) the flow of mortgage funds had fallen considerably beginning in Q2 2006 (see Chapter 3, Figure 3.3); and (3) new home unit sales had declined 35 percent during the previous seven quarters (see Chapter 3, Figure 3.2). Moreover, these patterns of decline were typical of post-war recessions and the Depression, although it is evident that they were not part of the traditional Federal Reserve economic or macroeconomic thinking and modeling.

The CDS market grew from only $631.5 billion in notional value in the first half of 2001 to more than $62.1 trillion in notional value in the second half of 2007.[6] How could such a large market – exploding a hundred-fold in six years – develop and accumulate so much risk without participants in that market becoming anxious about their exposure and taking action to reduce their risk? Based on this chapter's opening quotations from Summers at the U.S. Treasury (1998) and the Federal Reserve chairman (2005), it is evident that the industry's failed perception of risk (captured in the quote about

---

[5] The CDS market, however, did not function as effectively as an early-warning mechanism as did many other "information markets" or "prediction markets," such as the IEM or InTrade, for reasons that we explore later in this chapter.

[6] The International Swaps and Derivatives Association publishes summary data on outstanding derivatives contracts, available at www.isda.org/statistics/pdf/ISDA-Market-Survey-historical-data.pdf.

the Fitch ratings by Rodriguez 2007) was widely shared and included the leading and most prominent public-policy experts. Summers was arguing for legislation that would maintain the exempt status of CDS, and Treasury ensured that the exemption would be strengthened with its support of the Commodity Futures Modernization Act (CFMA) of 2000. The persistence of that mindset is clear: Five years later, Bernanke was still defending derivatives contracts because he believed they did not create excessive risk.

The CDS market provided a vehicle whereby investors in the MBS market could hedge their risk of exposure to default on payment of interest and principal by household borrowers. MBS investor-buyers, however, misperceived the CDS hedge as "insuring" against mortgage payment defaults. We now ask why CDS instruments did not constitute insurance in the sense in which one insures against the risk of death or property loss due to fire, weather, and other natural hazards. Our answer comes in two parts: (1) the first is a general question concerning the incentive problems inherent in insuring against business risk and relates not to the CDS but rather to the elements that went into the creation of the MBS; and (2) the second relates to specific incentive flaws in CDS instruments.

7.2 Can You Insure Against Business Risk of Loss?

Essentially, the answer to this question is "no,"[7] which is why corporate risk of loss, as well as the rewards from profit, falls on equity shareholders – the claimants of last resort – who ultimately bear any risk of loss. Profitability or loss arises directly from the business decisions of managers, not only from external acts of nature. Applied to mortgage loans, this potential loss arises if the household as a firm fails "profitability" – that is, is unable to earn an income sufficient to meet its obligations.

In his classic work, Knight (1921) distinguished between insurable risks (based on "objective probability calculus") and uncertainty, which Knight viewed as the core of business-decision risk and beyond such a calculus. Developments in probability theory challenged Knight's distinction between risk and uncertainty, but the essence of his message remained intact. That essence was stated succinctly by Buchanan (1968, p. 425), as follows:

The fact remains . . . that there exist certain uninsurable uncertainties in the institutional environment of modern business operation. Moreover, the distinction retains

---

[7] We do not digress on the abstract solution based on Arrow-Debreu securities that presuppose with certainty that a decision maker can exhaustively specify and observe the finite set of all possible contingent events on which the profitability of an investment can depend.

its formal validity, despite modern notions of probability, when it is recognized that insurance against the possibility of making wrong decisions removes all content from decision itself... As Knight quite explicitly stated in this early work, "where there is no genuine uncertainty there are no decisions."

Knight's lesson becomes particularly relevant when we use it to think about the incentive problems of the mortgage originators who exposed the ultimate lenders to excessive and unknown risks because they did not share enough of the default risk to perform due diligence on the mortgages they issued. Someone in the supply chain connecting the primary borrower to the final investor in MBS must perform this due diligence, and no one should be better positioned than the local originator that – traditionally, at least – knew the community and its people.[8] Knight would not have been surprised to learn that "a funny thing happened" when the financing of local mortgages went national (and international) and originators were paid upfront origination fees. That is, mortgage-origination incentives were compromised because lender due diligence was no longer what it had been when uncertainty was borne by local-lender judgments based on local knowledge after an investigation of a borrower's circumstances. The ultimate lender was far removed from the mortgage originator, whose upfront reward was earned by making the loan, thereby removing "all content" from the risky mortgage origination decision process.[9]

---

[8] Bair (2012, pp. 59–60) observed that losses on foreclosed property sales routinely run 40 to 50 percent of the unpaid principal balance on the loan and are much higher when the borrower owes much more than the property is worth. Therefore, modifying the loan such that it will keep the borrower in the property meeting reduced payments is far preferable to foreclosure – an option still available if the borrower defaults on the modified loan. Bair noted perceptively that commercial real estate loan markets performed better than household mortgage markets when the bubble collapsed because many of these loans were originated and held by community banks "[t]hat have worked with their commercial borrowers to restructure the loans, under guidelines issued by the regulators."

[9] Rodriguez (2007) succinctly and presciently summarized the (incentive incompatibility) flaws in the mortgage origination process before the full impact of the collapse had been felt: "We are of the opinion that the distancing of the borrower from the lender has contributed to the development of lax underwriting standards. Each participant, in the securitization/origination process, takes their ounce of payment, but no one truly worries about the underlying credit quality since the loan will be sold. Furthermore, most participants are compensated on volume and not quality of loan originated. In our opinion, 'a rolling loan gathers no loss.' Possibly, with so many subprime originators failing because of loan put-backs to them, some degree of underwriting discipline will return to the market; however, with so many types of loan originators operating outside of the regulatory system with minimal capital, it is far better to originate a loan, capture the fee, and then get out of Dodge, should the business go bad. One can always return another day." The impact of this fiasco has been so severe that many of the key participants in the mortgage origination process will not "return another day," yet many of these

A Knightian solution to this incentive compatibility problem would require the originator's reward for closing a loan to bear the business uncertainty of a mortgage default over the life of the loan. The problem that any new institutional incentive arrangements had to solve was being sure that the transactions cost – legal, monitoring, and disciplining – did not exceed the social gains from the creation of a national and international mortgage market that securitization offers.[10] The moral hazard of this design failure was not in the models used by the rating agencies – they used historical data – but the applicability of that data subsequently changed with the erosion of due-diligence incentives as mortgage origination became increasingly separated from the lenders.

The rapid surge in lending, however, was a principle reason that house prices throughout the decade of 1997–2006 deviated from the historical pattern; therefore, any use of the historical house price pattern to justify additional lending was a serious mistake. The price pattern reflected a history that was changed by the fact that it was being used to justify increased lending. This is precisely the type of process that helps to generate self-reinforcing expectations of rising prices. Assuming that historical default rates would hold when there was a significant increase in lending and house prices assumes, in effect, that default rates are independent of the level of mortgage finance and the path of price appreciation. However, such a large increase in mortgage lending would almost surely lead to a reduction of credit quality, and the extreme price increases were, at the same time, requiring payments that absorbed a larger fraction of household income. Both of these effects were sure to increase default rates eventually.

Successful institutional innovations come neither easily nor quickly, and the pathway can be expected to be strewn with the "litter" of trial-and-error learning and modification in the midst of failures. The MBS–CDS nexus has been a particularly costly social experiment.[11]

---

people, such as Angelo Mozzilo (Countrywide), Richard Fuld (Lehman Brothers), and Joe Cassano (AIG Financial Products) remain extremely wealthy to this day, whereas the economy languishes as a result of a calamity to which they contributed heavily. One of the most egregious examples of the breakdown of underwriting standards was Quick Loan Funding. Ivry (2007) reported that Daniel Sadek, founder of Quick Loan Funding, boasted that "I never wrote a loan that Wall Street wouldn't buy."

[10] Coase (1960) made this general point in other contexts.

[11] Our emphasis is on the incentive incompatibility of upfront mortgage origination fees that "fanned the flames" of the bubble, but other accumulated incentive incompatibilities plagued the process of loan restructuring in the aftermath of the bubble's crash. Bair (2012, pp. 60–2) referred to two that were especially troublesome. (1) Mortgage servicers were paid a flat fee for collecting the mortgage payments and passing them through to investors.

7.3 Flaws at the Center of CDS Instruments

The second part of our answer – why the CDS failed to insure mortgage investment risk – is the main focus in this section. There are two principle problems with the way derivative contracts were used. First, those who bet in favor of the MBS by selling a CDS reaped rewards for years while the housing market continued to rise. Anyone who sold one of these "insurance" contracts received the upfront cost of the contract from the buyer and, in addition, regular premiums. Morgenson (2008) describes the benefits reaped by AIG Financial Products (AIG F.P.), which wrote about $441 billion in CDS on MBS. Morgenson notes that this small division, which had only 377 employees in 2008, received between $423 million and $616 million in compensation each year between 2001 and 2007. In 2005, the revenue of AIG F.P. reached $3.26 billion and its profit margin reached 83 percent; in that year, it contributed 17.5 percent of the total profit of all of AIG, with its 116,000 employees. Each employee of AIG F.P. contributed about $7.2 million to the profit of the firm; each employee of AIG outside AIG F.P. contributed about $110,000 to firm profit. Whereas the bet in favor of MBS was attractive to those who could not see the risk, or who could personally lock in great rewards before their company collapsed, the demands of investors for short-term performance by fund managers made the contrarian bet a difficult sell. Lewis (2010) tells the stories of many fund managers whose investors were very reluctant to bet against the housing market or who lost their nerve and their patience as the costs of an uncertain gamble accumulated. The asymmetry between the two sides of the bet implies that those who view the market favorably can enter the market at almost any scale, whereas those who want to bet against it have to cajole their investors for capital. This asymmetric incentive is related to the other problem with CDS as an information market. If the "insurers" had been required to post collateral, then they would have tied up some of their capital, which would have raised the cost of each CDS issued. At AIG, with $441 billion in CDS on MBS – and ultimately about $50 billion

They had no incentive to work with a delinquent borrower to modify the loan, and they were contractually required to continue to advance mortgage payments to the investors. However, in foreclosure, a servicer would be paid off the top of the sale proceeds, leading him to prefer foreclosure to loan modification no matter how more efficient it might be. (2) Investors in the senior (i.e., AAA rated) tranch of MBS shared any reduced income from loan modification with holders of the subordinate tranches but, in foreclosure, they had strict priority over the subordinates. Consequently, they were well incentivized to prefer foreclosure over loan modification regardless of the efficiency advantages of the latter.

in losses on those contracts – the incentives would have been different had they been required to set aside 5 or 10 percent of their insured value in reserves. The firms that issued the CDS "insurance" would almost surely have scrutinized the loans in the MBS more carefully, which would have resulted in stricter underwriting standards among loan originators. CDS contracts were routinely not collateralized and the buyer was exposed to the prospect that the CDS seller would not be able to deliver on the default contract obligation. For example, if AIG was the seller, performance in the event of default depended on the liquidity and solvency of AIG – a time-variable characteristic resulting from a host of other AIG business decisions and fortunes – with no dedicated, relatively liquid reserves for the CDS it had written. CDS sellers, comfortably confident that house prices would not fall, did not want to reduce their investment returns by immobilizing funds in CDS collateral. These "sophisticated investors" in what are plainly information market instruments – that is, side bets on a credit default event – do not want to incur the opportunity cost of holding reserves against them in the unlikely "tail probability" event that the reserves will be needed to cover losses. The plain fact is that the event occurred and the Fed and Treasury intervened – that is, bought MBS at face value – using public reserves (against future central bank or taxpayer liability) to substitute for the missing private reserves. Private investors had enjoyed the higher returns from being fully invested and kept the profits, and the tail cost was shifted to the public's account (i.e., "socialized") (see Chapter 8).

Hence, calling a CDS contract "insurance" is an abuse of ordinary language; insurance companies must hold reserves against storms or other hazards to collateralize their obligations to insured buyers. Moreover, there is a historical database allowing storm probabilities, as external acts of nature, to be estimated and that guides the risk calculation in these contracts. The buyer of storm insurance is not exposed to the same type of business counterparty risk, generated by the internal decisions and actions that characterize the firms that write CDS contracts.

It also may be helpful in understanding the hazards of the exempt-status CDS contract and its market to see how it has been avoided elsewhere in financial markets: Stock brokers have long successfully hedged their loan risk when customers buy securities on margin. Brokers not only require collateral to be posted to the account in the form of the customer's portfolio of securities held in the name of the broker; they also value that collateral based on daily mark-to-market prices. The broker's advance of credit to the customer is literally a "call" loan empowering him or her to sell the customer's position to insure recovery of the loan amount. This is why the loss burden of stock market crashes is borne directly by investors with minimal damage to bank balance sheets. As stock prices fall, margin debt is continuously adjusted downward, in step with falling asset values. The emergent contract provisions governing margin requirements and mark-to-market call loan rules have provided an institution through which the risk in such loans is strictly confined to the contracting parties and does not directly undermine bank balance sheets. That tradition later became codified under regulation T by the Federal Reserve System pursuant to the Securities Exchange Act of 1934 (see Chapter 8).

To the extent that classes of securities (i.e., derivatives) and classes of investors (i.e., hedge funds and private equity funds) have emerged to limit downside risk and are exempt from these restrictions, the financial system has been gradually more and more exposed to these risks and made them "systemic."

Information markets such as political stock markets are examples in which side-bet contracts are traded; however, unlike CDS markets, they were fully collateralized. Experimental economists at the University of Iowa developed the Iowa Electronic Market (IEM), which enables the first information market to be made in shares on the popular vote outcome in the 1988 presidential election.[12] This market and the hundreds of political and other event-contingent information markets run since 1988 provide a means by which individuals can make side bets on the proportion of the popular vote that will be obtained by each candidate. The IEM today also runs "winner-take-all" markets in contracts on election outcomes and the federal funds rate. Formally, these side bets on the occurrence of an uncertain event are similar to a CDS contract except that they are (1) standardized bets identical for all traders, and (2) exchange traded on the IEM and fully (i.e., 100 percent margin) collateralized by cash deposits to cover all contract liabilities. The organizers of these markets were well motivated to require traders to collateralize their positions for the same reason that stock, commodity, and options exchanges require it.

7.4 The Gathering Storm and the Collapse of the CDS, MBS, and Loan Origination Markets

In 2006, the mortgage market collapse had not yet begun, but the warning signs were there. The median price of existing homes fell from $230,000 in July to $217,300 in November 2006. By the beginning of 2007, the

[12] See, for example, Forsythe et al. (1992).

Case-Shiller U.S. National Home Price Indices for Boston and San Diego had been falling for more than a year; the indices for San Francisco and Washington, DC, had been falling for six months. Prices were also falling in thirteen of the other sixteen cities in the Case-Shiller Home Price Index. Only the housing markets in Miami, Seattle, and Portland had not turned down by December 2006.

Measures of serious mortgage delinquency spiked noticeably during the same period, especially for subprime ARM loans. In Q2 2006, 6.52 percent of these loans were seriously delinquent; by Q3 2006, the figure was 7.72 percent; and by Q4 2006, it reached 9.16 percent.[13] Kelly (2007) related how Goldman Sachs avoided the fate of many of the other investment banks. In January 2006, a small group in Goldman's mortgage department – that is, the structured-products trading group – began trading Markit ABX CDS indices. In December 2006, Goldman's CFO, David Viniar, pushed these traders to hedge the firm's long positions in MBS with ABX indices. They loaded up on an index called ABX-HE-BBB–2006–2. This asset, which started trading in July 2006, is tied to the performance of subordinate (i.e., BBB–rated) tranches of an index of twenty MBS issued in the first half of 2006. When the price of an ABX index falls, the cost of insuring MBS rises. The price of an ABX index approximately equals the expected percentage payoff on the twenty MBS in the index. If the index stands at 100, the aggregated market belief is that there will be no losses at all. If it falls to 90, the market believes that losses on the security will be 10 percent. However, this is only an approximation because a Markit ABX index also has a coupon, which is an annual premium. For the ABX-HE-BBB–2006–2 issue, the coupon was 242 basis points; thus, insuring $10 million of BBB–rated MBS cost $242,000 per year when the index was first issued. Every price drop of one unit below the par value of 100 adds an increment of $100,000 to the cost of $10 million of insurance.

Goldman Sachs anticipated large losses on these assets and began to purchase insurance (with Markit ABX CDS indices) when their prices reflected market expectations of losses that were well below the losses that Goldman expected.[14] As the prices of ABX derivatives collapsed, the cost of insuring

---

[13] These figures on serious delinquency (defined as mortgage payments more than ninety days past due plus foreclosures in process) are taken from the Q3 2006 and Q4 2006 National Delinquency Survey published by the National Association of Realtors.

[14] Goldman Sachs was not the only firm that made extensive bets against the subprime market. Pittman (2007) recounted the steps that J. Kyle Bass at Hayman Capital Partners followed to trace down the source of some of the worst subprime loans – which he found at Daniel Sadek's mortgage "chop shop," Quick Loan Funding, Inc. – and bet against them with

new MBS skyrocketed. Goldman Sachs had loaded up on these derivatives – that is, it had increased its insurance against declines in the underlying value of its MBS – between early December 2006 and late February 2007, as the price dropped from 97.70 on December 4 to less than 64 by February 27. Normally, buying an asset with a falling price is not a good idea, but the ABX index pays off when MBS suffer losses. At a price of 97.70, it cost $230,000 plus the annual premium of $242,000 to insure $10 million of BBB– rated tranches; at a price of 64, the same insurance cost $3.6 million (plus the same annual premium). By getting into this market early, Goldman Sachs had obtained the insurance for a much lower fixed cost.

The insurance premiums on new residential mortgage-backed securi-ties (RMBS) skyrocketed, which precipitated a rapid decline in mortgage financing from these securities. In 2006, $483 billion in new subprime MBS was issued; by Q4 2007, the figure had fallen to $11.9 billion.[15] Other mea-sures of new loan originations were falling at the same time. By 2006, the characteristics and performance of many of these securities were extremely poor. For example, on August 17, 2006, Goldman Sachs issued a security (i.e., GSAMP Trust 2006-S5), which consisted of 5,321 second-lien mort-gages with a principal balance of $338,442,653. The loan-to-value ratio on the pool was 98.7 percent, the average FICO score of the borrowers was 666, and the average loan term remaining on the second-lien mortgages at the time the security was issued was 25.25 years.[16] The two top tranches of the bond, A1 and A2, were rated AAA by Moody's and by Standard & Poor, and these tranches amounted to $231,571,000. Thirty-nine days later, in the September 25, 2006, Form 10-D distribution report filed with the SEC, $26,129,089 of the loan pool was delinquent. By the end of 2006, more than $40 million was delinquent. In September 2008, Standard & Poor estimated that total losses on GSAMP Trust 2006-S5 would reach 68 percent; losses were expected to dig deep into the AAA tranches. SEC filings are replete with comparable loan pools that started to stink as soon as they were issued. When that happened, important links in the chain from securitization back toward origination buckled.

---

synthetic collateralized debt obligations. Lewis (2009) told a similar story for FrontPoint Partners (with his characteristically compelling exposition). Weiss (2009) described the bets made by John Paulson against both subprime mortgages and the firms that wrote them.

[15] These figures are taken from *Inside Mortgage Finance* (2008, Vol. II, pp. 149–50).

[16] Data on the characteristics of loans in GSAMP Trust 2006-S5 are drawn from SEC form FWP filing dated August 26, 2006, in the Edgar system, available at http://edgar.secdatabase .com/956/88237706002830/filing-main.htm.

Consequently, as the liquidity that generated the housing market bubble evaporated, new buyers disappeared, housing prices declined, and subprime and ARM delinquencies rose. Therefore, Goldman Sachs – acting on the belief that the housing market was headed for trouble – bought more insurance on MBS. This raised the price of insurance on these securities, which decreased the flow of capital to lenders and mortgages to households.[17] The actions of firms like Goldman Sachs were criticized for hastening the trouble that they anticipated and making money from the economic collapse. However, such actions to "short" the market served to stanch the hemorrhaging of capital into this destructive housing market bubble. Of course, home buyers, builders, loan originators, banks, real estate agents, MBS investors, and even the insurers of MBS – every node in the supply chain – were making money betting on increasing house prices, and critics were few, although the euphoria could not be sustained. That euphoria made it all the riskier to bet against the MBS market. If counterbets were to pay off, it was not enough to see that the market was overvalued – the timing had to be right; otherwise, the cost of carrying the short position would not be profitable. The long gravity-defying upswing in home prices meant that betting against it at any particular point in time was not a "slam dunk."

Many firms with major exposure to subprime and ARM RMBS that failed to notice the weakness in the housing market – or that noticed the developing signs of weakness but failed to balance their exposure to it – were drawn into the undertow from the collapsing housing market. Bear Stearns, Lehman Brothers, Merrill Lynch, AIG, Citigroup, Washington Mutual, and Wachovia had all been absorbed into other firms on the brink of collapse, failed, or been rescued by the federal government as a result of their exposure to the mortgage crisis.[18]

---

[17] By betting against the market, Goldman Sachs, Hayman Capital Partners, FrontPoint Partners, and Paulson & Co. made tens of billions of dollars, but their bets drove up the cost of insurance on new MBS to a level that deterred the flow of capital into these securities.

[18] Lehman Brothers went into bankruptcy. Bear Stearns, Merrill, and Wachovia were all taken over by other firms in the face of imminent collapse. Washington Mutual was seized by the Office of Thrift Supervision and placed into receivership with the FDIC in late September, filed for bankruptcy, and had major assets taken over by JPMorgan Chase. The latter also prevailed in competitive bidding in taking over Wachovia. Bair (2012, ch. 8), in her fascinating chapter titled "The Wachovia Blindside," discussed the internal pressure put on her agency (i.e., the FDIC) to provide sufficient guarantees (of depositors and bondholders) to enable Citibank to acquire Wachovia, whereas the lower offer from JPMorgan Chase was without government help.

As reported in our *Critical Review* article, beginning in late 2005 AIG Financial Products (F.P.) had discontinued writing CDSs on RMBS, also noting that "curiously, AIG saw the problems more than a year before Goldman Sachs, but did nothing during an eighteen-month period when they could have taken steps to reduce their exposure."[19] Lewis (2009) provided a fascinating "inside view" of AIG that resolves the curiosity only by introducing another curiosity, which ties back to the enigma posed in Chapter 2: the mystery, documented in the many laboratory asset market studies, of why intelligent people get caught up in self-reinforcing expectations of rising prices. Thus, according to Lewis (2009) (see also the quotation in Chapter 2):

Joe Cassano (former head of the AIG Financial Products unit) agreed to meet with all the big Wall Street firms and discuss the logic of their deals – to investigate how a bunch of shaky loans could be transformed into AAA-rated bonds. Together with Park[20] and a few others, Cassano set out on a series of meetings with Morgan Stanley, Goldman Sachs, and the rest – all of whom argued how unlikely it was for housing prices to fall all at once. "They all said the same thing,"[21] says one of the traders present. "They'd go back to historical real-estate prices over sixty years and say they had never fallen all at once." (The lone exception, he said, was Goldman Sachs. Two months after their meeting with the investment bank, one of the AIG F.P. traders bumped into the Goldman guy who had defended the bonds, who said, "Between you and me, you're right. These things are going to blow up.") The AIG F.P. executives present were shocked by how little actual thought or analysis seemed to underpin the subprime-mortgage machine: it was simply a bet that U.S. home prices would never fall. Once he understood this, Joe Cassano actually changed

---

[19] See Gjerstad and Smith (2009, footnote 10).
[20] Gene Park was an employee in the AIG F.P. Connecticut office who "put two and two together and guessed that the nature of these piles of consumer loans insured by AIG F.P. was changing, that they contained a lot more subprime mortgages than anyone knew, and that if U.S. homeowners began to default in sharply greater numbers AIG didn't have anywhere near the capital required to cover the losses" (Lewis, 2009, p. 8).
[21] This belief seems also to have led to actions that prevented all of the participants from seeking accurate information on the extent of the preponderance of subprime loans in their portfolio: First, "Park decided to examine more closely the loans that AIG F.P. had insured. He suspected Joe Cassano didn't understand what he had done, but even so Park was shocked by the magnitude of the misunderstanding: these piles of consumer loans were now 95 percent U.S. subprime mortgages. Park then conducted a little survey, asking the people around AIG F.P. most directly involved in insuring them how much subprime was in them. He asked Gary Gorton, a Yale professor who had helped build the model Cassano used to price the credit-default swaps. Gorton guessed that the piles were no more than 10 percent subprime. He asked a risk analyst in London, who guessed 20 percent. He asked Al Frost, who had no clue, but then, his job was to sell, not to trade. 'None of them knew,' says one trader. Which, in retrospect, sounds incredible. But an entire financial system was premised on their not knowing – and paying them for their talent!" (Lewis, 2009, p. 10).

his mind. He agreed with Gene Park: AIG F.P. shouldn't insure any more of these deals. And at the time it didn't really seem like all that big of an issue. AIG F.P. was generating around $2 billion a year in profits. At the peak, the entire credit-default-swap business contributed only $180 million of that.

Therefore, Goldman Sachs was simply an exception in acting aggressively to short the CDS market "herd."[22] AIG merely stopped writing new CDS contracts, and Lewis (2009, p. 11) notes that: The big Wall Street firms solved the problem by taking the risk themselves. The hundreds of billions of dollars in subprime losses suffered by Merrill Lynch, Morgan Stanley, Lehman Brothers, Bear Stearns, and the others were hundreds of billions in losses that might otherwise have been suffered by AIG F.P. Unwilling to take the risk of subprime-mortgage bonds in 2004 and 2005, the Wall Street firms swallowed the risk in 2006 and 2007.

Yes, these actions can be described as "irrational" or less euphemistically as "stupid," but it was what otherwise intelligent real people actually were doing.[23] Here were the "largely sophisticated financial institutions that would appear to be eminently capable of protecting themselves" (Summers, 1998). The problem was not a lack of transparency. Anyone could as easily have done what Park did and quickly learned from the data that MBS portfolios had become saturated with subprimes. No training in structured finance is required to solve this problem. The SEC filings (described in footnote 18) indicate the credit characteristics of the borrowers, the locations of the properties, the amounts loaned, and other relevant information needed

---

[22] However, the quotation suggests that Goldman Sachs probably was suspicious that the CDS market was in trouble well before it acted in December 2006. This likely reflects the simple fact that believing correctly that a market is in trouble is not alone sufficient to profit from it. Good timing also is needed. Shorting too soon lengthens the cost of holding the position until it yields a payoff. Goldman shorted in December 2006 and a decline in prices in the lower-rated tranches of the Markit ABX CDS index began in January 2007.

[23] People were telling stories about housing prices not falling that applied only to their home mortgage CDS "insurance," not to their consumer credit loans. Thus, Lewis (2009, p. 9) also reported that early in the 2000s, Wall Street firms began "to apply technology that had been dreamed up to redistribute corporate credit risk to *consumer* credit risk. The banks that used AIG F.P. to insure piles of loans to IBM and G.E. now came to it to insure much messier piles that included credit-card debt, student loans, auto loans, prime mortgages, and just about anything else that generated a cash flow. 'The problem,' as one trader puts it, 'is that something else came along that we thought was the same thing as what we'd been doing.' Because there were many different sorts of loans, to different sorts of people, the logic applied to corporate credit seemed to apply to this new pile of debt: it was sufficiently diverse that it was unlikely to all go bad at once. But then, these piles, at least at first, contained almost no subprime-mortgage loans." Apparently, the belief was that *credit performance of all kinds* would not suffer a reversal, not only that the housing-mortgage market would not reverse.

to determine the risks. The "Goldman guy" got it; Gene Park figured it out; even Cassano understood. This is a powerful "real world" illustration of the kind of market myopia that can infect asset trading and perpetuate the perception that a thing must surely be "worth" the price at which it trades. We recall the lessons from Chapter 2 – the contrast in behavior between the flow markets for perishables and the markets for assets. Perishable markets require almost no transparency because of each participant's repeat experience, whereas experimentalists discovered quite unexpectedly that asset markets are riddled with bubble propensities even with complete transparency, provided only that there was easy money or cash available or flowing in. Moreover, the uncertainty of when the momentum will stop is so great that, although knowing the facts as Park did might engender caution, it was not sufficient to yield a contrarian profit unless the timing was right. "Timing" means knowing *when* others will know what you have figured out and that they are about to act on that knowledge in numbers sufficient to turn the market around.

Returning to our larger theme concerning how the crisis unfolded, as of February 2007, the mortgage market was not yet in free-fall: Insurance on the AAA rated tranches of RMBS remained inexpensive. At the end of February, the cost of $10 million of insurance on the AAA rated portion of an index of RMBS issued in the first half of 2006 was only $68,000 (plus a $9,000 annual premium). It is true that significant concerns had emerged about the viability of the BBB–rated tranches; investment banks were reluctant to buy new subprime and ARM loans issued by originators with poor risk-management practices (e.g., Countrywide and Ameriquest). Still, no major players were concerned yet about the AAA rated tranches, which would face losses only after all of the subordinate tranches had been wiped out. That soon changed. By July 2007, prices of the cheapest homes in San Francisco were down by almost 13 percent from the peak; in San Diego, they were down by 10 percent. Serious delinquency on subprime ARM loans had reached 9.16 percent by Q4 2006 and had increased to 12.40 percent by Q2 2007.

Between July 9 and August 3, 2007, the cost of insuring $10 million of AAA rated tranches of MBS went from $50,000 (plus a $9,000 annual premium) to more than $900,000 (plus the premium). Because the cost of insuring MBS provides a measure of the estimated losses on them, the rising insurance cost not only left many of the bad assets stranded in the hands of the subprime originators. It also signaled to the market that assets that already had been acquired by banks and other financial institutions were at risk of substantial losses. By this time, expected losses at the bottom of the investment grade (i.e., BBB–rated subprime RMBS had reached 40 to 60 percent, depending on the issue date of the securities. Expected losses at the top end of the investment-grade (i.e., AAA rated) portions of the securities were in the 5 to 10 percent range. Because about two thirds of each security issue is investment grade, the expected losses had surged between January and July of 2007 from less than 2 percent to more than 20 percent. Meanwhile, the market for mortgages issued by subprime lenders was completely frozen by August 3; on August 9 BNP Paribas suspended withdrawals from investment funds exposed to the U.S. subprime market; and Countrywide was considered a bankruptcy risk by August 10.[24]

Figure 3.3 (see Chapter 3) displays the quarterly net flow of mortgage funds through Q4 2008. The data show clearly that after its recovery in the first half of 2007 from a sharp decline in 2006, the final and sudden collapse of the flow of mortgage funds began in Q3 2007, when fears about subprime mortgage delinquencies and defaults became acute.

In retrospect, it is transparent that the residential mortgage processing chain from origination to repackaging as MBS, to rating, resale, and "insuring" via CDS contracts, was inherently unstable. The chain was inadequately collateralized at the front by the incentive failure of mortgage originators to better screen and hold home buyers to higher down payment and amortization standards and, in the final link, by the failure to require that CDS issuers collateralize their insurance against mortgage default. What is remarkable is that this chain remained suspended for so long in a kind of false common-expectations equilibrium that could not be supported by the underlying market conditions.

The timeline of collapse began when housing prices started their decline in January 2006, ten years after the year that marked the beginning of their ascent (1997); mortgage delinquencies began rising; and the credit system froze in August 2007, followed by the stock market decline in Q4 2007. Figure 7.1 charts the Case-Shiller U.S. National Home Price Index, the Dow Jones Industrial Average, and the KBW BKX index of bank stocks: house prices peaked in 2006; bank stocks peaked in early 2007, reflecting the developing

---

[24] As discussed in Chapter 8, August 10, 2007, is also the date that the Federal Reserve finally reversed its thinking on monetary policy and went into "liquidity enhancement" mode, a *modus operandi* that would prove inadequate to stave off the inherent and growing insolvency of financial market institutions as overvalued homes plummeted in price relative to fixed mortgage principal in household and bank balance sheets.

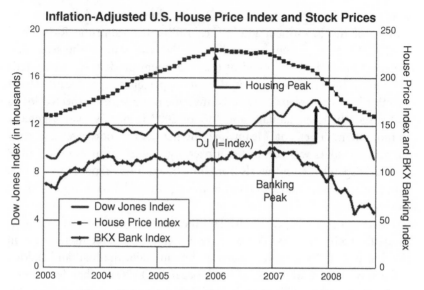

Figure 7.1. Chart showing how the housing downturn (2006) spread to banks (2007), to stocks (2007), and finally to recession in December 2007.

bank balance sheet crisis; and the Dow Jones peaked in October 2007. The National Bureau of Economic Research (NBER) subsequently declared that the recession began in December 2007.

7.5 Cry in the Wilderness: The Commodity Futures Trading Commission Raises Key Questions, Summarily Rejected, Subsequently Vindicated

Ten years before the crisis reached a critical stage, the U.S. Treasury, the Federal Reserve, and the SEC had gone to great lengths to ensure that neither they nor the one federal agency that considered revisiting the exempt unregistered status of the CDS market – the Commodity Futures Trading Commission (CFTC) – would have the information that they needed to assess the risks of derivatives. On May 7, 1998, the CFTC issued a Concept Release to solicit input regarding potential prospective regulatory oversight of the derivatives markets, including markets for CDS. In its press release accompanying the Concept Release, the CFTC explained its rationale for a regulatory review[25]:

---

[25] The Concept Release press statement is available at www.cftc.gov/opa/press98/opa4142–98.htm. The press release is available at www.cftc.gov/foia/fedreg98/foi980512a.htm.

The goal of this reexamination is to assist [CFTC] in determining how best to maintain adequate regulatory safeguards without impairing the ability of the OTC derivatives market to grow and the ability of U.S. entities to remain competitive in the global financial marketplace.

In that context, the Commission is open both to evidence in support of broadening its existing exemptions and to evidence of the need for additional safeguards. Thus, the concept release identifies a broad range of issues in order to stimulate public discussion and elicit informed analysis. The Commission seeks to draw on the knowledge and expertise of a broad spectrum of interested parties, including OTC derivatives dealers, end-users of derivatives, other industry participants, other regulatory authorities, and academicians.

The concept release seeks comment on a number of areas where potential changes to current CFTC exemptions might be possible, including eligible transactions, eligible participants, clearing, transaction-execution facilities, registration, capital, internal controls, sales practices, recordkeeping and reporting. The release also asks for the views of commenters as to whether issues described in the release might be addressed through industry bodies or self-regulatory organizations.

We can only be impressed by the benign and unthreatening tone of this concept release; taken at face value, this seemed to be an agency seeking knowledge with an open mind and a willingness to reconsider broadening or narrowing the exempt status of derivatives. Remarkably, Treasury Secretary Robert Rubin, SEC Chairman Arthur Levitt, and Federal Reserve Board Chairman Alan Greenspan issued a terse joint statement on the same day that questioned the authority of the CFTC to review the markets. They stated that the Fed, the SEC, and the Treasury had "grave concerns about this action and its possible consequences. The OTC derivatives market is a large and important global market. We seriously question the scope of the CFTC's jurisdiction in this area, and we are very concerned about reports that the CFTC's action may increase the legal uncertainty concerning certain types of OTC derivatives."[26]

More than a year earlier, Greenspan (1997) gave a speech on regulation and derivative contracts in which he provided a careful history of their origins and development. He also expressed his considered view that:

In the case of the institutional off-exchange derivatives markets, it seems abundantly clear that private market regulation is quite effectively and efficiently achieving what have been identified as the public policy objectives of government regulation... prices of off-exchange contracts are not used directly or indiscriminately as

---

[26] See www.treasury.gov/press-center/press-releases/Pages/rr2426.aspx for the joint statement from Treasury Secretary Rubin, Federal Reserve Board Chairman Greenspan, and SEC Chairman Levitt.

the basis for pricing other transactions, so any price distortions would not affect other buyers or sellers of the underlying asset and certainly would not affect the economy as a whole. Institutional participants in the off-exchange derivative markets also have demonstrated their ability to protect themselves from losses from fraud and counterparty insolvencies. Participants in those markets have insisted that dealers have financial strength sufficient to warrant a credit rating of A or higher . . . Thus, there appears to be no need for government regulation of off-exchange derivative transactions between institutional counterparties.

Contrary to the accepted wisdom of the time, many of the issues raised in the Concept Release ultimately proved to be at the heart of the problem with the derivatives market, which contributed to the spread of the riskiest subprime and ARM lending practices. AIG and many other insurers of MBS had inadequate capital to meet the obligations they had undertaken with CDS; regulators had an inadequate understanding of these risks due to their exempt status; and investors (e.g., AIG, Ambac, and MBIA) had an inadequate understanding of the risks they faced due to the lack of disclosure and collateral requirements.[27]

The CDS derivatives were exempt instruments and were not exchange-traded under standard private-exchange transparency rules. The lack of standardization, registration, disclosure, and capital-reserve requirements made them more complex and – as we have now learned – inherently more unstable than futures and options markets for commodities and equities. We cannot know, of course, what would have been the outcome if the CFTC public discussion had gone forward under Chairwoman Born.[28] Instead, Congress passed the CFMA in which Section 103 provided "Legal Certainty for Excluded Derivative Transactions." CDS continued to be exempt from the registration and margin rules that applied to other securities.

---

[27] Summers spearheaded opposition to the regulatory review of the derivatives market proposed by the CFTC and was the spokesperson for and the apparent architect of derivatives market deregulation. (See his July 30, 1998, congressional testimony in the quote used for this chapter.) However, in an interview with George Stephanopoulos on March 15, 2009, Summers signaled a change of heart in noting that "there are a lot of terrible things that have happened in the last eighteen months, but what's happened at AIG . . . *the way it was not regulated*, the way no one was watching . . . is outrageous" (italics added).

[28] We note that Brooksley Born is a retired partner of Arnold and Porter LLP, where "She was the head of the firm's derivatives practice and represented domestic and international clients in legislative, litigation, regulatory, and transactional matters involving derivatives transactions and financial markets." Available at www.arnoldporter.com/professionals .cfm?action=view&id=557. As such, she was particularly well qualified based on her litigation experience to know the hazards of CDS instruments when the CFTC issued its statement in 1998; none of her detractors seem to have had comparable experience at that time and were unwilling to listen and perhaps learn from her experience.

7.6 Other Warnings as Catastrophe Neared

With the hindsight we now enjoy, it is possible to identify scholars who expressed concerns about the institutional and technological changes that engulfed the financial industry – in particular, the traditionally risk-avoiding behavior of commercial banking. The following quote from Rajan (2005) provides an example based on a perceptive analysis of the changing incentives faced by bank managers:

The knowledge that managers are being evaluated against others can induce superior performance, but also a variety of perverse behavior. One is the incentive to take risk that is concealed from investors – since risk and return are related, the manager then looks as if he outperforms peers given the risk he takes. Typically, the kinds of risks that can be concealed most easily, given the requirement of periodic reporting, are risks that generate adverse consequences with small probability but, in return, offer generous compensation the rest of the time. These risks are known as tail risks. A second form of perverse behavior is the incentive to herd with other investment managers on investment choices because herding provides insurance the manager will not underperform his peers. Herd behavior can move asset prices away from fundamentals. Both behaviors can reinforce each other during an asset price boom, when investment managers are willing to bear the low-probability tail risk that asset prices will revert to fundamentals abruptly, and the knowledge that many of their peers are herding on this risk gives them comfort that they will not underperform significantly if boom turns to bust... even though some risk has been moved off balance sheets, balance sheets have been reloaded with fresh, more complicated risks. In fact, the data suggest that despite a deepening of financial markets, banks may not be any safer than in the past. Moreover, the risk they now bear is a small... tip of an iceberg they have created.

Rajan's paper anticipated both the greater potential risk that bank managers may incur in the new financial environment and how this can exacerbate self-reinforcing asset price bubbles. No one seems to have anticipated the severity of the impact of the mortgage market crash on the banking sector and the economy. Managerial corruption, as in the Enron case (as well as the Fannie Mae and Freddie Mac accounting scandals), is normally a matter of self-dealing or risk taking that is "concealed from investors." It was not realized or even thinkable that managers would self-deceptively take risks that they concealed from themselves! With rare exceptions, managers behaved as if their actions in the CDS market "insured" them against tail risks, dismissing systemic risk with the belief that national housing prices could not fall. The money was to be made in continued expansion of long positions, not in timing short positions on unpredictable tail events. This belief pattern thickened the tail.

Others saw the looming crisis but they were on the ground in the industry, not policy makers. For example, Robert Rodriguez, CEO of First Pacific Advisors, in a speech in June 2007, described problems discovered by his firm in 2005 with mortgage securities that they owned (for the full speech, see Rodriguez, 2007):

> Two years ago, we noticed a problem developing in our bond portfolios involving Alt-A securities. Despite having average FICO scores of 718 on the underlying loans, these securities experienced rapidly escalating delinquencies and defaults after just nine months. We sold them since we did not want to wait around to find out the reason why this was happening. Our worst fears were recently confirmed in a study by First American Financial entitled, "First American Real Estate Solutions Report, Alt-A Credit – The Other Shoe Drops?" . . . What is interesting is that the origination volumes for the last two years, when the most egregious deterioration in underwriting standards occurred, total more than the previous seven years of originations combined. Of further interest, Dale Westoff, senior managing director of Bear Stearns, Inc., estimates that 25.8 percent of subprime and 41.2 percent of Alt-A originations were in California; the combination of these total 33.7 percent of the total subprime/Alt-A universe. For 2006, subprime/Alt-A represented approximately 40 percent of total mortgage originations. I reference this Alt-A underwriting data because I believe it reflects the wider trend of underwriting deterioration throughout the entire mortgage universe. Because of a laxness in credit-underwriting standards, along with an accommodative Fed, the housing-price bubble was magnified and, thus, it has spread into the asset-backed securitizations market.

7.7 Complexity Surges: The Dodd-Frank Fix

On July 10, 2009, the Obama Administration's Treasury Secretary Geithner proposed to "require that all 'standardized' instruments be traded on a regulated exchange or through a central clearinghouse. Participants would have to disclose more information about their transactions, and they would have to meet strict new capital requirements."[29] Apparently, the intention was to expose derivatives to the same rules as in securities markets, implying that investors would have to post collateral similar in spirit to that applying to broker margin accounts. Because CDS instruments are heterogeneous bilateral contracts, the details are unclear. Geithner's call culminated in the Dodd-Frank Wall Street Reform and Consumer Protection Act (2010), but the Act "punted" on the details of implementation, leaving them to the

---

[29] *New York Times* report, available at www.nytimes.com/2009/07/11/business/economy/11treasury.html.

regulators. All of the action at the time (September 2010) was on the desks of the regulators who had to figure out what to do and who had to seek public comment on rule making. Paletta and McGrane (2010), in a *Wall Street Journal* article, noted that:

Banks, companies and trade associations challenged federal regulators Friday over the controversial question of how to regulate derivatives under the new Dodd-Frank financial revamp, the first big day of posturing since the law was enacted last month. The meetings, particularly a three-hour roundtable hosted jointly by the Commodity Futures Trading Commission and the Securities and Exchange Commission, illustrate how Wall Street's attention has shifted from Congress to the federal agencies that have to interpret the law by writing hundreds of new rules. Perhaps nowhere is the attention to detail more apparent than the focus on complex financial instruments known as derivatives, in part because the rules will impact scores of companies and can affect how hundreds of billions of dollars in credit moves through the economy. The law pushed for more disclosure and in some cases restrictions on how derivatives are traded amid concerns that if risks weren't overseen, it could pose a threat to the broader financial system. But many business groups and banks have said overly stringent rules make it harder for firms to access credit and potentially threaten the economic recovery.

As of May 2013, the SEC had implemented four sets of rules. These covered the definitions of swap dealers and major participants (644 pages), joint rules with the CFTC regarding definitions of swaps and recordkeeping related to swaps (600 pages), rules for clearing (214 pages), and rules covering risk management practices for swap dealers (254 pages). There are also twelve sets of rules under development on a broad range of issues, including confirmation of transactions; fraud and manipulation; registration; reporting; confidentiality; relationships of dealers with state and local governments, pension plans, and endowments; conflicts of interest; capital and margin requirements; and cross-border swaps.[30] Many of these issues arose in the Concept Release fifteen years earlier. The process of rule implementation under Dodd-Frank continues to be factious; if the tone of the 1998 CFTC Concept Release is an indication, the process may have been more thoughtful, inclusive, and rational under the guidance of the CFTC and Brooksley Born, and the problems of the explosive growth of the MBS market and the collapse of AIG under the weight of its uncollateralized CDS obligations may have been averted.

---

[30] For a list of implemented and proposed rules on derivatives, see www.sec.gov/spotlight/dodd-frank/derivatives.shtml.

7.8 Origins in Financial Market Legislation of the 1980s

The case can be articulated for the proposition that the subprime lending and mortgage credit expansion excesses had critical legal origins in federal legislation in the early 1980s.[31] Before commenting on the institutional change implicit in this legal history, we digress briefly to the 1970s era of regulatory reform in the transportation industry, which foreshadowed and helped to initiate the wave of changes that moved into banking and mortgage finance.

Although there were clear antecedents in earlier administrations, it was the Carter Administration that "gave wings" to a bipartisan movement for regulatory reform in the airline industry, which subsequently spread to trucking and then to railroad, natural gas, and wholesale-power markets in the 1980s. Airline deregulation – opposed by nearly all of the airlines – was supported by Senator Ted Kennedy most likely because, in the end, it was seen as beneficial to the consumer and therefore appealed to the politics of consumer protection (consumer advocate, Ralph Nader, also was a supporter).[32]

It is commonly acknowledged that a key action by President Carter was the appointment of Alfred Kahn as Chairman of the Civil Aeronautics Board (CAB).[33] Reagan, whose presidency may have been more a result than a cause of these trends, was publicly associated with this movement – perhaps because the prescheduled "sunset" of the CAB occurred during his tenure and Reagan's skills with free-market rhetoric.[34]

These transportation economic reforms have persisted and, in this sense, can be considered a success quite apart from the largely favorable academic and political opinion toward them at the time. Moreover, we recall that transportation services are a perishable and belong to the class of goods and

---

[31] See McCoy and Renuart (2008).
[32] See Derthick and Quirk (1985, pp. 40–1).
[33] Kahn (2008, p. 622) referred to himself "[a]s a self-proclaimed twentieth-century liberal, I have long been an antitrust true believer of the pre-Chicago variety, emphasizing its role as proscription of anti-competitive *conduct*." However, he became "the father of airline deregulation" because "of my realization that there was no acceptable halfway house between the thoroughly cartelistic regulatory regime I inherited in the spring of 1977 and the legislative triumph of deregulation in the fall of 1978" (p. 616). His appointments of Betsy Bailey, Mike Levine, and Darius Gaskins – who moved from the CAB to ICC and became chairman in 1980 – became legion.
[34] Contrary to this rhetoric, according to Niskanen (1988), a member of the Council of Economic Advisors under Reagan, "The reduction in economic regulation that started in the Carter Administration continued, but at a slower rate . . . Deregulation was clearly the lowest priority among the major elements of the Reagan economic program."

services whose markets have long been stable, well behaved, and responsive to the repetitive conditions of supply and demand. Reform had created new delivery systems in which – consistent with the properties of such markets – prices were more responsive to consumer demand and supplier costs. It was in this atmosphere that the regulatory-reform movement turned to banking and financial markets late in the Carter Administration.

The 1970s and 1980s also brought unprecedented inflation rates. One consequence was a collision between rising mortgage interest rates and heterogeneous state usury laws governing (nominal) interest rates; a second consequence was the welter of limits on bank time deposits. Savings and loan deposit rates became unworkable and clearly needed to be reexamined. Reform was badly needed, but state usury laws had been a functional, if blunt, mechanism for consumer (i.e., borrower) protection that involved more than simply interest rate ceilings. President Carter and Congress responded with the Depository Institutions Deregulation and Monetary Control Act of 1980. The new law abolished interest ceilings for primary mortgages on residences, ostensibly setting the stage for more competitive financial markets but also opening the door to subprime lending at higher rates in an environment fraught with incentive incompatibilities in which the higher risks of such loans were not borne by the mortgage originators. Essentially, restrictions on prices (i.e., interest rates) and entry were removed in the loan market, much as had occurred with the airline industry, but the institutional structure and the nature of the product in the two cases were quite different. The terms of a loan contract specify not only the interest charge but also the equity stake in the investment provided by the borrower. The lender's specification of a required level of equity as well as the loan amount – that is, rationing – is part of the lender's due diligence on the default risk associated with the particular borrower. Interest rate ceilings, it can be argued, have the effect of reducing any temptation by the lender to substitute a higher interest charge for less equity, thereby increasing the default risk and lending too much.[35]

---

[35] That interest rates fail to serve adequately as a standalone price for clearing loan markets is a proposition going back at least to Adam Smith, who was aware that direct forms of rationing in addition to the interest price were essential in efficient loan markets: "The legal rate, it is to be observed, though it ought to be somewhat above, ought not to be much above the lowest market rate. If the legal rate of interest in Great Britain, for example, was fixed so high as eight or ten per cent, the greater part of the money which was to be lent, would be lent to prodigals and projectors, who alone would be willing to give this high interest. Sober people, who will give for the use of money no more than a part of what they are likely to make by the use of it, would not venture into the competition. A great part of the capital of the country would thus be kept out of the hands which were most

How important were these structural differences between the transportation and financial industries? What new institutional property rights structures were needed to replace and improve the old state-regulated system? That system had the merit of blocking subprime loan expansion to a high-risk group but may not have been sensitive to within-group differences. To be efficient, the net benefits of an alternative system must exceed the higher transactions cost of implementing it. The state system had evolved gradually and we must assume that it captured substantial experience that was not oblivious to efficiency and transactions-cost considerations. However, for better or worse, the new legislation swept it aside.

Two years after President Carter's action, President Reagan and Congress passed the Alternative Mortgage Transactions Parity Act of 1982. This law removed previous restrictions barring banks from making mortgage loans other than the conventional fixed-rate type. Again, the intention was to promote market flexibility and competition by removing the rigidity that fixed mortgage rates imposed asymmetrically on the borrower–debtor relationship (1) when inflation set in, and (2) when Fed monetary policy raised or lowered interest rates, as follows:

- With inflation, borrowers gain relative to lenders in real terms and have an incentive to cling to these favorable earlier contracts. One implication for the economy is that it reduces labor mobility – a "lock in" that provides a disincentive to move to a better job opportunity because buying a new home incurs a larger mortgage loan interest cost.
- Similar "lock in" effects follow when the Fed raises interest rates: And a lowering of rates gives borrowers an incentive to refinance, and lender returns are pressured by declines in interest earnings. (Ferreira et al., 2008, pp. 3–4)

The effect of the law change was to launch experiments in nonfixed and more sophisticated contract variations: (1) ARMs, (2) interest-only

likely to make a profitable and advantageous use of it, and thrown into those which were most likely to waste and destroy it. Where the legal rate of interest, on the contrary, is fixed but a very little above the lowest market rate, sober people are universally preferred, as borrowers, to prodigals and projectors. The person who lends money gets nearly as much interest from the former as he dares to take from the latter, and his money is much safer in the hands of the one set of people, than in those of the other. A great part of the capital of the country is thus thrown into the hands in which it is most likely to be employed with advantage" Smith (1776/1981). Hence, Smith seems to have had a clear and articulate understanding that the effect of a legal ceiling is to restrain lenders from any temptation to simply charge a higher rate to "prodigals and projectors" instead of performing due diligence in identifying the "sober people" more likely to make profitable use of the capital. Default risk of this type is formally modeled in Quirk (1960) and Smith (1972).

mortgages, combined with (3) balloon payments, and (4) negative-equity loans (i.e., option-ARM) with payments below interest and with a consequent increase in principal owed for the early years of the loan. The objective was to refinance with a more conventional mortgage once the home appreciated in value or otherwise pay off the loan. In theory, each innovation defined a niche arrangement that would allow the market to fine-tune mortgages to the circumstances of individual borrowers. ARM, interest-only, and balloon payments provide potential economies to those with higher and more reliable incomes; negative equity makes sense for those who face high average but volatile income. However, institutions had to emerge for implementing the information and due-diligence requirements for fitting the different contract arrangements to individual circumstances. None of these arrangements may be suitable for the typical uncalculating, unsophisticated borrower for whom even a simple fixed-rate mortgage is a cognitive challenge. Effective property rights systems cannot be oblivious to people's capacity for rational understanding of their circumstances – any more than it can absolve people of responsibility for their own actions because of ignorance. How property rights balance these considerations has important implications for the stability of financial markets.

We offer the hypothesis that the diversity of state usury and consumer protection laws evolved in a world of fixed rate mortgages that, however imperfectly, were serving an institutional purpose: Loans to uninformed high-risk borrowers were simply denied rather than being ideally fine-tuned to borrower circumstances. Hence, preempting those laws – in the absence of replacing them with an institutional process for discovering an incentive-compatible substitute – opened up the system to a disequilibrating price bubble and balance sheet damage that could be corrected only through widespread de facto bankruptcy.[36]

7.9 Conclusions

Although financial innovation in the form of MBS was not new, this market grew to unprecedented levels and, together with derivatives "insurance," became the financial engine that maintained house price momentum into the frothy years of 2002–2006. In this chapter, we ask fundamental

---

[36] The way things have evolved may reflect ecologically rational mechanisms invisible to constructivist reason, and the state laws in question may be a prominent example. (For many other examples, see Smith, 2008.) The research questions we raise are deeper than we could hope to investigate very far herein.

incentive questions (reminiscent of Knight) concerning the insurability of these types of business risks. However, even if this hurdle is crossed, derivatives were flawed in their basic property rights structure in not being collateralized; unlike other securities, these instruments could be purchased with large amounts of "other people's money." Mortgage markets were flawed by an unsustainable, destabilizing chain from mortgage origination – badly incentivized with upfront origination fees – through mortgage securitization insured by uncollateralized derivative instruments and rated by agencies whose models had a built-in allowance for price appreciation. This chain remained suspended by ebullient expectations until its collapse in 2007.

In 1998, long before the derivatives market collapsed, the CFTC under Brooksley Born raised key questions for public comment that proposed to revisit the exempt status of derivatives. CFTC Chairwoman Born, who had private litigation background experience with the downside hazards of these instruments, failed to prevail over the policy leaders of the federal agencies who opposed any public discussion of the issue: Greenspan at the Federal Reserve, Rubin at Treasury, and Levitt at the SEC. Moreover, through testimony by Summers from Treasury, "the boys" prevailed in blocking any further such action by the CFTC, and Congress passed the CFMA, in which Section 103 provided "Legal Certainty for Excluded Derivative Transactions." Other warnings, however, were also perceptive, particularly those of Rajan (2005), who echoed Born but emphasized the incentive incompatibilities that had overtaken the banking and financial sector. But intelligent people everywhere were riding what was somehow perceived as a new gravity-defying norm.

Ultimately, Dodd-Frank became the heavy-handed expression of congressional dissatisfaction with the world they had so prominently helped to create. Provisions of the bill – designed to correct all the "errors," whether primary, secondary, or peripheral, of the great housing bubble and collapse – led to proposed rulemaking that continues in a state of political controversy. At the foundation of disagreement is the continued poor performance of the economy and a sense that correctional actions inhibit the short-run need for housing recovery "stimulus." The lesson seems to be that there is never a good time to get the rules right: In good times, we must not interfere with the ongoing prosperity; in bad times, we must not interfere with the recovery.

We also raise questions about the origins of the housing–mortgage market bubble in the financial market legislation of the 1980s. We offer the hypothesis that the enormous and justifiable success of the transportation market liberalization movement under President Carter and continuing under President Reagan, extended that framework to financial markets without adequate appreciation of their fundamental differences.

References

Bair, Sheila (2012). *Bull by the Horns.* New York: Free Press.
Bernanke, Ben S. (2005). "Nomination of Ben S. Bernanke." Hearing before the Committee On Banking, Housing, and Urban Affairs, United States Senate, Senate Hearing 109-551, November 15. Available at www.gpo.gov/fdsys/pkg/CHRG-109shrg26610/html/CHRG-109shrg26610.htm.
Boysen, Louis K. (1931). "A History of Real Estate Bonds." *Chicago Real Estate Magazine,* 6 (23 May), pp. 12–13.
Buchanan, James (1968). "Knight, Frank H." *International Encyclopedia of the Social Sciences.* Vol. 8, p. 425. Macmillan: London.
Coase, Ronald (1960). "The Problem of Social Cost." *Journal of Law and Economics,* 1, pp. 1–44.
Derthick, Martha, and Paul J. Quirk (1985). *The Politics of Deregulation.* Washington, DC: The Brookings Institution.
Ferreira, Fernando, Joseph Gyourko, and Joseph Tracy (2008). "Housing Busts and Household Mobility." Federal Reserve Bank of New York, Staff Report No. 350, October.
Fitzpatrick, Dan (2012). "Bank of America's $40 BillionMistake." *Wall Street Journal,* July 1. Available at http://online.wsj.com/news/articles/SB10001424052702303561504577495332947870736.
Forsythe, Robert, Forrest Nelson, George Neumann, and Jack Wright (1992). "Anatomy of an Experimental Political Stock Market." *American Economic Review,* 82, pp. 1142–61.
Gjerstad, Steven, and Vernon L. Smith (2009). "Monetary Policy, Credit Extension, and Housing Bubbles: 2008 and 1929." *Critical Review,* 2–3, pp. 269–300.
Greenspan, Alan (1997). "Government Regulation and Derivative Contracts." Financial Markets Conference of the Federal Reserve Bank of Atlanta, February 21.
Hilsenrath, Jon (2010). "I Didn't Recognize All the Weaknesses." *Wall Street Journal,* June 18.
Ivry, Bob (2007). "'Deal with Devil' Funded Carrera Crash before Bust." *Bloomberg,* December 18.
Kahn, Alfred E. (2008). "Reflections of an Unwitting 'Political Entrepreneur'." *Review of Network Economics,* December.
Kelly, Kate (2007). "How Goldman Won Big on Mortgage Meltdown." *Wall Street Journal,* December 14.
Knight, Frank (1921). *Risk, Uncertainty and Profit.* New York: Augustus M. Kelley, Bookseller.
Lewis, Michael (2009). "The Man Who Crashed the World." *Vanity Fair,* August. Available at http://www.vanityfair.com/politics/features/2009/08/aig200908.
Lewis, Michael (2010). *The Big Short: Inside the Doomsday Machine.* New York: W.W. Norton & Co.

Lowenstein, Roger (2000). *When Genius Failed.* New York: Random House.

McCoy, Patricia A., and Elizabeth Renuart (2008). "The Legal Infrastructure of Subprime and Nontraditional Home Mortgages." Joint Center for Housing Studies, Harvard University, UCC08–5, February.

Morgenson, Gretchen (2008). "Behind Insurer's Crisis, Blind Eye to a Web of Risk." *New York Times*, September 27, p. A1.

Niskanen, William (1988). *Reaganomics.* The Concise Encyclopedia of Economics, Library of Economics and Liberty. Available at www.econlib.org/library/Enc1/Reaganomics.html.

Paletta, Damian, and Victoria McGrane (2010). "Fighting Flares on New Rules for Street." *Wall Street Journal*, August 21.

Pittman, Mark (2007). "Bass Shorted 'God I Hope You're Wrong' Wall Street." *Bloomberg*, December 19.

Quirk, James P. (1960). "Default Risk and the Loan Market." *Journal of Finance*, 15, pp. 575–6.

Rajan, Raghuram G. (2005). "Has Financial Development Made the World Riskier?" Federal Reserve Bank of Kansas City, pp. 316–17.

Rodriguez, Robert L. (2007). "Absence of Fear." CFA Society of Chicago speech, June 28. Available at www.fpafunds.com/docs/special-commentaries/absence_of_fear.pdf?sfvrsn=2.

Smith, Adam (1776/1981). *An Inquiry into the Nature and Causes of the Wealth of Nations, Vol. I.* Ed. R. H. Campbell and A. S. Skinner, Vol. II of the Glasgow Edition of the Works and Correspondence of Adam Smith. Indianapolis, IN: Liberty Fund.

Smith, Vernon L. (1972). "A Theory and Test of Credit Rationing: Some Generalizations." *American Economic Review*, 62, pp. 477–83.

Smith, Vernon L. (2008). *Rationality in Economics: Constructivist and Ecological Form.* New York: Cambridge University Press.

Summers, Lawrence (1998). "Testimony before the Senate Committee on Agriculture, Nutrition, and Forestry on the CFTC Concept Release." U.S. Department of Treasury, July 30. Available at www.treasury.gov/press-center/press-releases/Pages/rr2616.aspx.

Weiss, Gary (2009). "The Man Who Made Too Much." *Upstart Business Journal.* January 7. Available at http://upstart.bizjournals.com/executives/features/2009/01/07/John-Paulson-Profits-in-Downturn.html?page=all.

8

Blindsided Experts

The rise in subprime mortgage lending likely boosted home sales somewhat, and curbs on this lending are expected to be a source of some restraint on home purchases and residential investment in coming quarters. Moreover, we are likely to see further increases in delinquencies and foreclosures this year and next as many adjustable-rate loans face interest-rate resets. All that said, given the fundamental factors in place that should support the demand for housing, we believe the effect of the troubles in the subprime sector on the broader housing market will likely be limited, and we do not expect significant spillovers from the subprime market to the rest of the economy or to the financial system. The vast majority of mortgages, including even subprime mortgages, continue to perform well. Past gains in house prices have left most homeowners with significant amounts of home equity, and growth in jobs and incomes should help keep the financial obligations of most households manageable.
– Ben Bernanke, May 17, 2007

Although I was concerned about the potential fallout from a collapse of the housing market, I think that it is fair to say that these costs have turned out to be much greater than I and many other observers imagined. In particular, I and other observers underestimated the potential for house prices to decline substantially, the degree to which such a decline would create difficulties for homeowners, and, most important, the vulnerability of the broader financial system to these events.
– Donald L. Kohn, Board of Governors of the Federal Reserve System,
November 19, 2008

I got back and I called some friends in the Federal Reserve. "How big is this subprime mortgage thing?" I must admit, the answer I got from them first was, "I don't know." Then, they called me back later, and they told me, "Well, it looks like it's over a trillion dollars." I had no imagination that this subprime mortgage thing was over a trillion dollars.
– Paul Volcker interview (Feldstein, 2013, p. 114)

As the current crisis reached one critical stage after another, the FOMC reacted with evident surprise to the sudden disarray in mortgage-financial markets that resulted from the accumulated losses and risks in the financial sector.[1] This surprise accounts for the chasm separating Bernanke's thoughts quoted here, which were recorded in 2007 three months before he began the largest (and continuing into 2012) Federal Reserve intervention in history, and those of his vice chairman, who was willing to write candidly from the perspective of hindsight after only an additional eighteen months. Volcker is referring to a conversation in the spring of 2007.

8.1 From Monitoring Events and Fighting Inflation to Surprise and Adaptation

Although the Fed was monitoring housing and financial markets, it under-estimated (as stated in Kohn's acknowledgment) and did not anticipate (1) the rapidity and severity with which those developments would burst on the financial world in 2007 and be transmitted to the broader economy in late 2007 and 2008; and (2) the magnitude of FMOC action that ultimately would be considered necessary. Throughout 2007 and 2008, the grasp of the state of financial and economic affairs by the FOMC, as well as that of the financial and economic community at large, seems clearly to have lagged behind developing market events.

Against this backdrop, we recall from Chapter 3 that unit home sales had reached a peak in 2005 and began their decline in Q4 2005; housing expenditures and the flow of mortgage funds both began declining in Q2 2006; and house prices had flattened and started to decline in 2006 but then declined rapidly beginning in 2007. For easy reference in Figure 8.1, we chart home sales (S), flow of mortgage funds (M), Case-Shiller Home Price Index (P), and housing investment (H) as percentage changes relative to the levels in Q4 2007. The Federal Reserve's primary responses were expressed in two parts: In the figure, the first Fed action event is labeled "I" in August 2007 and the second is labeled "II" in October 2008.

These two events correspond to abrupt turning points in FOMC expec-tations and reveal how those expectations about events – inflation, the severity of the housing slump, the collateral damage from the expansion in mortgage debt, and the capacity-output gap – turned out to be wrong, and well outside the range of FOMC expectations. The specter of inflation began to diminish and ultimately translated into concerns about deflation;

---

[1] See www.federalreserve.gov/newsevents/press/monetary/20070817b.htm. All references to FOMC monetary press releases in this chapter can be accessed at www.federalreserve.gov/newsevents/press/monetary/2014monetary.htm.

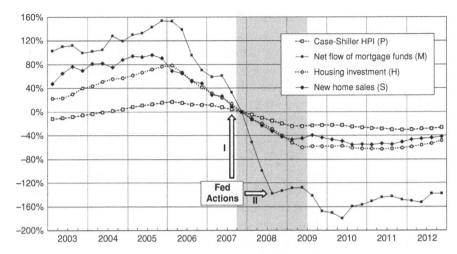

Figure 8.1. The housing and mortgage bubble and Fed actions.

a continuing slump in housing culminated in a crash; the collateral damage to bank balance sheets from overvalued collateral pledged against mortgage and other loans was revealed to be staggering; and excess industrial capacity ultimately would result from a rapid decline in demand. These lags reflected, in part, the uncertainty and unpredictability that resulted from a cascade of unfamiliar and dramatic events.

Models fitted to the historical data on accounting flows were not reflecting the unusual character of recent balance sheet deterioration. Private sector expectations also were failing to reflect these underlying risks; for example, firm investments continued to rise right up until the start of the recession, and even then declined less than 1 percent by the middle of 2008. As a consequence, the FOMC was focused on inflationary concerns while household and bank balance sheets were developing gaping holes. As a result, the FOMC went through two sharply defined reversals as it saw the bank stresses break into the open: first in early August 2007 and then in September–October 2008.

Long before mid-2007, the Fed indicated that it was monitoring the housing sector conditions that would eventually cause so much damage in the collapse, but they always assumed that the problems would be contained. Beginning with its May 10, 2006, press release and continuing throughout 2006, the FOMC recorded its expectation of a more moderate and sustainable pace of growth "partly reflecting a gradual cooling of the housing market"; then, in its January 31, 2007, press release, the FMOC saw "somewhat firmer economic growth, and some tentative signs of stabilization have appeared in the housing market"; and in its March 21, 2007, press release, it recognized that "the adjustment in the housing sector is ongoing." However, this record is not that of a committee of monetary experts who had been primed by a long history of awareness of the persistent role that housing has had as a precursor of the Depression and most of the postwar recessions. This interpretation essentially is confirmed by the dramatic about-face expressed in the FMOC press releases of August 10 and 17, 2007. Suddenly, the force of events in housing, mortgage, and derivative markets made the committee aware that financial markets generally were in trouble, the likes of which had not been seen since the early 1930s. Yet, at this point, new home unit sales had entered the eighth straight quarter of decline, and home investment expenditures had begun the sixth quarter of decline – very pronounced indicators of looming economic decline based on the postwar historical record (as discussed in Chapter 5).

Both the uncertainty perceived by Federal Reserve policy makers and the nagging residue of their preoccupation with inflationary concerns had been expressed in Bernanke's statement before Congress on March 28, 2007 (Bernanke, 2007a):

At this juncture, however, the impact on the broader economy and financial markets of the problems in the subprime markets seems likely to be contained.... Although the turmoil in the subprime mortgage market has created severe financial problems for many individuals and families, the implications of these developments for the housing market as a whole are less clear. . . . The near-term prospects for the housing market remain uncertain.

Thus, Bernanke, who was obviously following housing developments carefully if somewhat routinely, saw no problems for the mortgage market, financial system, or economy that could not be contained. He restated this expectation in mid-May (Bernanke 2007b), as follows:

[W]e believe the effect of the troubles in the subprime sector on the broader housing market will likely be limited, and we do not expect significant spillovers from the subprime market to the rest of the economy or to the financial system. The vast majority of mortgages, including even subprime mortgages, continue to perform well. Past gains in house prices have left most homeowners with significant amounts of home equity, and growth in jobs and incomes should help keep the financial obligations of most households manageable.

Moreover, in this view, Bernanke was joined by Secretary of Treasury Henry Paulson, who had a tendency to exhibit significantly less discipline than

Bernanke in his public pronouncements, as the following statements from Secretary Paulson indicate:

"I don't see (subprime mortgage market troubles) imposing a serious problem. I think it's going to be largely contained." (Reuters, April 20, 2007)

July 12, 2007: "This is far and away the strongest global economy I've seen in my business lifetime." (Kirkland, 2007, July 12)

"I see the underlying economy as being very healthy." (Lawder, 2007, August 1)

We think it is fair to say that these statements from Secretary Paulson credibly reflect what was generally believed in the business community at the time.

In earlier statements on March 21, May 9, June 28, and again on August 7, the FOMC reiterated verbatim that "the Committee's predominant policy concern remains the risk that inflation will fail to moderate." However, the August 7 release acknowledged a change in financial market conditions and simultaneously reaffirmed its expectations of economic stability:

The Federal Open Market Committee decided today to keep its target for the federal funds rate at 5-1/4 percent.

Economic growth was moderate during the first half of the year. Financial markets have been volatile in recent weeks, credit conditions have become tighter for some households and businesses, and the housing correction is ongoing. Nevertheless, the economy seems likely to continue to expand at a moderate pace over coming quarters, supported by solid growth in employment and incomes and a robust global economy.

Readings on core inflation have improved modestly in recent months. However, a sustained moderation in inflation pressures has yet to be convincingly demonstrated. Moreover, the high level of resource utilization has the potential to sustain those pressures.

Although the downside risks to growth have increased somewhat, the Committee's predominant policy concern remains the risk that inflation will fail to moderate as expected. Future policy adjustments will depend on the outlook for both inflation and economic growth, as implied by incoming information.

8.1.1 Federal Reserve Adaptation I: Concerns Switch from Inflation to the Provision of Liquidity

As is evident in Figure 8.1, by August 7, the net flow of mortgage funds had declined dramatically from the peak in Q1 2006 and housing prices had picked up substantial downward momentum, returning to the level in Q2 2005. August 9, 2007, was a watershed day. BNP Paribas announced that day that they would suspend redemptions from three funds that were heavily

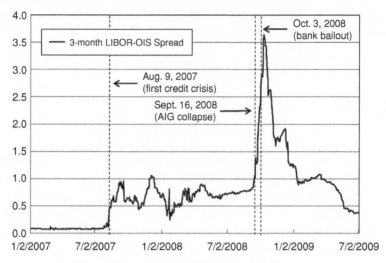

Figure 8.2. The LIBOR-OIS spread.

invested in U.S. subprime securities because "the complete evaporation of liquidity in certain market segments of the US securitisation market has made it impossible to value certain assets fairly regardless of their quality or credit rating." On the same day, the LIBOR-OIS spread tripled, from 13 basis points to 40 as indicated in Figure 8.2.[2] The next day, on August 10, the FOMC announcement signaled an abrupt change in Fed thinking and the course it would now pursue:

[T]he Federal Reserve will provide reserves as necessary through open market operations to promote trading in the federal funds market at rates close to the Federal Open Market Committee's target rate of 5-1/4 percent. In current circumstances, depository institutions may experience unusual funding needs because of dislocations in money and credit markets. As always, the discount window is available as a source of funding.

---

[2] The London Interbank Offered Rate (LIBOR) refers to the interest rate at which banks borrow wholesale from other banks for a specified term (e.g., three months). Overnight Index Swaps (OIS) refers to the overnight indexed swap rate, the rate a bank receives on a derivative contract on the overnight rate (i.e., the effective federal funds rate in the United States). OIS is a side bet in which one party agrees to compensate the other for the difference between the term OIS rate and the geometric average of the overnight federal funds rate over the term of the contract. The OIS spread indicates banks' expectations of interest rates, whereas the LIBOR incorporates both interest rates and default risk, because the lending bank may not be able to recover the loan amount if the borrowing bank is unable to repay. Empirically, it is a responsive indicator of bank exposure to financial market stress. See Sengupta and Tam (2008).

The Fed appears to have been misled by its monetarist (liquidity) preconceptions. Depository institutions were encountering significant stress because banks were reluctant to either lend to one another or to publicly advertise their distress by borrowing from the Fed.[3] The LIBOR-OIS continued to deteriorate, even after the announced liquidity enhancement measures Adaptation I by the FOMC coincides with the abrupt leap in this spread in early August 2007, which prompted the FOMC release on August 10. The spread then became erratic during the remainder of 2007 (see Figure 8.2).

The mortgage market was in disarray, Countrywide was collapsing, and it clearly was not turning out to be the familiar world in which the financial system merely needed a shot of short-term liquidity, as the Fed treated it. It was a crisis of confidence in the banks' own assets (Taylor 2009; Taylor and Williams 2009), based on a widespread realization that a growing number of subprime borrowers might not be able to pay back their loans, and that default was likely to reach much higher up the MBS tranche structure than anyone had expected. This was precisely the mortgage-market expectations environment in which the reversal of the housing-mortgage bubble would accelerate its downward momentum.

Seven days later, on August 17, the FOMC further confirmed that "financial market conditions have deteriorated." A month after that, the FOMC reacted to the continuing deterioration by lowering the target funds rate to 4.75 percent – even as it cautioned (perhaps only in deference to its own past pronouncements) that "some inflation risks remain."

There followed a continued lowering of the target funds rate into 2008, and numerous open-market operations in 2008 continued to facilitate short-term liquidity. The intentions of these monetary actions were explained in an FOMC press release on August 5, 2008, as follows:

Economic activity expanded in the second quarter, partly reflecting growth in consumer spending and exports. However, labor markets have softened further and financial markets remain under considerable stress. Tight credit conditions, the ongoing housing contraction, and elevated energy prices are likely to weigh on economic growth over the next few quarters. Over time, the substantial easing of monetary policy, combined with ongoing measures to foster market liquidity, should help to promote moderate economic growth.

Inflation has been high, spurred by the earlier increases in the prices of energy and some other commodities, and some indicators of inflation expectations have been

---

[3] Cecchetti (2009, p. 55) discussed reasons that banks may be reluctant to borrow at the discount window.

elevated. The Committee expects inflation to moderate later this year and next year, but the inflation outlook remains highly uncertain.

Although downside risks to growth remain, the upside risks to inflation are also of significant concern to the Committee.

From August 10, 2007, through and beyond the August 5, 2008, announcement, the Fed acted on the premise that short-term liquidity, not solvency, was the problem. The standard tools were being used because anything stronger was seen as potentially inflationary – still named as a "concern." Bernanke (1983) was applying his well-learned lessons from the Great Depression, wherein the Federal Reserve had not responded properly to what in retrospect had been seen as a "liquidity crisis" – an interpretation that we revisit in Chapter 4. As we read the previously mentioned record, it appears that the FOMC – faced with growing financial market stress in the midst of mixed signals on the state of the economy – had done its best to employ the traditional tools of liquidity enhancement based on traditional thinking. However, these tools had been woefully inadequate to stem the tide of rising balance sheet stress as asset values declined against fixed debt.

The economy was being undermined by weak balance sheets throughout the banking and household sectors.

The Fed was not prepared to take steps to address the underlying balance sheet problems because that has never been its mandate and it has never before pursued that course. This is reflected, although qualified, in the following excerpt from Bernanke's speech on October 15, 2007:

[I]t is not the responsibility of the Federal Reserve – nor would it be appropriate – to protect lenders and investors from the consequences of their financial decisions. But developments in financial markets can have broad economic effects felt by many outside the markets, and the Federal Reserve must take those effects into account when determining policy. In particular, as I have emphasized, the Federal Reserve has a mandate from the Congress to promote maximum employment and stable prices, and its monetary policy actions will be chosen so as to best meet that mandate Bernanke (2007b).

8.1.2 Federal Reserve Adaptation II: An Implicit Acknowledgment That It Was a Solvency Crisis

The policies that had been implemented by time-honored Fed principles were due for another and even more abrupt change as the second moment of truth arrived. If the first shock to the financial system was an unexpected outsized wave, the second was a tsunami.

This is indicated by the unprecedented number as well as the changing content of the 145 monetary press releases by the FOMC in 2008;[4] in fact, the releases exhibited a progressive expansion in the use of liquidity-enhancement tools, then changed gears to redefine the very meaning of Fed "monetary action." In January and February, four separate releases announced that "The Federal Reserve will conduct two auctions of twenty-eight-day credit through its Term Auction Facility." Each auction was for a $30 billion credit enhancement. In March and April, these amounts were raised to $50 billion per auction; in May and June, several more were offered in amounts of $75 billion. These actions had perhaps helped to contain the greatly increased volatility of the LIBOR in 2007 and 2008, but this important indicator of counterparty risk among the banks suffered a sharp spike in late September–October 2008 that rivaled the similar movement in 2007 (see Figure 8.2) but starting from a much higher baseline level. New initiatives announced on September 14 and 19 allowed Federal Reserve loans to be collateralized by "all investment-grade debt securities" and to "finance . . . purchases of high-quality asset-backed commercial paper." Then, on October 6, it was announced that the Federal Reserve would pay interest on both the required and the excess reserves of their deposit institutions. The Fed was rescuing the banks from the "black hole" of negative equity precipitated by growing homeowner negative equity, which had shaken financial market expectations in 2007 and induced the collapse of the MBS and CDS markets.

This crescendo of events, in which a de facto unrecognized problem of insolvency was being addressed by aggressive but traditional forms of liquidity enhancement, culminated in the October 14, Joint Statement by Treasury, Federal Reserve, and FDIC (2008):

Today we are taking decisive actions to protect the U.S. economy, to strengthen public confidence in our financial institutions, and to foster the robust functioning of our credit markets. These steps will ensure that the U.S. financial system performs its vital role of providing credit to households and businesses and protecting savings and investments in a manner that promotes strong economic growth in the United States and around the world. The overwhelming majority of banks in the United States are strong and well capitalized. These actions will bolster public confidence in our system to restore and stabilize liquidity necessary to support economic growth.

First, Treasury is announcing a voluntary capital purchase program. A broad array of financial institutions is eligible to participate in this program by selling preferred shares to the U.S. government on attractive terms that protect the taxpayer. Second,

---

[4] This compares with eighty-two press releases in 2007 and sixty-two in 2006.

after receiving a recommendation from the boards of the FDIC and the Federal Reserve, and consulting with the President, Secretary Paulson signed the systemic risk exception to the FDIC Act, enabling the FDIC to temporarily guarantee the senior debt of all FDIC-insured institutions and their holding companies, as well as deposits in non-interest-bearing deposit transaction accounts. Regulators will implement an enhanced supervisory framework to assure appropriate use of this new guarantee... Third, to further increase access to funding for businesses in all sectors of our economy, the Federal Reserve has announced further details of its Commercial Paper Funding Facility (CPFF) program, which provides a broad backstop for the commercial paper market. Beginning October 27, the CPFF will fund purchases of commercial paper of three-month maturity from high-quality issuers.

Together these three steps significantly strengthen the capital position and funding ability of U.S. financial institutions, enabling them to perform their role of under-pinning overall economic growth. These actions demonstrate to market participants here and around the world the strength of the U.S. Government's commitment to take all necessary steps to unlock our credit markets and minimize the impact of the current instability on the overall U.S. economy. The actions taken today are a powerful step toward restoring the health of the global financial system.

At this point, Fed monetary authorities had been in policy-transition mode for more than fourteen months, as revealed by the trend discussed previously in increased levels of liquidity enhancement. However, because these actions were short-term, self-liquidating arrangements (e.g., repurchase agreements), they had left a near-zero trend mark on the Fed balance sheet. This is shown in the data chart in Figure 8.3 for the period from June 2007 through September 2008. These liquidity-enhancement actions did nothing of consequence to the banks' implicit and growing negative equity problems. The episode ended as abruptly as it began when financial markets registered even more strongly than in August 2007 that household and therefore bank balance sheets were in deeper trouble than previously imagined. The October 2008 crisis was reflecting the fact that by Q4 2008, the housing data would show that home values had fallen to less than $16 trillion from $22 trillion in Q4 2006. This had an unprecedented impact on bank balance sheets by undermining the value base for the entire MBS and CDS markets. The impact on homeowner balance sheets was staggering: During the same two-year period, home equity fell from $12.5 trillion to $6 trillion. With such significant deterioration of household and bank balance sheets, and such widespread insolvency, the usual liquidity enhancement measures were not working. This is the background for the shift from Bernanke's earlier statement that "it is not the responsibility of the Federal Reserve – nor would it be appropriate – to protect lenders and investors from the consequences

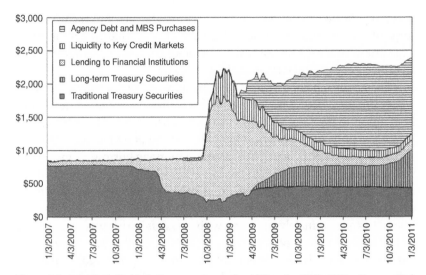

Figure 8.3. Principal Federal Reserve assets (in billions), 2007–2010. *Source:* Federal Reserve Bank of Cleveland, Credit Easing Policy Tools. Data available at www .clevelandfed.org/research/data/credit_easing/index.cfm.

of their financial decisions" to their decisions to begin filling holes in the balance sheets with capital investments in financial institutions. He was in the center of a collapse that was similar to the Depression-era world that he knew well. But his knowledge of it was from the strictly academic perspective "to know that," and he was now learning in real time about the far more difficult problem "to know how."[5] Critics of Bernanke's action at this point should ask: What would they have done, given the circumstances, whatever might have been any previous mistakes that had become relevant only to history?

In retrospect, it seems likely that the Greenspan Fed had gone too far in easing monetary policy after the dotcom bubble burst, and this may have strengthened the Bernanke Fed's subsequent resolve to avoid premature easing of money. Neither is it by any means evident that reverting to a policy of ease earlier than August 2007 would have had any effect beyond

[5] In his discussion of "know how," Hayek (1967, p. 44) observed that "German . . . has three terms for the English 'to know': *wissen,* corresponding to 'know that', *kennen,* corresponding to 'be acquainted with', and *können,* corresponding to 'know how'." The latter "consists in the capacity to act according to rules which we may be able to discover but which we may not be able to state in order to obey them." These last are the rules of the craftsman, learned from being immersed in much practical experience; central bankers only rarely encounter episodes like those from 1929–32 and 2007–10.

stretching the housing bubble still farther – the damage had been done; the surge of "water under the bridge" had already occurred as a result of the large inflow of foreign investment aided, abetted, and further leveraged by an expansionary monetary policy in 2002–2004.

If Fed actions in context seemed to be fully justified – even inevitable – it does not mean that it was all happening without creating future hazards. In addition to the long-run moral hazard of bailing out home buyers and banks – victims of their own folly – there is the potential error of seeing systemic risk where there is only private risk among borrowers and lenders who must bear the burden of its own actions. In light of Bernanke's (2007b), concern that the Fed should *not* "protect lenders and investors from the consequences of their financial decisions," it seems clear that he (and the FMOC) came ultimately to the view that systemic risk was so great that he had to do what had been repugnant to his principles. Switching in time but not too soon is also important in minimizing the Fed's reputation risk: Criticism of the Bernanke Fed has been nothing compared with the firestorm that would have followed if the banking system had suffered a collapse. However, as discussed in Chapter 10, alternative policies directed to restructuring bank balance sheets through bankruptcy may be advantageous in returning the economy more quickly to its natural growth path.

That the Fed moved decisively after September 2008 is reflected in its unprecedented acquisition of the overvalued asset holdings of private financial and public housing agency institutions.[6] Households, banks, and other financial industry segments all faced one overriding problem in the 2007–2008 meltdown: Their balance sheets were inadequately reserved. In effect, in Q4 2008, the Bernanke Fed moved to reserve them all, creating reserve deposits far beyond what was required to service current levels of demand for new private lending activity. The chart in Figure 8.3 shows the approximate $1.3 trillion increase in the Fed's acquisition of mortgage, commercial paper, and federal housing agency debt, in less than three months. It was a new world; the previous episode of liquidity enhancement had been inadequate, ending as abruptly as it had started as the Fed moved decisively to rechart its course. Whatever we might think about Bernanke, he had not

---

[6] Much controversy has surrounded the Lehman Brothers Chapter 11 bankruptcy filing of September 15, 2008, and the Fed AIG bailout on September 16, 2008, to prevent its bankruptcy, as precipitating events. However, MBS asset values and their derivatives had been eroding under pressure from housing price declines since early 2006, and this had widespread insolvency implications that sooner or later were certain to come to a head. We think the Lehman Brothers and AIG events were only the messengers of tidings that were sure to break through somewhere.

Table 8.1. *Treasury and Federal Reserve Purchases, GSE-Guaranteed MBS and GSE-Issued Debt, 2008–2010 ($ billion)*

Action	Period	Freddie Mac	Fannie Mae	Ginnie Mae	FHLB
Treasury Purchase MBS	December 2008 to March 2010	105.9	114.8	NA	NA
Federal Reserve Purchase MBS	January 5, 2009, to March 31, 2010	432.3	703.6	114.0	NA
Federal Reserve Purchase GSE Debt	December 2008 to March 2010	67.1	67.4	NA	37.7
Total (All: 1,642.2)		605.3	885.8	114.0	37.1

Source: Federal Housing Finance Agency. Available at www.fhfa.gov/Default.aspx?Page=70.

been an ideologue committed to the new path he had chosen in August 2007. In fact, beginning in Q1 2008, the Fed had already been switching out of its traditional holdings of short-term Treasuries and increasing its lending to financial institutions, while keeping its overall level of asset holdings constant (see Figure 8.3).

The $1.3 trillion jump in Fed asset holdings after October 2008 was concentrated in the categories of "lending to financial institutions" and providing "liquidity to key credit markets" (e.g., commercial paper). Both of these actions would prove to be relatively short-lived because these direct forms of support to the private sector started to wane by February 2009. Overlapping this decline, both the Fed and the Treasury began purchasing GSE-guaranteed private MBS instruments as well as GSE debt issues used to finance their own MBS instruments.

Total acquisitions for the account of the U.S. Treasury and the Federal Reserve are shown in Table 8.1, listed by period of purchase and the various GSE entities. Freddie Mac and Fannie Mae were by far the largest, totaling more than $1.6 trillion.

The storm's fury may have been dampened by these actions, but the Fed did not see the danger as having passed. Bernanke's actions continued to reflect a pessimistic view, even if overlaid by pronouncements of hope.

The massive bubble in housing prices based on price expectations supported by expansionary credit, undisciplined by traditional equity requirements, had all depended on continuance of these forces. When that momentum turned negative, buyers of homes, mortgages, and bank obligations reined in their activity; the stock market plummeted; and monetary policy was impotent to stem the economic consequences of balance sheet changes. Monetary policy was "pushing on a string" that only absent buyers could pull. Too many buyers were living in homes with deepening negative equity, and monetary policy was caught in what was – not very informatively – called "the liquidity trap."

The Fed's asset purchase actions after Q3 2008 lifted much of the weight – it is impossible to know exactly how much – of overvalued mortgage assets off bank balance sheets. Those assets were carried at their original face value on the bank books. By replacing those assets with deposits in the Federal Reserve at their full face value, the banks were made more nearly whole in the sense that the bank liabilities were more closely aligned with the market worth of their assets.

There followed much agonizing in the press, with responses by the Fed to the following question: What will be the Fed's exit strategy, or how will the Fed unwind its massive, potentially inflationary creation of excess reserves? However, all of those concerns disappeared like phantoms in the night: By Q4 2010, two years after the great Fed rescue of the banks, the economy remained mired in low growth, bank lending was still negative on net, and there was 9.6 percent unemployment – dismal but much better than 20 percent at a comparable point in the Great Depression.

8.2 Continuous Adaptation: Still More Fed Easing Was to Follow

By November 2010, about 23 percent of homes were in negative equity, which for most households means negative net worth. These households were relatively frozen into their current locations and jobs; they hunkered down to pay off debt, implying that we were facing a long hard slog of slow recovery.[7] The Fed seemed to have recognized this, revealing its deepest fears – either a protracted recovery or a double-dip 1980s-style recession – by proposing (in November 2010 but previously advertised as a "coming attraction") a $600 billion program of market purchases of longer-term Treasury bonds; this was known as QE2 (i.e., quantitative easing part 2). This was in addition to the previous announcement that $300 billion of income from the Fed's holdings of MBS would be reinvested in Treasuries. In effect, during the eight months of the program, the Fed would purchase nearly

---

[7] As we suggested in a *Wall Street Journal* article in 2010: "[I]t appears that those who see signs of a recovery may be grasping at straws. What one should hope is that this time it is different from every one of the past fourteen U.S. downturns, but those who believe this have the weight of past experience against them" (Gjerstad and Smith, 2010).

all of the new Treasury bonds that were expected to be issued to finance the government's projected expenditure needs (Hilsenrath, 2010; see also Reddy, 2010). In effect monetizing all new Treasury debt during an eight-month period brought an outcry from many concerning its inflationary implications, showing only the extent to which people were underestimating the inevitable consequences of a severe balance sheet recession. Monetary inflation cannot be forthcoming in these circumstances as long as the banks are not lending – the monetary consequence of Fed action was to simply pump up the level of idle bank reserves.

The effect of these new initiatives is reflected in Figure 8.3 by the surge in Fed "long-term treasury purchases" after November 2010, raising total Fed holdings of its major asset categories to roughly $2.9 trillion, which was $2 trillion more than total holdings in September 2008. The Fed balance sheet had tripled in magnitude in three years, resulting mostly in near-zero interest rates, high bank profitability, and an economy with too many people owing more than their assets were worth. Neither could anyone be sure that this purchase program would be sufficient and that the Fed would not buy even more Treasuries or take new actions as the fallout continued from the 2007 crash of the great housing-mortgage market bubble.

That it was not deemed sufficient was clear in the Board's FOMC press release of January 2012, when it expressed the likelihood that the long period of exceptional monetary ease would continue for another two years:

[T]he Committee decided today to keep the target range for the federal funds rate at 0 to 1/4 percent and currently anticipates that economic conditions – including low rates of resource utilization and a subdued outlook for inflation over the medium run – are likely to warrant exceptionally low levels for the federal funds rate at least through late 2014.

8.3 Why Do Housing Market Crashes Bring Recession but Stock Market Crashes Do Not?

In the dotcom crash of 2000–2002, $10 trillion came off the value of securities, yet that decline hardly made a dent in bank balance sheets and it was associated with only a mild recession – caused in the opinion of the Greenspan Fed by a slump in nonresidential fixed investment. Similarly, the stock market crash of October 19, 1987, did not lead to a recession. However, when the value of all U.S. homes declined by $4 trillion in 2006–2007, whereas fixed nonresidential investment was increasing, the banks buckled, the Fed began (in August 2007) its year-long program of "liquidity enhancement," and the Great Recession was underway. Why this difference?

That a difference was not recognized by sophisticated analysts is illustrated by an examination of potential consequences for the economy and for Fed policy of a reversal in the long run-up in housing prices. The occasion was a 2005 meeting of the FOMC devoted to five presentations on the special topic "Housing Valuations and Monetary Policy" by senior Fed research personnel. This research established the proposition that home prices had risen unsustainably relative to home rentals, thereby constituting a price bubble. John Williams, a senior vice president at the Federal Reserve Bank of San Francisco at the time, used the impact of the 2001–2002 stock market crash to estimate the fallout from a potential 20 percent drop in housing prices based on how changes in wealth impact household spending (Williams, 2005, p. 18):

There is considerable uncertainty regarding the magnitude of the effects of changes in stock market and housing wealth on household spending; nonetheless, it seems clear the magnitude of the current potential problem is much smaller than, and perhaps only half as large as, that of the stock market bubble.

This statement is oblivious to the distinct balance sheet effects of stock market and housing price declines. The contrast between the dotcom crash (2000–2002) and the housing collapse (2007–2009) renews an important lesson going back to the 1920s and 1930s. Whenever stocks fall "off the cliff," the combination of tough margin requirements and callable loans serves well to confine the balance sheet damage to investors with minimal impact on their lenders. However, when housing prices collapse against fixed long-term mortgage obligations, household equity falls dollar for dollar with the declining home prices. The resulting household balance sheet damage extends directly to the banks, causing them to severely restrict new loan activity.

As discussed herein, mortgage loans became highly leveraged, especially in the second phase of the recent housing bubble. Figure 3.7 (see Chapter 3) shows the collapse in market value of homes against fixed mortgage debt that accounted for the rapid onset of household negative equity and the parallel stress on bank balance sheets. On stocks, a margin loan can be called within twenty-four hours, whereas an "underwater" mortgage goes unrecognized as long as the bank receives loan payments. Mortgage-lender risk accumulates if the collateral values continue to erode against fixed debt, threatening financial system solvency and economic distress for the innocent and profligate alike. However, in stock market crashes, loan obligations are flexible downward as assets are liquidated against debt; this feature removes the onus of negative equity from future decisions for both debtor and creditor.

Figure 8.4. S&P 500 Index and total margin debt, 1959–2013. Margin debt closely tracks the rise and fall of the S&P 500 Index.

The downward flexibility in stock market debt is illustrated in Figure 8.4, which plots the S&P 500 stock index since 1957 and margin debt during the same period. In contrast to Figure 3.7 for housing mortgage debt, stock margin debt not only rises in step with stock index value in market booms, it also declines symmetrically in step with market collapses.[8] Hence, balance sheets are continually marked to market with equity losses incurred in real time. The decline in equity is arrested and does not accumulate to dampen forward-looking decisions to spend or lend.

By 1934, we had the rules right for containing the fallout from stock bubbles, and we stayed within those rules; soon thereafter, we found and then ultimately lost a stabilizing approach to mortgage market rules. Why?

Stock Markets. Beginning in April 1928, a year and a half before the 1929 crash, brokers had – in their own interest and under pressure from banks that lent to them – increased margin requirements from about 25 to 50 percent on Dow-Jones stocks – and much higher on riskier stocks (*New York Times,* 1928a, 1928b, 1928c). After the October 1929 crash, margins returned to their pre-1929 level of 25 percent. Then, in 1933, for the first time, the New York Stock Exchange (NYSE) required all of its members to

---

[8]   NYSE margin debt figures are from the *NYSE Factbook.* S&P 500 Index values are from the St. Louis Federal Reserve Economic Data (FRED), available at http://research.stlouisfed .org/fred2/series/SP500.

fix margin requirements for their customers (*New York Times*, 1933a). Soon after the NYSE took steps to restrict margin purchases, federal regulation was proposed (*New York Times*, 1933b). Regulation T, fixing minimum margin requirements (today at 50 percent), was implemented by the Federal Reserve Board on September 27, 1934, under the Securities and Exchange Act (*New York Times*, 1934a) and became effective on October 15, 1934 (*New York Times*, 1934b). Hence, the NYSE and then Congress codified the property right rules that first emerged in financial practice in the brokerage and banking industry.

All of this institutional learning about stock market credit has become cast in concrete, and it accounts for the fact that securities market crashes, such as the dotcom crash, have been confined primarily to investors. These crashes have done minimal collateral damage to the credit system and the economy.

Mortgage Markets. Housing investment reached peak levels in 1925 and 1926 of nearly 60 percent higher than when the Depression began in 1929, and it would decline another 85 percent before bottoming out in 1933 (see Figure 4.1 in Chapter 4). Prices and sales volumes also fell after 1926. Savings and loan banks had long amortized practically all mortgage loans, but 85 percent of mortgage loans by insurance companies and 88 percent by commercial banks were non-amortizing or only partially amortizing between 1925 and 1929 (Grebler et al., 1956, p. 231). By the late 1930s, all major classes of lenders had adopted strict amortization requirements. High mortgage standards for both federal and privately financed homes remained the norm for decades but began to erode in the 1990s, with the growing political consensus and widespread private financial accommodation that U.S. society should be more aggressive in mortgage lending to low- to middle-income families.

Derivatives pose the same problem as stocks and mortgages: Financial stability requires them to be collateralized. Otherwise, as discussed in Chapter 7, they further the instability of the banking system. Their exempt status insulated them from the institutional learning that had long confined the burden of stock market crashes to stock market investors.

Tough margin rules have not and cannot prevent stock market bubbles and crashes, but they have demonstrably controlled external damage to banks and the economy. Lax mortgage standards can and have brought great unintended harm, even to those it was hoped would be made to prosper. The reasons are evident: Strong political constituencies existed to alter mortgage "margin requirements" – that is, to support low down payments for home buyers and exempt status for derivatives.

8.4 Pause for Reflection

The next two chapters change direction to examine two questions. Chapter 9 addresses what might be done; the policy discussion is largely in the specific context of the U.S. experience. Chapter 10 inquires about what might be learned from foreign economic crises. Both chapters, however, continue to use the framework of analysis that we use throughout the book. Therefore, at this juncture, readers may find it helpful to review where we have been by referring to Sections 11.1 through 11.10 in the final chapter, "Summarizing: What Have We Learned?"

References

Associated Press (2007). "Fed's Bernanke: Subprime Mortgage Problems Contained." March 28. Available at www.ar15.com/archive/topic.html?b=1&f=5&t=913103.

Bernanke, Ben S. (1983). "Nonmonetary Effects of the Financial Crisis in the Propagation of the Great Depression." *American Economic Review* 73, pp. 257–76.

Bernanke, Ben S. (2007a). "The Economic Outlook," before the Joint Economic Committee, U.S. Congress. Board of Governors of the Federal Reserve System, March 28. www.federalreserve.gov/newsevents/testimony/bernanke20070328a.htm.

Bernanke, Ben S. (2007b). "The Subprime Mortgage Market." Federal Reserve Bank of Chicago, 43rd Annual Conference on Bank Structure and Competition, Chicago, May 17.

Bernanke, Ben S. (2007c). "The Recent Financial Turmoil and its Economic and Policy Consequences." Economic Club of New York, October 15.

Cecchetti, Stephen G. (2009). "Crisis and Responses: The Federal Reserve in the Early Stages of the Financial Crisis." *Journal of Economic Perspectives*, 23, pp. 51–75.

Feldstein, Martin (2013). "An Interview with Paul Volcker," *Journal of Economic Perspectives* 27 (4) pp. 105–20.

Gjerstad, Steven, and Vernon. L. Smith (2010). "Why We Are in for a Long, Hard Economic Slog." *Wall Street Journal,* September 10.

Grebler, Leo, David M. Blank, and Louis Winnick (1956). *Capital Formation in Residential Real Estate.* Princeton, NJ: Princeton University Press.

Hayek, Friedrich (1967). "Rules, Perception and Intelligibility." In *Studies in Philosophy, Politics and Economics.* Chicago: University of Chicago Press, pp. 43–65.

Hilsenrath, John (2010). "Central Bank Treads into Once-Taboo Realm." *Wall Street Journal,* November 4.

Joint Statement by Treasury, Federal Reserve, and FDIC (2008). Board of Governors of the Federal Reserve System, October 14, 8:30 a.m., EDT. Available at www.federalreserve .gov/newsevents/press/monetary/20081014a.htm.

Kirkland, Rik (2007). "The Greatest Economic Boom Ever." *Fortune,* July 12. Available at http://money.cnn.com/magazines/fortune/fortune_archive/2007/07/23/100134937/index.htm.

Kohn, Donald L. (2009). "Monetary Policy and Asset Prices Revisited." *Cato Journal*, 29, 1, pp. 31–44. Speech at the Cato Institute 26th Monetary Policy Conference, Washington, DC, November 19, 2008.

Lawder, David (2007). "Strong World Econ Containing Subprime Risk: Paulson," *Reuters*, Beijing, August 1. Available at www.reuters.com/article/2007/08/01/us-usa-paulson-subprime-idUSBJC00005820070801.

New York Times (1928a). "Exchange Houses Tighten Margin." April 18, p. 35.

New York Times (1928b). "Brokers Increase Margins on Stocks." October 7, p. N9.

New York Times (1928c). "Margin Requirements Raised by Brokers." November 1, p. 42.

New York Times (1933a). "Stock Exchange Curbs Gambling; High Margins Set, Pools Checked." August 3, p. 1.

New York Times (1933b). "Brokers Expect Federal Control." October 29, p. N7.

New York Times (1934a). "Text of the Federal Reserve's Regulations on Margin Dealing on the Stock Exchange." September 28, p. 40.

New York Times (1934b). "Stock Margin Rules Become Effective Today." October 15, p. 27.

Reddy, Sudeep (2010). "Q&A on QE2: What a Fed Move Would Mean." *Wall Street Journal, Real Time Economics*, September 3. Available at http://blogs.wsj.com/economics/2010/11/03/qa-on-qe2-what-a-fed-move-would-mean/.

Reuters (2007). "Treasury's Paulson – Subprime Woes Likely Contained." New York, April 20. Available at http://uk.reuters.com/article/2007/04/20/usa-subprime-paulson-idUKWBT00686520070420.

Sengupta, Rajdeep, and Yu Man Tam (2008). "The LIBOR-OIS Spread as a Summary Indicator." Federal Reserve Bank of St. Louis, Economic Synopses, Number 25.

Taylor, John B. (2009). "Economic Policy and Financial Markets: An Empirical Analysis of What Went Wrong." *Critical Review*, 21, 2–3, pp. 341–64.

Taylor, John B., and John C. Williams (2009). "A Black Swan in the Money Market." *American Economic Journal: Macroeconomics*, 1, 1, pp. 58–83.

Williams, John C. (2005). "Monetary Policy Implications of a House Price Bubble." FOMC, Transcript of the Meeting, June 29–30. Transcripts and Other Historical Materials, Board of Governors of the Federal Reserve System. Available at http://federalreserve.gov/monetarypolicy/files/FOMC20050630meeting.pdf.

9

What Might Be Done?

This is the paradox at the heart of the financial crisis. In the past few years, we've seen too much greed and too little fear; too much spending and not enough saving; too much borrowing and not enough worrying. Today, however, our problem is exactly the opposite.

The President's recovery strategy is addressing the housing market. The vicious cycle of rising foreclosures leading to declining home prices, leading to rising foreclosures – must be contained. This problem is at the heart of our economic crisis.

Through direct interventions, using the GSEs to bring down mortgage rates and make possible refinancings for creditworthy borrowers who have lost their home equity as house prices decline, and through setting standards and providing significant financial subsidies for measures directed at payment relief to prevent foreclosures, we are achieving several objectives.
 – Lawrence Summers at The Brookings Institution, March 13, 2009

The curious task of economics is to demonstrate to men how little they really know about what they imagine they can design.
 – Friedrich A. Hayek, *The Fatal Conceit*, 1988, p. 76

In 2009, President Obama's chief economic advisor saw a sudden, paradoxical, 180-degree shift in what had been wrong with the American economy in the past "few" years: (1) "too much greed" (i.e., incentives that were incompatible with stable growth); (2) "too little fear, not enough worrying, and too much borrowing" (i.e., inadequate provision for and protection against balance sheet risk); and (3) "too much spending and not enough saving" (i.e., inadequate investment from current income). However, now the problems were exactly the opposite. Summers' Paradox is that the solution to a housing market collapse – expanded credit support to artificially stimulate housing demand – is what has been universally acknowledged as the original problem.[1] Missing from both Democratic and Republican economic policy was recognition of the severe disequilibrium in the economy: Housing prices, fueled by credit, were far too high relative to the prices of other consumer goods including labor. Normal self-sustaining demand could not be restored until this imbalance was corrected. Missing from models of the economic cycle was acknowledgment that the economy was in a balance sheet recession, much like that of the Great Depression and, although far less severely than in the Great Depression or the Great Recession, housing had been a key problem in most of the postwar recessions. Moreover, normal household demand would not be restored until mortgage debt was aligned with current housing prices (i.e., excessive leverage had to be deleveraged). Normal credit supply in the economy would not be restored until the balance sheets of households and banks improved, either from mortgage principal repayments or from house price appreciation, or a combination of the two.

9.1 Incentives and Human Betterment

If we begin with the proposition that human economic betterment depends on the existence of private incentives supporting work, saving, investment, and entrepreneurship – including human capital development and innovation – then it is desirable for public policy to avoid structural forms that are contrary to those incentives. Although a free society promotes opportunities, it is individuals and organizations that decide how much to work, save, learn, and venture. Within this framework, we also must ask which policies might support financial and economic stability because the extremes of inflation and wasted excess capacity also clearly interfere with self-propelled forms of human economic betterment.

Regardless of political opinion, all shades of it surely must appreciate the inherent contradictions in an enlarged stock of unsold, empty, and foreclosed homes juxtaposed with families doubling up and desirous of more accommodative living quarters but even more concerned about reducing their burden of household debt. The questions are how to (1) escape the balance sheet hole with minimum long-term damage to moral hazard incentives; and (2) restore a semblance of equilibrium to an economy battered

---

[1] As in Gilbert and Sullivan's *The Pirates of Penzance*, Act II:

"A most ingenious paradox!
We've quips and quibbles heard in flocks,
But none to beat this paradox!"

by disequilibrium from the undisciplined flow of credit into both housing demand and supply; followed by paralyzing balance sheet distortions in households, banks, and commercial property portfolios; and the real sector marking time as income is diverted into deleveraging.

This chapter discusses policies that we think have a reasonable chance of being incentive-compatible for work, saving, investment, entrepreneurship and human capital development as well as consistent with long-term stability. The policies are based on our reading of experience: Past institutions found but also lost and the recurrent sources of instability; they are therefore subject to error in our interpretation or in the extrapolation of measures of past experience. Error in basing policy (private or public) on historical experience arises when the policy itself misconstrues or changes the nature of the historical measures. Historically, mortgage default experience reflected the due diligence of local loan originators that were also the lenders. However, the practice of paying upfront fees for mortgages that originated locally and were sold to distant lenders threatens to undermine due-diligence incentives and to alter subsequent default experience.

In this chapter, we discuss monetary and taxation policy as well as "regulation" as a property rights issue. The perspective is, in part, that of promoting stability in the sense that although asset bubbles are an inevitable feature of human and social behavior in modern financial economies, the collateral damage done to the economy and to those who are more or less innocent bystanders must be minimized. Thus, under existing institutions that firmly established securities margin requirements going back to the late 1920s, the bursting of an equities bubble primarily impacts only those who have chosen to invest in equities (although secondarily there are negative wealth effects). However, when a housing-mortgage bubble "turns south" because of unfathomably relaxed down payment requirements and inadequately reserved financial institutions and instruments, it adversely impacts all bank depositors, most of whom may be innocent of these excesses. Therefore, the discussion, in part, addresses broader issues of human welfare. The policies discussed range from the economically ideal to those that may be within the range of practical politics, but the discussion is not constrained by what might be feasible within the current high volatility of political opinion (e.g., political sentiment for stimulus spending in 2008–2009 turned to sentiment for austerity in 2012–2013). We do not find excusable the existence of risk-blinded banks, profligate borrowers, or government programs that aided and abetted home buyers to live beyond their means, joining the many other private and public entities that rode the bubble with so little forward thought but now are anxious to find who (excluding themselves) is most blameworthy.

Many of the policy issues we discuss, such as the need to address the negative equity problem in household and bank balance sheets, is years overdue. In fact, as Chapter 10 shows, the events during the Great Depression and the Great Recession in the United States are not uncommon. These events have been occurring frequently during the past several decades; they affect the country that suffers an asset market collapse and the countries that lend to them. Moreover, many countries that confront asset market collapses and financial crises also experience sharp currency depreciation, which affects their competitors and suppliers in international markets. The linkages among economies are abundant, and capital inflow-supported asset bubbles and collapses, financial crises, and the effects of responses to these events have become a recurring part of the global economic environment in past decades. Understanding the course of these events is crucial for stabilizing the global economy.

9.2 The Blame Game

Because it is so prominent – if orthogonal to our own intentions – we briefly summarize and comment on the widespread dominant political and journalistic question discussed in the bubble's aftermath and published in outlets ranging from traditional academic journals to the media: Whom are we to blame?

The issues here are simplistically stated, as follows (Stiglitz, 2009, pp. 329–30):

> The search is on for whom to blame for the global economic crisis. It is not just a matter of vindictiveness; it is important to know who or what caused the crisis if one is to figure out how to prevent another, or perhaps even to fix this one . . . causation is, however, complex. Presumably, it means something like: "If only the guilty party had taken another course of action, the crisis would not have occurred" . . . But I would argue that blame should be placed primarily on the banks . . . and the investors.

Of course, good regulations mean good property rights – required and prohibited actions that favor stability – but forming institutions with rights that foster orderly wealth creation is a challenge facing countries around the world. Finding blame in private or public opportunists who come and go without end does not confront the imposing task of achieving lasting rules and casting institutions from them that live across transient generations and adapt to changing circumstances.

Interventionists are deluded with images of ideal regulation imposed by a benevolent government that can implement the continuous monitoring, surveillance, and information that its objectives would require. Free-market opponents of any and all "regulation" leave us without guidelines for defining the property rights within which markets and choices are to be free but constrained to be efficacious to do their best work in furthering human betterment. One day, we are scandalized by Fannie and Freddie accounting, another day by "the banks" and by Madoff; in many cases, the individuals involved are already accountable in that they have violated existing property rights restrictions that limit fraud and the bearing of false witness, although loopholes may sometimes require new legislation. Otherwise, there is enough blame to go around for the millions (e.g., from borrowers, mortgage originators, securitizers, raters, ideological regulators, to CDS "insurers") who may have nurtured self-delusions that they were acting in good faith and within the rules but were inadequately reserved or inappropriately incentivized or misunderstood the dynamics of the market. Better than the goal of determining which were the principals and which the accessories to the crime of "killing the economy" is to seek a rule regime that achieves for housing-mortgage markets what registration and minimum margin rules have achieved for securities markets. That is not an easy task and will certainly be prone to error: Securities and housing have quite disparate properties.

9.3 "Regulation" as Incentive-Compatible Property Rights

Regulations are about defining property rights – that is human rights to act – because it is not possible to speak of inanimate "property" as having rights to act; the essence of such rights is that they be fitting and proper.[2] What went wrong in the world of banking and finance – broadly construed to include depository institutions, investment banks, "shadow" banking, and exempt investment vehicles – was the widespread commitment by individuals and financial institutions to obligations that were insufficiently

---

[2] This essence is indicated by their origin in the phrase "propriety rights." Thus, " . . . in seventeenth-century usage . . . the interchangeability of 'propriety' and 'property' is well illustrated by Locke himself: after showing an initial preference for 'propriety' in much of his work, he changed many references to 'property' in later versions" (Buckle, 1991, pp. 172–3). By the eighteenth century – for example, in the writings of David Hume and Adam Smith – the term used is "property rights," but what these scholars meant is clearly indicated by their idea that such rights arise by consent in social groups that have suffered the repeated experience of violating them.

reserved to buffer their obligation to pay out of projected income or assets against unforeseen changes in the debtor or payer's economic circumstances. If changed circumstances for individuals impacted only the fortunes of those affected, then these costs to the creditor-payee might simply be captured in the equilibrium price terms of the applicable contracts. However, there are systemic and correlated forms of contagion risk in asset markets that make such responses inadequate. Hence, one person's insufficiently collateralized promise to pay (e.g., a home buyer) becomes another's (e.g., a bank's) insufficiently collateralized ability to fulfill his or her promise to pay a third party (e.g., a depositor), and so on – each having acted solemnly in good faith *but without adequate reserves.*

Reserves are a convention, emerging from experience and designed to cushion the fulfillment of promises when the best of good-faith intentions fail. This proposition applies to the relationship between the assets and liabilities of all entities: mortgage borrowers, bank lenders, federal housing agencies, buyers and sellers of CDS, and nonbank financial firms that borrow short and lend long (e.g., they issue money-market instruments, buy MBS, and count on rolling over those instruments in stable markets).

Since the onset of the crisis – first confronted by the FOMC on August 10, 2007 (see Chapter 8) – public policy has intervened with the intention of arresting the decline in financial and economic activity in ways that often justify, reward, and continue the same excesses that led to the original crisis. Given the systemic severity of the housing-mortgage market crash, this does not mean that some intervention was without merit and that it should not have been undertaken.

Rather, our essential point is that those conditions that exacerbated the bubble must be avoided in the first place – before asset markets are running amuck and there are no desirable choices left – through institutional learning in the form of constraints on individual access to credit. Otherwise, contradictions abound: Summers (2009) described his response to his "most ingenious paradox."

1. Public-housing policy (c. 2009) sought to stimulate housing demand with relaxed down payment and mortgage amortization require-ments, incentives, and subsidized low-interest loans. Summers argues that "steps to support incomes, increase the flow of credit and normalize housing market conditions address each of the vicious cycles . . . leading to decline." To do this, he sought to increase the flow of mortgage credit through the GSE. However, two years before the collapse of the housing-mortgage market, Frame and White (2005,

p. 173) had argued that [t]he United States has too much housing... and federal sponsorship of Fannie Mae and Freddie Mac exac-
erbates this problem. Moreover, Fannie Mae and Freddie Mac do not
do an especially good job of focusing on the low- and moderate-
income first-time buyer, where the social argument for support of
homeownership is strongest."

2. Summers also noted that "[t]he President's approach rests on two
pillars... [t]he first is provision for a trillion dollars or more for
financing, for purchasing mortgages... and other financial instruments through... the government-sponsored enterprises in the mortgage area... for establishing realistic asset valuations so that markets
can function, and enabling banks to divest toxic assets." Apparently,
because the mortgage assets that the banks had created did not command good prices in the markets, the government would be able to help
out. "The second pillar of our program is assuring that our banking
system is well capitalized."

Government bailouts of large banks and massive lending on toxic
collateral by the Fed were emergency measures by policy makers
defended as essential to rescue the economy from the onslaught of
a depression. The rescue "medicine" necessarily assures that financial
entities, whose primary concern is managing downside risk exposure,
are rescued from the consequences of their own decisions in the rush to
prevent home price decline and deterioration in bank balance sheets.
As discussed in Chapter 8, what Bernanke thought he could avoid –
that is, protecting investors from the consequences of their decisions –
was ultimately embraced.

Summers has been among the strongest proponents of privatized gains
and socialized losses. Obviously, when systemically important institutions
are unable to meet their current obligations, in order to arrest contagion,
forceful, timely action is necessary. Yet this does not imply that the government needs to provide new capital to the firms, or take "toxic" assets off
of their balance sheets. In Chapter 10, we consider a variety of approaches
that have been followed in other countries. The Swedish response, in which
equity holders lost their stake in a number of institutions, was among the
most successful. After the balance sheets were restored to good condition,
the institutions were restored to private ownership.

We propose another more market-oriented approach. For systemically
important institutions, we propose creation of a new class of bonds
that is subordinated to normal bonds but senior to equity, comprising

approximately 8 percent of the firms' liabilities, which for expositional purposes we refer to here as Mezzanine Bonds. If the equity position of the firm
is impaired because of poor management decisions, poor asset performance,
or other adverse conditions, as in 2008, and the equity capital of the firm as
a percentage of total liabilities falls below a preestablished threshold (e.g., 2
or 4 percent), then the Mezzanine Bondholders would form a bondholders'
committee and make contingency plans for their takeover of the firm. These
contingency plans would include formation of a new board of directors and
plans for the replacement or retention of senior management. If the firm
reaches a point at which it is unable to meet current obligations and collapse
of the firm is imminent – such as Long-Term Capital Management reached
in September 1998 that Bear Stearns reached in March 2008 and that AIG
and Lehman Brothers reached in September 2008 – rather than follow ad
hoc procedures, such as a takeover coordinated by the Federal Reserve (as
in the case of LTCM), or asset guarantees in a sale of the firm (as with Bear
Stearns), or a capital infusion from the Federal Reserve and the U.S. Treasury (AIG), or a Chapter 11 bankruptcy (Lehman Brothers), we propose a
new form of legal restructuring that can be completed in a matter of hours.
Once the firm is unable to meet its obligations, the board of directors would
be dismissed (under a new chapter in the bankruptcy code), the equity
position would be eliminated, the Mezzanine Bonds would be converted to
equity, and the Mezzanine Bondholders would establish their new board of
directors and their new senior management team. At that point, the firm
would have equity capital of approximately 8 percent, the liabilities of the
firm would be substantially reduced (by the conversion of Mezzanine Bond
debt into equity), the old management and board of directors will have been
cleared away, and the public purse does not assume responsibility for the
poor decisions of the departed management.

In the remainder of this section, we review other changes that we believe
are needed.

9.3.1 Mortgages

First, meaningful down payments must be made in cash or its near-cash
liquidity equivalent. No one can be sure of the precise requirement, but
the traditional rule of at least 20 percent seems experienced-based and
proper. Nothing in the new world of alleged financial "magic" indicates the
existence of a better alternative for cushioning each node in the mortgage
lending network against negative shocks. However, down-payment rules
alone are not enough.

Second, a rule requiring loan amortization with principal declining with payments would not be optimal for every borrower (see Chapter 7, Section 7.8). However, implementing a more detailed property rights structure is costly and may not be feasible.[3]

Third, whereas the loan originator compensation fee should be determined by the market, its time distribution must be geared to the time profile of borrower payments. Any upfront component of the fee must be proportional to the cash down payment, with the remainder proportioned to principal payments and impounded in escrow payments to the originator. Under these fee rules, an originator cannot off-load the risk to a third-party lender; loan default must have consequences for the originator of the loan and induce due diligence in the originator's own self-interest. Under this proposed distribution rule, it may or may not be efficient to separate lending from origination; however, if such separation occurs, the lending and origination functions would be incentive-compatible. Problems of "predatory lending behavior" are simply symptoms of incentive-incompatible institutional rules. The need is to address the incentive causes of poor decision making, not the symptoms by trying to impose complicated new and untested constraints on the consequences of agent responses to their incentives for personal gain. Otherwise, originators simply will find imaginative new ways to maximize their upfront payments and others, downstream, will have to suffer the consequences of due-diligence failure at the critical loan origination stage.[4]

---

[3] The final rules under Dodd-Frank do not require amortization but rather specify detailed provisions designed to govern the definition of a "qualified mortgage." Thus, lenders are required to satisfy eight minimum standard factors. That amortization is part of the core standard is contained in the following provision: "The rule provides guidance as to the application of these factors under the statute. For example, monthly payments must generally be calculated by assuming that the loan is repaid in substantially equal monthly payments during its term" (*Federal Register*, Consumer Financial Protection Bureau, January 30, 2013). However, these micromanagement provisions are administratively costly both to the regulator (i.e., taxpayer) and the regulated: They represent a further attempt to change incentives by imposing external input constraints rather than focusing on internalizing rules that align agent-consequential outcomes with the desired social outcomes. Thus, as discussed herein, bank-originated loans have been incentive-compatible (under traditional FDIC bank supervision; see Bair, 2012) and have not been a problem, unlike the loans of third-party originators. In the FDIC, we already had in place bank-supervision rules to govern risk. New rules need not displace or duplicate existing rules and institutions.

[4] Other suppliers of services to the housing-mortgage industry, in addition to mortgage originators, are in need of incentives equivalent to those of the lenders: mortgage service firms and investors were motivated by incentives that favored foreclosure over loan

9.3.2 Derivatives

Derivatives are securities and should not be exempt from registration and margin-collateral requirements even if buyers imagine that they can safely forgo such requirements. Institutional rules and traditions have the capacity to incorporate constraints that are wiser than myopic individual expressions of reason because institutional controls can account for more facts and experience than any individual mind.[5] Derivatives should not be exempt from collateral rules because the ability of the buyers of CDS to keep their commitments to others may fail if the sellers default on their payment obligation under the terms of the CDS. This is the essence of balance sheet interdependence, and the connection nodes must be secured by experienced-based collateral rules.[6] Otherwise, there is nothing inherently wrong with derivatives as potentially useful information markets, and there is no reason to discourage them per se. Although the CDS market signaled financial market stress at a late date, it was much earlier than the Fed's expectations based on its sophisticated econometric modeling and supplemented by access to the best and most recent data. We cannot help wondering, however, why the long lead-time declines in new home sales and housing investment expenditures had not set off louder and clearer warning signals in the Fed's policy research shop.

---

modification, contrary to achieving an efficient outcome (see Bair, 2012, pp. 60–2). Again, "regulation" here means only incentive-compatible property rights rules.

[5] To quote Hayek (1988, p. 75), "knowledge . . . is obtained not from immediate experience or observation, but in the continuous process of sifting a learnt tradition . . . The process of selection that shaped customs and morality could take account of more factual circumstances than individuals could perceive, and in consequence tradition is in some respects superior to, or 'wiser' than, human reason . . . This decisive insight is one that only a very critical rationalist could recognize."

[6] Investment bankers and other investors will lobby and complain against such collateral rules because it immobilizes funds that could be earning higher immediate private returns; this unrestraint was the source of the high profitability of the financial industry right up to the edge of the collapse. However, the profits were implicitly distorted; they were not burdened by a reserve against downside risk. This was precisely where myopic individual incentives were progressively accumulating the enormous risk of a collective cascade of plummeting asset values – a risk that is not simply an independent, euphemistic "fat tail." Good rules serve to protect investors from their own folly but, more important, protect others and the economy from the external consequences of that folly; exempt investors will strongly oppose collateral rules because the consequent opportunity costs are visible to them, whereas the benefits in avoiding collapse are not and, in the midst of chaos, are too easily handed to the Fed or the Treasury.

9.3.3 Rating Agencies

If the CDS market is repaired as discussed previously, then rating agencies are not needed; they are obsolete. Hundreds of laboratory experiments and applications in the field have shown that relative to centralized alternatives, information markets are more effective mechanisms for aggregating dispersed information on event outcomes, including MBS default (Arrow et al., 2008).

9.3.4 Transparency

Although programs to increase transparency in lending and other financial markets are welcome, we caution against the belief that a lack of transparency was in any primary sense a cause of the housing bubble. The asset market experiments in Chapter 2 can hardly be more transparent, but this does not prevent the formation of self-reinforcing expectations of rising prices. Caught in the center of an advancing price bubble, people – borrowers, lenders, originators, rating agencies, insurers, regulators, and politicians – do not have difficulty rationalizing their beliefs and their actions based on those beliefs.

9.3.5 Proprietary Trading and Depository Institutions (the Volcker Rule)

An issue that may not be resolved for some time, if ever, concerns the culpability for the Great Recession of the fact that commercial banks engaged in "proprietary trading" or for-profit trading for their own account (as distinct from commission trading for the accounts of others). The premise of the federal government's support for commercial banking (i.e., depository institutions) is to provide "a stable and efficient payments mechanism, a safe depository for liquid assets, and the provision of credit to individuals, governments and business" (Volcker, 2012, p. 1). Because of the speculative (i.e., capital-gains–driven) nature of proprietary trading, the Volcker Rule would restrict such trading by depository institutions with their access to Federal Reserve credit, depository insurance, and emergency support in unusual conditions. We refer readers to the full statement by Paul Volcker tendered before the deadline in the matter of public comment on implementing the Dodd-Frank legislation (Volcker, 2012).

More recently, here is Volcker's response to the question from Feldstein (2013, pp. 115–6):

> How important was proprietary trading, which I take it is the essence of the Volcker Rule . . . as a cause of the crisis?"
>
> I don't know whether I'd rank it as a prime cause of the crisis, but it was a contributing factor in the sense it led to a lot of . . . exposure on proprietary trading and money market funds, and hedge funds.
>
> . . . I have seen figures that say the banks collectively lost as much money in 2008 as they made on proprietary trading and hedge funds in the whole previous decade all in one fell swoop. But obviously the weakest part of the banking system was bad loans.
>
> The difference is banks are there to make loans. That's an essential part of the economy. They're not there, in my opinion, to trade for their own account basically. That's a distinction that I try to make. That's obviously a complicating factor, if it wasn't the prime factor, in the crisis.
>
> The worst part of it in a way, in my view, is a cultural, a psychological question. It's not just the risks that are involved directly for the whole institution.
>
> Take this JPMorgan thing. They lost $6 billion . . . with one little play in the derivatives market . . . They can survive $6 billion. But what is the psychology that leads people to take that kind of risk? Traders know that the rewards are huge – of a kind that have not been at all normal commercial banking now or in history. When you've got that kind of cleavage between the culture on the investment banking side of the house and the traditional banking side of the house, obviously the people in the commercial banking side say, "I want to make money, too. Maybe I can make some big risks and I'll get some mortgages together, and I'll package them up. Let's securitize them and stick them out. We'll make a commission on it. It's not a relationship matter. We're going to stick this out, we'll stick somebody else with it." It's a different culture.

9.3.6 The Fed Rewrites Its Rules

We note without comment that the Fed is reported to be quietly rewriting its rule book, as follows (McGrane and Hilsenrath, 2012):

> While many Americans may not realize it, the Fed has taken on a much larger regulatory role than at any time in history. Since the Dodd-Frank financial overhaul became law in July 2010, the Fed has held forty-seven separate votes on financial regulations, and scores more are coming. In the process, it is reshaping the U.S. financial industry by directing banks on how much capital they must hold, what kind of trading they can engage in, and what kind of fees they can charge retailers on debit-card transactions.

The Fed is making these sweeping changes – the most dramatic since the Great Depression – almost completely without public meetings... since July 2010... forty-five of forty-seven of the draft or final regulatory measures during that period, they (the governors) have emailed their votes to the central bank's secretary.

The votes, in turn, weren't publicly disclosed until last week, after *The Wall Street Journal* requested the information for this article. On February 14, for the first time, the Fed posted on its website the names of the Fed governors voting for or against each closed-door regulatory action on Dodd-Frank since July 2010, when that law was enacted.

"People have a right to know and hear the discussion and hear the presentations and the reasoning for these rules," Sheila Bair, the former chairwoman of the Federal Deposit Insurance Corp., said in an interview. "All of the other agencies which are governed by boards or commissions propose and approve these rules in public meetings," she said. "I think it would be in the Fed's interest to do so as well."

9.4 Bailouts: Banks but Not Homeowners?

As in the Great Depression, both banks and households have suffered from negative equity balance sheets since the onset of the crisis in 2007.[7] In a fractional reserve banking system, the banks are particularly vulnerable to panic behavior. Deposit insurance can reduce this downside risk to individuals; however, the flipside of deposit insurance is a reduced concern for caution in periods of credit expansion. If, indeed, the Fed played a dual role in saving both individual banks from their own folly and the economy from systemic risk by acquiring a substantial amount of the banks' non-performing assets at more than their market worth, then the action also served to restore bank profitability and system stability. (However, the action still left some of the largest banks with underperforming loans and mortgage assets carried at above market book values.) If we also are correct in our view that the recovery of normal income-driven demand to the housing industry requires

---

[7] One of the hidden costs of household negative equity on economic growth is a substantial lock-in effect on labor mobility (Ferreira et al., 2008, pp. 3–4). Relative to the empirical baseline the authors use, having negative equity reduces the two-year household mobility rate by 50 percent. This compares with a 25 percent reduction in mobility from a higher real mortgage interest rate. The latter especially kicks in when, after a long period of low mortgage rates, economic recovery and tightened monetary policy result in higher interest rates. Homeowners are then reluctant to move and forgo their low mortgage rate. Reduced mobility will be the hidden cost of current Fed policy, announced as extending its 0 to 0.25 percent interest rates into 2014.

housing prices to fall relative to the prices of other goods, then there are three policy options, as follows:

(1) Inflate the prices of all other goods including labor, thereby lowering the burden of debt relative to home prices, and extricate housing demand from its negative equity loop. Inflation "solutions" are hardly desirable, but we have not been left with any good options. The Fed's policy has been consistent with this objective since 2007 with little evidence of success; Keynesians call it the "liquidity trap."

(2) Allow the household deleveraging process to grind through an extended period of low GDP growth and high unemployment until the economy gradually recovers. This option surely will succeed in due time, but not without high annual opportunity cost in terms of lost output and employment. (See, however, the Chapter 10 discussion of Japan, where low growth has persisted for fifteen years after its real estate collapse was followed by policies designed to protect banks from bankruptcy and asset restructuring.) This is the low-growth path we have followed even with extreme monetary ease, government fiscal stimulus, and housing stimulus in the form of subsidies to first-time buyers. Now, at the end of 2013, it appears that home prices bottomed out in Q4 2011 at approximately the same level as in Q1 1999 (and at the same levels as Q1 1990 and Q1 1987 in inflation-adjusted terms). (See Figures 3.1 and 3.2 in Chapter 3.) Once again, they are on the rise, restoring equity in both household and bank balance sheets. This was fueled by five years of extremely low interest rates – in the now-classic Fed style of being part of initializing a typical housing-economic cycle. These rates are now thought to be on target to increase; however, in a more typical cycle, interest rates do not rise before there are solid signs of inflation.

(3) Do for households what the Fed sought for the banks: The Fed, via bank capital requirements and facilitative maintenance of high excess reserves, enables the banks to restate the principal on current negative equity mortgage loans, thereby restoring them to new mark-to-market zero-equity baselines. Forgiving loans is never good economic policy, but recall that we are discussing a world in which there are choices only among bad options. Forgiveness, however, was not inevitable: Many households with subprime loans were still paying in 2007 and in need of loan modifications that would save 40 to 50 percent of the unpaid principal balance – if modification could avoid foreclosure (Bair, 2012, p. 59).

The third option, in principle, seeks to reboot homeowners' damaged balance sheets in an effort to arrest a prolonged deleveraging process and more quickly restore household demand to levels no longer dominated by negative home equity. It is analogous to a mortgage "margin call" through Federal Reserve Bank private capital regulations, which – given the severity of bank balance sheet damage – almost certainly meant large bank failures.

As early as 2007, Sheila Bair called for a subprime loan modification effort, described in detail at the time as follows (Bair, 2007; see also Bair, 2012, and Chapter 6):

There have been many proposals to deal with the problems in the mortgage market. But the best place to begin is by looking at . . . the troubling loans called 2/28 and 3/27 subprime hybrids. They have starter interest rates of 7 percent or more for the first two or three years, and "resets" that raise rates to as much as 12 percent, causing monthly payments to increase by at least 30 percent. When housing prices were rising, borrowers could sell or refinance their homes to pay off the loans before reset and avoid crippling monthly payments. But this year, as prices have dropped, more than $150 billion in these loans have undergone reset, and an additional $300 billion will do so before the end of 2008 . . . A government bailout is not the answer. Bailouts erode market discipline, raising the likelihood of repeat episodes. And efforts to expand refinancing options will help only those borrowers who have enough equity to refinance. What happens to those who are unable to refinance and cannot afford the rate resets? Most of their loans are managed by firms called servicers. Typically, servicers sit back and wait for people to default, then foreclose and sell the properties. But in today's troubled housing market, widespread foreclosures will only maximize losses for servicers. Renegotiating terms loan by loan is too costly and time consuming. Servicers have modified only 1 percent of these mortgages that reset in early 2007. So subprime servicers should take a more standardized approach: restructure all 2/28 and 3/27 subprime hybrid loans for owner-occupied homes in cases where the borrower has been making timely payments but can't afford the reset payments. Convert these to fixed-rate loans at the starter rate. . . . Billions in savings would be generated by avoiding the administrative, legal, marketing, and other costs of foreclosure, which can run to half or more of the loan amount. And avoiding foreclosure would protect neighboring properties and hasten the recovery of markets burdened by an excess supply of houses.

Politically, addressing household-bank balance sheet repair was an option explored by trial balloons that came from both political camps in 2008, but it gained no traction. Potentially, it was a surgical strike but lost out to the scattergun of stimulus spending. Thus, in February 2008 (before the NBER named the recession start date as Q4 2007), Alan Blinder (2008), long an advisor to leading Democrats, articulated the case for buying up negative equity mortgages and replacing them with new market-based mortgages.

The proposal was reported as being favored by former Democratic Senator Christopher Dodd. The thrust of the proposal was to resurrect a version of the HOLC, which was established in 1933 to address the foreclosure problem by purchasing mortgages in default from the banks using Treasury bonds and issuing new mortgages to the owner-occupants.[8] Blinder reported that the HOLC processed 1.9 million homeowner applications and granted about 1 million new mortgages.[9] Blinder correctly perceived this action as striking directly at the impact that foreclosures would have on household demand, while simultaneously addressing stability problems in the banking and financial system. We perceive it as going to the heart of the household-bank balance sheet problem – the Fed's action directly addressed only the bank balance sheets.

At the time, Blinder estimated the cost at $300 billion and the number of homes affected as ranging from 1 million to 2 million. Presidential candidate John McCain also referred to a cost of $300 billion when he unveiled a version of the same policy at the second debate between the presidential candidates in October 2008.[10] (The estimate was likely too low.) McCain's proposal failed along with his presidential bid. In this case, the election format turned out to be inimical to bipartisan action on the central problem of the Great Recession.[11] McCain also championed the plan as a twin-pronged means of eliminating economic uncertainty about defaults and simultaneously unfreezing mortgage markets. Apparently, the resurrection of some version of the HOLC option never made it to the new president's desk or, if it did, it never survived the

---

[8] We note – without claiming a unique causal connection with HOLC – that new housing expenditures, which declined steadily from 1926 through 1933, turned upward in 1934.

[9] Following is a brief background on HOLC. Just as in the Great Recession, from 1931 to 1933, the high cost of implementing foreclosure proceedings meant that lenders preferred to modify loans. In a New York study, loan modifications exceeded foreclosures by an average of more than seven to one; some 96 percent of them stretched the period of the loan, only 10 percent lowered the interest rate, and none lowered the principal. Yet, nationwide, foreclosures escalated, 1930–1932, along with a great increase in borrowers falling behind in their payments. HOLC purchased 1,017,881 mortgages out of 1,885,356 applications from distressed borrowers, in trouble "through no fault of their own." The mortgages were reissued with emphasis on longer (15-year) terms, amortized (equal) payments, and a maximum loan of 80 percent of appraisal – significantly larger than available in private lender markets. Some loans received a reduction in principal, but appraisals were typically above what current market prices could realistically command. (See Fishback, Rose, and Snowden, 2013; and Chapters 5, 6, and 7.)

[10] "McCain Announces $300 Billion Homeownership Plan." *WSJ Blogs*, Washington Wire, October 7, 2008. Available at http://blogs.wsj.com/washwire/2008/10/07/mccain-announces-homeownership-resurgence-plan/.

[11] In contrast, Bill Clinton's campaign promise to allow homeowners to be exempt from capital gains on home resales led to the bipartisan Tax Relief Act of 1997.

perceived better idea of rounding out the Bush stimulus spending to about $1 trillion.[12]

Most mortgages refinanced through government and bank programs have simply stretched out the terms of the loans with lower payments, without altering the principal balance. Consequently, homeowners still faced a slow period of balance sheet recovery that constrains their demands, creates a lock-in to their current location, and constitutes a drag on the mobility demands of a growing economy. One study (Haughwout et al., 2009, p. 30) reported a high redefault rate on mortgages on which payments were lowered by reducing interest and stretching the term of the loan but a lower rate when principal was lowered, as follows:

Our analysis of those modifications in which payments were meaningfully reduced indicates that redefault rates – around 56 percent in the first year – are distressingly high. Yet the magnitude and form of modifications make a difference. Mortgages that receive larger payment reductions are significantly less likely to redefault, as are those that are modified in such a way as to restore the borrower's equity position. Of course, these kinds of modifications are not mutually exclusive since reductions in mortgage balances offer both increased equity and reduced payments.

Total national negative equity was estimated (as of July 2010) at $771 billion for 14.7 million homes.[13] For seriously delinquent mortgages, the restoration of household balance sheets was underway – if at a snail's pace relative to the need – through the ongoing process of foreclosures and short sales that Blinder, McCain, Hillary Clinton, and others in both parties sought to moderate. From the beginning (i.e., 2007), however, there has been a private decentralized initiative quietly underway, specifically for owner-occupied homes at risk of but not yet in default (see Hagerty, 2010). Private investors and funds specialized to this objective buy mortgages at deep discount from the banks and renegotiate the principal and loan terms with the owner-occupiers at rates reflecting a home's market valuation.[14]

---

[12] Hillary Clinton (2008) also had proposed reviving HOLC; but as an erstwhile Democrat presidential candidate, her views here seemed to have little influence on President Obama. Available at http://online.wsj.com/article/SB122230767702474045.html.

[13] Media references are all to a congressional briefing that cited a Zandi spreadsheet, available at www.calculatedriskblog.com/2010/07/negative-equity-breakdown.html. Core-Logic estimates, Q3 2011, showed that it reduced to about $700 billion (i.e., 10.7 million or 22.5 percent of all residential properties). Available at www.corelogic.com/about-us/news/corelogic-third-quarter-2011-negative-equity-data-shows-slight-decline-but-remains-elevated.aspx. By Q3 2013, the value of homes in negative equity was $397 billion and expected to continue falling (Corelogic, 2013).

[14] For example, Archbay Capital was formed in 2007 specifically to acquire troubled mortgages. On July 15, 2009, DataGrant Venture Capital news reported that Archbay bought $600 million in mostly nonperforming subprime loans at $0.35 on the dollar face value.

The balance sheet revaluation process has been indirectly facilitated by Congress through the Mortgage Forgiveness Debt Relief Act (2007), which forgives the tax that a homeowner would otherwise owe on any portion of a mortgage loan that has been restated downward by the lender. Such forgiven amounts are routinely treated as income by the Internal Revenue Service; relief under this Act is restricted to primary residences and does not apply to secondary residences or rental properties.

Although the amount is minor relative to total holdings, BAC announced on December 13, 2010, that it would sell $1 billion worth of mortgage assets, including mortgage servicing rights – described as previously written off – to private bidders Kosman and DeCambre (2010). BAC is the largest U.S. mortgage investor. At the end of 2010, BAC had $1,044 billon in mortgage assets; it achieved that distinction on acquiring Countrywide and Merrill Lynch, both casualties of the housing-mortgage market meltdown. From the end of 2010 to the end of 2012, BAC managed to reduce its mortgage holdings by $808 billion.

In September 2011, two years after Hillary Clinton and John McCain had proposed it, the Obama Administration designed an FHA program that addressed the need to reevaluate mortgages (Timiraos, 2010a and 2010b). The program targets occupant-homeowners who are current on their mortgage payments but have negative equity. The borrower is refinanced with an FHA-guaranteed loan meeting traditional FHA-conforming standards. Both the lender and the loan service agency must agree to reduce the principal balance by at least 10 percent so that the new loan does not exceed 97.75 percent of the current value of the home.

However, the most serious deterrent to realigning house value and mortgage debt began in late 2010 with the evidence in foreclosure cases of mortgage-service companies failing to document a paper trail of transfers from the original lender to the foreclosing lender. In February 2012, the Obama Administration reached a $26 billion relief settlement with five banks (i.e., BAC, JPMorgan Chase, Wells Fargo, Citigroup, and Ally Financial). Approximately 1 million homeowners are projected to have their debt reduced, with the reductions distributed over three years (*New York Times*, 2012).

9.5 Monetary Policy

Monetary policy had a part in the current crisis and needs to be reformed based on fundamental rethinking. We make only the following three points:

Available at www.bizjournals.com/triad/stories/2009/07/13/daily35.html. See also Kouwe (2009).

(1) In view of the persistent connection in the past fourteen recessions between housing industry decline and recovery and subsequent declines and recovery in the economy, it is not practical to maintain the fiction that the Fed does not target particular industries. It already has and does, implicitly even if not explicitly. It is not evident to us – given the long-standing connection among Fed policy, interest rates, and housing cycles – that monetary policy has been effective in anticipating the course of the economy, particularly its own effect on that course as an equilibrium outcome. The FOMC, with all of its access to data and professional econometric methodology, did not and could not anticipate the mortgage-financial market events to which it responded in early August 2007, or the even more dramatic mortgage-financial market decline to which it responded massively after September 2008. In both cases, it was private market signals of extreme, sudden, "tipping point" distress that "jump-started" its action. With this track record, why would anyone suddenly expect this lagged trend-following to miraculously change and the Federal Reserve System to finally acquire prescience? Bernanke can harbor these hopes, but his warnings and his rapid adaptation once financial markets had spoken suggest that he has been hanging onto events by his fingernails.

(2) Evidence presented in Chapters 3 and 10 shows that an important source of fuel for the housing bubble was the inflow of capital from foreign countries due to the U.S. current account deficit. Although this capital may flow primarily into U.S. Treasury and federal agency bonds, it lowers the return to these investments making other investments, such as housing and securities, more attractive. Therefore, the Fed cannot ignore these flows or treat them as external effects in setting monetary policy. What are the instruments that will guide Fed policy in getting the adjustment right in a manner that anticipates its own effect? Is it an endemic feature of Fed policy that it is always in the ex post position of learning about what it did not consider earlier that exacerbated a new experience in economic instability?

(3) In the aftermath of the stock market decline that followed the tech sector bubble, Bernanke (2002) addressed the issue of whether the Federal Reserve should take a proactive policy to attempt to contain asset market bubbles. His position is that the Federal Reserve cannot reliably identify bubbles and cannot control one without doing excessive collateral damage to the rest of the economy, so that "if a sudden correction in asset prices does occur, the Fed's first responsibility is to do its part to ensure the integrity of the financial

infrastructure . . . [and] the Fed should provide ample liquidity until
the immediate crisis has passed." Provision of ample liquidity following a crash has often been called the "Greenspan put" because
of its analogy to a "put option" in which an asset holder has a floor
price that the asset can be sold at, even if the asset value falls below
that floor. In this case, the liquidity that the Federal Reserve provides
reduces the cost of funding for depository institutions. In the case
of U.S. banks, their cost of funds is close to the rates on short-term
U.S. Treasury debt because the two are close substitutes for depositors. During the feverish period of the housing bubble, profits of the
financial sector in the United States reached $375 billion in the peak
year of 2006; the recovery to comparable profits levels was quick and,
in the four quarters ended in Q3 2013, had reached $447 billion.
There has been much discussion of the "moral hazard" problem of
bailouts, but the effects of the "Greenspan put" have been profound.
The financial sector earned an average of $294.9 billion per year from
2001 through Q2 2008. Since the beginning of 2009, the financial
sector has earned an average of $380.0 billion per year. In effect, the
"Greenspan put" is a guarantee that no matter how recklessly the
financial sector operates, and no matter how disastrous the consequences are, the Federal Reserve will create an environment in which
they can only prosper, and for an indefinitely long time, largely at the
expense of savers.

9.6 Taxation Policy

There has been resurgent academic interest in the refreshingly modern tax
proposals of Irving Fisher in the 1930s and 1940s. Because most of the core
principles that apply to the taxation of income and of businesses arise in the
context of this proposal, our discussion focuses on that development.

9.6.1 Household Income Taxes

Fisher and Fisher (1942) argued for a progressive consumption (called
a "spendings") tax that would be implemented by allowing all forms of
household savings and direct investment to be deducted from household
earnings to determine the net inflow received that is subject to tax. In this
conception, all durable consumer goods – including houses and interest
on their purchases – are consumption, subject to tax.[15] In our view, this

---

[15] For a contemporary review of their proposals, see Shoven and Whalley (2005) and the two
comments that followed their paper.

proposal is the proper response to concerns for the long-term problem of an inadequate savings rate, but the Fisher arguments penetrated far beyond any such concern to broadly encourage work, saving, economic growth, education, health, and other investment.

The tax form that Fisher and Fisher proposed focuses on listing income sources, exactly as in current practice, and then listing and deducting all savings and direct investments. The latter is also current practice in the calculation of capital gains. Finally, total consumption is computed as the residue of income receipts after savings and investments are deducted. This consumption residue would then be subject to a progressive tax, as existing law now applies to income. The particular composition of the consumption spending is irrelevant. Deductible "investments" in the Fisher proposal included tuition and books for schooling but not room and board because a student would have to incur them without the direct expense of education. The Fisher proposal clearly perceived education as investment long before the concept of human-capital development had become part of standard economics. He also would allow medical expenses to be deducted as part of the need to maintain an individual's productivity and capacity to earn income and to enjoy after-tax consumption.

Under the current tax code, when a household uses some of its income for savings or investment, it pays taxes on the income and, therefore, on the part that is saved or invested. When the investment or savings produces earnings, those earnings are taxed again, and so on. Fisher's proposal avoided this multiple taxation of capital investments, which – after all – are the source of increases in productivity and future output. In this conception, the calculation of income for the year includes not only ordinary income – that is, wages, dividends, interest, rent, and other direct payments for services and investments – but also sales minus purchases of investments, itemized by source. No distinction is made between income and capital gains in listing income sources and neither is such a distinction needed.[16] To the extent that capital gains are reinvested or saved, no tax is levied because it has not been withdrawn from the economy in the form of consumption. To the extent that capital gains are not reinvested, then – of course – they are taxed as consumption.[17]

---

[16] To the extent that capital gains tend to be reinvested under current law and are subject to a lower tax rate, the distinction is an important – if crude – means of correcting flaws in current tax law. However, Fisher would allow all incoming net receipts that are invested (reinvested) to go tax-free; therefore, the distinction becomes entirely irrelevant.

[17] If this seems strange to modern economics, it is because of Fisher's clear realization of the ambiguity of the concept of "income." In Fisher's view, consumption withdrawals from the production of goods and services was itself the only unambiguous way to define "income."

Thus, we suppose a person has ordinary income from all sources of $200,000. In addition, we suppose he sells assets with a market worth of $1 million and reinvests $900,000. We suppose further that his cash balance from the previous year is $50,000 and his new end-of-year cash balance is $200,000. Then, he pays taxes at a progressive rate on his (consumption) expenditure, computed as the residue, as follows: taxable expenditure = $200,000 + $1,000,000 − $900,000 + $50,000 − $200,000 = $150,000. On his individual tax form, he itemizes ordinary income by source, cash received from investments by source, less the cash outgo for investments, plus (or minus) any reduction in cash balances. The consumption-expenditure residual, after accounting for net investments and subtracting an increase in idle cash balances, is $150,000. In arriving at the residue of Fisher's taxable "spendings," it makes no difference whether he bought a yacht, a home, hamburgers, or clothing or dined at high-end restaurants.

We note that the fundamental principle underlying Fisher's taxable spending is that a person's gross income is the market worth of what the individual contributed to all others in the economy. From this income is subtracted the value of that portion of income that the individual leaves unconsumed to work in the economic system for all.[18] The residual difference is withdrawn from the economy, is not available to work for others, and is consumed – that is, the resources used to produce the hamburger that is eaten are forever unavailable to support future economic output. Only the aggregate of these consumption withdrawals is taxed, and it is taxed at whatever is the applicable progressive rate.

Fisher's principles of capital preservation apply naturally to death (i.e., estate and inheritance) taxes. Intergenerational wealth transfers are in the form of capital assets or, most prominently, the equity and debt claims on them. The act of transfer converts *none of this wealth into consumption* and, under those principles, would be transferred tax-free. Insofar as the transfer includes consumer durable goods – for example, automobiles, homes, and yachts – the tax has already been paid on the entire future

---

[18] Investment as representing resources left in the economy to work for poor and rich alike is reminiscent of Adam Smith (1759/1976, pp. 184–5) in *The Theory of Moral Sentiments*, in which he states rather flamboyantly that "The rich only select from the heap what is most precious and agreeable... and in spite of their natural selfishness and rapacity, though they mean only their own conveniency... they divide with the poor the produce of all their improvements. They are led by an invisible hand... without intending it, without knowing it, (to) advance the interest of the society, and afford means to the multiplication of the species."

flow of consumption services from these consumer durables. If the heirs in a subsequent year sell any of their claims on capital assets and purchase consumer goods for any part of it, they pay taxes on that part in that year. No withdrawal of resources from production escapes without being taxed.

9.6.2 Business Income Taxes

All business receipts – that is, net of payments to other businesses for goods and services – accrue to individual households in the form of wages, rents, profits, interest, and dividends; any tax on business income falls with unknown incidence on individuals who receive correspondingly smaller payments. Under Fisher's proposal, all business income would be taxed only once at the individual household level insofar as it was consumed; hence, all business taxes would be abolished (user fees such as emission charges are not business taxes). Because corporations commonly retain a portion of their profits for reinvestment, this represents the return of resources to the generation of future output and would not be taxed. Corporate retained earnings, therefore, are savings until reinvested by the firm and would not be taxed.

To the extent that businesses incur food and entertainment (or nonbusiness-related transportation) expenditures for employees and customers, even if defended as increasing goodwill, they would be taxable – martinis in the two-martini lunch as well as the lunch would both be taxed. Otherwise, a business becomes a loophole that allows consumption goods and services to escape taxation. These expenditures are analogous to room and board for university students that are subject to tax in the Fisher scheme because they are consumption whether at work or in school.

9.7 Business Policy: Entry Cost by New Firms Should Be Low

By far, the most important business policies that would support the recovery of employment and the resumption of long-term growth would be those that remove tax- and transactions-cost barriers to the formation of new businesses.

This consideration is most evident in the data provided by recent studies of new-firm formation, or startups, from 1980 to 2005 by the U.S. Census Bureau and the Kauffman Foundation. The studies demonstrate that, *ceteris paribus*, without the employment growth afforded by the entry of new firms, total employment growth would be negative. Haltiwanger, Jarmin, and Miranda (2009) described the finer structure of shifts in employment as firms enter, grow, and exit, as follows:

The fraction of employment accounted for by U.S. private-sector business startups over the 1980–2005 period is about 3 percent per year. This measure is interpretable as the employment-weighted business startup rate for the United States. While this is a small fraction of overall employment, all of this employment from startups reflects new jobs. As such, 3 percent is large compared to the average annual net employment growth of the U.S. private sector for the same period (about 1.8 percent). This pattern implies that, excluding the jobs from new firms, the U.S. net employment growth rate is negative on average. This simple comparison highlights the importance of business startups to job creation in the United States.

Although this comparison is dramatic, we must suppose that in the absence of the entry of new firms and the creation of new jobs, the process whereby new firms bid workers away from old firms would not be in play. In the absence of new entrants, wages would have been lower and fewer workers would have been diverted from old jobs to new. Workers move between old firms, as well as between old and new. In fact, as Table 9.1 shows, most hiring is done by older firms. On average during those 25 years, there were 104.9 million people employed in private enterprises in the United States. In a typical year between 1987 and 2011, there were almost 9.5 million hires by firms that had existed for more than ten years. However, this is a somewhat misleading picture of the contributions of older firms relative to younger firms in the growth of the labor market. The older firms had a negative contribution to job growth. In fact, every vintage of firms contributed negatively to growth except for new firms.

Table 9.1 indicates the dynamic character of the labor market, with constant turnover as new jobs are created and workers are continually rematched to jobs. In the past twenty-four years, total employment has grown at about 1.2 percent per year. However, this net percentage rate of employment growth is only the surviving tip of a process of hiring and job separation that is far larger. The labor market is a churning "turmoil" that involves new firms entering the market, older firms exiting the market, existing firms moving people into and out of jobs, and employees shifting among jobs and firms. Surviving firms of all ages contribute to net employment growth and to output (at rates that decline with age), but job losses from business closures exceed the job growth at surviving firms. Consequently, every vintage of firms other than new ones contributes negatively to employment growth. Survivors generate high employment at the same time that failing firms contribute to job loss. However, taken together, job gains from

Table 9.1. *Hires and separations by firm age*

Firm age category	Percent of labor force	(A) Hires	(B) Separations	(A-B) Net hires	Job separations from firm closure	(C) Separations among survivors	(A-C) Net hires among survivors
Less than 1	2.9	2,987,318	0	2,987,318	0	0	2,987,318
Less than 2	2.8	841,130	912,273	−71,144	511,092	401,181	439,948
Less than 3	2.6	598,966	788,984	−190,018	405,445	383,539	215,427
Less than 4	2.5	508,863	648,577	−139,714	306,148	342,429	166,434
Less than 5	2.4	449,734	570,788	−121,055	251,489	319,299	130,435
Less than 6	2.3	412,317	509,070	−96,753	212,991	296,079	116,238
Less than 10	10.3	1,647,680	1,994,901	−347,222	750,071	1,244,830	402,850
More than 10	74.2	9,455,827	10,026,205	−570,378	2,927,573	7,098,633	2,357,195
ALL	100.0	16,901,834	15,450,799	1,451,035	5,364,810	10,085,989	6,815,845

Source: U.S. Census Bureau, Center for Economic Studies, Business Dynamics Statistics.

247

existing firms fall short of job losses from those firms in all firm-age categories except new firms.

The fine structure sources of this turnover is shown in Table 9.1,[19] which lists hires, separations, and net employment changes for firms of various vintages. Separations are further categorized as those due to firm closure versus those from existing firms. For example, firms exiting after one year account for 511,092 of 5,364,810 job losses due to firm closure (9.5 percent of) and for 4.0 percent of job separations from existing firms. Churning is evident in the high number of hires; at 16.9 million hires per year, hires amount to 16.1 percent of all jobs each year. Separations also are high: the 15.45 million separations per year amount to 14.7 percent of all jobs. The column "Net Hires," however, shows that no firm vintage other than newly formed firms contributes to job growth; whereas the column "Net Hires among Survivors" shows that continuing firms of all ages continue to grow.

The public-policy implications are obvious: Barriers to the formation of new firms are inimical to job growth and wealth creation. We should make it easy to start new firms and focus on taxing business income after it accrues as income to individuals. We also should avoid subsidizing or trying artificially to save failing firms; probing the innovation frontier is an essential part of the process of discovery and creation, and some of this exploration will not be fruitful. When losses occur in failed undertakings, jobs are reallocated from exiting firms to surviving and entering firms, generating new net wealth.

References

Arrow, Kenneth J., Robert Forsythe, Michael Gorham, Robert Hahn, Robin Hanson, John O. Ledyard, et al. (2008). "The Promise of Prediction Markets." *Science*, 320, pp. 877–8, May 16.

Bair, Sheila (2007). "Fix Rates to Save Loans." *New York Times, Opinion.* October 19.

Bair, Sheila (2012). *Bull by the Horns.* New York: The Free Press.

Bernanke, Ben S. (2002). "Remarks by Governor Ben S. Bernanke before the New York Chapter of the National Association for Business Economics." October 15. Available at www.federalreserve.gov/boarddocs/speeches/2002/20021015/.

---

[19] The table is compiled from data collected by the U.S. Census Bureau, Center for Economic Studies, Business Dynamics Statistics, available at www2.census.gov/ces/bds/firm/bds_f_age_release.xls. The data in the table indicate the average number of employees in each age category and each classification for the years between 1987 and 2011. The category "Less than 1" lists firms that were not yet one year old as of March of the year; the category "Less than 2" lists firms that existed in the dataset in the previous March but had not yet reached two years old; and so forth.

Blinder, Alan (2008). "From the New Deal, a Way out of a Mess." *Economic View, New York Times,* February 24. Available at www.nytimes.com/2008/02/24/business/24view .html.

Buckle, Stephen (1991). *Natural Law and the Theory of Property.* Oxford: Clarendon Press, pp. 172–3.

Clinton, Hillary (2008). "Let's Keep People in Their Homes." *Wall Street Journal,* September 15.

Corelogic (2013). "CoreLogic Reports 791,000 More Residential Properties Return to Positive Equity in Third Quarter of 2013. December. Available at www.corelogic. com/about-us/news/corelogic-reports-791,000-more-residential-properties-return-to-positive-equity-in-third-quarter-of-2013.aspx.

Federal Register (2013). "Ability-to-Repay and Qualified Mortgage Standards under the Truth in Lending Act (Regulation Z)." A Rule by the Consumer Financial Protection Bureau. Available at www.federalregister.gov/articles/2013/01/30/2013-00736/ ability-to-repay-and-qualified-mortgage-standards-under-the-truth-in-lending-act-regulation-z.

Feldstein, Martin (2013). "An Interview with Paul Volcker." *Journal of Economic Perspectives* 27 (4) pp. 105–20.

Ferreira, Fernando, Joseph Gyourko, and Joseph Tracy (2008). "Housing Busts and Household Mobility." Federal Reserve Bank of New York, Staff Report No. 350, October.

Fishback, Price, Jonathan Rose, and Kenneth Snowden (2013). *Well Worth Saving.* Chicago: University of Chicago Press.

Fisher, Irving, and Herbert W. Fisher (1942). *Constructive Income Taxation: A Proposal for Reform.* New York: Harper and Brothers.

Frame, W. Scott, and Lawrence J. White (2005). "Fussing and Fuming over Fannie and Freddie: How Much Smoke, How Much Fire?" *Journal of Economic Perspectives,* 19, pp. 159–84.

Hagerty, James R. (2010). "Vultures' Save Troubled Homeowners." *Wall Street Journal,* August 18. Available at http://online.wsj.carticleom// SB10001424052748704720004575377022447064474.html.

Haltiwanger, John, Ron Jarmin, and Javier Miranda (2009). "Business Dynamics Statistics Briefing: Jobs Created from Business Startups in the United States" (January). Available at www.issuelab.org/resource/business_dynamics_statistics_briefing_jobs_created_from_business_startups_in_the_united_states

Haughwout, Andrew, Ebiere Okah, and Joseph Tracy (2009). "Second Chances: Subprime Mortgage Modification and Redefault." Federal Reserve Bank of New York, Staff Report No. 417. December; revised August 2010.

Hayek, Friedrich A. (1988). *The Fatal Conceit.* Chicago: University of Chicago Press.

Kouwe, Zachery (2009). "Banks Begin Quietly Selling Toxic Mortgages." *Dealbook, New York Times,* August 13.

Kosman, Josh (2010). "Bank of America to Sell $1B in Toxic Paper." *New York Post,* December 13. Available at www.nypost.com/p/news/business/bank_of_america_to_ sell_in_toxic_FYFnXNncpp9NNjQSaBa9uM#ixzz180X1qmRG.

McGrane, Victoria, and Jon Hilsenrath (2012). "Fed Writes Sweeping Rules from Behind Closed Doors." *Wall Street Journal,* February 21.

New York Times (2012). "Foreclosures (2012 Robosigning and Foreclosure Abuse Settlement)." February 17. Available at http://topics.nytimes.com/top/reference/timestopics/subjects/f/foreclosures/index.html.

Shoven, John, and John Whalley (2005). "Irving Fisher's Spendings (Consumption) Tax in Retrospect." *American Journal of Economics and Sociology,* 64, pp. 215–35.

Smith, Adam (1759/1976). *The Theory of Moral Sentiments.* Indianapolis, IN: Liberty Fund.

Solomon, Deborah, and Dan Fitzpatrick (2010). "Fed Orders 2nd Round of Stress Tests." *Wall Street Journal,* November 18. Available at http://online.wsj.com/article/SB10001424052748704648604575620732161392908.html.

Stiglitz, Joseph (2009). "The Anatomy of a Murder: Who Killed America's Economy." *Critical Review,* 21, pp. 329–39.

Summers, Lawrence (2009). "Responding to an Historic Economic Crisis: The Obama Program." Washington, DC: The Brookings Institution, March 13. Available at www.brookings.edu/~/media/events/2009/3/13%20summers/20090313_summers.pdf.

Timiraos, Nick (2010a). "Government to Deploy Broader Mortgage Aid." *Wall Street Journal,* September 4. Available at http://online.wsj.com/article/SB10001424052748704323704575461920164400014.html.

Timiraos, Nick (2010b). "The FHA's 'Short Refinance' Program: Frequently Asked Questions." *Wall Street Journal Blogs, Developments,* September 6. Available at blogs.wsj.com/developments/2010/09/06/the-fhas-short-refinance-program-frequently-asked-questions/.

Volcker, Paul A. (2012). "Commentary on the Restrictions on Proprietary Trading by Insured Depository Institutions." Available at http://online.wsj.com/public/resources/documents/Volcker_Rule_Essay_2-13-12.pdf.

10

Learning from Foreign Economic Crises

Consequences, Responses, and Policies

So, any interesting model must be a dynamic stochastic general equilibrium [DSGE] model. From this perspective, there is no other game in town. ... If you have an interesting and a coherent story to tell, you can do so within a DSGE model. If you cannot, it probably is incoherent.

... [T]he models are not well suited to analyze extremely rare events.
  – V. V. Chari, Testimony before the Committee on Science and Technology,
            U.S. House of Representatives, July 20, 2010

All of the papers employ simple applied dynamic general equilibrium models ... to decompose changes in output into three portions: one due to changes in inputs of labor, another due to changes in inputs of capital, and the third due to the changes in efficiency with which these factors are used.
  –Timothy J. Kehoe and Edward C. Prescott, from the introduction to *Great Depressions of the Twentieth Century*

10.1 Introduction and Overview

Our overriding objective in this book has been to show that unusual credit flows frequently produce asset bubbles; when those assets are highly leveraged, immobile, and illiquid, borrowers and the financial system often suffer severe balance sheet deterioration in a collapse. Moreover, the economy is left saturated with an excess of produced assets, so that output is reduced. We have described the Great Recession as the result of a balance sheet crisis. In this chapter, we examine several even more severe downturns and show that all resulted from a collapse in the production of fixed assets. The opening quotes for this chapter argue for the view that the source of severe economic downturns lies in reductions to inputs of labor and capital and a reduction in the efficiency of these factors of production. Although this

251

view is not "the only game in town," it is arguably the dominant view in macroeconomics. In this book, we have sought to present evidence that supports an alternative view. Our argument is that when a bubble has pushed asset prices above fundamental value, production of those assets grows rapidly, but when asset prices become noticeably disconnected from fundamentals, financing for purchases of those assets collapses, asset prices collapse, and their production collapses too. When that happens, the economic downturn can be severe. The economic collapse does have noticeable effects on inputs of labor and capital and their efficiency, but changes to those factors are not causal. If many severe economic downturns result from a collapse of fixed investment, then it is not surprising that measured inputs of labor and capital "are not well suited to analyze extremely rare events."

Because extreme economic collapses have been rare in the United States in the past century, in this chapter we examine several comparable events from around the world. These cases provide further evidence that these downturns are associated with rapid collapses of fixed investment and also indicate which policies are associated with rapid and sustained recovery and which lead to prolonged stagnation. Notoriously, monetary policy does not have its normal effect during a balance sheet crisis, and many economists argue that we must resort to government stimulus spending for a recovery. We provide direct evidence that fiscal stimulus has not been a part of the recovery process in many countries that experienced robust recoveries following a balance sheet crisis. In fact, most countries that recovered rapidly reduced both government expenditures and government deficits; Japan increased both and then logged nearly two decades of poor performance.

We identify and discuss three recovery-response regularities that emerge from our examination of countries that suffered the seriously impaired balance sheet consequences of a financial crisis like the Great Recession. The emergent responses are partly through natural economic and market processes and partly in the form of constructivist policy interventions but also through "forbearance" – that is, the absence of intervention. Our purpose is to study these cases as forms of experience that inform understanding, not primarily to define what policy should be. Policy choice is more complex but surely dependent on prior understanding, including an assessment of the longer-term moral hazards that a choice might create. None of these responses is painless. Ideally, such crises would be avoided in the first place. Because the alternatives all have undesirable features, the question is whether we can ultimately chart a pathway that seems to be the least damaging, as follows:

- The first approach uses the process of default and bankruptcy to confront the need to repair and reboot balance sheets, to restore health, and to enable the resumption of growth. We use Sweden in the 1990s as an example in which this route was aggressively followed and the economy recovered quickly. In the United States, the FDIC followed this course where it had jurisdiction, but its health-restoration accomplishments were limited to smaller regional banks and gained no significant traction for the largest banks, even though they faced the same problems.
- The second approach seeks to shore up financial institutions by protecting creditors and investors from default with the hope or expectation that recovery will bring economic growth that gradually repay the loan losses accumulated during the asset market collapse. This is the model that was applied to the large banks in the United States. Many years earlier, Japan allowed its banks to stretch out recognition of losses on bad assets; the country subsequently experienced nearly two decades of anemic growth. We chart and discuss the Japanese experience because it is relevant in understanding the U.S. economic experience since 2007.
- The third approach is found in the history of many smaller countries with flexible currency regimes in which market depreciation plays a key role. We discuss and chart three disparate examples – Finland, Thailand, and Iceland – that illustrate and explicate common recurring features in a host of similar countries.

Fiscal responses also have differed widely. Most countries that experienced an asset market bubble and collapse incurred government deficits of about 10 percent of GDP per year afterward due to declining revenues and increased expenditures. Large deficits consistently develop after an asset market collapse and financial crisis. But some countries take measures quickly to sharply reduce or even eliminate deficits, whereas others embrace them as "Keynesian stimulus." Japan is an extreme example of Keynesian deficit spending that continued for two decades after the crisis began. At the other extreme, some countries brought deficits below 2 percent of GDP within two or three years. The results almost uniformly favored the countries that controlled their deficits in direct contradiction to the standard Keynesian economic prescription.

10.2 Bankruptcy and Default as a Healthy Balance Sheet Repair and Reboot Process

In financial crises, many banks suffer de facto loan losses large enough to wipe out their capital; however, the loss is not reflected in their accounting practices. Industry practice and regulatory procedures do not require the banks to mark down the accounting book value of a loan to approximate its market worth as long as it is a performing loan. Performing loans are those in which borrowers are making their payments or, after loan restructuring, are meeting their approved lower payments. Yet, the circumstances of the bank are such that in neither case is the market value of a loan expressed in its book value. Why might this be a problem, especially in a balance sheet crisis like the Great Recession?

The explicit recognition of such loan losses is essential for raising new capital under these circumstances. Loan losses of 10 to 15 percent of GDP are not unusual in serious banking crises. For example, in Sweden from 1990 to 1994, loan losses amounted to 10.6 percent of GDP and a slightly larger percentage of total loans.[1] For many banks, losses significantly exceeded capital. Protective support for the interests of existing shareholders and bondholders reduces the incentive of prospective new capital investors to recapitalize the banking sector. The economy suffers from the absence of lending and the recovery is postponed.

The extreme case of completely privatized losses illustrates the benefits from achieving a write-down of bad loans in which those losses are borne by shareholders and bondholders. Suppose that all bad loans are written down, the losses wipe out a bank's capital, and the bondholders take whatever "haircut" is necessary for liability claims to equal asset value; then, the bank's balance sheet is clean. In this context, as new investors provide new capital for the bank, that capital does not need to be applied to fill in historical losses in the balance sheet. Neither is the new investment diluted by claims on new earnings from the previous shareholders because their interest in the firm is wiped out when the firm fails.

In the United States, this is the FDIC model for failing banks. The model was applied to 465 small- to medium-sized regional banks from 2008 to 2012 (but, of course, not to the bailed-out largest banks, which were managed by the Treasury and the Fed and protected from failure). In this model, all shareholders, bondholders, and creditors other than prepaid insured

---

[1] See "Financial enterprises, annual financial data" from Statistics Sweden. Available at www .scb.se/fm0402-en.

depositors are at risk of losing part or all of their investments depending on how serious is the failure of a particular bank. All banks that survive this process as "whole banks" or in merged, restructured form emerge with clean, ready-to-lend balance sheets. Their burden is left behind but, most important, the economy can move forward with the creation of new income.[2]

The alternative in which bank losses are not fully recognized is much less attractive for new capital investors and is inimical to the entire economic recovery process. This is because new capital investment is being diverted to filling in the historical-loss holes in the balance sheet. If previous shareholders are protected from loss, new investors have to share future earnings with the incumbent equity holders and, as a result, they receive a lower return from their capital investments, and their incentive is to provide less new capital (if any). The objective of restoring the financial system to health, as well as reviving its capacity to lend, is obviously facilitated by requiring loan losses to be borne by incumbent shareholders on whose watch the losses occurred. In Sweden, although a failing bank's equity losses might be borne by shareholders, the state assumed bad assets to protect bondholders from loss.[3] The overall result of the Swedish approach, however, was favorable for its economy: Loan losses declined sharply after they spiked from 1991 to 1993. By 1994, they were at a level only slightly above their more normal levels prior to the crisis. Once the bad loans were written off and new capital was raised, banks could begin lending again. Bank lending bottomed out at

---

[2] As Chairwoman of the FDIC, Sheila Bair understood that it was important in restructuring the loans of failed banks to also address the need to minimize their losses in bankruptcy. Any such savings helps investors and uninsured creditors of a failing bank and reduces the cost to the FDIC of processing the deposits it insures. The high cost of processing foreclosures – 40 to 50 percent – of unpaid principal balances argues for working with borrowers who are still able to pay a portion of their monthly loan obligations to reduce those payments and preserve value by avoiding the high cost of foreclosure. However, any such monthly payment reduction needs to be applied to lowering the borrower's principal balance if it is to help repair homeowner balance sheets. If the payment reduction is financed only by lowering interest on the loan and/or stretching the term from ten to twenty years, this only serves to prolong the homeowner's "underwater" burden without changing the net flow of payments to the bank. (See Bair, 2012; and Chapters 6, 11, and 13 for a discussion of these issues.)

[3] We consider it a mistake to make an exception for bondholders. The practice still works to restore a private bank's balance sheet, but transfers to the government losses for which incumbent bondholders should be responsible as part of the risk they voluntarily accepted to bear after equity capital were exhausted. More serious for the recovery, the transfers of these losses to the government become an additional burden to future taxpayers and carry historical claims forward to burden future growth.

the end of 1994 and then gradually rose until 1999, when it began a sharp rise that continued unabated for ten years.[4]

In summary, when banks recapitalize through private markets, with new capital going into restructured balance sheets unencumbered by the liability claims and investors of the past, the consequence is to greatly facilitate recovery and restoration of growth in the economy. The Swedish stock market and house price indices both increased sharply once lending recovered. The house price increase also would have helped to restore the damaged balance sheets of households. Although the 29.2 percent fall in house prices in Stockholm was almost as great as the U.S. national decline, house prices had recovered to their pre-crisis peak by 1998, only five years after the trough.[5] Recovery in the stock market was faster. The contrast with Japan, where bank losses were papered over by accounting devices, is stark.

10.3 Protecting Incumbent Investors from Losses: Recipe for Postponing Recovery?

Protecting incumbent creditors and investors from the consequences of excesses in housing-mortgage markets became the centerpiece of U.S. policy beginning in October 2008: first with the Fed action to relieve the banks of large amounts of their toxic loans, and then with Treasury implementation of a "too-big-too-fail" program. The Japanese response to bad loans and to bank insolvency in the 1990s was generically and substantively equivalent to the U.S. approach but contrasts sharply with that of Sweden, as discussed previously. Hence, the path followed by Japan provides evidence relevant to understanding why the U.S. economy remained mired in a low-growth rut at least through 2013.

House prices in Japan peaked in the fall of 1990 and then fell 25 percent within two years. After fourteen consecutive years of decline, house prices had fallen 65 percent by 2004. After house prices began to fall in 1990, nonperforming loans continued to escalate throughout the decade. Various types of distressed loans remained significant in 1998, eight years after the initial downturn in the real estate market. One category of loans, which Packer (2000) called "support loans," was extended to distressed borrowers so that they could continue to make their loan payments. In 1998, these loans amounted to about 6.5 percent of all loans issued by major Japanese

---

[4] For credit market lending, see, e.g., Table H in Sveriges Riksbank (2007).
[5] Real estate prices are from Statistics Sweden, available at www.scb.se/bo0501-en.

banks. After a support loan was issued, the original loan could technically avoid classification as a distressed asset.

This and other forms of forbearance from mark-to-market accounting allowed Japanese banks to stretch out write-downs of ¥95 trillion in loan losses – about 20 percent of annual GDP – during a period of twelve years from 1993 to 2004. One objective of this strategy was to allow Japanese banks to offset their losses from bad assets with earnings from sound assets as those earnings declined. The de facto losses thus were concealed by official bank "sleight-of-hand" accounting, but the resulting poor incentives for growth recovery were fully revealed in the prolonged poor performance of the Japanese economy. The serious consequence of this accounting legerdemain is that Japanese banks remained "hunkered down" and unwilling to lend for fifteen years. Whether it was the loan supply or demand (or both) that collapsed, the contrast between the outcomes in Sweden and Japan suggests that the combination of regulatory forbearance and bailouts of incumbent shareholders and bondholders is the less effective policy. The flow of funds indicates the severity of the downturn in Japanese lending: Total lending by private financial institutions fell at an annual rate of 1.7 percent per year between 1992 and 2007. This fifteen-year decline in lending resulted from the unresolved losses of the banks and was an important cause of the extremely sluggish economic growth in this period.

Figure 10.1 is a chart of inflation-adjusted GDP, government revenue, and government expenditures, all measured annually for Japan from 1976 through 2012. Robust Japanese growth in GDP between 1976 and 1991 slowed to a crawl from 1992 onward despite the large and growing government deficit in which government expenditures trended upward, whereas tax revenue flattened or declined. The real GDP growth rate in Japan between Q1 1997 and Q3 2012 was 0.5 percent. During a period of 15.5 years, the total real growth of GDP amounted to only 8.1 percent.

As we have argued, one source of this poor performance is the failure of Japan to recognize the large de facto losses plaguing their banking sector: Protecting incumbent investors from their enormous real estate losses became a millstone on the economy from which it has yet to free itself. In addition, however, as Figure 10.1 demonstrates, throughout this period of sluggish growth, Japan faithfully adhered to the Keynesian prescriptions of deficit-financed government spending. The results certainly do not provide any support for the Keynesian prescription. As discussed in this chapter, countries that pursued the opposite approach have fared much better, provided that they have their own flexible currency so that they can jump-start their economy with an export boom.

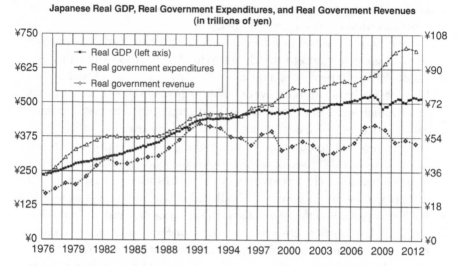

Figure 10.1. Deficit spending has not generated a robust recovery in Japan: Two decades of lost growth.

Going back at least as far as the Depression, there is a widespread intuition that naively associates failing enterprises, particularly banks, with economic decline. However, these correlated symptoms of stress in no sense imply that the economic decline can be arrested by bank loan loss avoidance – that is, by hiding bank losses in overstated book values. Rather, it is quite the reverse: Bankruptcy is a process for "healing the wounds" of broken balance sheets enabling banks, firms, and households to resume normal economic growth unencumbered by negative equity. This interpretation is consistent with the experience of many smaller countries that suffered an investment and real estate boom and collapse. In these cases, however, an important part of the adjustment process is the result of market currency depreciation.

10.4 Learning from Market Currency Depreciation in Three of Many Countries: Finland (1990–1993), Thailand (1994–2003), and Iceland (2007–2010)

Countries with flexible currency regimes (and also countries with a pegged currency that are forced to abandon the peg) provide a record of market adjustment to balance sheet crises that inform a pathway to rapid recovery. Through market forces, these countries have seen resources channeled into new sources of growth, a process that also addresses the problem of balance sheet repair. We briefly review Finland, Thailand, and Iceland as three of many examples that illustrate this market-correction process. The original excesses in these economies were a consequence of large, unsustainable flows of capital into fixed investment (including housing) that ultimately were reversed, leading to economic collapse. However, in each case, that reversal led to currency depreciation as investors abandoned the currency, and the depreciation initiated a period of export-led growth. The associated declines in the country's currency brought a reversal of the current account deficit, which in turn aided the balance sheet recovery in a way that government borrowing cannot.

One common objection to treating these countries as models for recovery is their small size. However, in 1996, Thailand, Malaysia, Indonesia, and South Korea had a combined GDP of $1.07 trillion; the composite of these economies would have been the seventh largest in the world at that time. All four countries experienced financial crises and currency depreciations in the same narrow window of time. Between June 1997 and June 1998, the Thai baht, Malaysian ringgit, and South Korean won all depreciated between 36 and 42 percent, and the Indonesian rupiah depreciated 82 percent. During the same period, Indonesia, Thailand, and South Korea had improvements in their net export positions, varying from 13.1 to 17.5 percent of GDP. From the 1997 to the 1998 calendar year, Malaysia experienced an improvement in its net export position of 21.9 percent of GDP.[6]

This process contrasts sharply with the plight of Portugal, Ireland, Italy, Greece, and Spain, which no longer have a separate currency and whose idiosyncratic economic excesses cannot lead to a market currency response independent of the stronger Eurozone economies such as Germany. The U.S. analogy is represented by Michigan, which has seen its share of national product decline – from 3.8 to 2.6 percent in the past quarter-century – and has had its share of population decline, from 3.8 to 3.2 percent. Hence, adjustments can occur only through the exit-entry migration decisions by businesses and people with limited moderating effects resulting from price level responses.

Our point is not about exchange rate regime policy – that is, whether any country should or should not be on a flexible currency, which has

[6] For Thai GDP and net export figures, see the Thai National Accounts from the Office of the National Economic and Social Development Board, available at http://eng.nesdb .go.th/Default.aspx?tabid=317. For Indonesian and South Korean figures, see the Quarterly National Accounts in the OECD database, available at stats.oecd.org. For Malaysian figures, see Department of Statistics Malaysia, available at www.statistics.gov.my/portal/ download_Economics/files/DATA_SERIES/2011/pdf/01Akaun_Negara.pdf.

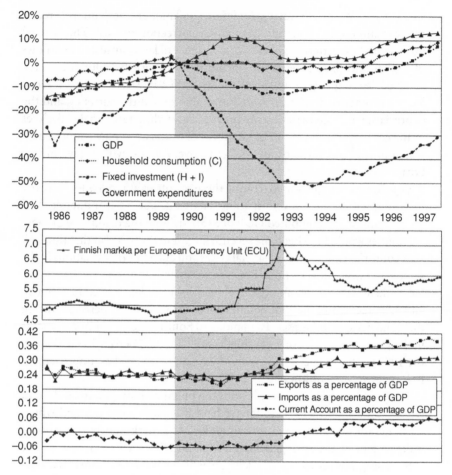

Figure 10.2. Changes in GDP and the current account in Finland, 1986–1997.

important political dimensions. Rather, it is about understanding the work accomplished by the currency depreciation adjustment process in cases of severe balance sheet crises.

10.4.1 Finland

Finnish fixed investment (including housing) started to collapse in Q1 1990 after a long increase accompanied by rising capital inflows and an increasing current account deficit. Figure 10.2 shows both the rapid rise in fixed investment between 1986 and 1989 and the developing current account deficits. Investment peaked in Q4 1989 at 30.4 percent of GDP and then declined more than 30 percent by the autumn of 1991, when a banking crisis ensued from major deterioration in bank balance sheets. In a typical pattern, which suggests nervous investors, capital inflows diminished before the crisis. Exports had long been declining gently as a percentage of GDP. Three years after the currency devaluation in November 1991 and two years after the currency depreciation in 1992, exports surged from 20 to 35 percent of GDP and moved sharply ahead of the growth in imports.

The fundamental dislocation during the crisis and depression was a collapse of fixed investment; the recovery consisted primarily in filling this gap with export growth. In Finland, during the three years before the peak of its economic cycle in early 1990, 61.4 percent of growth was in fixed capital investment. During the next four years, fixed investment fell 51.4 percent; most of the GDP decline could be accounted for by this decline. GDP fell by 12.4 percent, whereas fixed investment fell from 29.7 percent of GDP, when the downturn began, to only 18.2 percent of GDP 6.5 years later.

A common objection to "depreciation" is that it will set off a series of competitive devaluations in which countries, in succession, follow a "beggar-thy-neighbor" strategy – that is, taking export market share away from other countries. In the eight years preceding devaluation, real imports in Finland grew 4.1 percent (only 0.5 percent per year); in the first four years after depreciation, real imports grew 38.2 percent (8.4 percent per year); and in the first eight years after depreciation, real imports grew 73.2 percent (7.1 percent per year). In most of the serious downturns that we examine – including Thailand, South Korea, Malaysia, Argentina, and Mexico – imports increased as a percentage of GDP following depreciation. Therefore, the beggar-thy-neighbor objection to depreciation has no empirical support in the crisis countries that we evaluate. The common consequence of market currency depreciation is an increase in a country's trade.

10.4.2 Thailand

For many years prior to 1986, Thailand was the fastest growing economy in the world. The late stage of this boom was augmented by a current account deficit averaging 7.2 percent of GDP between 1993 and 1996, which contributed capital for the boom in fixed investment. Investors eventually grew skittish and withdrew. Figure 10.3 shows Thailand's stagnant exports and growing imports prior to the crisis. As in Finland, rapidly declining construction and investment were key factors in the downturn. The collapses in construction and fixed investment (down 44 and 20 percent, respectively,

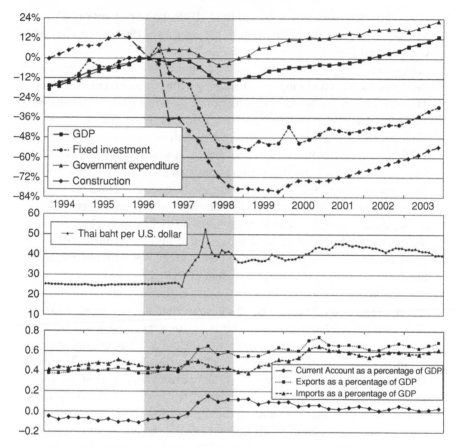

Figure 10.3. Changes in GDP and the current account in Thailand, 1994–2003.

from their peak by the time of the currency collapse) were pronounced and appeared in advance of the financial and balance-of-payments crises.

In Thailand, the same sequence played out as in Finland. If we examine the changes in Thai output during the boom, the collapse, and the recovery, we see that fixed investment contributed importantly to both the boom and a significant portion of the decline. Thai GDP fell 14.9 percent in the downturn. At the peak in Q3 1996, fixed investment comprised 39.6 percent of Thai output. GDP first recovered the 1996 peak 5.5 years later, in Q1 2002. By that time, fixed investment was only 23.0 percent of GDP. As in Finland, the decline of fixed investment was comparable to the total decline in GDP, and the increase in net exports accounted for most of the recovery. During the same 5.5-year period of collapse and recovery, exports increased by

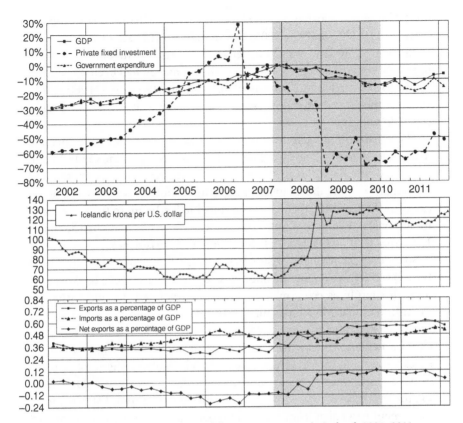

Figure 10.4. Changes in GDP and the current account in Iceland, 2001–2011.

23.9 percent of GDP, whereas imports increased by 10.6 percent of GDP, which increased net exports by 13.3 percent of GDP – almost enough to account for the entire recovery. As in Finland, currency depreciation led to an increase in imports. Between the peak of the economic cycle in Q3 1996 and the recovery to the peak in Q1 2002, Thai imports grew from 43.7 to 54.3 percent of GDP.

10.4.3 Iceland

The more recent Icelandic crisis was preceded by several years of extraordinary capital inflows that fueled the boom in fixed investment. The top panel in Figure 10.4 shows the boom in fixed investment; the bottom panel shows the rapid increase of the trade deficit. At its maximum, the gap between imports and exports reached 20.4 percent of GDP in Q1 2006. These capital inflows supported equally extraordinary growth of fixed investment. Between Q1 2002 and Q4 2006, the annual growth rate of private fixed investment in Iceland was 31.3 percent.[7] When this investment bubble burst, the collapse was even faster than the expansion had been – real fixed capital formation fell 78.2 percent in only nine quarters from Q4 2006 to Q1 2009; by then, fixed capital investment was below its level when the rapid expansion began.

The expansion of fixed investment was accompanied by a huge increase in deposits in the Icelandic banking system. According to the Central Bank of Iceland, the liabilities of the banking system reached 13.2 times GDP immediately before the financial crisis. Three months later, the value of the assets in the Icelandic financial system had fallen by more than five times the annual GDP of the country.[8] (For comparison, U.S. banks had liabilities 1.19 times GDP in Q3 2008, when the financial crisis struck.)

Soon after the financial crisis entered its final stage in the United States (i.e., Q4 2008), the value of illiquid assets in the Icelandic banking system fell sharply as economic conditions deteriorated. Iceland turned to the International Monetary Fund (IMF) for loans, and the IMF required fiscal consolidation as a condition of the loans. The krona began to depreciate immediately before fiscal consolidation was undertaken, and exports quickly overtook imports. As in Finland and Thailand, the improvement in net exports was the major contributor to the recovery into 2012. During the nearly seven years since fixed investment peaked in Q4 2006, fixed investment had fallen from 34.8 to 11.0 percent of GDP – a decline of 23.8 percent of GDP. In that same period, exports and imports increased by 27.3 percent of GDP and imports fell by 1.5 percent of GDP; therefore, net exports increased by 28.8 percent of GDP. The improvement in net exports can account for the entire recovery of Icelandic output to a level that it first attained only one quarter before the peak of the economic cycle.

10.5 Fiscal Consolidation versus Fiscal Stimulus and Deficit Spending

The discussion of Finland, Thailand, and Iceland in the previous sections focuses on the restructuring of their economies from growth of fixed

---

[7] For figures on Icelandic trade, investment, and GDP, see Statistics Iceland, National Accounts, available at www.statice.is/Statistics/National-accounts-and-public-fin.

[8] Summary financial accounts for Icelandic financial corporations are available from Statistics Iceland, National Accounts, available at www.statice.is/Statistics/National-accounts-and-public-fin.

investment to growth in exports, imports, and net exports, as well as the role of currency depreciation in that process. However, the data that we provide for these countries also demonstrate that growth of government expenditures – so-called fiscal stimulus – did not have a role in any of these recoveries. Most developed countries that experience a financial crisis also face a surge in government deficits soon afterward. However, many of the countries where those deficits persisted also had poor growth records.

Finnish deficits soared after the financial crisis, from a deficit of 0.4 percent of GDP in 1991 to 9.0 percent of GDP in 1993. However, real government expenditures peaked in Q3 1991, and deficits began to fall in 1994. Between 1993 and 1997, government expenditures were reduced by 8.6 percent of GDP; by 1997, the deficits were brought down to 1.6 percent of GDP, well below the growth rate. Hence, government debt began to decline as a percentage of GDP. During the first five years of the Finnish recovery, the growth rate averaged 4.2 percent per year; during the first ten years, growth averaged 3.7 percent per year.

The Finnish experience stands in stark contrast to the Japanese experience. Japanese government deficits grew rapidly after Japan's financial crisis in 1997 and continued at an elevated level for fifteen years. According to the Japanese Ministry of Finance, central government debt grew from 49.5 percent of GDP in 1997 to 147.8 percent of GDP in 2012. Annual deficits averaged 6.8 percent of GDP during that period, whereas the growth rate of GDP averaged 0.5 percent per year. In Finland, the growth rate during the first fifteen years after its financial crisis was 3.6 percent and the government had, on average, a small surplus of 0.5 percent of GDP.

In Thailand, after international financial inflows ceased, IMF assistance was sought. Loan funds from the IMF were provided with the stipulation that government finances remain on a solid foundation. By mid-August 1997, about six weeks after the collapse of the baht, the government had implemented tax increases and finalized spending cuts as the first steps in its fiscal consolidation plan. Just as the government curtailed its expenditures, the Thai net export position began to improve dramatically. In only two quarters (i.e., Q2 1997 to Q4 1997), exports increased by 22.5 percent of GDP, whereas imports increased by only 6.9 percent of GDP in the same two quarters. In the five years after the Thai crisis, government borrowing averaged less than 2 percent of GDP per year. During the fourteen-year period from the end of the crisis in 1998 to 2011, government borrowing averaged 1.1 percent of GDP, and the average growth rate in Thailand was 3.6 percent.

In the United Kingdom, which Krugman (2012) suggested has undergone an austerity program, deficits peaked at 11.4 percent of GDP in 2009 and remained elevated at 8.3 percent of GDP in 2011. With significant deficit spending and an increase in government expenditures of 4.6 percent, the growth rate in the United Kingdom was only 0.9 percent per year since output peaked in Q1 2008.

This evidence indicates flaws in the argument that government spending can substitute for private demand or that tax cuts can stimulate the economy after a sharp downturn due to a balance sheet crisis. We see in numerous cases a clear relationship between deficit spending and prolonged stagnation, and we also see evidence that fiscal consolidation is related to renewed growth.

10.6 Conclusion

Much of the dislocation during some of the most severe economic downturns in the developed and developing world during the past twenty years arose when asset prices collapsed and the fixed investment sector of the affected economy suffered a sharp reduction in output. The Keynesian prescription is to increase government expenditures and reduce taxes to stimulate growth. However, we describe evidence from several countries that the contrary approach was successful. A combination of revenue enhancements and expenditure reductions by the government that reduces fiscal deficits seems to support a reduction of capital inflows, currency depreciation, and net export growth. Countries that followed this approach experienced a return to strong and sustained output growth and generated the foreign income to reduce accumulated debts. Although many of the countries that followed this path were small- to medium-sized economies, the composite of South Korea, Thailand, Malaysia, and Indonesia was large, and they all quickly controlled government expenditures and deficits and all returned quickly to strong and sustained growth. The Keynesian prescription, which was followed most extensively by Japan, led to extreme public-sector indebtedness and is associated with a prolonged record of extremely poor growth.

References

Bair, Sheila (2012). *Bull by the Horns*. New York: The Free Press.
Chari, V. V. (2010). "Testimony before the Committee on Science and Technology, Subcommittee on Investigations and Oversight, U.S. House of Representatives." Available at www.gpo.gov/fdsys/pkg/CHRG-111hhrg57604/pdf/CHRG-111hhrg57604.pdf.

Gjerstad, Steven, and Vernon L. Smith (2013). "Balance Sheet Crises: Causes, Consequences, and Responses." *Cato Journal*, 33, pp. 437–70.

Kehoe, Timothy J., and Edward C. Prescott (2007). *Great Depressions of the Twentieth Century*. Minneapolis, MN: Federal Reserve Bank of Minneapolis.

Krugman, Paul (2012). "The Austerity Agenda." *New York Times*, May 31, p. A27.

Packer, Frank (2000). "The Disposal of Bad Loans in Japan: The Case of the CCPC." In *Crisis and Change in the Japanese Financial System*, ed. T. Hoshi and H. Patrick, pp. 137–57. Boston: Kluwer.

Sveriges Riksbank (2007). "The Swedish Financial Market 2007." Available at www .riksbank.se.

11

Summary: What Have We Learned?

11.1 Balance Sheet Crises and Housing: Definition and Occurrence

In the United States, balance sheet crises have occurred as a consequence of a decline in housing market values against fixed mortgage debt. Many household balance sheets are thereby plunged into negative equity, and the lenders suffer parallel balance sheet damage as the underlying value of their mortgage loans declines in step with house prices. Under these conditions, households have strong precautionary incentives to reduce their expenditures and banks to reduce their lending as both sectors seek to rebuild their lost equity and avoid incurring new risks. Although this net-debt-reduction process increases the availability of funds for investment, those channels are simultaneously experiencing expectations of declining returns to new investment opportunities and falling interest rates, even in advance of policy shifts toward monetary ease.

Fortunately, such crises are rare, having occurred in the United States only twice in seventy-eight years – the downturn in 1929 and again in 2008 – culminating in the Great Depression and the Great Recession. Both episodes were preceded by three-year substantial declines in new housing expenditures in 1927–1929 and again in 2006–2008. Perhaps because of their rarity, they are not part of standard macroeconomic or general microeconomic equilibrium models; neither are they part of conventional thinking in monetary and fiscal policy.

11.2 Housing Leads in Most Recessions

Most of the twelve smaller recessions between the Great Depression and the Great Recession also were preceded by declines in housing investment. Housing decline is a consistently superior indicator of both the duration and the depth of recession than declines in firms' fixed investments. By our reckoning, housing has been a leading indicator and implicated as proximal cause in eleven of the past fourteen recessions, starting with the Great Depression. Even more impressive, thirteen of the past fourteen recession recoveries were accompanied by rapidly increasing expenditures on construction of new housing. The single exception is the Great Recession, from which (in 2013) the recovery has been weak, exhibiting neither a customary recovery surge in growth nor a return to previous long-term growth trends. Hence, based on the past fourteen recessions, we conclude that if there is no recovery in housing, then there is either no recovery or, unusually, an extended period of substandard economic growth.

11.3 Two Types of Markets in Experiments and the Economy

Experimental research informs the study of recessions and vice versa, greatly enhancing our understanding of the incentive and performance characteristics of markets and demonstrating the key proposition that not all markets are created equal.

There are two fundamental types of markets, the performance of which has been studied in the laboratory, as follows:

1. The first type is supply-and-demand markets that are repeated as flows of goods or services during successive time periods. Experimental tests of these markets began in the 1950s and 1960s. Equilibrium price discovery in these markets occurs rapidly under strictly privately dispersed information on buyer (consumer) value and seller (producer) value. These markets tend to converge quickly.

   Special features of these markets, however, are of key importance to make note of, as follows:

   • The items in the particular experiments we discuss are not retradable.
   • Before entering the market, all traders know their role as either a buyer or seller. Although the amounts bought or sold may depend on price, unit costs, and value – as well as the individual's available units of capacity to buy or sell – participant roles do not depend on price.
   • The items disappear from the market when sold, with buyer and seller each recording the dollar value of the utilitarian surplus received from the exchange for consumption.

2. The second type is asset-market experiments, which began in the 1980s. In these investigations, the items exchanged "lived" as long as

an experiment lasted and could be freely retraded across all periods of the experiment, within the constraining limits on cash and asset stock held by each individual. At the end of each period, there is a "dividend" realization on all units held by each trader corresponding to a current utility value enjoyed by the possessor of units of the asset. Each trader is provided an initial endowment of asset units and cash, informed of the dividend distribution, and – with complete transparency – informed and reminded each period of the declining fundamental (i.e., dividend-holding) value as the number of periods remaining diminishes.

Corresponding to these two distinguishing types of experimental markets, several of their broad features are shared with key components of national macroeconomic accounts in the United States and other countries (see Chapters 3–5 and 10).

1. Nondurable consumer goods and services: In the aggregate, we label this "C" in our chart of the Great Depression Figure 4.1. Predominantly, they share with experimental supply-and-demand studies the perishability, buyer-seller role specialization, and nonretradability of the items. Moreover, C is the dynamically stable component of private domestic final product and, by far, the largest, accounting for about 75 percent of annual private final output.
2. At the opposite end of the spectrum from consumer nondurable goods and services are expenditures on new single-family and multifamily housing that we label "H" in our charts of twelve of the past fourteen U.S. recessions. These consumer goods are typically and, we think, misleadingly treated as capital or investment goods. Rather, they are plainly the longest-lived of all consumer goods and are almost always bought with a large percentage of "other people's money" (e.g., bank loans). As a direct consequence of these properties, such goods are recurrent sources of dynamic instability in economies the world over.

It is a puzzle why people in laboratory asset-market experiments, as well as their "sophisticated" counterparts in economies today, become entangled in self-sustaining expectations of escalating prices; however, they do so reliably. There are important parallels in behavior between experimental price bubbles and those in the housing market, as follows:

- As in the laboratory, money matters; the availability and aggressive marketing of mortgage credit supported the housing bubble until credit started to be withdrawn.

- In experiments, at or near the peak in contract prices, asking prices continue to rise but with fewer accepted. Hence, volume tends to decline.
- This stickiness of prices was evident in late 2005 and early 2006 in the housing market as unit-sales volume declined even as prices rose or flattened out, while sellers kept their home on the market longer, reluctant to cut prices until it became essential to secure a sale.

11.4 Build-Up and Collapse: Overview of the Great Recession

Real estate asset values began their ascent in 1997 and expanded in two phases. Phase I, from 1997 to 2001, carried inflation-adjusted national housing prices to their previous peak in 1989. Phase II, in which prices continued their ascent into early 2006, was directly financed by a bulge in the net flow of mortgage credit to households and indirectly by an equally rapid increase in the inflow of foreign investment (see Figure 3.3).

Over the long build-up from 1997 to 2006, the U.S. housing market bubble expansion was unprecedented in national post war housing experience. Moreover, that the bubble was driven largely by momentum was revealed by the fact that the median U.S. home price was rising at an increasing rate over much of this ascension. In contrast, during previous recent home price bubbles, peaking in 1979 and 1989, prices had risen through most of the bubble at a decreasing rate (see Figure 3.1). Similarly, in laboratory asset price bubbles, prices typically rise at a decreasing rate (see Figures 2.6 and 2.8).

This unusual price pattern, with prices rising at an increasing rate, was already well entrenched before the widespread adoption of alternative mortgage products – such as adjustable rate mortgages, interest-only mortgages, and negative equity mortgages – and before derivative "insurance" had become prominent markers of the greatest of all national housing bubbles. Hence the bubble was exhibiting clear evidence of the presence of price momentum – buying in proportion to price increases – in the years before the mortgage market's structural features had become prominent; before the Fannie Mae and Freddie Mac scandals of 2003 and 2004; and before 2005 when 45 percent of first-time home buyers paid no money down. This momentum-driven acceleration in home prices was therefore part of the expectations environment before the radical changes in the mortgage market that subsequently dominated so much of both media and professional comment.

Throughout the entire period of 1997–2006, aggregate inflation-adjusted real estate equity – the primary source of net real wealth for most households – more than doubled, to about $13 trillion. The ensuing collapse in real estate asset values in 2007 against fixed mortgage debt continued until Q4 2011, with devastating consequences for real estate equity: In Q4 2011, households' inflation-adjusted real estate equity reached its post-bubble minimum of $5.6 trillion, which was identical to its level in Q2 1985, more than twenty-six years earlier! These movements were reflected in the national income accounts in the form of rising expenditures on new home construction that reached a peak in Q1 2006 seven quarters before the recession began in Q4 2007. All other components of GDP had been steady or increasing, reversing course only after the recession began – a lag consistent with the "surprise" character of the Great Recession for consumers and businesses as much as for the "blindsided" policy makers (see Figure 3.8). Only the collapse in 1929 into the Great Depression was comparable.

In comparison with the Great Depression, however, the Great Recession was far better documented in public and private statistical records. The much better statistical record of the Great Recession, which illuminates its dynamics, also guides a reexamination of the Great Depression.

11.5 Revisiting the 1920s and the Depression

The justifiably influential research of Friedman and Schwartz led to the interpretation that the Depression was predominantly a monetary phenomenon ensuing from the failure of the monetary authorities to provide badly needed liquidity in the critical period, 1929–31, thus causing the economy to escalate from a solvable illiquidity problem into a solvency crisis. That the monetary authorities appear not to have acted appropriately in light of subsequent economic history leaves unanswered the question about the origins of the Depression.

Was the Depression an ordinary recession that spun out of control because of inadequate monetary action? If so, how can we be more assured of this interpretation? That narrative does not account for the comparatively sharp decline in household consumption in 1930 in advance of the banking system collapse. Particularly unusual, in comparison with all other downturns in the last century (except 2009; see footnote 12 on p. 93), was the decrease in nondurable consumption, C, in 1930, which suggests quite unusual and presumably sudden consumer belt-tightening (see Figure 4.1).

Following is what the record shows for the period from 1922 to 1933:

- Annual housing construction expenditures rose 60 percent from 1922 through 1925, held steady in 1926, declined in both 1927 and in 1928, returned to its 1922 baseline level in 1929, and then declined an additional 46 percent in 1930 alone. By 1933, new housing expenditures were 88 percent below the level in 1929 (see Figure 4.1). However, from the well-documented experience of the Great Recession, we now appreciate how sensitive household demand can be to declines in housing prices against fixed mortgage debt. We offer the hypothesis, and corroborating evidence, that prior to 1929–30, household balance sheets reflected a cumulative build-up in leverage that, with the reversal of a rapidly expanding housing market dependent on the continued flow of mortgage credit, could account for the sudden household belt-tightening. Thus, from 1921 to 1925, the net flow of mortgage funds tripled while new construction rose 60 percent.
- These high mortgage flows continued essentially unchanged from 1925 through 1928. Yet, the peak net mortgage flows in 1927 and 1928 were running against the tide of declining new construction (compare Figures 4.1 and 4.2). With the increasing flow of net mortgage credit greatly exceeding new construction expenditures from 1922 through 1928, we can infer that the build-up in household real estate leverage had a six-year run in advance of the economic downturn from 1929 to 1930 and the subsequent collapse from 1931 to 1933. These developments implicate housing in the origins of the Great Depression, although there were important differences from the Great Recession – both loan-to-value ratios and bank participation in mortgage lending were smaller on average in the boom years of the 1920s. However, we summarize new and old but neglected data, making it clear that a significant percentage of homeowners had low and diminishing levels of equity before 1929–30 (see Chapter 4).
- Indications of rapid deterioration in real estate and banking in 1930 included (1) the bankruptcy of the Bank of United States, which had 45 percent of its assets in real estate; and (2) the distress in the Chicago mortgage-bond market, where defaults jumped to fifty in 1930 from twenty-two in 1929; only seven defaulted from 1925 to 1928.

11.6 Household Equity: Depression versus Great Recession

Compared with the pre-Depression 1920s, there was a more significant run-up in real estate prices in advance of the Great Recession, although both suffered major price collapses. Is a large price bubble a necessary condition

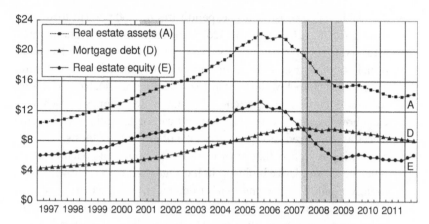

Figure 11.1. Real estate assets, debt and equity, 1997–2012.

for a severe subsequent economic downturn? We suggest that this is not the case. Our hypothesis is that the critical necessary condition is an expansion in the output of long-lived goods financed disproportionately with mortgage loans dependent on refinancing, leading to a collapse in prices against fixed debt. Thus, if the supply of new housing is relatively elastic, price increases will be smaller; the implication is that the aggregate-leverage accumulation will be smaller per home but dispersed across more units. If, however, the supply is relatively inelastic, prices will increase more, construction output will be more restrained, and leverage will be larger per home. In either case, a large subsequent decline in home prices will disproportionately reduce equity values and can plunge many households into negative equity.

In both episodes, the consequences of a long build-up in household balance sheet leverage and subsequent deleveraging are reflected in the time paths of real estate equity (Figures 11.1 and 11.2). In the Great Depression, real estate equity declined about one third from its peak in 1929 to its bottom in 1932; whereas in the Great Recession, real estate equity declined 58 percent from its peak in Q1 2006 to its trough in Q4 2011.

If 1922 and 1997 are considered beginning years in their respective cycles in real estate equity, then the percentage rise – trough to peak – was much smaller in the Great Depression than in the Great Recession. However, the pattern over time, trough to trough (1922–33 and 1997–2009) and the subsequent decline, follow similar paths. In both cases, households were left with less equity after a decade-long bubble and collapse; in both cases, they had substantially more mortgage debt at the end of the cycle.

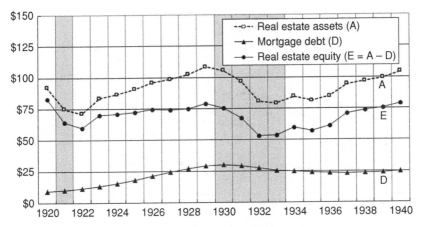

Figure 11.2. Real estate assets, debt and equity, 1920–1940.

11.7 The Post–World War II Recessions

In the post–World War II period, housing was a prominent leading indicator of recession, with a 10 percent decline in housing expenditures foreboding an economic downturn. However, the consequences were far less severe than in the Great Depression or the Great Recession. Particularly prominent is a recurrent interaction between housing investment and monetary policy in defining the pattern of economic cycles. The cycle begins with low inflation and interest rates and new housing construction expanding. Housing continues to expand, but at a slower pace, and inflation begins to set in. In response, monetary policy is tightened, housing declines more sharply, and durable goods spending declines. This reduces inflationary pressure but also leads to a turn in the investment cycle as firms encounter reduced demand. The combination of this household expenditure cycle and the investment cycle form an economic cycle (see Chapter 5).

The recession of 1953–54 followed this typical pattern except that the recession was delayed after a substantial and sharp decline in housing due to the major expansion in national defense expenditures in anticipation of the Korean conflict (see Figure 5.4). In our view, this example illustrates the proposition that government fiscal policy can be effective in offsetting other expenditure declines, provided that household balance sheets are healthy and unburdened by negative equity. The 2001 recession also deviates from this pattern but, as indicated in Chapter 3, the pattern was disrupted by the huge influx of foreign investment that directly and indirectly supported the surge in mortgage lending.

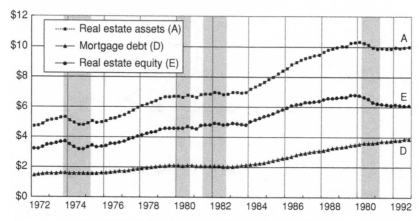

Figure 11.3. Real estate assets, debt and equity, 1972–1992.

Figure 11.3 is a chart of real estate assets, debt, and equity for the period 1972–92 to compare with the Depression and Great Recession in Figures 11.1 and 11.2. Similar to all other post–World War II recessions, the four recessions shown in Figure 11.3 exhibit only minor declines (if any) in equity, and they stand in sharp contrast with both the Great Recession and the Depression. Their ordering is clear: The Great Recession equity decline by far is the worst; followed by the Depression, a strong second; and then a sharp drop to the post – World War II recessions, in which the real estate equity hit is comparatively minor indeed. (A similar chart for the four recessions in the period 1952–72 is even smaller than those depicted in Figure 11.3, and we do not include it.)

11.8 The Housing Bubble: Were There Triggers?

We divide the course of the housing bubble into two five-year intervals for examination: (1) from 1997 to 2001, when the national median price of a home accelerated, growing at an increasing rate to its previous inflation-adjusted high; and (2) from 2002 to 2006, when the median price of homes continued this surge to a new historical high, then flattened before collapsing into the Great Recession. Although bubbles are not fundamentally caused or driven only by external circumstances, we first identify several promising "triggers" in both the public and private sectors that either coincided with or preceded the 1997 takeoff as an "incubation interval" (see Chapter 6).

These events or developments included the bipartisan Taxpayer Relief Act of 1997 that exempted home resales from capital gains taxes up to $500,000.

Both the timing of this event and the substantial tax incentive it provided for the diversion of capital investment into homes combined to make it a prime trigger suspect. Incentives matter and the problem with the Act is the differential treatment of houses relative to productive capital investments, channeling savings and borrowings into house consumption.

Although there can be no question that the housing bubble excesses were aided by continuing public subsidy programs – that is, the GSE and Ginnie Mae – these programs had long been creating perverse potential housing stimulus incentives. The evidence we provide is consistent with the proposition that to compete with these programs, the private-label lenders expanded more prominently into riskier segments of the mortgage markets. These risks were self-deceptively camouflaged by (1) the false perception that MBS were safely hedged by derivative insurance, and (2) the failure of lenders to adapt to the poor upfront incentives for loan originators to conduct due diligence in evaluating borrowers – issues that are examined in Chapter 7.

The CRA became a well-intentioned but insidious new source of potential risk enhancement in the 1990s by using threats of coercion to influence bankers to expand loans in LMII neighborhoods, especially without better controls for the increased risk incurred. As we interpret the evidence and testimony, the CRA can neither be absolved of a contributing role in the crisis nor faulted as a root cause.

11.9 The Great Recession: Incentives, Mortgage-Backed Securities, and Derivatives

The evolution of a national (and then international) mortgage market had the efficiency advantage that differential regional housing demand no longer depended on local sources of finance. Along with that development, however, mortgage origination became separated from lending, and originators were paid upfront fees that provided them with no built-in incentive for due diligence comparable to the incentives faced by a mortgage lender. The mortgages were sold to companies that combined blocks of them into MBS "tranches," most of which were rated AAA even though they included high percentages of risky subprime loans. The MBS tranches were hedged by derivatives in the form of CDS that were considered to be "insurance" against default.

These derivatives, however, were exempt from registration as securities and were not subject to collateral requirements. The overall consequence of this rapid institutional change in response to growing mortgage

markets was that the residential mortgage-processing chain – from origination through repackaging as MBS, to rating, and "insuring" the MBS
via CDS contracts – was inherently unstable. The chain was inadequately
collateralized all the way from home buyers (because mortgage originators
failed to screen and hold home buyers to higher down payment and amortization standards) to the final link in the chain in which the CDS issuers
were not required and chose not to collateralize their default insurance on
mortgages. Remarkably, the chain remained suspended in a kind of false
common-expectations equilibrium that depended on further increases in
home prices to justify housing commitments beyond what could be sustained out of current income. Prices had only to stop growing to precipitate
defaults because recently issued mortgages precariously depended on some
accumulation of equity so that they could be refinanced into fixed-rate
mortgages.

11.10 The Great Recession: Economic Policy Lags the
Housing-Mortgage-Market Decline

In 2006, the aging housing market boom was starting to weaken: Prices
peaked in the first half of 2006 and then began to decline. Subprime and
ARM defaults were on the rise and, from December 2006 into February
2007, the insurance cost of BBB – rated MBS increased sharply. Throughout
the first half of 2007, the Federal Reserve – although recognizing that the
housing market was going through an adjustment – did not anticipate the
unraveling of financial markets that erupted suddenly in July and August
of 2007 (see Chapters 7 and 8). In 2007, it took only three days, August
7–10, for the FOMC to shift from a stance of continuing concerns about
inflation to the recognition that financial markets were in disarray, with
banks reluctant to lend overnight funds to other banks. Financial entities,
seeing the strains in their own balance sheets (i.e., long-term asset values
declining against short-term liabilities), were reluctant to extend funds to
others who were likely to be in similar straits. Based on the lessons from
the Friedman and Schwartz interpretation of the Depression, Bernanke and
other FOMC members exhibited great flexibility in moving decisively after
the August 2007 credit market seizure – albeit in traditional ways for the first
year – to "enhance" bank and financial market liquidity. Chapter 8 refers to
this as "Fed Adaptation I" (labeled "Fed Action I" in Figure 8.1).

Bernanke was not going to make the same policy mistake, widely believed
to have been made in 1929–31, of failing to provide emergency liquidity as
needed. Hence, from August 2007 through September 2008, in the face of

increasingly jittery financial markets, the Fed steadily expanded both the size and term structure of its short-term liquidity injections. These actions served to stabilize financial market expectations, which had crumbled in Q3 2007. However, liquidity alone could not overcome the effects of the continued deterioration of the housing market and the damage its collapse was doing to household and bank balance sheets. Reminiscent of 1929, output (GDP) and firms' nonresidential fixed investment (I) simultaneously reached peaks in Q4 2007, consistent with the proposition that businesses were taken by surprise in the sudden turn of economic events (see Figure 3.8).

However, because of escalating mortgage market defaults in 2007–2008, households and their banks had a solvency crisis that came to a head: By October 2008, the credit market dysfunction could no longer be interpreted as a liquidity crisis. We call this "Fed Adaptation II" because the Fed (joined by Treasury) intervened massively to provide reserves to the banking system and to lift undercollateralized depreciating mortgages and other bad assets off bank balance sheets at face value (labeled "Fed Action II" in Figure 8.1). This action became known popularly as the "too-big-to-fail" bailout of the largest banks. The Fed's Adaptation II implicitly recognized the failure of the Fed's previous liquidity moves from August 2007 to October 2008. From the beginning, the Fed had faced an unrecognized insolvency crisis that could not be papered over by "liquidity enhancement," although its consequences could be and were postponed by these actions.

In all of the minor recessions of postwar history, conventional monetary ease was effective because household and bank balance sheets were predominantly in positive net equity positions. Consequently, monetary ease and reduced short-term interest rates opened up a gap between the mortgage rates that banks could charge and their short-term cost of funds. This gap stimulates their mortgage lending and housing demand. Through this mechanism, the Federal Reserve maintained control over the recovery. This time, it was much different: In balance sheet crises, many households and banks are in negative net equity; there are large inventories of homes on the market; and the Fed loses control over housing and mortgage markets and therefore has limited ability to stimulate a recovery. Government deficit spending, long thought to be the main recovery avenue when monetary policy fails, is likewise ineffective for the same reason: Too many households and banks are mired in negative equity, and the financial system stalls in the slow process of diverting income into debt reduction. The idea that fiscal policy is effective when monetary policy is not derives from the association between the end of the Great Depression and the beginning of

World War II military spending. However, in 1940, the United States had experienced a decade of balance sheet repair, and it does not follow that increased government spending could have revived the economy in 1930.

Federal Reserve easing has continued into 2014. However, when Bernanke reviewed the past decade in his GWU lectures, he would not mark the beginning of the Fed's response policies until the large-scale bank lending program in October 2008 (see Figure 8.3). What we call Fed Adaptation I, and interpreted as a test of the Friedman-Schwartz hypothesis, does not even register in recounting the Fed's response history in the Bernanke lectures; neither is the Friedman-Schwartz work mentioned. If liquidity enhancement could have averted the Great Depression, why did it not work between August 2007 and September 2008? We perceive this as casting aside a key episode that is rife with lessons that deserve to be remembered and carefully examined.

11.11 International Crisis-Management "Experiments" Supplement the Limited U.S. Experience: Sweden versus Japan; Finnish, Thai, and Icelandic Fiscal Discipline

We present data contrasting the experience of Sweden and Japan in the 1990s, which followed opposite approaches to losses in the banking sector. We also contrast Japan with Finland, Thailand, and Iceland, which followed opposite fiscal policy approaches from Japan. All three of these countries reduced government expenditures, reduced deficits quickly, and resumed a path of growth after their severe downturns. Furthermore, in all three, it was their currency depreciation that catalyzed a surge of export-led growth that was sustained for many years.

Japan and Sweden both experienced major real estate investment bubbles but followed diametrically opposite bank and government fiscal policies. In Sweden, the government put the banks through a bankruptcy process that zeroed-out their negative equity, with shareholders bearing the consequences of poor management. In Japan, the banks were permitted to carry real estate loans at book value; they even issued "support loans" that amounted to more than 6 percent of total bank loans to enable distressed borrowers to continue making payments. In Sweden, bank lending recovered along with the economy; whereas in Japan, new bank lending eroded and economic stagnation was endemic for more than fifteen years despite government deficit spending.

Finland, Thailand, and Iceland each illustrate the experience of a host of smaller countries with flexible currencies that encountered crises resulting from a large investment boom and collapse. Recovery in each case was driven by substantial market-driven currency depreciation, followed by increases in net exports characterized by surging exports and a smaller increase in imports. Moreover, in each case, the recovery did not depend on government deficit spending.

11.12 Thinking about What Might Be Done

We suggest three areas of reform that help avoid mortgage and housing market bubbles and the financial crises that so frequently follow them. These fall into three broad categories. The most significant failures in the U.S. housing bubble fell into the category of inappropriately defined property rights. The second is monetary policy that has not adequately accounted for (1) the role of housing and mortgages in the economic cycle, and (2) has not yet adapted to the impact of international capital flows on investment and the economic cycle. The third area for reform is a tax policy that has favored consumption. This section reviews these three areas.

11.12.1 Thinking in Terms of Incentive-Compatible Property Rights, Not Politically Charged "Regulation"

Both popular and academic reactions to the Great Recession are preoccupied with assessing blame – a stance that is particularly distracting in this case because there is more than enough blame to go around. Reform should be concerned with modifying incentives via the restructuring of property rights: The performance and functioning of every market depends on rules that define the rights of individuals and organizations to take action. Rules are essential if individual incentives are to be compatible with socially desirable outcomes (see Chapter 9). Posing the problem as "regulation versus deregulation" tends to immediately appeal to political opinion – the choosing of sides and asking which conclusions are acceptable – before any of the relevant issues and evidence are even on the table.

In mortgage markets, surely that means stricter down-payment rules. When down payments are too small, borrowers and lenders place other parties at risk, including depositors and other investors who are not informed of the decision made by lenders. Even if the borrower and lender agree on the terms of the loan, third parties are affected. The proposition that housing-mortgage markets will function effectively based on freely negotiated terms between borrowers and lenders was tested and failed miserably. No one can know the best rules. The rule that mortgage, property insurance, and property taxes should not exceed 30 percent of income is not "sacred," but it has tradition and experience behind it. Rapid departures from established standards are likely to propel a surge of new borrowers into the market, destabilizing prices. If those borrowers are unprepared for the commitments they undertake, then price increases will reverse. Additionally, we have seen the hazards of interest-only and negative-equity loans with balloon payments, especially when borrowers with those loans need to refinance. Fixed monthly mortgage payments with full amortization provided stability to the mortgage and housing markets for a half-century. Requiring amortization is not optimal for those with volatile sources of income, but those special cases have a general consumption-smoothing problem – housing consumption especially – that other financial market institutions can address.

A particular source of external damage to others in the housing-mortgage market nexus was the unintended consequence of the separation from lending of the specialized mortgage origination industry. We argue that the loan originator compensation fee should be determined by the market but constrained by a rule that distributes the fee over the life of the loan in proportion to the time profile of borrower payments. The upfront component would be proportioned to the cash down payment, with the remainder proportioned at the same rate to principal payments and impounded in escrow payments to the originator. An originator therefore cannot offload all of the risk to a third-party lender. Loan origination then has the same due-diligence incentive as a lender. The market would determine the fee level and also whether origination would be separated from lending. Problems of "predatory lending" are simply symptoms of incentive-incompatible practices; the need is to modify incentives rather than addressing only the symptoms by imposing new untested constraints on agents whose incentives encourage behavior with destructive consequences. Incentives should encourage due diligence at the critical loan-origination stage, whether it is originated by the lender or a third-party specialist.

A sensible policy for derivatives is as plain as for mortgage origination: They are securities and, as such, require registration and should be subject to collateralization rules like those faced by any insurer. Derivatives listing and trading provide valuable forms of information markets. The latter – in the laboratory, in the field (e.g., political stock markets), and in the so-called natural experiments (e.g., the Florida Orange Juice Futures market and racetrack betting) – have served well as predictors when prediction is possible.

A corollary of the case for derivative-securities markets is that rating agencies are rendered obsolete. A rating agency has one centralized model for generating a rating (see the quote by Robert Rodriguez at the opening of Chapter 7). However, a derivatives market has as many models as trading agents, all of whom would have their own collateralized incentive for good performance. Moreover, information markets appear not to be subject to bubbles, although research is continuing as to why, if this is true. In Florida Orange Juice Futures, racetrack betting, and laboratory and field experiments, part of the answer may be found in the near-endpoint realization of the event outcome, which may serve to dampen trading motivated by endogenous expectations of changes in retrading value.

Although programs that call for greater transparency are welcome, it would be wise to maintain a healthy skepticism that bubbles in the housing and mortgage markets are due to a lack of transparency. Laboratory asset market experiments reported in Chapter 2 could not be more transparent, and the excesses in the mortgage market can hardly be said to have been invisible to the participants. Transparency may improve the performance of rational forward-looking agents but may have little effect on myopically rational agents that are surrounded by people caught up in expectations of rising prices and the belief that they can get out before others when the inevitable collapse arrives.

In the aftermath of balance sheet crises like the Great Recession, we argue the case for variety in public policy that includes directly targeting homeowners' negative equity. Preferably, this would be done through a process of large-bank recapitalization and restructuring similar to what took place for the 465 failed smaller banks closed by the FDIC between 2008 and 2012. If the political exigencies require such relief to involve the public purse, then such debt-financed expenditures merit priority over government deficit-stimulus spending: The former jointly addresses both the household and bank problem of negative equity; stimulus spending addresses neither. The $1 trillion Bush-Obama stimulus would have directly covered 2010 estimates of total household negative equity. Our preferred approach is to correct these imbalances through bank failures that restructure the balance sheets of both banks and households, positioning them for a return to growth.

11.12.2 Monetary Policy Needs to Account for Its Own Effect and that of Foreign Investment

Our review of the past fourteen recessions strongly suggests the need for monetary policy reform. Here, we highlight two persistent problems that require attention, as follows:

- The first is the Fed's role in the interplay between housing industry decline and recovery, and subsequent declines and recovery in the economy: It is a fiction to pretend that Fed policy does not target particular industries. Implicitly, this is the effect of the persistent cycle connecting policy, interest rates, and housing cycles. Monetary policy has not been effective in anticipating this regularity in the course of the economy, particularly in adjusting for its own effect on that course as an equilibrium outcome. The Federal Reserve, with its access to current data and professional econometric methodology, did not anticipate the mortgage- and financial-market events in the summer of 2007 or the insolvency events to which it responded massively after September 2008. In both cases, it was private market signals of extreme, sudden, "tipping point" distress that jump-started its action. Can the Federal Reserve do nothing to correct its lagged trend-following response to the long-persistent housing-finance industry cycle?
- We summarize evidence that an important source of fuel for the housing bubble was the inflow of capital from foreign countries arising from the U.S. current account deficit. (International capital flows also are implicated in cross-country housing bubbles.) Therefore, the Fed cannot ignore capital inflows as exogenous sources of monetary ease in determining its policy.

11.12.3 Consumption and Growth-Focused Tax and Business Policies

The Clinton Administration's politically popular bipartisan Taxpayer Relief Act of 1997 increased the return on funds invested in housing. Analysis of that policy focused on the anticipated increase in house prices that would result in equilibrium but did not examine how that shift might affect investors who were attracted by capital gains. Between the mortgage interest deduction and the capital gains exemption, tax policy in the U.S. strongly favors consumption.

Irving and Herbert Fisher proposed a practical tax policy that instead taxes consumption. Their proposal provides incentives for work, saving, economic growth, and investment. The underlying principle derives from Fisher's elementary insight that there is no unambiguous definition of society's income in the current period other than society's consumption withdrawals from the total production of goods and services. An individual's gross income is the market value – that is, wages, interest, rents, and profits – of what the individual supplies for the economic betterment of all others in the economy. All nonconsumption uses of output necessarily remain in the economic system to enhance future output and are not taxed until they are withdrawn from the circular flow to be consumed. A tax on any income receipts that continues to supply goods and services to the economy is necessarily a tax on future output and human economic betterment.

Under Fisher's proposal, income from all sources – including capital gains minus losses – would be calculated as it is today. No distinction is made between income and capital gains in listing income sources; neither is a distinction needed. Deductible from such income are all forms of saving regardless of whether it is held in bank deposits, invested in new capital goods, or used to buy common stocks or bonds. The residue after all of these savings-investment deductions is taxed as consumption, regardless of what form the consumption takes – buying a Ford, a yacht, hamburgers, clothing, or groceries, or making a down payment on a home. We note that capital gains are not taxed if reinvested because the resources continue to work in the economy and are taxed only if consumed, as with any other income source.

As a practical matter, 401(k) plans shelter saved income from taxes. A substantial expansion of this section of the tax code, to allow many additional permitted forms of investment and saving, to remove limits on maximum contributions into accounts, and to allow withdrawals at any age (with taxation on withdrawal but without penalties), would be a reasonable step to move toward incentives for saving.The same logic implies that all business income would be taxed only once at the individual-household level and only insofar as it is consumed. Hence, all business taxes would be abolished. Because corporations commonly retain a portion of their profits for reinvestment, this represents the recycling of resources into the generation of future output and would not be taxed. Corporate retained earnings are savings until reinvested by the firm and would not be taxed. To the extent that businesses incur food and entertainment expenditures for employees and customers, they would be taxable for the same reason that room and board would be taxable while attending college.

Perhaps the most important business policy is a direct implication of the output and employment characteristics of firms entering and exiting the economy. It is well documented that U.S. private-sector business startups minus exits for the period 1980–2005 generated net new jobs at the rate of about 3 percent per year. Because average annual net employment growth for the entire private sector for this period was about 1.8 percent, there is

Rethinking Housing Bubbles

a clear case for public policies that avoid taxing or making it unnecessarily costly and burdensome for people to create new enterprises.

11.13 Conclusions

For more than sixty years, Federal Reserve intervention in the market for Treasury securities has been used as the principle monetary policy instrument in the United States. We show that these interventions, which alter short-term interest rates, had their primary impact on residential mortgage lending until the Great Recession. One effect of overuse of this instrument was an excessively volatile residential construction sector. More recently, the policy has generally led to high volatility in house prices, household wealth, and economic activity. The problems of housing market and asset market instability are exacerbated by large and persistent trade and current account deficits. Deficits on the current account are balanced by investments from outside of the country, and these investments naturally flow into secured assets (e.g., mortgages, bonds, equity, and foreign direct investment). Excessive and chronic capital inflows lead inevitably to inflated asset prices. Policies that contribute to these capital inflows should be identified and moderated. Preliminary examination of data from many countries that have experienced asset market collapses and financial sector turmoil indicates that fiscal expansion is not associated with recovery. It is also reasonable to conclude that excessive monetary accommodation will not help either, because central bank absorption of fiscal deficits delays the adjustments required to eliminate current account deficits. The fundamental lesson that we see in these episodes is that policies that facilitate large capital inflows into specific asset markets should be watched carefully. If excessive flows occur and financial market turmoil develops, the best solution is to allow capital flows to reverse so that export growth can replace the asset and fixed investment growth that has collapsed. Extraordinary measures by monetary and fiscal authorities lead to prolonged stagnation.

Index

A.I.G., 185, 186, 214
affordability (housing), 67–70
Agarwal , S., 165
Ally Financial, 240
Alternative Mortgage Transactions Parity Act (AMTPA, 1982), 198
American Recovery and Reinvestment Act (2009), 6
amortization, 282
    negative, 68
Archbay Capital, 239
Argentina, 261
Arnold and Porter LLP, 192
auction, 46
    buyer-bid (English, or progressive), 29
    Federal Reserve 28-day, 211
    open-outcry continuous double, 25

Badgley, L. Durward, 109
Bailey, Betsy, 196
bailouts, 13, 229, 235–40, 279
Bair, Sheila, 60, 174, 178, 235, 237, 255
balance sheet
    bank, 113, 116–18, 205, 212
    crises, 190, 251, 266
    defined, i
    housing and, 268
    disequilibrium, 170
    financial interdependence, 232
    household, 12–14, 51, 55, 56, 80, 82, 85, 90–1, 113, 114–15, 119, 212, 218
    inadequate reserves and, 214
    of Federal reserve, 241
    of Federal Reserve, 217
    recessions, 3, 6–18, 224

repair and reboot with bankruptcy and default, 256
    risk, 205, 223
Bank of America Corporation (BAC), 13, 174, 240
bankruptcy, 174, 199, 214, 236, 242, 253, 255–6
    Bank of United States and, 273
    Lehman Brothers, 175, 179, 185, 214
    negative equity and, 258, 280
    roles of, 13
banks
    bailouts, 235–40
    collapse of, 173–201
    illiquidity and, 70, 76, 81, 88, 117
    insolvency and, 5, 86, 88, 211, 256, 279
    losses and, 255, 256, 258
    negative equity and, 7
    receivership and, 88
    zombie, 13
Barnd, Merle O., 111
Bass, J. Kyle, 183
Bear Stearns, 175, 182, 185, 194
Bernanke, Ben, 117, 139, 204, 212, 229, 241, 278
    1 July 2005 interview, 20
    15 October 2007 speech, 210, 214
    28 March 2007 congressional testimony, 206
    9 June 2008 speech, 2
    derivatives and, 177
    Friedman-Schwartz hypothesis and, 5
    GSEs and, 150
    liquidity and, 278
    on the September 2008 meltdown, 14
    policy reversal and, 3
    Recession of 2008 and, 1
    subprime mortgages and, 203